HARVARD GSD FALL 2013

Evening Program

9/3 Award Ceremony
Veronica Rudge Green Prize in Urban Design
Eduardo Souto de Moura, Souto Moura Arquitectos, Porto
João Velez de Carvalho, Metro do Porto
Alejandro Echeverri, Alejandro Echeverri Arquitectos, Medellín
Margarita María Ángel Bernal, Empresa de Desarollo Urbano, Medellín
Hosted by Rahul Mehrotra, Professor of Urban Design and Planning and Chair, Urban Planning and Design Department
gsd.harvard.edu/green-prize-2013

9/4 Lecture
Eduardo Souto de Moura
Souto Moura Arquitectos, Porto

9/10 Lecture
Mark Jarzombek
Professor in the History and Theory of Architecture, MIT School of Architecture + Planning, Cambridge

9/12 Lecture
Sheila O'Donnell and John Tuomey
O'Donnell + Tuomey, Dublin

9/13–14 Colloquium
Ecology for Land and City: Exploring the Confluences of Landscape, Road, and Urban Ecology
Convened by Richard T.T. Forman, Research Professor of Advanced Environmental Studies in the Field of Landscape Ecology, and Jane Hutton, Assistant Professor of Landscape
Co-sponsored by Harvard Museum of Comparative Zoology, The Harvard Forest, and Harvard University Center for the Environment.
gsd.harvard.edu/ecology-land-city

9/19 Lecture
Richard Sennett
PhD '69, Professor of Sociology, New York University and London School of Economics

9/18
Panel Discussion: Frontiers of Design Criticism
Mimi Zeiger
critic and journalist, Los Angeles
Alexandra Lange
2014 Loeb Fellow
Florencia Rodriguez
2014 Loeb Fellow

9/30
John T. Dunlop Lecture
J. Ronald Terwilliger
MBA '70, Enterprise Community Partners; Trammell Crow Residential
Presented by the Joint Center for Housing Studies with support from the National Housing Endowment and the John T. Dunlop Professorship in Housing and Urbanization

10/3 Olmsted Lecture
Rod Barnett
School of Architecture, Planning and Landscape Architecture, Auburn University

10/8 Lecture
Takaharu Tezuka
Tezuka Architects, Tokyo

10/10 Symposium
Roots of a 21st Century Urbanism: The Vision of Manuel de Solà-Morales
Organized by Joan Busquets, Martin Bucksbaum Professor in Practice of Urban Planning and Design
gsd.harvard.edu/sola-morales

10/15 Conversation
Mohsen Mostafavi
Dean and Alexander and Victoria Wiley Professor of Design
Nicholas Negroponte
Professor of Media Arts and Sciences and Chairman Emeritus, MIT Media Lab

10/18 Lecture
Robert Wilson
Artist, New York
Supported by the Rouse Visiting Artist in Residence Fund

10/22 Lecture
Denise Scott Brown
Venturi Scott Brown Architects and Planners, Philadelphia

10/24 Conversation
Theaster Gates
Artist, Chicago; 2011 Loeb Fellow
Walid Raad
Artist, New York

11/1
Open House Lecture
Philippe Rahm
Philippe Rahm Architectes, Paris

11/7 Alumni Insights Lecture
Sharon Johnston
MArch '95
Mark Lee
MArch '95
Johnston Marklee, Los Angeles

11/14
Airport Landscape Keynote Lecture
Adriaan Geuze
West 8, Rotterdam / New York

11/14–15 Conference
Airport Landscape: Urban Ecologies in the Aerial Age
Sponsored in part by the Graham Foundation with additional support from the Massachusetts Port Authority/Logan Airport.
gsd.harvard.edu/airport-landscape

11/19 Lecture
Majora Carter
Majora Carter Group, New York

11/22
Margaret McCurry Lectureship in the Design Arts
Antony Gormley
Artist, London
Organized by the Loeb Fellowship Program

Noontime Program

9/5 GSD Talks
Alejandro Echeverri
Alejandro Echeverri Arquitectos, Medellín

9/10 Innovate
Salmaan Craig
Foster + Partners, London

10/10 GSD Talks
Chad Oppenheim
Oppenheim Architecture + Design, New York
Eric de Broche des Combes
Luxigon, Paris

10/28 Innovate
Frank Barkow
MArch '90, Barkow Leibinger, Berlin

11/12 Innovate
Anton Garcia Abril
Ensamble, Madrid; MIT POPlab, Cambridge

11/14 Alumni Insights
Alex Krieger
MCPUD '77, Professor in Practice of Urban Design and member, U.S. Commission of Fine Arts
Elizabeth Meyer
FASLA, Professor, Department of Landscape Architecture, University of Virginia and member, U.S. Commission of Fine Arts
Thomas Luebke
MArch '91, FAIA, Secretary, U.S. Commission of Fine Arts
Supported by the Rachel Dorothy Tanur Memorial Lectureship Fund

Exhibitions

8/26–10/13
Transformative Mobilities: Porto and Medellín
Curated by Rahul Mehrotra, MAUD '87, Professor of Urban Design and Planning, and James Whitten, MAUD '13
Veronica Rudge Green Prize in Urban Design Exhibition

8/31–10/6
The Generic Sublime: Utopioids
Curated by Ciro Najle, Design Critic in Architecture

8/31–10/6
Composites: Renewed Optimism in the Age of Digital Fabrication
Curated by John Nastasi, MDesS '03, Lecturer in Architecture, and Rachel Vroman, MArch '10, Fabrication Manager and Digital Fabrication Technical Specialist

10/16–12/19
Airplot and Other Aerial Obsessions
Curated by Luis Callejas, Lecturer in Landscape Architecture

10/16–12/19
From Airfields to Greenfields: A Genealogy of Airport Landscape
Curated by Sonja Dümpelmann, Associate Professor of Landscape Architecture

10/16–12/19
Altitudes of Urbanization
Curated by Pierre Bélanger, MLA '00, Associate Professor of Landscape Architecture

10/16–12/19
ORD: Documenting the Definitive Modern Airport
Curated by Charles Waldheim, John E. Irving Professor of Landscape Architecture

10/30–12/19
Airport Landscape: Urban Ecologies in the Aerial Age
Curated by Charles Waldheim and Sonja Dümpelmann

For up-to-date information:
gsd.harvard.edu/events
gsd.harvard.edu/exhibitions

Anyone requiring accessibility accommodations should contact the events office two weeks in advance at 617 496 2414 or events@gsd.harvard.edu

Harvard University
Graduate School of Design

Core Studios

Option Studios

Theses

Electives

Doctoral Dissertations

Research Labs

@GSD

© Justin Knight, 2013. On the trays

MArch I Construction Lab class final review

HARVARD UNIVERSITY GRADUATE SCHOOL OF DESIGN

Drew Gilpin Faust President of Harvard University
Mohsen Mostafavi Dean of the Graduate School of Design
Patricia Roberts Executive Dean
K. Michael Hays Associate Dean for Academic Affairs
Beth Kramer Associate Dean for Development and Alumni Relations
Benjamin Prosky Assistant Dean for Communications

2013–2014
Iñaki Abalos Chair of the Department of Architecture
Rahul Mehrotra Chair of the Department of Urban Planning and Design
Charles Waldheim Chair of the Department of Landscape Architecture
Martin Bechthold Co-director of the Doctor of Design Program
Pierre Bélanger Co-director of the Master in Design Studies Program
Anita Berrizbeitia Director of the Master in Landscape Architecture Program
Felipe Correa Director of the Master of Architecture in Urban Design and the Master of Landscape Architecture in Urban Design Programs
Ann Forsyth Director of the Master in Urban Planning Program
Kiel Moe Co-director of the Master in Design Studies Program
Mark Mulligan Director of the Master in Architecture Programs
Erika Naginski Co-director of the PhD Program in Architecture, Landscape Architecture, and Urban Planning
Antoine Picon Co-director of the PhD Program in Architecture, Landscape Architecture, and Urban Planning and Doctor of Design Program

GSD PUBLICATIONS TEAM

Jennifer Sigler Editor in Chief
Melissa Vaughn Senior Editor
Leah Whitman-Salkin Associate Editor
Meghan Sandberg Publications Coordinator

PLATFORM 7 EDITORIAL AND DESIGN TEAM

Leire Asensio Villoria Faculty Editor
Melissa Vaughn Senior Editor

Georgios Athanasopoulos MAUD
Patrick Burke MArch I AP
Jisoo Kim MLA I
Elizabeth Wu MLA I AP

GRAPHIC DESIGN CONSULTANTS

Laura Grey
Zak Jensen

FRANCES LOEB LIBRARY STUDENT WORK COLLECTION

Ann Baird Whiteside
Janina Mueller

PHOTOGRAPHY

Anita Kan

ADDITIONAL PHOTOGRAPHY

Jenn Alton
Iwan Baan
Frank Braman
Maggie Janik
Nathan King
Justin Knight
Jozef Sulik
Yusuke Suzuki
Katherine Taylor

ACTAR TEAM

Ramon Prat
Nuria Saban

IMPRINT

Published by the Harvard University Graduate School of Design and ActarD

Production by ActarD Inc.

Printed in China

GSD *Platform 7* represents selected studios, seminars, research, events, and exhibitions from the 2013–2014 academic year.

For additional information and a more comprehensive selection of student work, please visit gsd.harvard.edu.

ISBN 978-1-940291-43-7

The Harvard University Graduate School of Design is a leading center for education, information, and technical expertise on the built environment. Its Departments of Architecture, Landscape Architecture, and Urban Planning and Design offer masters and doctoral degree programs, and provide the foundation for the School's Advanced Studies and Executive Education programs.

DISTRIBUTION

Actar
151 Grand Street, 5th floor
New York, NY 10013
T 212-966-2207
F 212-966-2214
salesnewyork@actar-d.com
www.actar-d.com

SPECIAL THANKS

We would like to thank the following individuals, for without their efforts this publication would not have been possible:

Mohsen Mostafavi, Patricia Roberts, Dan Borelli, David Zimmerman-Stuart, David Mah, Ann Forsyth, Hanif Kara, Andreas Georgoulias, Ciro Najle, George L. Legendre, Sergio Lopez-Pineiro, Jose Mayoral Moratilla, Hal Gould, Mark Hagen, Trevor O'Brien, Anita Kan, Shantel Blakely, Christine G. O'Brien, Erica L. George, Julia Villoria Rodriguez, and Lucas Asensio-Mah.

A CIP catalogue record for this book is available from the Library of Congress, Washington, D.C., USA.

Letter from the Dean

Imagine a recording of a piece of classical music—or any musical recording, for that matter. As you listen, the emphasis is invariably on the sounds heard, apprehended, and felt by your ears, mind, and body. Separated from the performance that led to the making of the recording, your focus and experience is limited to the auditory outcome of the act of performing.

Now picture yourself at a live performance—say, of a chamber ensemble, jazz trio, or rock group—and then it becomes impossible to separate the sensorial experience of the performance before you from the qualities of the sounds produced as a consequence.

Playing music is both a physical and a participatory act. The making of chamber music, for example, is deeply intertwined with the movements of the body, the gestures of the hand, the rhythm of breathing, and the visual as well as sensory acknowledgment of the temporal responsiveness to others that is a prerequisite for the act of playing together.

The making of this book is in some ways akin to making a recording. This volume documents a series of activities and events—all performances of a sort—and their outcome at the Harvard Graduate School of Design during the past academic year. It brings together the work of a multitude of designers, authors, and makers, and in the process represents the work within the logics and limits of producing a book. I am grateful to Leire Asensio Villoria and the group of students who collaborated with her on the selection, assembly, and organization of content from the large body of available material.

Building on previous years' advances, this has been a time of deliberate transition, change, and transformation at the GSD, including the launch of numerous pedagogic and research initiatives. Many of these projects reflect the School's desire to have global impact and transform the built environment for the better. Like music, these projects have often been created through a combination of individual effort and collaborative practice, with a mindfulness of their reception and consequences for others. We feel compelled to highlight both the autonomy of the output as presented and the performative, circumstantial, and globally responsive conditions of its making. It is very important for us that the work of students and faculty is situated in the world and in the process rethinks and remakes that world.

It was thus particularly valuable for the School to take part in this year's Venice Biennale of Architecture, titled "Fundamentals." Our participation was based on two semester-long GSD studios in Rotterdam led by Professor Rem Koolhaas, who curated the Biennale. These studios provided much of the content for the "Elements of Architecture" exhibition held at the Central Pavilion in Venice.

Similarly, another group of students spent the spring semester in Los Angeles, investigating the "architecture of urbanism" in a studio led by Michael Maltzan in collaboration with Mia Lehrer, working across the scales of architecture, landscape, and urban design.

In Cambridge, the appointments of Iñaki Abalos as chair of the department of architecture, Grace La, and Ali Malkawi have enriched our commitment to practice, building systems, and the thermodynamics of architecture, a fact most clearly demonstrated in the School's support for the newly established Harvard Center for Green Buildings and Cities.

Our engagements with other parts of the University are beginning to produce interesting results. These include research on health and urbanization in collaboration with the Harvard School of Public Health and a proposed master's degree in Design Engineering with the School of Engineering and Applied Sciences. It was also rewarding for us to be able to cosponsor the Deans' Design Challenge, "Urban Life 2030," at the Harvard Innovation Lab; this project brought together students from across the University to collaborate on innovations for the future of our cities. These efforts parallel the success of the D-Labs, our faculty and student design research platforms that are undertaking significant investigations of the built environment from multiple perspectives and at multiple scales.

The carefully curated and dynamic offering of events in the School—lectures, conferences, symposia, and exhibitions—together with our publications provide an important context for showcasing the creative work of our students and faculty. This past year a diverse array of individuals including Denise Scott Brown, Robert Wilson, and Kanye West gave lectures or presentations. For me personally, however, one of the most rewarding parts of each year is to witness the incredible achievements and contributions of our students, faculty, and staff. The building of the beautiful Horizon House in rural Hokkaido and the proposals for the devastated Tohoku region (also in Japan), both by faculty-led student groups, are just two examples of the GSD's globally responsive accomplishments.

It would be impossible for a publication to document all of the School's work, collaborations, performances. This volume attempts to record a selective yet representative sample of the GSD's wide-ranging design proposals and activities.

A recording—a book—has led, in the process of its own making, to the production of a new view, with its own logics of affiliations, proximities, and connections.

Mohsen Mostafavi
Dean and Alexander and
Victoria Wiley Professor of Design
August 2014

Letter from the Editor

To communicate life at the GSD through a publication, even if limited to consideration of a single academic year, presents an engaging yet daunting exercise. There is certainly no scarcity of compelling design production, observable on even a casual stroll through the trays. Nor is there an absence of captivating lectures, conferences, symposia, and even gossip floating throughout the rooms and corridors at the School.

Yet to isolate a number of clear and common themes that allow for the unambiguous aggregation of various aspects of the GSD's creative activities into neat chapters can be elusive, and the ambition to do so capricious. How one decides on criteria for organizing such an overwhelming amount of activity and production is, unsurprisingly, not immediately obvious. Given such a mandate, I opted to use this year's *Platform* to communicate the very broadest range of work and events at the School.

It began for me with the simple organization of this year's content into straightforward categories. Studios, courses, lectures, exhibitions, and thesis projects are all sponsored by the three departments at the School and have been used as some of the specific sections of *Platform 7*. This clear-cut arrangement offered us an opportunity to place analogous work from the different departments in close proximity. An example of this can be seen with the core studios of all departments, which have been combined into a shared chapter, giving us a window into the distinct issues that are addressed in the core design sequence of each particular discipline. This grouping also allows us to recognize some unexpected moments of overlapping interests or commonality, a finding that extends across the curriculum and in the many events hosted by the GSD.

And this for me is one of the more absorbing aspects of the work and life here, where the diversity and breadth of the activity can be attributed to a combination of both highly specific and disciplinarily bounded explorations and something that emerges from collaboration and influence across disciplines. Unlike many other architecture schools that encompass a range of departments, the GSD is exceptional in the ease with which it appears to maintain a careful balance between having three departments with distinctive identities while also being the site where so much compelling collaborative work is nurtured. To highlight this condition, we used the color pink to distinguish some of the particularly noteworthy instances of cross-disciplinary exploration.

In many ways this intellectual duality resonates with the material reality of life at the GSD. Gund Hall's accommodation of students, staff, and faculty of all departments under one roof may be the most immediately evident illustration of this idea. The vast building places all three departments in close contiguity, enabling each department to find its own zone of operation, while also offering a shared setting within which the disciplines can collaborate, discuss, and be inspired by one another.

We kick off this year's volume of *Platform* with interviews of several members of the GSD community. The interviewees were approached to gather their insights into the value of this diversity that we recognized. While all responded to the same set of questions, we believe that the assortment of ideas and opinions that emerges out of the exercise provides both an engaging read and a useful frame for the showcased work and record of events that follow.

To present a complete picture of the many facets of design exploration at the GSD, the burgeoning activities of the School's various research groups as well as GSD life have been included in this year's *Platform*. It is also precisely in areas like these, where the community comes together either socially or engages the wider world, that we can see more immediately the value of the rich diversity cultivated at the GSD.

Leire Asensio Villoria
Lecturer in Architecture and Landscape Architecture
August 2014

Photographer Iwan Baan sharing photography techniques with students

Seven Questions about the GSD

Mohsen Mostafavi
Dean and Alexander and Victoria Wiley Professor of Design

Iñaki Abalos
Professor in Residence and Chair of the Department of Architecture

Rahul Mehrotra
Professor of Urban Design and Planning and Chair of the Department of Urban Planning and Design

Charles Waldheim
John E. Irving Professor of Landscape Architecture and Chair of the Department of Landscape Architecture

Ann Forsyth
Professor of Urban Planning

Hanif Kara
Professor in Practice of Architectural Technology

Farshid Moussavi
Professor in Practice of Architecture

Krzysztof Wodiczko
Professor in Residence of Art, Design, and the Public Domain

Giancarlo Mazzanti
Design Critic in Urban Planning and Design

To kick off this year's edition of *Platform*, we approached nine members of the GSD community to answer seven questions. The respondents were selected to span a broad range of disciplines currently active at the School. The seven questions invite each interviewee to offer us their ideas, attitudes, and impressions on the core concerns of the various disciplines at the GSD and the potential value of cross-disciplinary collaboration or inspiration. We believe that the assortment of thoughts and opinions that emerged out of the exercise provides both an engaging read and a useful context for the showcased work and events that follow. It should be noted that the responses were edited for length and extracted from more extensive remarks.

1

As an architect, landscape architect, or urban planner or designer, what do you consider the core disciplinary knowledge or concerns of your field?

Mohsen Mostafavi
The core disciplinary knowledge of architecture, like that of other design disciplines, is in a constant state of flux. What we need to know today is always based on our knowledge of architecture from the past as well as the present. But this knowledge is also anticipatory and projective in the sense that contemporary issues invariably involve negotiations between what has been before and what is yet to come. The core of this knowledge necessitates a contemporary reimagining of the Vitruvian virtues or Triad. In short, the articulation of the imagination brings the knowledge of building, use, and beauty into new and evolving relations.

Iñaki Abalos
If I had to summarize, I would say that architecture needs a continuous contrast between disciplinary historical knowledge and contemporary technical knowledge. I believe that the right balance between these two areas in the discipline is what allows designers to advance.

Rahul Mehrotra
I am not an urban planner by training, but rather through practice. And as a practitioner, I see the core concerns of urban planning as being about creating a neutral or common ground for society. That is, urban planning is the common set of rules that address questions of the most efficient, sustainable (as well as equitable) modes by which we can deploy and share resources in the city and its hinterland, both addressing questions of the present as well as anticipating their implications on the future. Urban design, on the other hand, is a bridge practice that straddles the abstraction of planning and the site specificity of architectural practice. So intrinsically urban design as a practice is about creating crucial feedback loops between scales and different forms of protocols. Thus by nature it is about activism and about initiatives to create a better built world on our planet.

Farshid Moussavi
I consider the core disciplinary knowledge of architecture to be the history of architecture, and the core concerns of architecture to be contemporary problems and opportunities that are sparked extrinsically, such as shortage of housing, potentials of digital fabrication, global warming, security, the new workplace, etc.

Hanif Kara
My sense is that the core disciplinary concerns of an architect and architecture has not really changed—it requires mastering many spheres of thought and bringing them together in a cohesive way. What appears to have changed is that the role of the architects has been reduced and eroded in the recent past, and their lack of concerns and inability to deliver in practice have allowed that. The net effect is that many other disciplines get into that gap they leave behind; the latest example of this is how many recently got stuck in a tectonic discourse fueled by technology. They really need to hold the pencil or the mouse!

Charles Waldheim
While I am not a landscape architect, I have become convinced that the field holds particular relevance to the challenges of the contemporary city. The profession of landscape architecture was conceived in the nineteenth century as a new profession responsible for divining the shape of the city. In contemporary terms, this would entail the integration of social, ecological, and spatial conditions in the making of urban space as a cultural project. Olmsted's "New Art" was intended as an explicitly social and political project, and built upon antecedent practices in Europe. These commitments of the field to shaping the contemporary

city persist today, and I believe that the core disciplinary knowledge of landscape architecture encompasses the design of the city, in relation to its social, ecological, and cultural performance.

Ann Forsyth
Planning is a future-oriented field concerned with developing human settlements in the long-term public interest, with a particular focus on future generations and social equity. It is concerned with the interconnections between different issues as they play out in space—social practices, natural environment, economic activity, and built environments. One philosophy of planning focuses on creating a generalist with a specialty, and the generalist part is important for a field focused on making connections.

Giancarlo Mazzanti
It is the understanding of the everyday use process of public space. What does the design produce in terms of life, interactions, and how can we generate new behaviors instead of only physical elements?

2

What are the contemporary and/or imminent design issues or concerns that you think the architecture, landscape architecture, urban planning, and urban design disciplines and/or professions should be addressing actively?

Mohsen Mostafavi
Broadly speaking, one of the key issues for design is how to make design itself a more potent component of everyday life. This task is nothing less than changing design from mere service, albeit an aspect of our work that should not be forgotten, to being inextricably linked to civic and political life. The exciting prospects for design remain many. There are of course a lot of key issues like climate change, limitations of resources, etc., that require new responses, but what is critical is the need for the designer to see everything—every issue, every problem—with fresh eyes.

Iñaki Abalos
I would like to differentiate between urgent matters and important themes—and keep in mind that often the two collide. I believe it is urgent that architects begin to respond to the extreme scales that we are currently witnessing in the built environment. In some parts of the world, it seems that there is not the need to build a single square meter more, while in other parts of the world, literally 250 million dwellings are expected to be built in the next twelve years. Moreover, the quality of architects is not well distributed with respect to that demand. I believe that if we are unable to respond to the situation of mass construction in a way that creates a new notion of quality at the different scales, architects will stop being useful for society and run the risk of occupying a bubble, isolated from the most pressing issues in the built environment. Probably the single most important issue is the idea of quality. How much do we need to modify the patterns of what historically has being understood as interesting design? The other topic that I believe will continue to be important to address over time is what we have framed in the department under the umbrella of "thermodynamics." The term is not only a technical reflection but also a cultural reflection having to do with contemporary science. This topic is really all about how architects can integrate different understandings of material and physical entities, both visible and invisible.

Farshid Moussavi
I believe the world presents the architectural discipline with diverse problems, both in terms of subject as well as scale. It would only be possible to give greater urgency to some over the others if you frame the question geographically. In America, I would say, the re-

generation of post-industrial cities; in the UK, the quality of housing built by house builders.

Hanif Kara
I think contemporary issues and concerns such as ecology, economy, and obsolescence need to be tackled head-on by design; we need to remove the "opacity," "mystique," and "esoteric" projection of the discipline that alienates the consumers and users from architecture.

Charles Waldheim
Our profession has a particular relevance for, and concomitant obligation to, addressing the imbrication of cultural production and ecological performance. This addresses one of the more pressing concerns in design culture more broadly, namely the relationship between architectural culture's recent history of autonomy and criticality on the one hand, and the social as well as ecological imperatives of contemporary urbanization on the other. We are presently experiencing the tectonic shifts of architectural culture attempting to reconcile these two heretofore contradictory conditions.

Rahul Mehrotra
For me the most critical issues for urban planning and urban design have to do with equity and ecology. Equity in the broadest term that involves not only financial equity but equity in terms of access to resources both natural and man-made. And by ecology I mean thinking ecologically to understand the interconnectedness of our world and thus understanding the implications of any form of intervention—which is what planning and urban design are fundamentally about. Naturally the two are related and all-encompassing. But for these issues to be effectively addressed, urban planning and design must be more speculative and anticipatory. This shift to future speculation is crucial for urban planning and design to retain its cutting edge and relevance. Most institutionalized urban planning and design has unfortunately become retrospective and obsessed with the present and the past, so this cultural shift in the discipline must begin in the academy.

Ann Forsyth
There are some obvious big issues: environmental change, aging, continued poverty, the shrinking of populations in some areas and continued growth in others. A concern is creating places that support a decent quality of life in the context of this change.

Giancarlo Mazzanti
Design is not only a finished and touchable product but the production of new ways of coexisting with nature, with the context, and with other humans. The intangible product will be more valuable for people who will embrace the architecture rather than a brick or a door. The actions that architecture produces are beyond the physical construction; it encourages communities, changes of mind, activities, and events. What do we do with an empty building? It is not useful at all.

Krzysztof Wodiczko
I think the relationship between art and design is something that needs to be further explored, and to help in this direction we should look to the avant-garde tradition. The divisions were less fixed in Constructivist and Productivist work in the 1920s Soviet Union, and also to some degree with the Bauhaus, the Futurists, Fluxus, and the Situationist International. Design students aren't encouraged to operate as artists. This is true especially for future architects. They are not taught and inspired to consider other, more artistic paths in their design projects even as a parallel practice to an official "professional" one. Development and implementation of shorter-term, unsolicited projects, not commissioned by "clients," especially those developed with less privileged and fewer acknowledged potential users, collaborators, and producers in mind, are seldom encouraged and discussed. The fact that artists, even these who operate as designers, are rarely invited to teach or co-teach design studio courses in architecture, and design schools make the situation difficult to change. As a Professor in Residence of Art, Design, and the Public Domain here at the GSD, I feel privileged because I am in the unusual position of being able to encourage and inspire design

students to consider art as a way to expand and transform their field and challenge the limits of both art and design for the benefit of life. Such a challenge, however, is a difficult task even in my privileged situation, because the design profession is generally not open to temporary, interventional, and critical-political projects. Yet design can have a role in identifying those whose needs aren't recognized by the market, whose needs shouldn't exist but unfortunately do exist in our "civilized" world—the needs that, like wounds, need emergency bandages. These needs can be articulated by design, but at the same time, design should draw attention to their unacceptability and emphasize that the solution (the elimination of such needs) must come through other means.

3

Should these concerns be addressed within strict disciplinary boundaries, or may we benefit from an engagement with other disciplines?

Mohsen Mostafavi
There are certain types of disciplinary knowledge that are formal and more internal to a particular discipline. But contemporary practice is perhaps most productive when the knowledge of different disciplines is brought to bear on a particular problem or topic. This proximity and reciprocity between various fields is the only way for us to produce new outcomes and solutions that transcend the knowledge of a specific discipline.

Iñaki Abalos
From a strategic point of view, I believe that we are at a key moment to reconstruct the discipline. It is totally obvious that multidisciplinarity is the only way of working because of the technical, political, and social complexity that architecture has acquired. However, I believe that in architectural schools and other places where the discipline maintains its integrity, to be able to work consistently and in a multidisciplinary way it is essential to rebuild the discipline. In other words, it is essential to rebuild the authority of the architect, and the only way to rebuild the authority of the architect is through disciplinary knowledge.

Rahul Mehrotra
We would naturally benefit from interacting deliberately with other disciplines. In fact, I think, "disciplinary anxieties" are something we have to actively work toward dissolving. The obsession with branding, claiming terrains of knowledge, etc., are only self-serving and totally detrimental to the common good. This atmosphere of self-centric knowledge creation is myopic and dangerous in the academy, where we incubate planners and designers of the future. Instead a generosity, openness, and a culture of collaboration must be totally central to our values in articulating a sense of the discipline.

Charles Waldheim
While the challenges of the built environment generally, and cities in particular, rarely correspond to strict disciplinary or professional boundaries, those boundaries continue to shape our knowledge and practices. This relationship, between ongoing cultural, technological, environmental, and social change, and enduring disciplinary and professional identities, is among the most engaging set of questions for the design disciplines today. This necessarily involves reflection on the founding aspirations and conditions for each discipline, as well as ongoing, robust engagements within and between the professions responsible for the shape of the city as simultaneously a cultural and ecological project.

Ann Forsyth
Urban planning is extremely interdisciplinary. Planning students take courses across Harvard, not just across the GSD. Faculty collaborate with others in a wide variety of disciplines. Because of planning's interest

in interconnections and the wider public interest, planners need to know about many other fields.

Hanif Kara
There is no doubt in my mind that the most profit is extracted in the borders and boundaries between disciplines through filtering and exclusion, but it takes many confident disciplines to recognize these boundaries and extract the most creative and valuable contributions. In that regard, one should be an excellent architect but also have a good understanding of engineering or cost, for instance.

Farshid Moussavi
There is no simple answer to this. On the one hand, architecture's public dimension means that its discourse and practice are interrelated with those of so many other fields that are in themselves changing. Therefore changing areas of overlap can and should be subjects of research at the School. On the other hand, this can not be limited to simply identifying areas of overlap. It is necessary to develop tools to act upon them too, a process that is best done by each discipline separately. For example, the study of housing shortage may bring a sociologist, an economist, a politician, and an architect together to discuss the problem and identify the needs. But ultimately, the instruments of each of the experts are different. The architect's role has always been to synthesize and draw the various layers of a project together. So when it comes to constructing the actual project, I believe that he or she should focus on the architectural tools. Otherwise we can end up talking around the table and having great ideas, but finally implementing them in conventional ways.

Krzysztof Wodiczko
Of course the issue of cross-disciplinarity comes straight after this; the world is too complicated to work alone, so one must work with others and also learn other fields, because one field is not enough. The word "avant-garde" seems to be exhausted, but I think that it is important to bring it back and do more that is proactive, transformative, speculative—as some activity that transforms the world in a positional way rather than in a desconstructive way; that is something that I see as a task for avant-garde art. And design comes immediately as part of this. The moment that avant-garde art is proactive, it must become design—that is how I see it. Now that we are somehow working together, we have to really understand this agenda together—people in technology, social scientists, architects, designers, artists. But the issue is that art and architecture should be understood in many ways; one cannot simply combine things because we like cross-disciplinarity.

4

From your experience and observations as an active member of the GSD community, and in particular someone who works within Gund Hall (a building that houses a number of design disciplines under one roof), how valuable is the exposure and proximity to other design disciplines for the GSD as a whole?

Mohsen Mostafavi
The proximities, overlaps, negotiations, conflicts, disagreements, and conversations that occur within the GSD as a forum for multiple disciplines and areas of investigation are vital for a collaborative model of design education and research.

Iñaki Abalos
I believe that the interest in having almost 800 people working on three complementary disciplinary fields is embedded in the initials of the GSD: the word "design" links

us all. The most interesting thing is that our School is expanding and advancing the definition of design, and that is why the friction and proximity between disciplines is a way of feeding the system, which is very productive in that sense.

Rahul Mehrotra

I think it's critical. However, I believe that interdisciplinary work does not occur by throwing people from different disciplines in the same room, but by framing the problems in a robust and inclusive way such that it attracts interdisciplinary engagement. Picking and defining the problem is perhaps more important to facilitate interdisplinary work than believing we will solve it by making space for it to occur.

Charles Waldheim

It is among the defining characteristics of the GSD that it was founded explicitly under the rubric of "design" that the disciplines share, yet none own exclusively. Within that rubric, each discipline and profession bring distinct bodies of knowledge, practices, and preoccupations. Equally, each of the disciplines brings utterly distinct methods and cultural norms. The regular, rigorous, and ongoing interaction between the disciplines of the School makes for a richer and more diverse environment for graduate study in design.

Ann Forsyth

I'm sure it's valuable, and there's a relatively large amount of interaction at the GSD, inside and outside of courses. But it is also valuable to be exposed to disciplines outside of the GSD.

Farshid Moussavi

I think it is a key ingredient of the GSD's culture. In fact, I wrote a short article for *The Architectural Review* on the subject. The building of an architecture school— beyond the teaching staff, curriculum, etc.— is what makes the school what it is. The interplay between its spatial arrangement and pedagogical strategy embeds the school with a specific kind of habitus, which influences the kind of agency students take on in future practice. Gund Hall's single, large open-plan space, with cascading floors or "trays," embeds it with affect of collectivity and transparency. Its two flights of stairs that cut into the trays are instrumental in enabling students from the three disciplines to thread through each other's work, like a web of ideas. The building therefore situates students within disciplinary agendas in order to question the limits of each, but it also instills awareness of other agendas and dialogue across them. Of course mobile devices now provide the students with the possibility of working from anywhere. But part of going to architecture school is also learning to work and interact with others. The building allows you to interact with one another in ways that working remotely simply doesn't.

Hanif Kara

I am a proponent of "interdisciplinary practice" and distinguish this from a "multidisciplinary practice," for instance. In my version, one requires a deep knowledge of one's discipline, but also a knowledge of other disciplines and most of all an ability to communicate in that environment; therefore I think the Gund Hall model, with exposure to other disciplines, is invaluable.

Giancarlo Mazzanti

It allows that teachers as well as students consider the space as a sum of infinite variables and not as a unit to put an object on. Being all together in a building gives everyone the opportunity to interact, share knowledge, and learn continuously. The connection between urban design, architecture, and landscape is a huge asset that not all universities have, but they should.

Krzysztof Wodiczko

A very important contribution is coming from planning, and urban studies in general, simply because what we have learned from the work of people like Rahul [Mehrotra], Diane [Davis], and Neil [Brenner]. We have a lot in common—our focus on social relations, public space, cultural geography, historical geography, all of those things without which it is difficult to approach work in public space as a social project. Social relations from that space have something to do with the title of the concentration Art, Design, and the Public Domain; public domain is not the space as such, it is life and the way people make sense and use of that space as a stage, as a vehicle, for life together, communication, exchange, confronting each other's point of view— a dynamic full of friction and healthy conflict.

5

What other areas in the School or other departments within the University would you like to establish connections with in order to further advance the trajectory and knowledge of the department?

Mohsen Mostafavi
We have already established connections and collaborations with the School of Engineering and Applied Sciences, the School of Public Health, the Mahindra Center for the Humanities, the Faculty of Arts and Sciences, Harvard University's Committee on the Arts, Harvard Business School, the Harvard Law School, and the Wyss Institute for Biologically Inspired Engineering. Now we need to strengthen these relationships and make sure that they are sustainable in the long run. It is exciting to imagine the unexpected possibilities and outcomes of these collaborations for our students and our faculty.

Iñaki Abalos
I believe that the exchanges and collaborations that are the most interesting at the moment, not only for the Department of Architecture but for all the departments, are those having to do with the exterior world with its exterior knowledge. I am extremely interested in the reconstruction of the role of the subject, how we conceive humans relationships with the world. For this we need knowledge in the fields of neuroscience, medicine, and even ethics. There is a need to study how we move collectively and individually as mammals, since traditional distinctions between human and nonhuman have become less useful. As Giorgio Agamben says, how to exactly locate us as mammals to start a conversation about our socialization patterns.

Hanif Kara
I think the connection between "design" and "the business of design" could be stronger; perhaps the interaction with the business school should be on a par with access to MIT technology labs, for example.

Farshid Moussavi
Working alongside other disciplines is an unavoidable part of architectural practice. We don't need to recreate the environment of real practice at School. I am sure faculty will always collaborate with other departments when it is seen as useful. I personally believe that it is important to be exposed to other fields, but not necessarily to do work with other fields. Ultimately, every discipline needs to address the "common problems" with its own tools and instruments. However, it would be good to have access to a platform, where we can meet others and hear them in a less formal manner. Maybe there should be a Harvard café right in the center of Harvard Yard, with talks, interviews, and presentations every day, that anyone can pass through and be "touched by" other departments—something equivalent to the TED talks by Harvard, not within the bounds of any of the schools but somewhere neutral and open exclusively to the Harvard community. It could become an exciting think-tank space with no predefined agendas or goals. I would love to design such a space in the middle of the Yard.

Rahul Mehrotra
In the UPD department we have already actively done this. Over the last three years we have invited faculty from other departments across the University to become affiliates. We have made bridges to anthropology, divinity, sociology, law, government, history, public health, and economics. I think we need to build stronger ties with departments, looking at new technologies

and disciplines that could expose us more mindfully to the cultures of innovation—an infusion of which is something that urban planning (more than urban design) needs rather urgently!

Charles Waldheim
The Department of Landscape Architecture continues to benefit from its historical and ongoing relationships with the range of disciplines and professions represented in the School, as well as across campus. Going forward, we expect these connections to strengthen and multiply, particularly with respect to the intersection of architecture as a cultural form and processes of urbanization as examined across a range of disciplines in the School and on campus that are responsible for the city as an object of study.

Giancarlo Mazzanti
Architecture is not a lonely area; it should be supported by departments of anthropology, psychology, biology, sociology, philosophy, economy, law, arts, and many others. As we gather more and more information, design will be more usable and embraced because is dedicated to people and their context. Multidisciplinary research allows us to have a well-thought-out project instead of a soulless building.

6

What have you been excited by or enjoyed the most this year at the GSD (in relation to the previous questions or not)?

Mohsen Mostafavi
I enjoy seeing the ever-changing list of achievements of our students and faculty on the website. It is this sense of the School as a place where a plurality of individuals and groups are constantly producing interesting ideas and making important contributions to the built environment that is the most rewarding. It was, for example, inspiring to be present in Tokyo when a group of GSD students from various parts of the School won an international prize for their response to the disaster in the Tohoku region of Japan.

Iñaki Abalos
I have especially enjoyed the informal lectures in Loeb Library. The ground floor of the library is an incredible place that we are using more and more due to its informality. I like the contrast between the collective world of the trays and the spaces of isolation of the library. I believe that a school of architecture should be made out of spaces of isolation and spaces of intense friction. This school has these very good dualities. The space that I like the least is Piper. There are hundreds of auditoriums that are more empathetic and that foster discussion and participation that do not occur in Piper due to its rigidity. Even though Piper is very flexible in its format, it is hard to achieve a very participatory lecture.

Rahul Mehrotra
What I have been stimulated by the most are the things I have been doing as part of GSD's outreach program in the University. My time at the South Asia Institute, my participation in the course run by Michael Hays and Neil Levine for undergraduates that looks at landmark architecture around the world, the many seminars at Radcliffe—for me these forays into the wider universe of the University has been incredibly enriching.

Charles Waldheim
Among the many rewarding aspects of the past year has been the GSD's remarkable success in recruiting extraordinary students and faculty to join our community and contribute to the work of disciplinary and professional formation that is an ongoing project of the School. I am equally proud of the work of our faculty and students, as evident in this publication, and beyond. I am also pleased to participate in the intellectual life of the School, its publications program, exhibitions, and events.

Ann Forsyth
The planning program has been working

actively with an increasing number of new and established research centers and initiatives, including the Joint Center for Housing Studies, Transforming Urban Transport, the Health and Places Initiative, various labs, and cross-campus collaborations.

Giancarlo Mazzanti
Having the opportunity to meet people, experience speeches and ways of thinking that taught me many things. The multiplicity of elements and resources that are always available.

Krzysztof Wodiczko
The many beautiful exhibitions in Gund Hall, especially Cartographic Grounds, Airport Landscape—remarkable exhibitions. And of course as always, the rich number of lectures; I wish I could attend more of them. It is very hard to select something that was the most exciting; the place is exciting every day.

7

And what are you looking forward to next year?

Mohsen Mostafavi
The evolution of research and its links to pedagogy across all the departments is a very exciting topic, as is the shaping of the new masters program in Design Engineering in collaboration with the School of Engineering and Applied Sciences, and of course the development of the Center for Green Buildings and Cities.

Iñaki Abalos
I hope to see the consolidation of the program's modification that we have been working on since I joined the GSD as the chair of the Department of Architecture. My main interest has been the core courses within the field of design, and the reorganization of the areas of knowledge and the interrelation of lectures, courses, and seminars. These are the areas that I have been focusing on the most, and I believe that they can lead to a more updated and open design culture that is entirely focused on the importance and quality of design as the main benefit that we can offer as architects to the world.

Rahul Mehrotra
Like every year, what one really looks forward to is the array of option studios that will take place at the GSD and the many new visitors that will be present. It always feels like the GSD is a completely new place every year!

Charles Waldheim
I am looking forward to working with our colleagues to continue building disciplinary and professional capacity around questions that are central to the future of the design disciplines generally, and landscape architecture and contemporary urbanism more particularly. This entails the ongoing work of leadership with respect to recruiting and retaining the best and brightest across all stages of professional development.

Hanif Kara
The things that I enjoy the most at the GSD are the many symposiums and lectures that the School hosts; listening to the many different voices and perspectives is exciting.

Krzysztof Wodiczko
I am looking forward to my option studio and meeting guests that I have invited:Lucy Horta, N55, Marjetica Potr, Atelier van Lieshout. Also, we will develop a new project with students on campus, maybe as part of work on the architecture culture of prosthetics. I am looking forward even to the challenges that come with it.

Architecture's first year MArch I structures exercise

Nikon

Architecture I

Coordinators
Iñaki Abalos
Cameron Wu
Instructors
Katy Barkan
Jeffry Burchard
Kiel Moe
Megan Panzano
Ingeborg Rocker

The first core studio of the four-semester sequence of the MArch I program, Project may refer to fundamental modes of architectural representation, the mapping of the subject in the larger objective context, or a conceptual foray into territory unknown. A series of focused and intense design exercises required students to investigate disciplinary issues of architectural thought, practice, and representation. As the introductory studio in the first professional degree program, the curriculum addressed the varied educational backgrounds of incoming MArch I candidates. Specifically, students were encouraged to leverage their expertise in the sciences, humanities, and other disciplines to find provocative and perhaps unexpected motivations of architectural form.

PLATFORM 7

01 James Murray (MArch I)
02 See Hong Quek (MArch I)
03 Nastaran Arfaei (MArch I)
04 Johanna Faust (MArch I)
05 Yurina Kodama (MArch I)
06 Ben Halpern (MArch I)
07 See Hong Quek (MArch I)
08 Evan Farley (MArch I)
09 Justin Jiang (MArch I)
10 Justin Gallagher (MArch I)
11 Felipe Oropeza (MArch I)
12 David Hamm (MArch I)
13 Sean Chai (MArch I)
14 Felipe Oropeza (MArch I)
15 Justin Gallagher (MArch I)
16 Felipe Oropeza (MArch I)
17 Yurina Kodama (MArch I)
18 Olivia Heung (MArch I)
19 Felipe Oropeza (MArch I)
20 Sophia Panova (MArch I)
21 David Hamm (MArch I)
22 James Murray (MArch I)

01

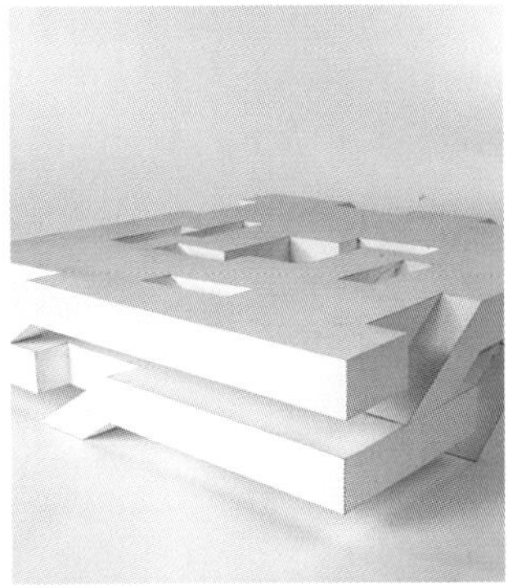
02

03

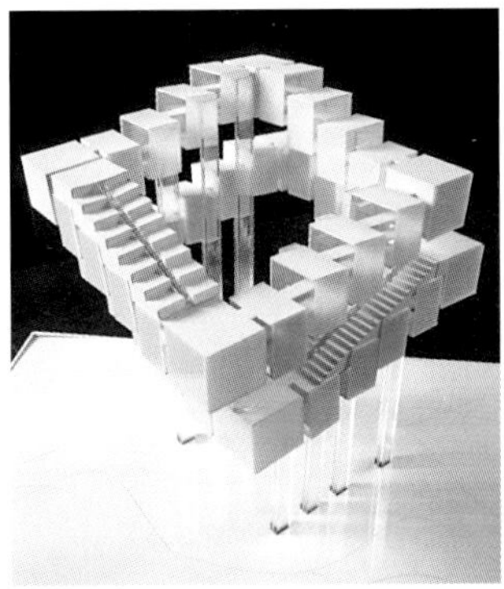
04

05

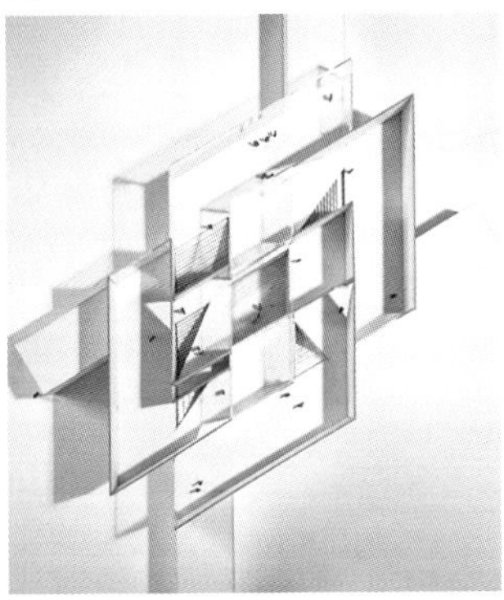
06

07

08

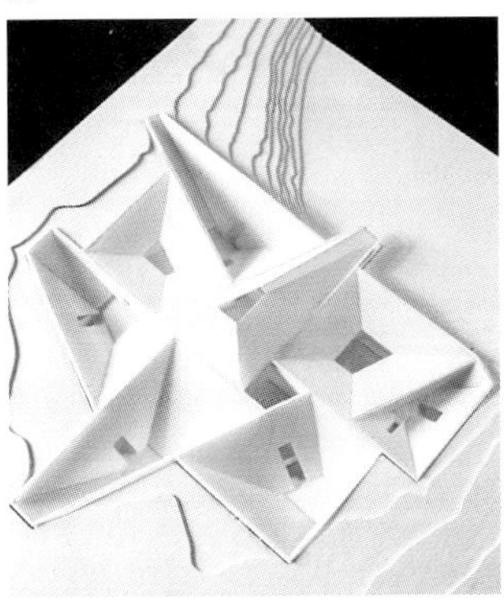
09

10

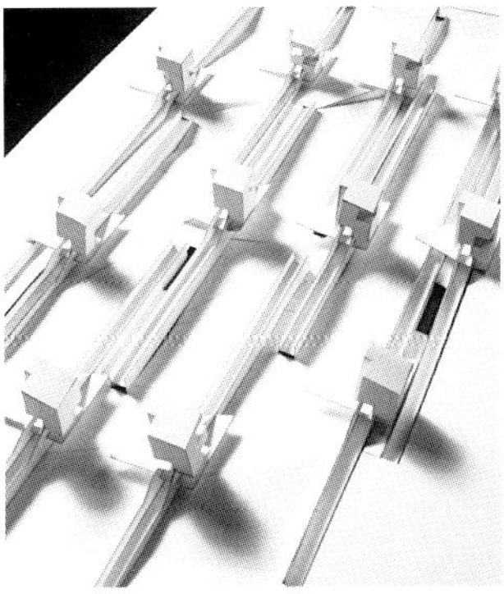

11

12

13

14

15

16

17

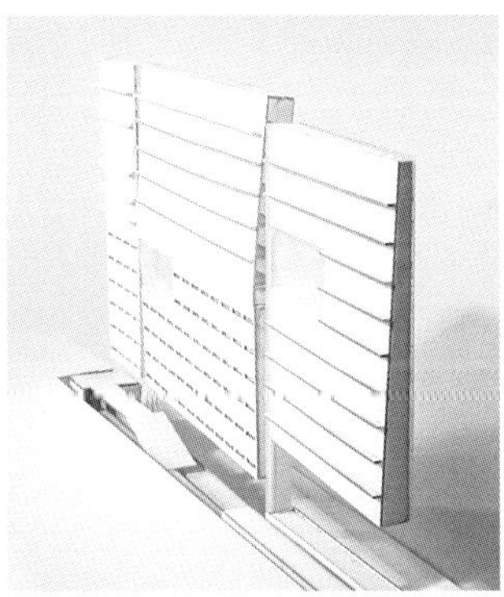

18

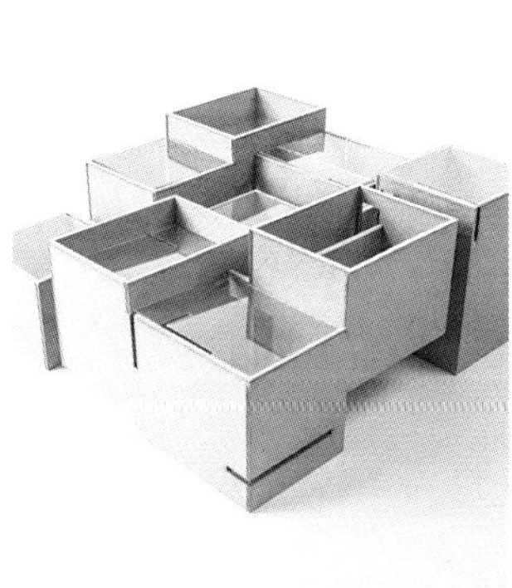

19

20

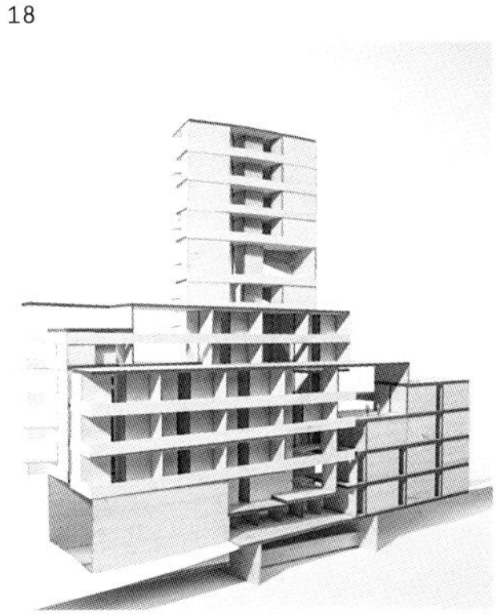

21

22

Gavin Ruedisueli (MArch I)
Instructor: Kiel Moe
01 Compact/Cold Plan 1
02 Compact/Cold Plan 2
01 Convoluted/Hot Plan 1
02 Convoluted/Hot Plan 2
05 Compact/Cold Section
06 Compact/Cold Section
07 Compact/Cold Section
08 Convoluted/Hot Section
09 Convoluted/Hot Section
10 Convoluted/Hot Section

Ben Halpern (MArch I)
Instructor: Katy Barkan
11 Transformation (A) along hinged dissection
12 Daytime thermo: mechanical, insulation, exposure
13 Nighttime thermo: radiant heat, thermal mass
14 Plan (A)
15 Daytime thermo: mechanical, insulation, exposure
16 Nighttime thermo: radiant heat, thermal mass
17 Transformation (B) along hinged dissection
18 Daytime thermo: mechanical, insulation, exposure
19 Nighttime thermo: radiant heat, thermal mass
20 Plan (B)
21 Daytime thermo: mechanical, insulation, exposure
22 Nighttime thermo: radiant heat, thermal mass

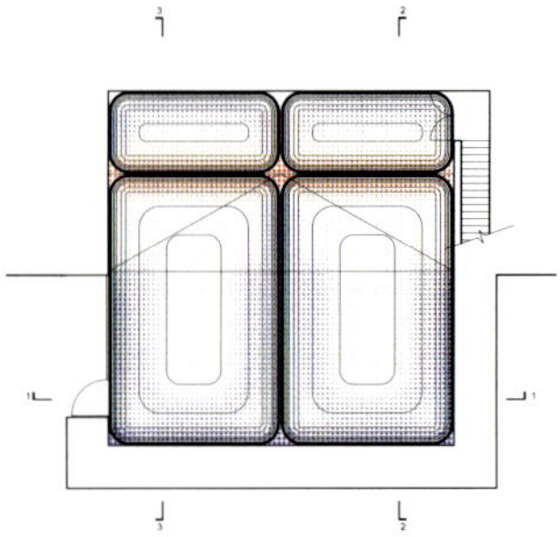

01

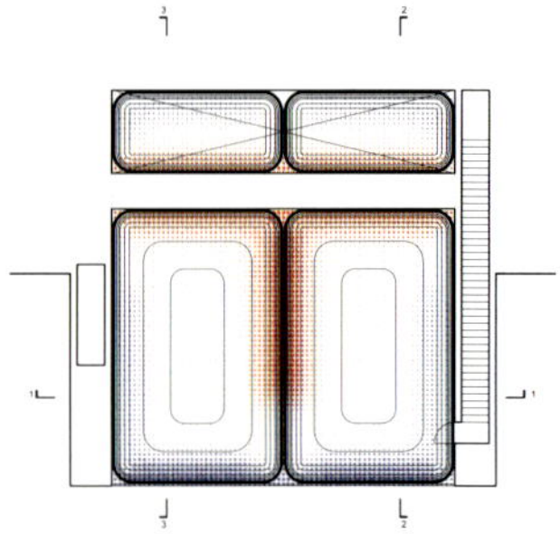

02

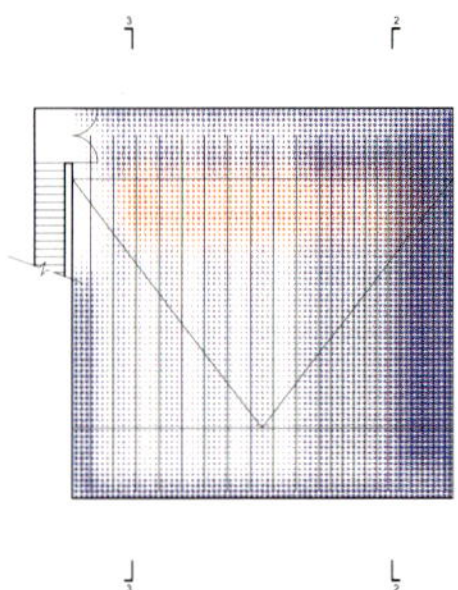

03

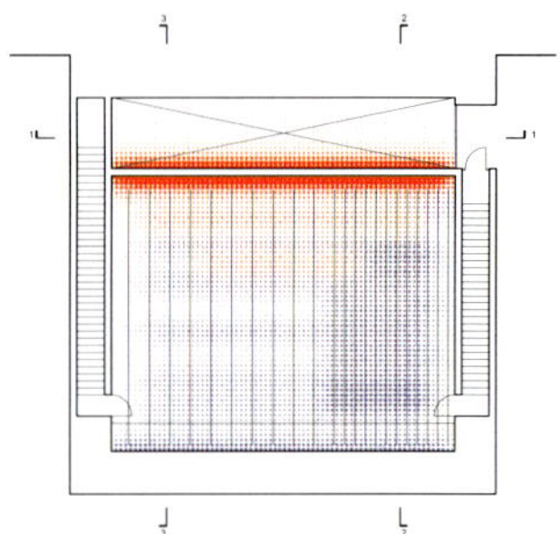

04

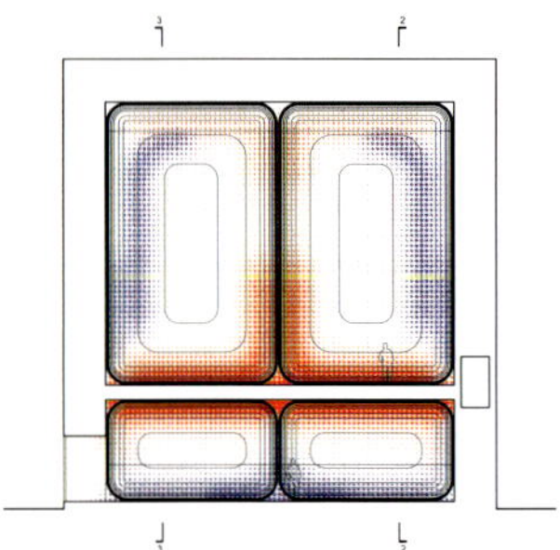

05

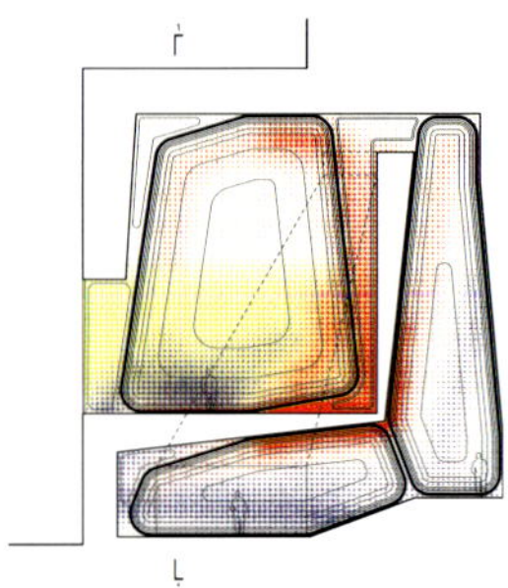

06

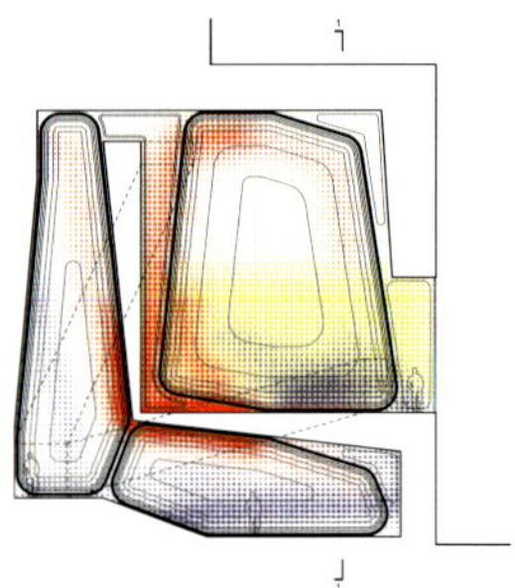

07

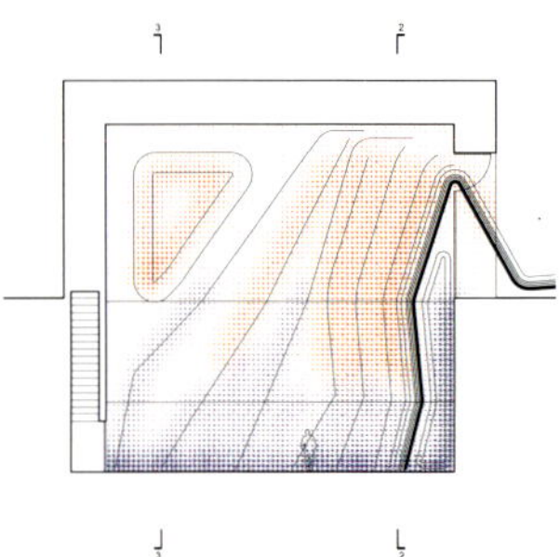

08

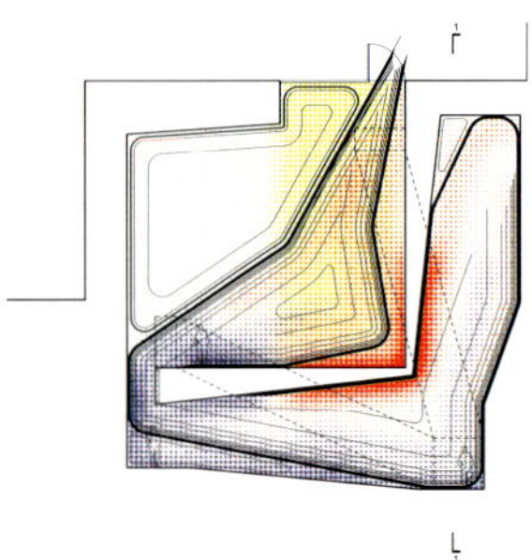

09

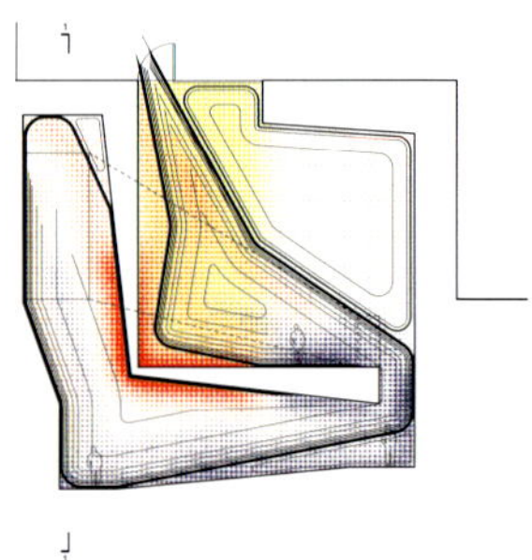

10

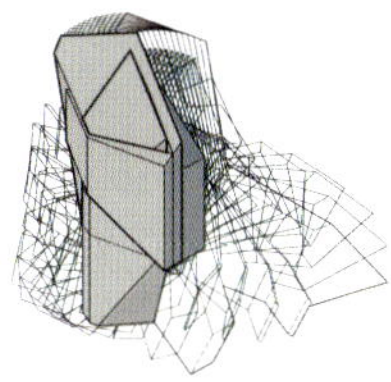

11

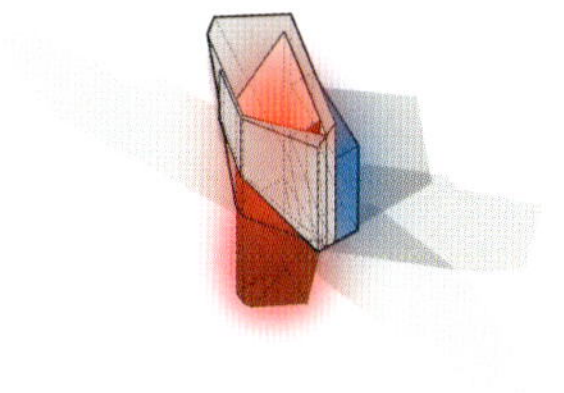

12

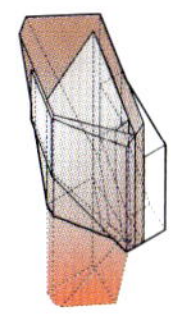

13

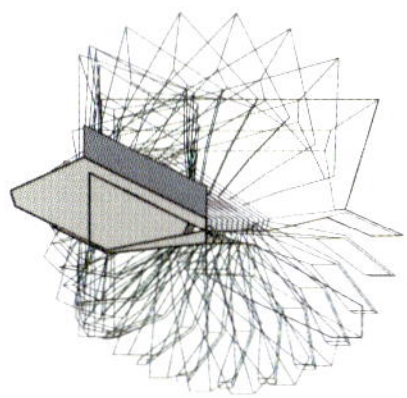

14

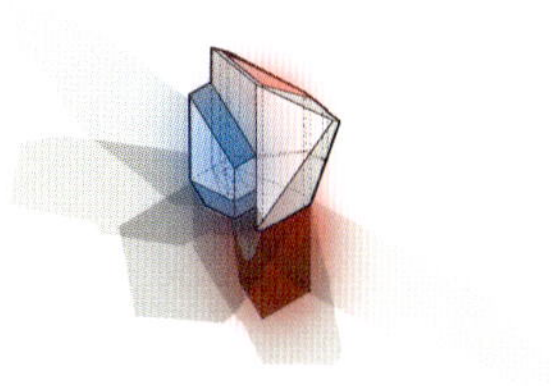

15

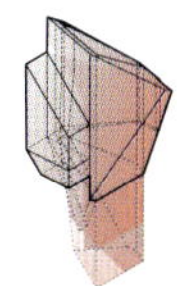

16

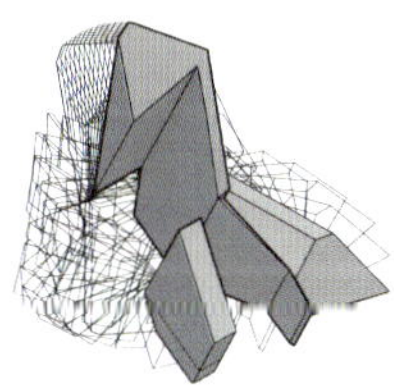

17

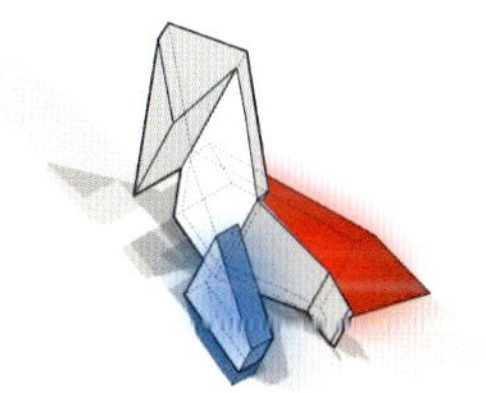

18

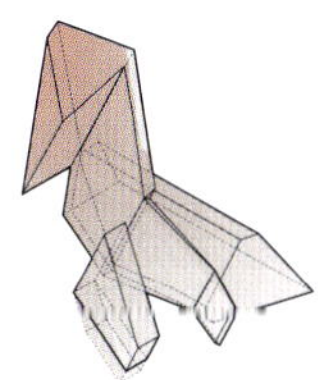

19

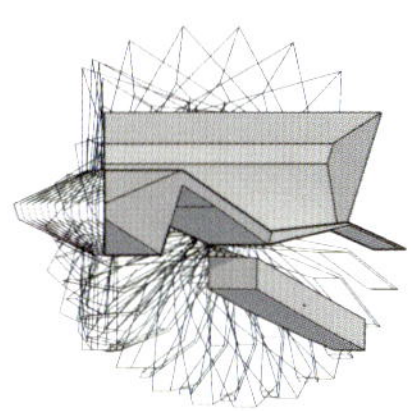

20

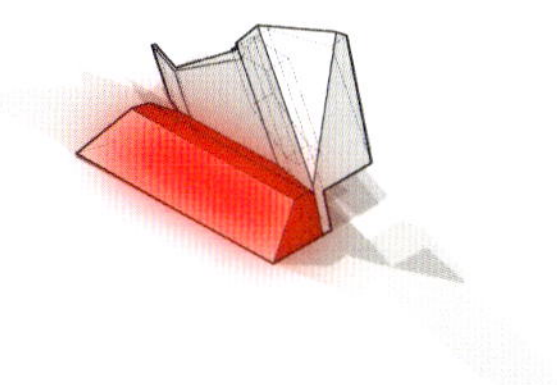

21

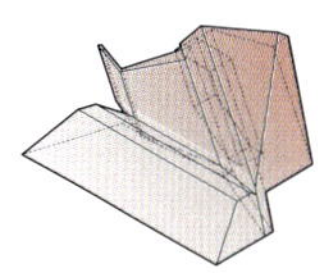

22

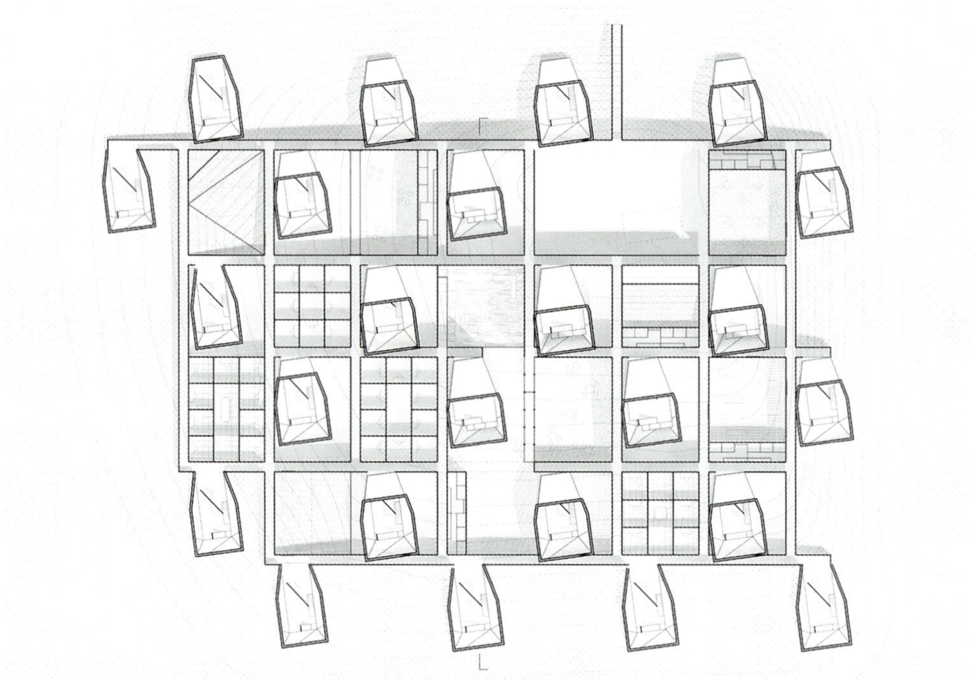

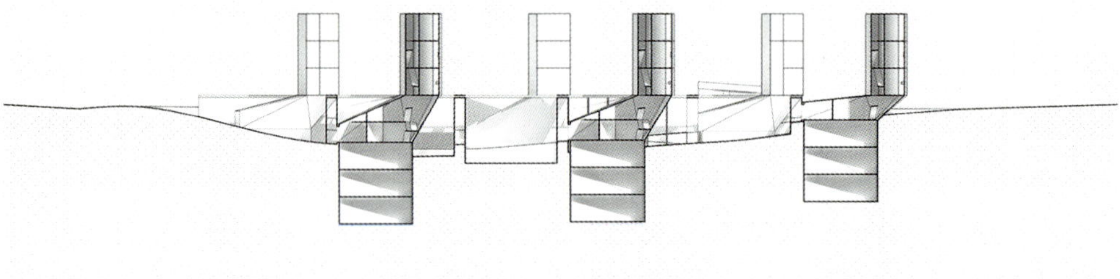

James Murray (MArch I). Instructor: Kiel Moe. Dispersed in a field condition, the labs construct a topography of difference. Towers array around an intuitive spacing of trees, casting shade on themselves but not on each other. With an approaching view of the laboratory, the grid of towers appears as a field of self-similar objects while in fact producing a terrain of diverse experiences and thermodynamic conditions through its relationship with the landscape.

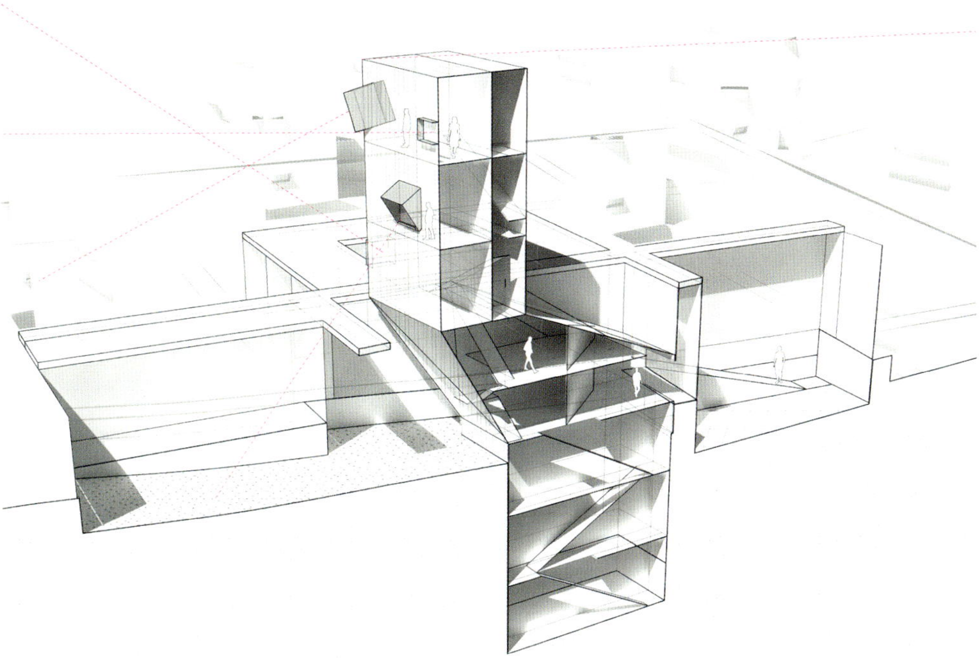

James Murray (MArch I). Instructor: Kiel Moe. The labs change shape to meet a sloping ground plane, connecting to a grid that frames an exploration of boundaries and follies. Thermal orientation is translated to an orientation of the inhabitants' experience by small apertures, demarcating their relation to courtyards and the field.

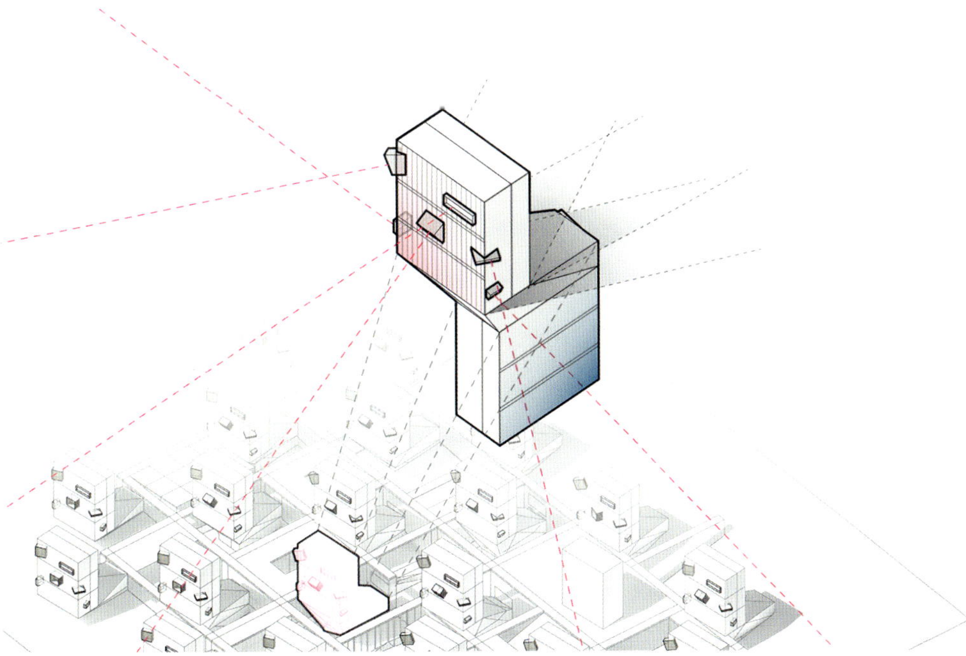

Coordinators
Gary Hilderbrand
Jane Hutton
Instructors
Silvia Benedito
Zaneta Hong
Workshops
Peter Beard
Michael Van Valkenburgh

Landscape Architecture I

This studio problematizes issues of orientation and experience, scale and pattern, topographic form, canopy and climatic influences, and varied ecological process that help define urban public space. As the first of a four-term sequence of design studios, the course encouraged students to develop spatial literacy, critical design thinking, and proficiency in diverse modes of representation in landscape architecture. The first studio exercises investigated a set of typological models rooted in historical and contemporary precedents. These underwent sequential transformations aimed at devising hybrid solutions to common conceptual design problems: conditions of stasis, movement, and change over time. Two workshops were conducted: a one-week engagement of specialized analog techniques of surface description, and a second week focused on conceptualizing coastal vegetative palettes. Throughout the course, the studio emphasized design as a performative venue for conceiving, interrogating, and elaborating concrete ideas about the role of the biophysical landscape in urbanization and urban life.

PLATFORM 7

01,22:
Jessica Booth (MLA I)
02,09:
Yong Uk Kim (MLA I)
03 Vipavee Sirivatanaaksorn (MLA I)
04 Sarah Bolivar (MLA I)
05 Andrew Boyd (MLA I)
06,16:
Zehao Xie (MLA I)
07,15:
Alicia Meza (MLA I)
08,13:
Yuanjie Li (MLA I)
10 Emily Allen (MLA I)
11,21:
Xinhui Li (MLA I)
12 Hui Wang (MLA I)
14 Ambrose Luk (MLA I)
17 Ivy Pan (MLA I)
18 Alexander Cassini (MLA I)
19 Azzurra Cox (MLA I)
20 Larissa Belcic (MLA I)

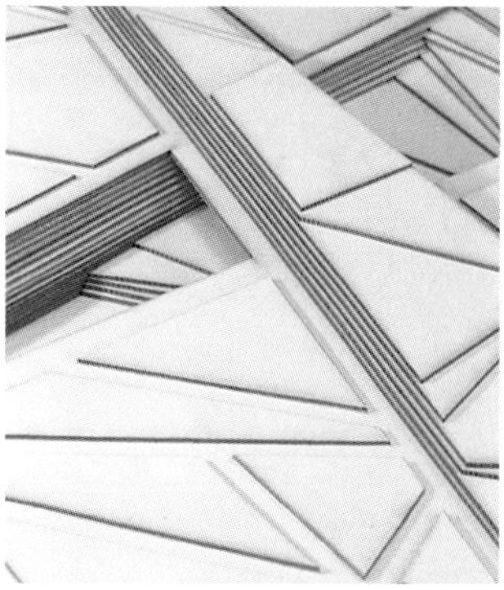
01

02

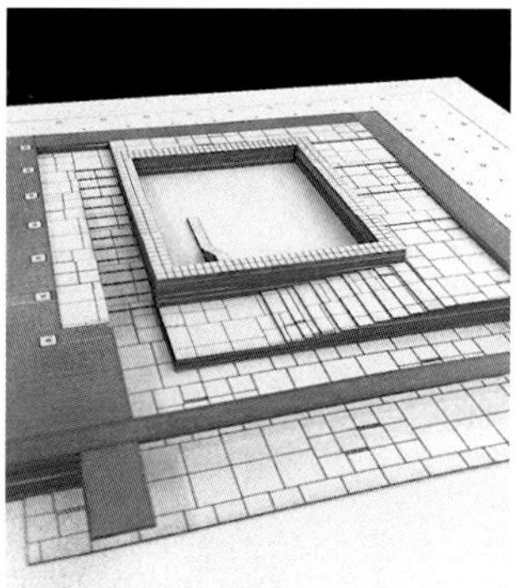
03

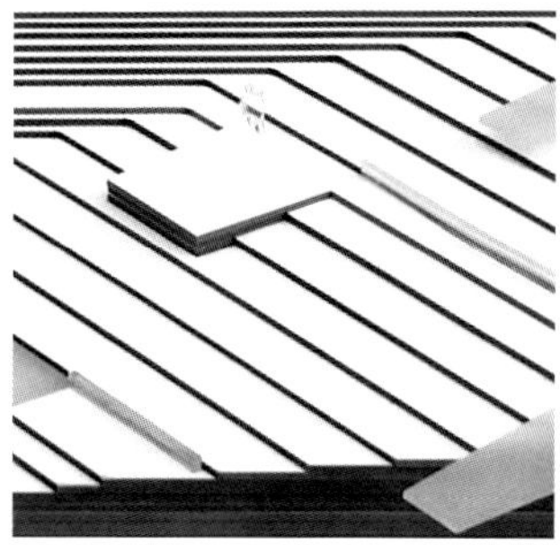
04

05

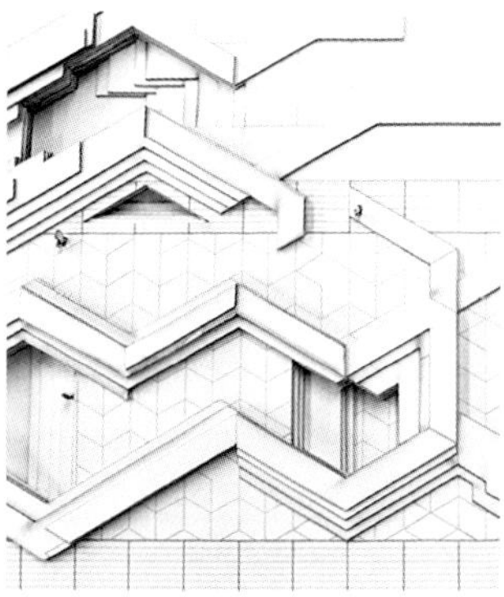
06

07

08

09

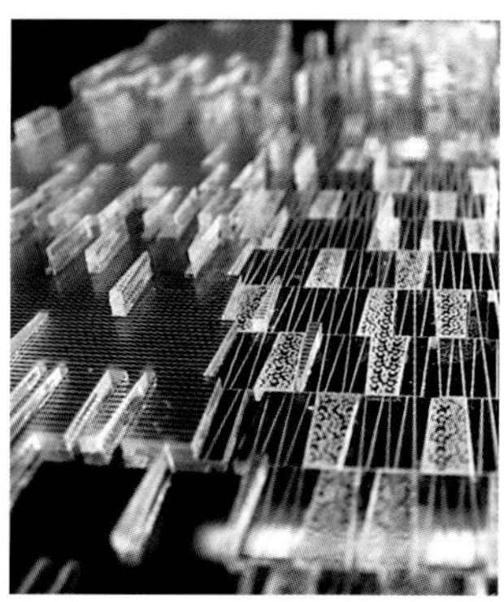
10

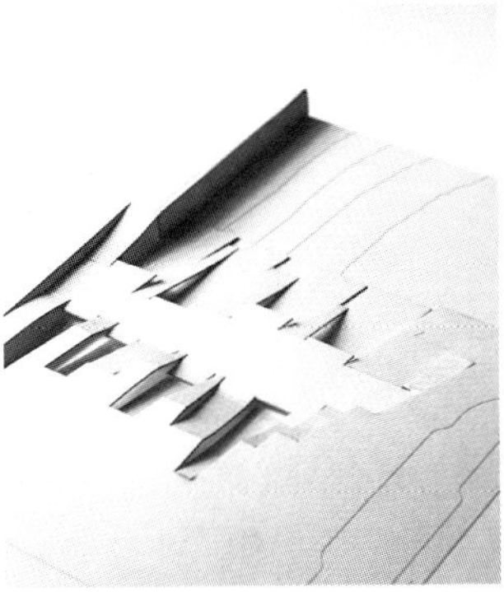

11

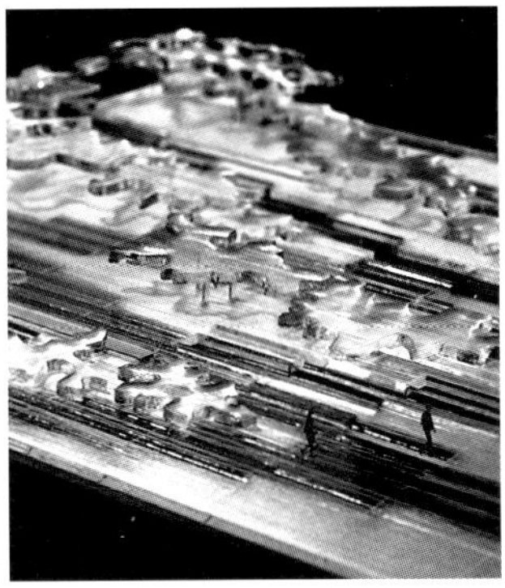

12

13

14

15

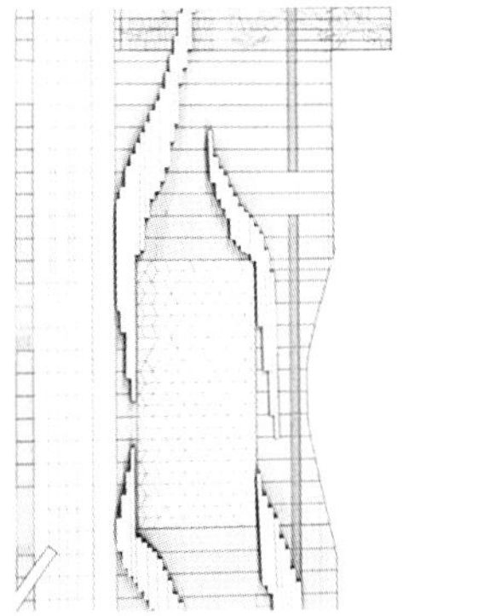

16

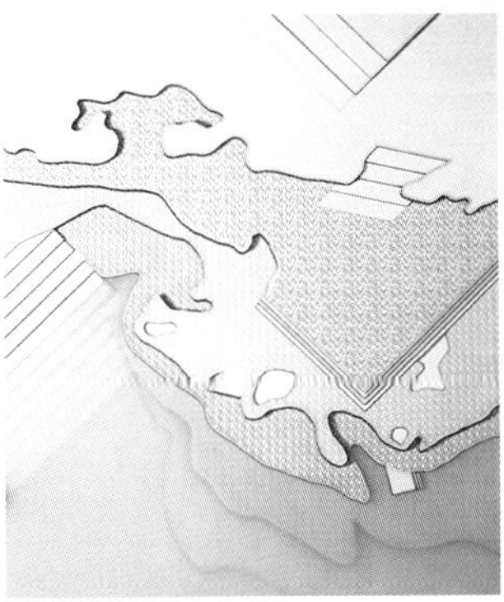

17

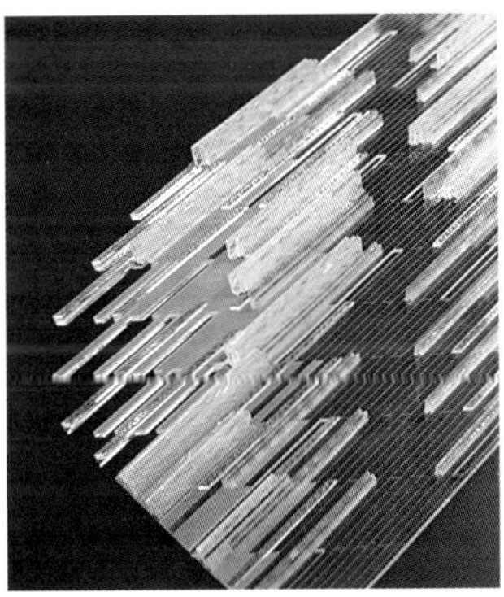

18

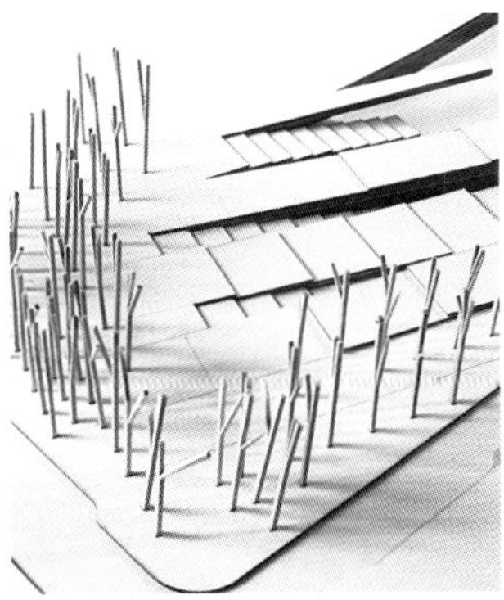

19

20

21

22

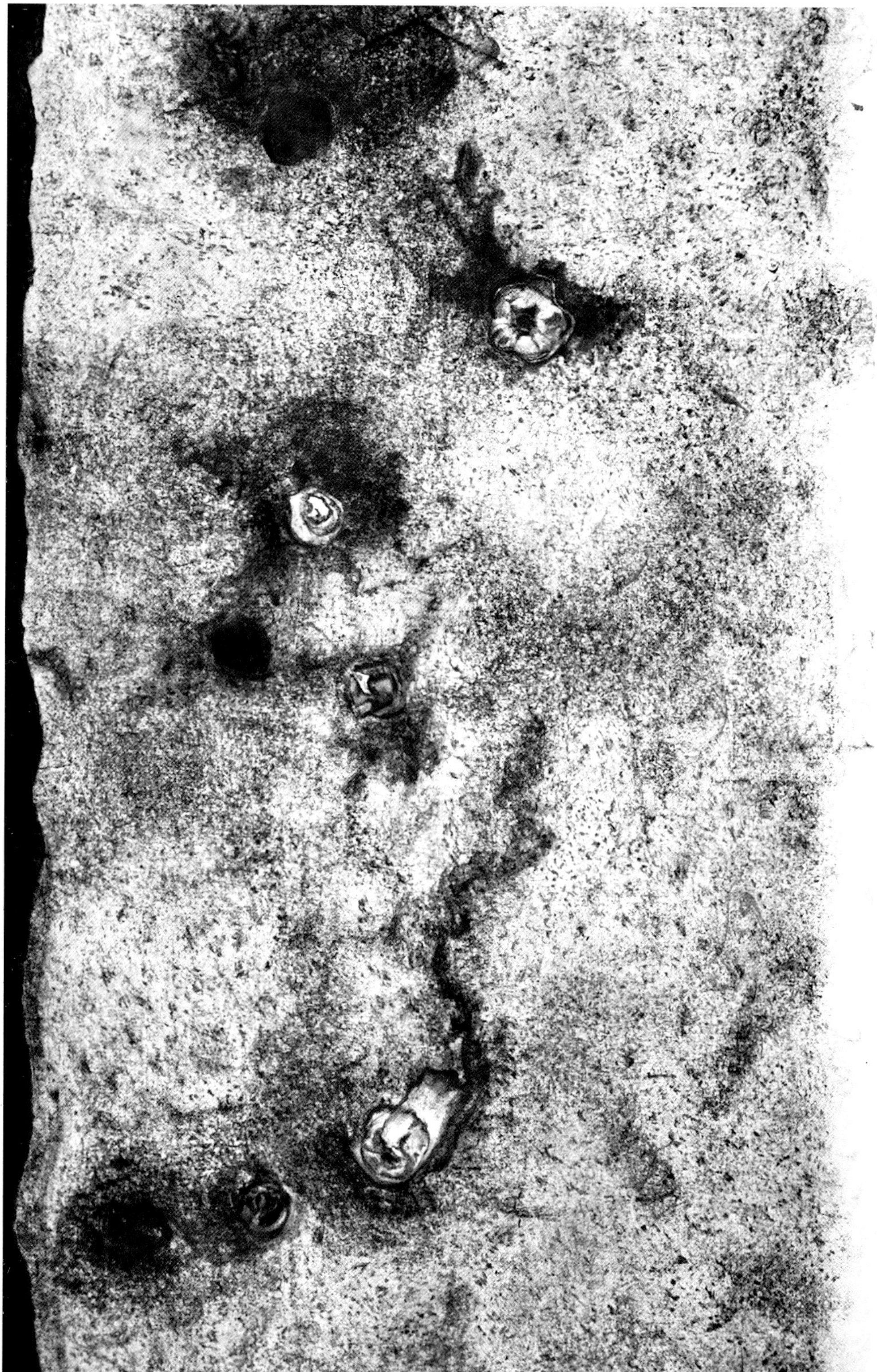

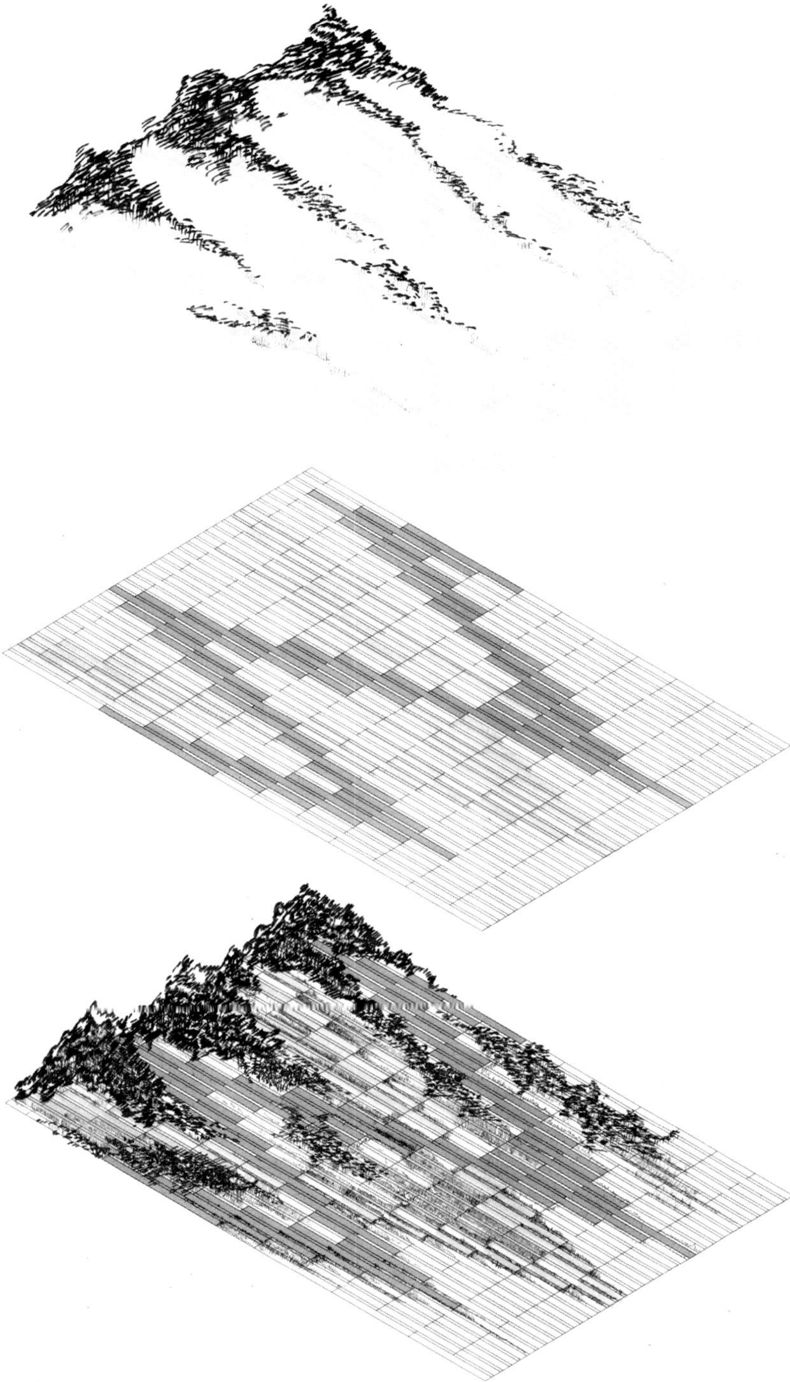

From Left: Azzurra Cox (MLA I), Michelle Shofet (MLA I), and Xinhui Li (MLA I); Drawing from Workshop with Peter Beard. Hui Wang (MLA I), Instructor: Zaneta Hong

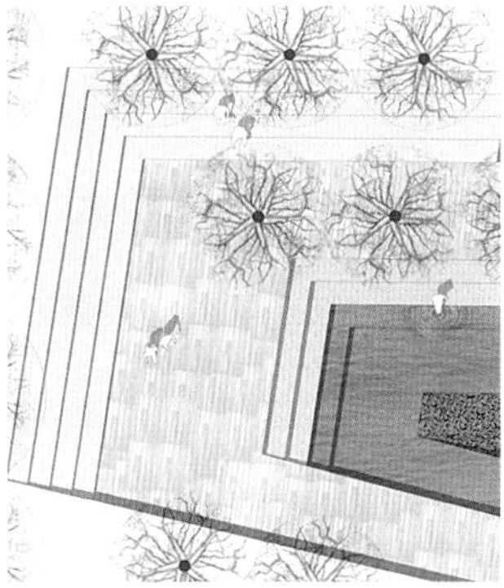

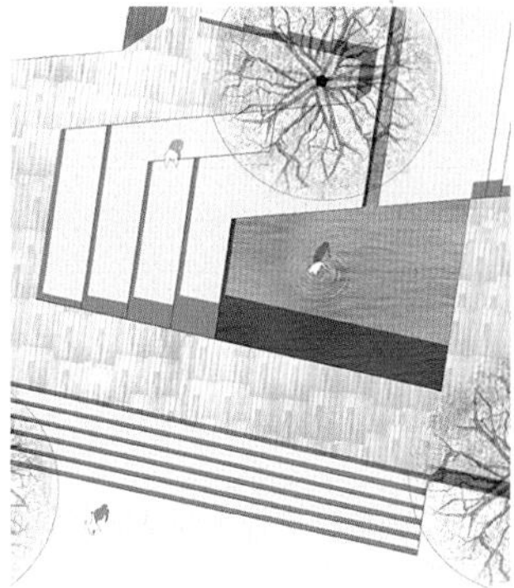

Ambrose Luk (MLA I). Instructor: Silvia Benedito

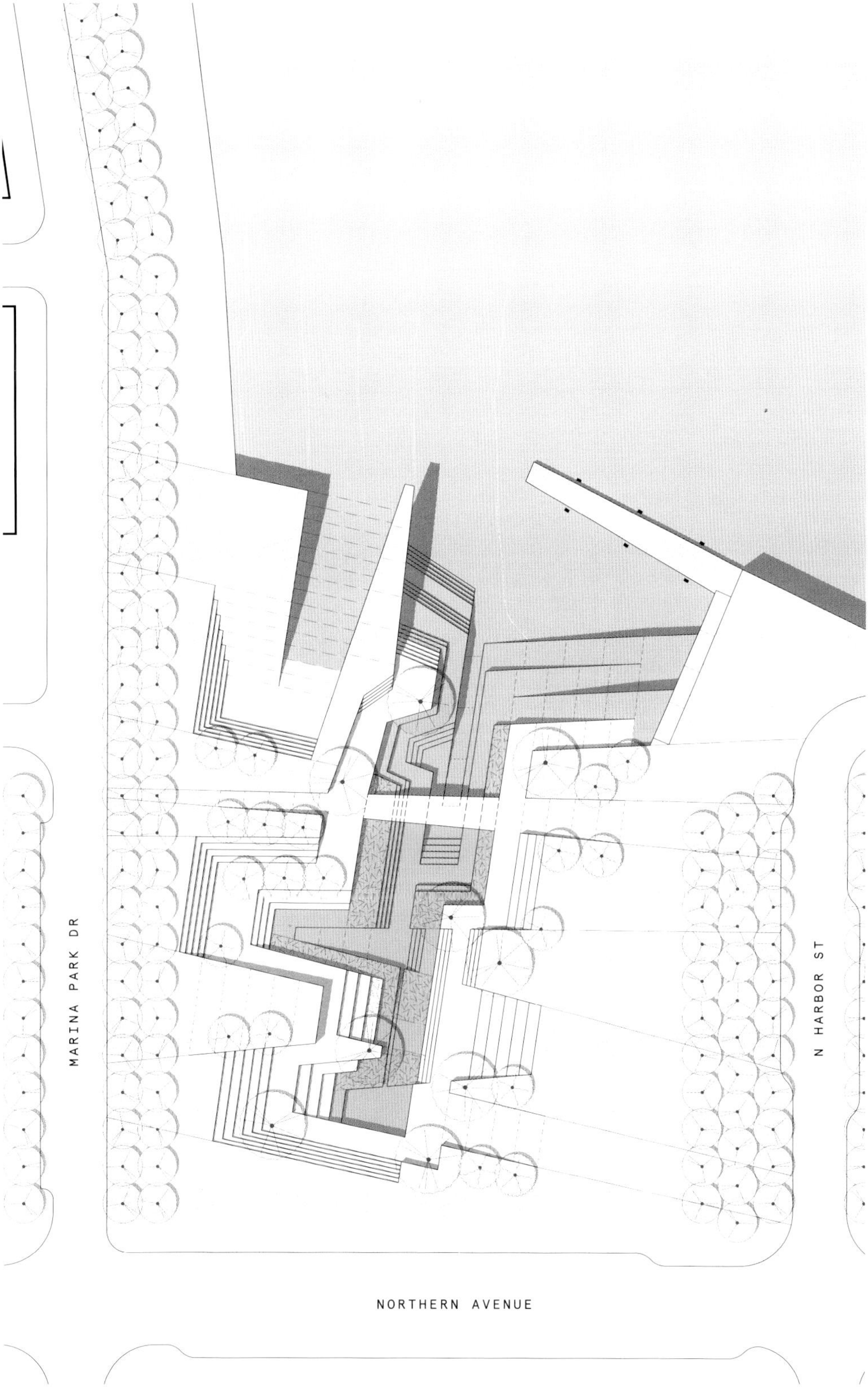
MARINA PARK DR
N HARBOR ST
NORTHERN AVENUE

Coordinator
Judith Long
Instructors
Ana Gelabert-Sanchez
Kathy Spiegelman

Urban Planning I

The first-semester core studio of the Master of Urban Planning program introduced students to the fundamental knowledge and technical skills used by urban planners to create, research, analyze, and implement plans and projects for the built environment. The studio used the City of Boston as the students' planning laboratory, and students were expected to understand the city through the lenses of planning elements such as demographics, economic attributes, market forces, and public and private stakeholder interests, all of which shape the city and inform decisions about land use, development, and infrastructure.

Kathryn Casey (MArch I/MUP)
Instructor: Judith Long
01 Parks and Gardens as Magnets, Filters, and Anchors
02 North End, Boston
03 Family Households per Block in the North End
04 Non-Family Households per Block in the North End
05 Boston Land Use
06 Circular Formation of Commercial Properties
07 Varying Lane Widths Cause Congestion in LMA
08 Existing Fens
09 Proposed Fens Phase 1, 2020
10 Proposed Fens Phase 2, 2022
17 Existing Bus Routes and Train Lines
18 Public Green Space in LMA
19 Final Proposal for LMA
20 Proposed Fens Phase 3, 2025
21 Proposed Fens Phase 4, 2027
22 Proposed Fens Phase 5, 2030

Margaret Scott (MUP)
Instructor: Ana Gelabert-Sanchez
11 Peripheral Mixed Use
12 Building Density
13 Targeting Huntington Ave.
14 Phase 1, 2020: Huntington & Tremont Aves.
15 Phase 2, 2030: Ruggles Ave.
16 Phase 3, 2040: Mass Ave.

01

02

03

04

05

06

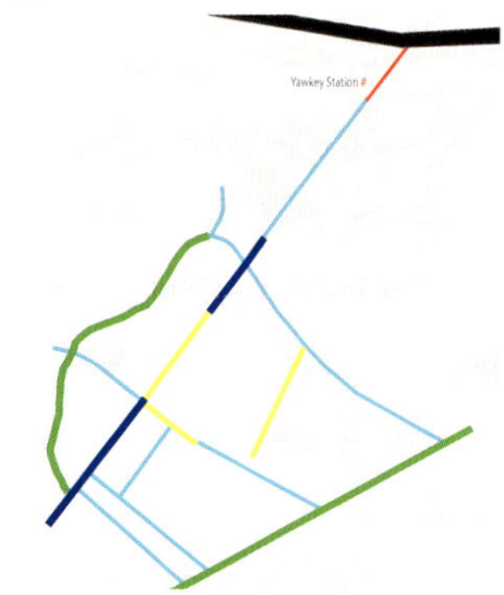

07

08

09

10

11

12

13

14

15

16

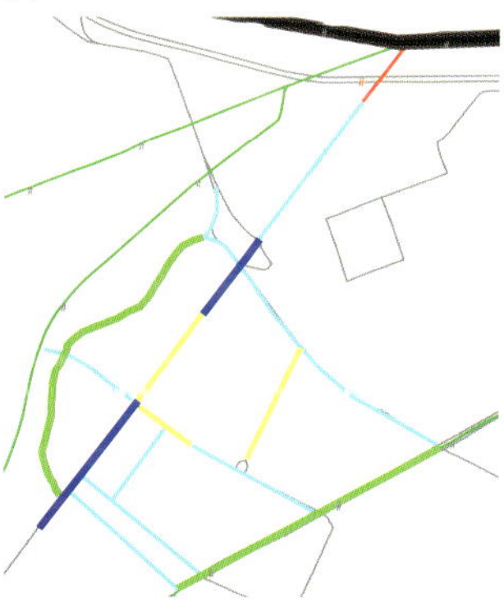

17

18

19

20

21

22

Building a Community Corridor: Leveraging Institutional Partnerships and Growth

Margaret Scott (MUP). "Building a Community Corridor"

Expected Employment + Population Growth by 2040

given 4% City of Boston growth rate and 13% + District growth rate per decade

15,000 + new residents

and 1100 new LMA employees per year

37,000 + new employees

40,000 +

new neighbors by 2040

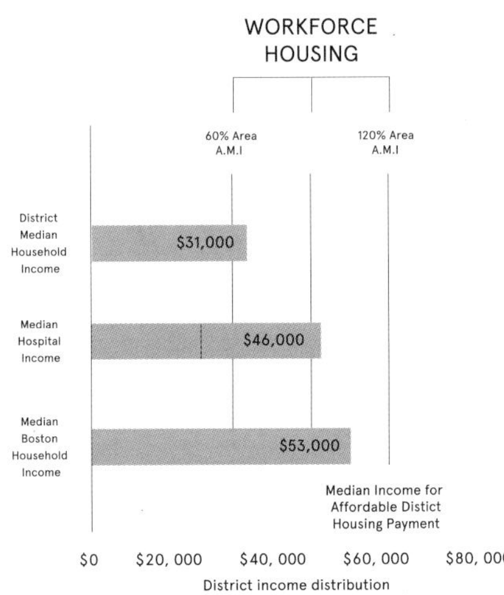

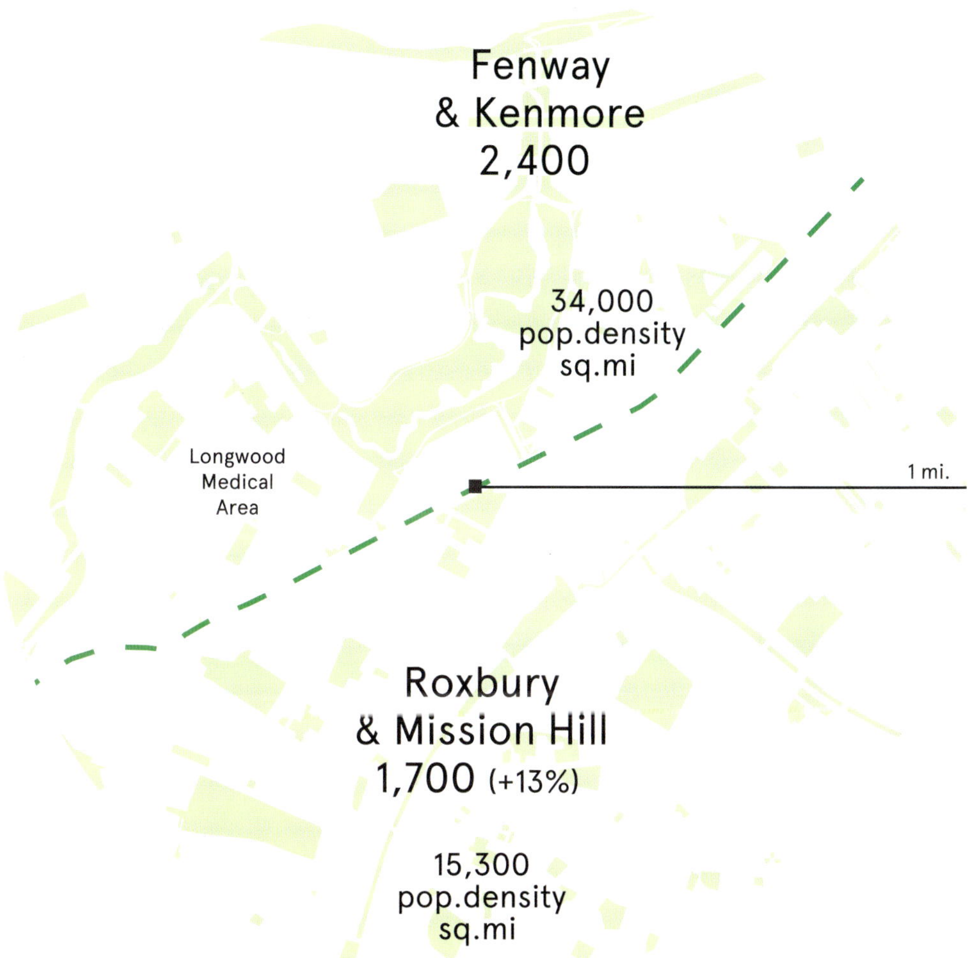
Fenway
& Kenmore
2,400
34,000
pop.density
sq.mi
Longwood
Medical
Area
1 mi.
Roxbury
& Mission Hill
1,700 (+13%)
15,300
pop.density
sq.mi

Kathryn Casey (MArch I/MUP). "Longwood Medical Area: Ameliorating Congestion, Increasing Respiration, and Helping the LMA Stand Taller"

PROPOSED DISTRICT PROGRAMMING CHANGES

SUB-DISTRICT ZONES	Existing Lot Coverage	Proposed Lot Coverage	Existing FAR	Proposed FAR	Proposed Height Max	Proposed Setbacks	Existing Parking	Proposed Parking	Existing Built Area (sf)	Proposed Built Area (sf)
Open Space OS Natural Landscape, Small Pocket Parks	100%	100%	0	0	X	0′	X	X	4,083,750	8,697,500
University Institutional SD1 Mixed-Use, Predominantly University & College	55%	55%	3.9	3.5	80′	20′	0.75 / 1000sf	0.55 / 1000sf	39,599,307	22,934,340
Residential Mixed-Use MXD Mixed-Use, Predominantly Residential	80%	70%	3.5	3.5	60′	12′	0.75 / 1000sf	0.75 / 1000sf	28,586,250	28,586,250
Healthcare Institutional SD2 Mixed-Use, Predominantly Hospitals, Research	85%	60%	4.0	8.0	200′	20′	0.65 / 1000sf	0.65 / 1000sf	15,028,200	32,670,000
Arts Area SD3 Art Museums & Cultural Institutions	60%	60%	2.5	2.5	75′	15′	0.75 / 1000sf	0.75 / 1000sf	1,633,500	1,633,500
Fenway Commercial BA1 Mixed-Use, Predominantly Commercial	80%	70%	2.6	4.0	80′	15′	0.75 / 1000sf	0.75 / 1000sf	5,945,940	9,147,600

Hard Edges
Soft Edges
Landscaped Edge
N 1:14,500

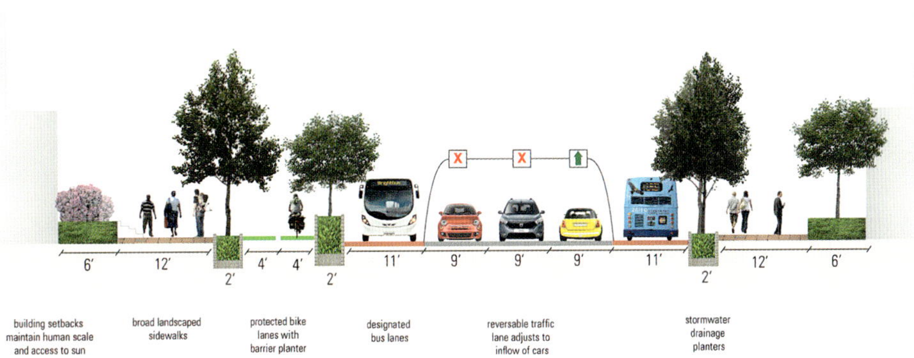
6'
12'
2'
4'
4'
2'
11'
9'
9'
9'
11'
2'
12'
6'
building setbacks maintain human scale and access to sun
broad landscaped sidewalks
protected bike lanes with barrier planter
designated bus lanes
reversable traffic lane adjusts to inflow of cars
stormwater drainage planters

Lecture: Denise Scott Brown
Mayhew's Architecture
October 22, 2013

"[The Pritzker] was a source of much pain for me in 1991, and then it kind of went away. And I got on with my life and my work. But really, with the petition [Harvard GSD Women in Architecture's petition to recognize Denise Scott Brown as a co-recipient of the 1991 Pritzker Prize], who needs the Pritzker? That's my prize. That's my reward. And just think what it will do for architecture."

"[...] A wise mentor to a young person can say, 'Be patient. You don't have to see everything at this point. Why would you? Why wouldn't you be going into the unknown at this point?' I used to say to Bob, as we were having all these troubles with getting work, 'Be patient, it's a long, low arc for us.' But I also think mine has three curves, on three continents."

"[...] Why should English people feel that they can be in South Africa and say they know the right way, and we colonials are crude and we have the wrong way? And their landscape is the pretty one, and ours is the ugly one? I used to see as a child, in South Africa, English people looking at a little bit of a veldt, 'This could be Surrey.' I say, well, 'Why does it have to look like Surrey to be beautiful? What's wrong with the veldt?' It's incredibly beautiful to me. So, long before I got to Las Vegas, I was thinking, what's wrong with our own local landscape?"

"When I got to England and I went to the AA, I found more mentors: Arthur Korn, another German refugee, teaching at the AA, an old Communist, and I started telling him, 'My life lacks structure.' He started taking me for coffee, one morning a week at the little Austrian café, and these seemed to be parallel conversations that I suspect helped us both. Because I came out of that with a lot of passion, and a lot of questions."

"Everyone knows that if you are a really good architect, you want to study urbanism. And so I came to study city planning in America [at UPenn]. We went to our student advisor, Dave Crane, and Dave Crane said, 'Stay with us. Stay in planning, because you're going to learn things that you need for going back to Africa.' So I say that if it hadn't been for Dave Crane, putting me in planning school, there would have been no learning from Las Vegas."

"We were very interested in the idea that there are patterns in activities. And the patterns we were studying in Las Vegas were of course the new patterns of the automobile city of the American West. [...] We architects have been criticized and quite rightly by sociologists, saying, 'You design spaces that no one uses. Why can't you go to spaces that people like? Therefore go to Los Angeles and Las Vegas and see why they go to those spaces instead of the spaces you design?' But I say, 'These are spaces that I have designed and they are full of people.' But there is a very special reason why they are full of people and it has to do with the patterns."

"I saw a bullfighter—and I am against bullfighting, but it is the most beautiful thing in the world, the most skilled thing in the world, and the most dangerous thing in the world—and they interviewed him and they said to him, 'And you want it to be beautiful too?' He answered, 'Of course!' We architects doing architecture can be splendidly beautiful too and still do our jobs and use our minds and our hearts, and I hope you do all that."

Architecture II

Coordinator
Grace La
Instructors
Katy Barkan
Jeffry Burchard
Max Kuo
Renata Sentkiewicz
Elizabeth Whittaker

The overarching pedagogical agenda for the second semester was to expand on the design methodologies developed in the first semester such that students acquired an understanding of the interwoven relationships among form, space, structure, and materiality. This semester extended the subject matter to include the fundamental parameters of site and program, considered foundational to the discipline of architecture. Through the design problems, students also engaged in multiple modes of analytical processes that inform and inspire the study of mass, proportion, and tactility.

01 Justin Gallagher (MArch I)
02 Maria Carriero (MArch I)
03 Jiayu Qiu (MArch I)
04 Maria Carriero (MArch I)
05 David Hamm (MArch I)
06 Justin Gallagher (MArch I)
07 Gavin Ruedisueli (MArch I)
08 John Going (MArch I)
09 Maria Carriero (MArch I)
10 Felipe Oropeza (MArch I)
11 Thomas McMurtrie (MArch I)
12 John Going (MArch I)
13 Niki Murata (MArch I)
14 Niki Murata (MArch I)
15 Justin Gallagher (MArch I)
16 Gavin Ruedisueli (MArch I)
17 Davis Owen (MArch I)
18 Maria Carriero (MArch I)
19 Felipe Oropeza (MArch I)
20 Lillian Taylor (MArch I)
21 Gavin Ruedisueli (MArch I)
22 Thomas McMurtrie (MArch I)

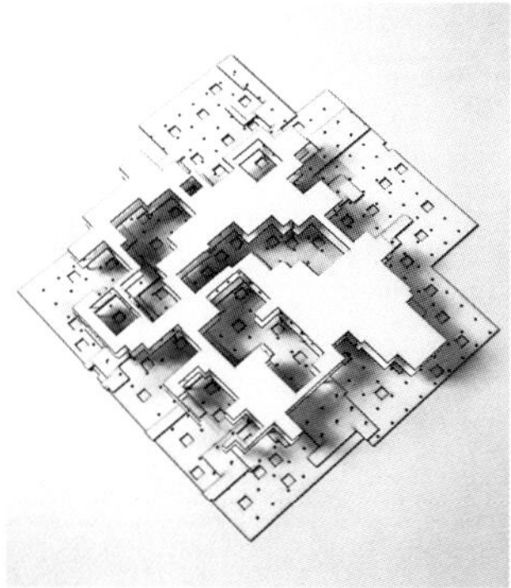
01

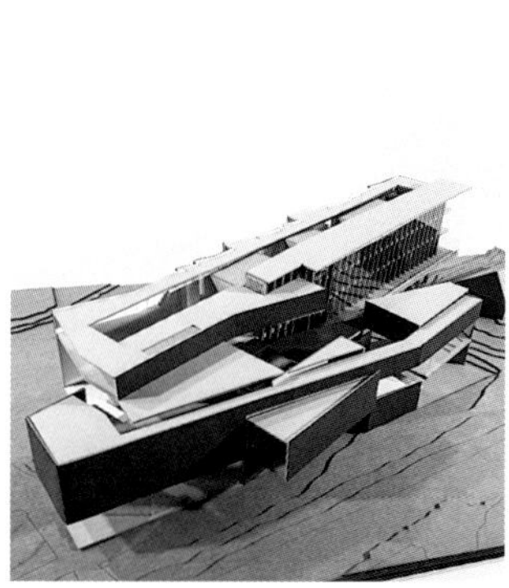
02

03

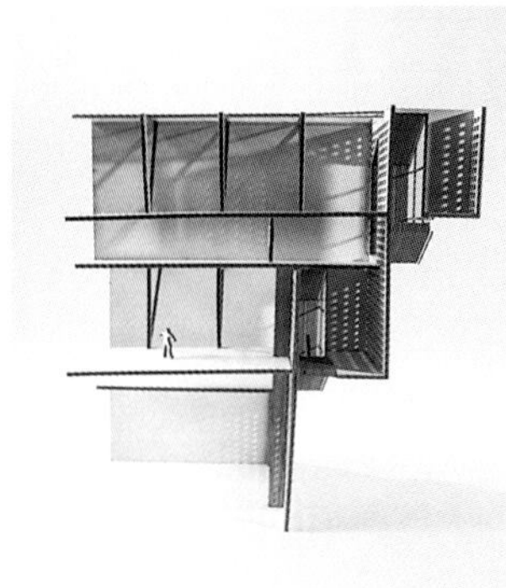
04

05

06

07

08

09

10

11

12

13

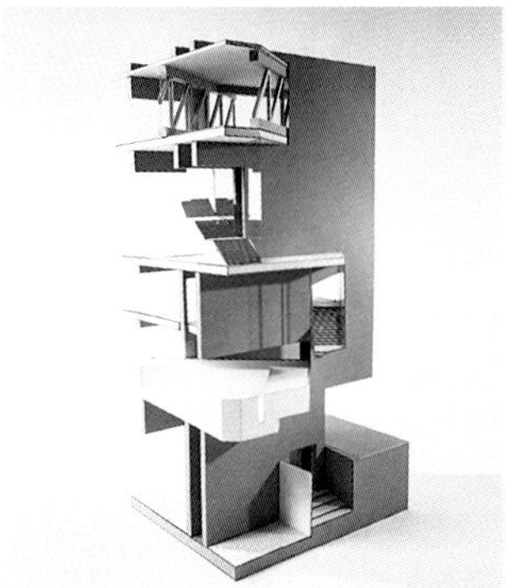
14

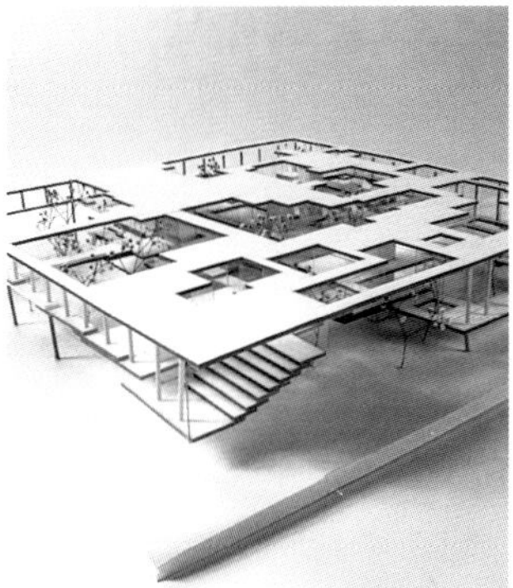
15

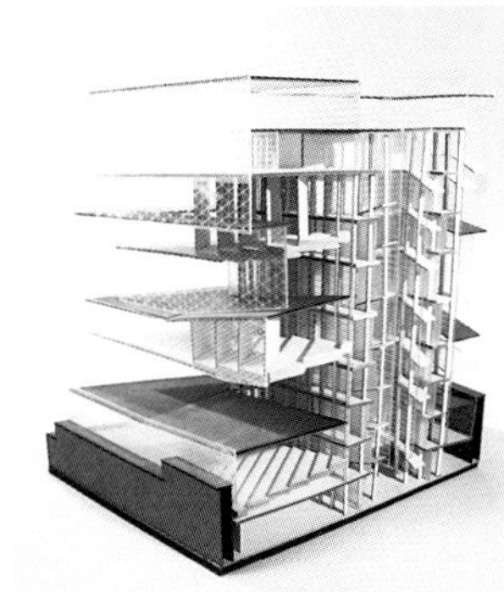
16

17

18

19

20

21

22

PLATFORM 7

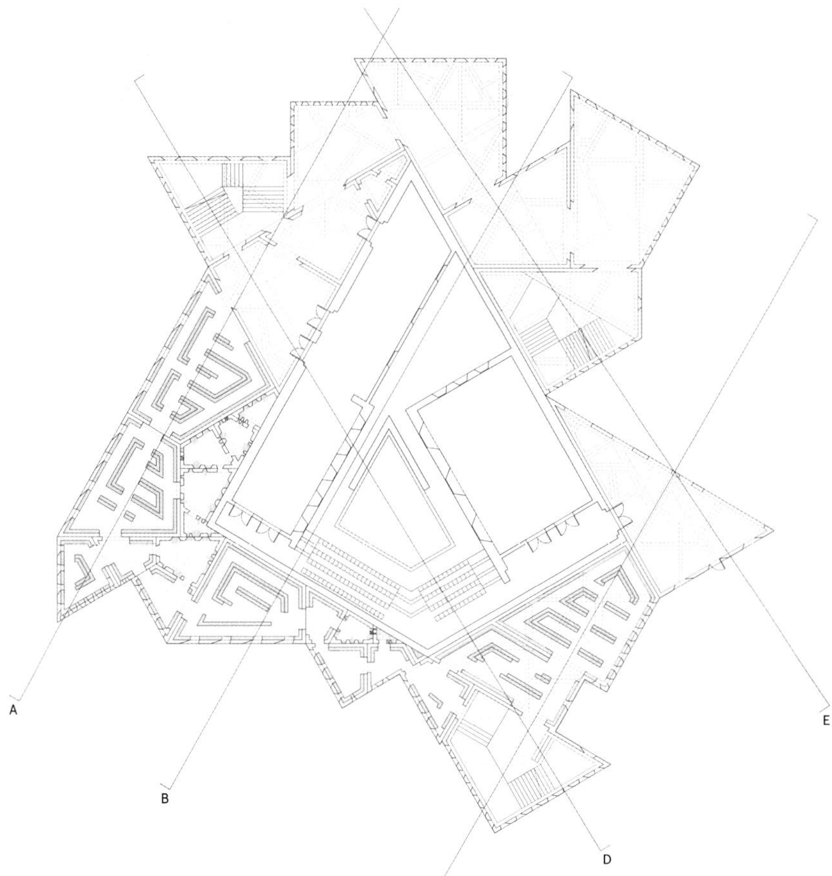

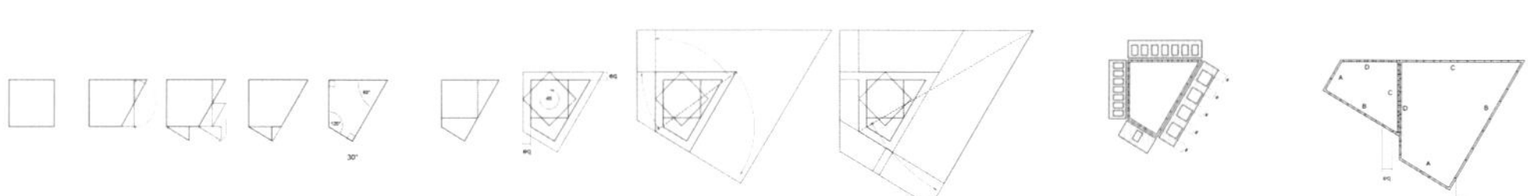

CORE II ARCHITECTURE

Felipe Oropeza (MArch I)
Instructor: Jeffry Burchard

01 Vestibule
02 Reception & Gallery
03 Theatre
04 Bookstore & Cafe
05 Reading Room
06 Reference Desk
07 Public Stacks
08 Circulation
09 Support
10 Research Stations
11 Multipurpose Rooms
12 Rare Book Stacks
13 Grand Staircase

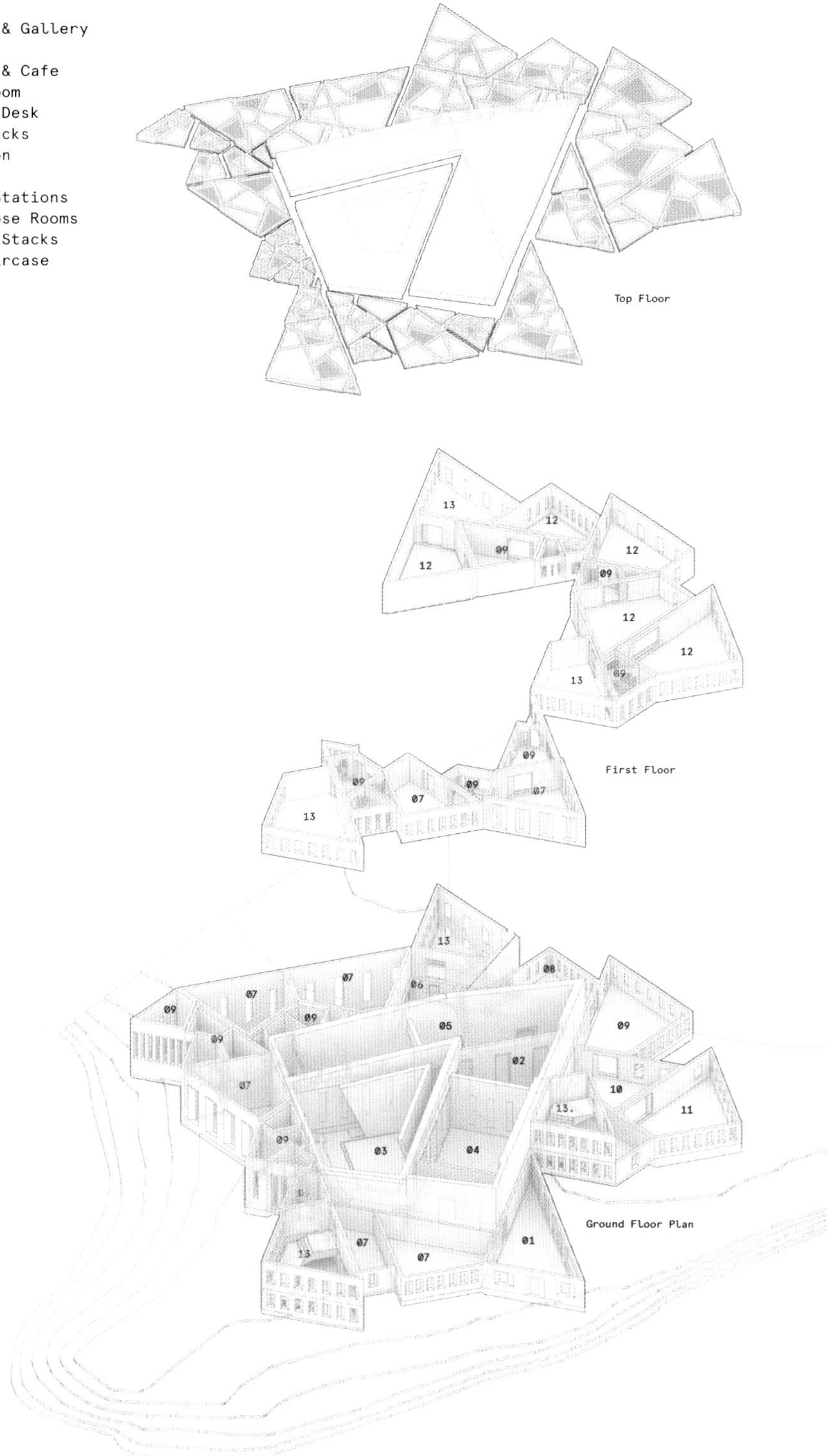

Justin Gallagher (MArch I). Instructor: Renata Sentkiewicz

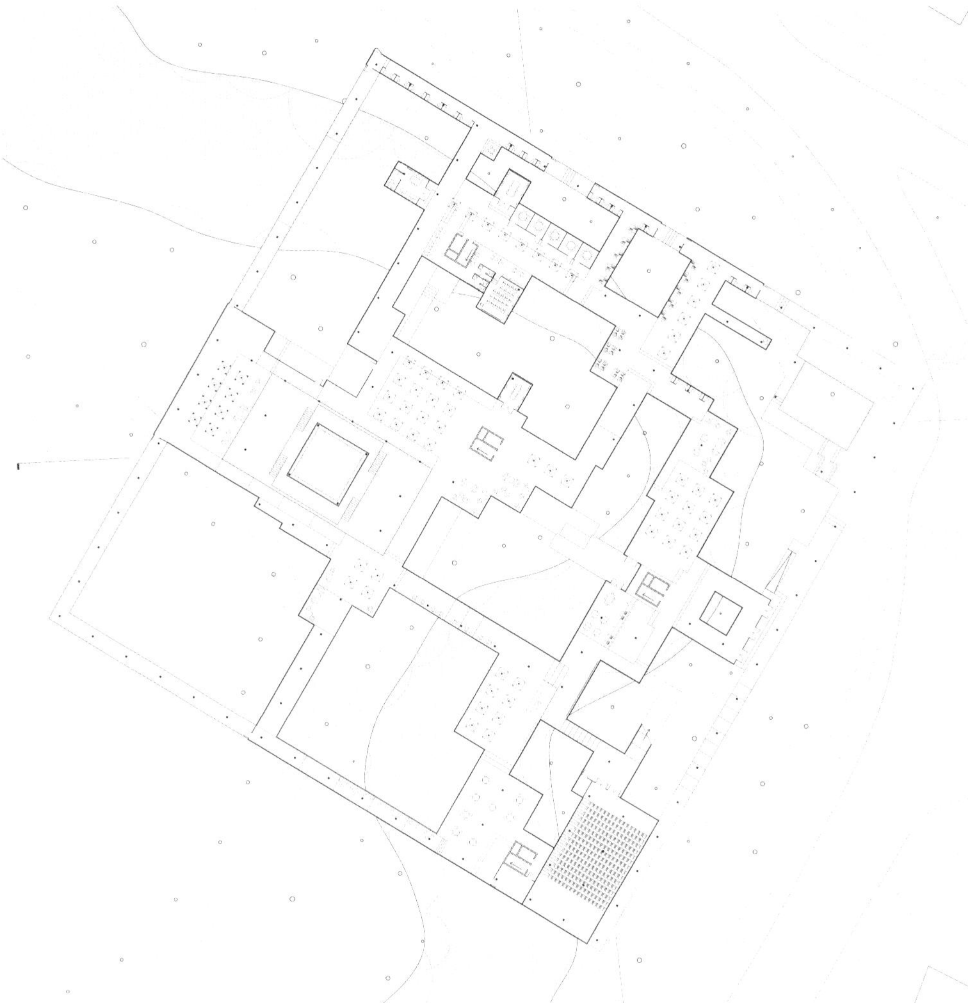

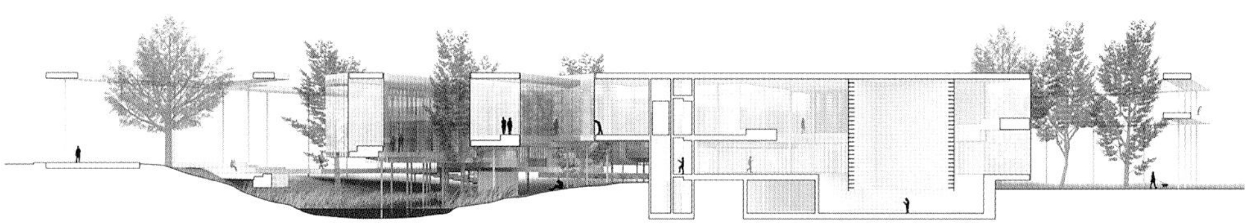

Landscape Architecture II

Coordinator
Anita Berrizbeitia
Jill Desimini
Instructors
Luis Callejas
Shauna Gillies-Smith
Workshop
Martha Schwartz

The second-semester core studio explored the research and design methods associated with interventions in complex urban conditions: sites layered with multiple interventions across a long span of history that present issues of connectivity, accessibility, identity, and need for contemporary programs. Students learned to apply various forms of research—historical, social, material, spatial, and technical—to the formulation of project arguments and strategies. The studio emphasized exploring the relationships among documentation, analytical research, and design through diverse conceptual frameworks and projective representational techniques.

01,02:
Foad Vahidi (MLA I)
03 Clementine InHye Jang (MLA I)
04,14-16:
Alexander Cassini (MLA I)
05-07:
Xinhui Li (MLA I)
08-10:
Sarah Canepa (MLA I)
11-13:
Vipavee Sirivatanaaksorn (MLA I)
17-19:
Ivy Pan (MLA I)
20-22:
Maria Arroyo (MLA I)

01

02

03

04

05

06

07

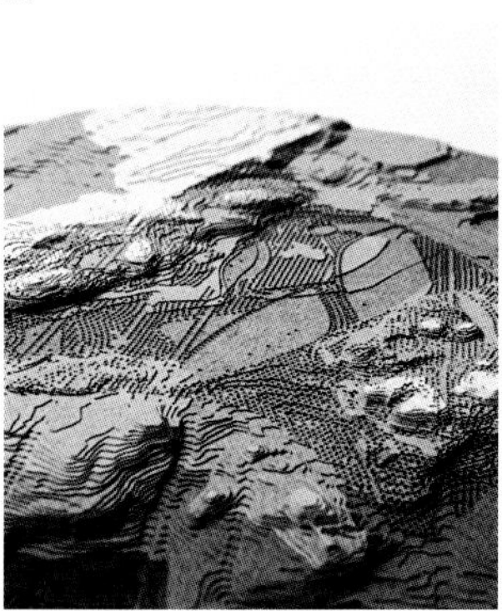

08

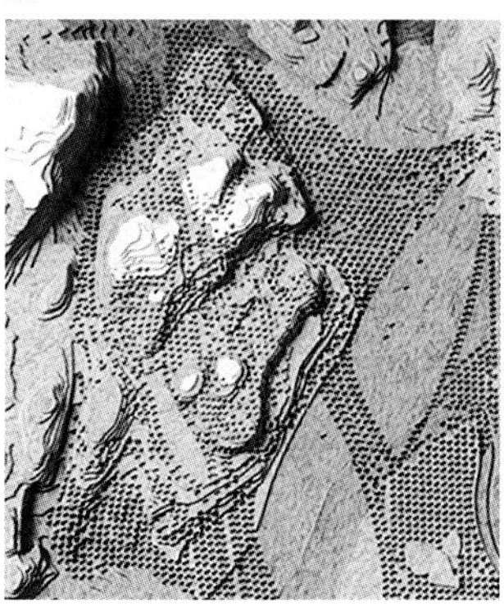

09

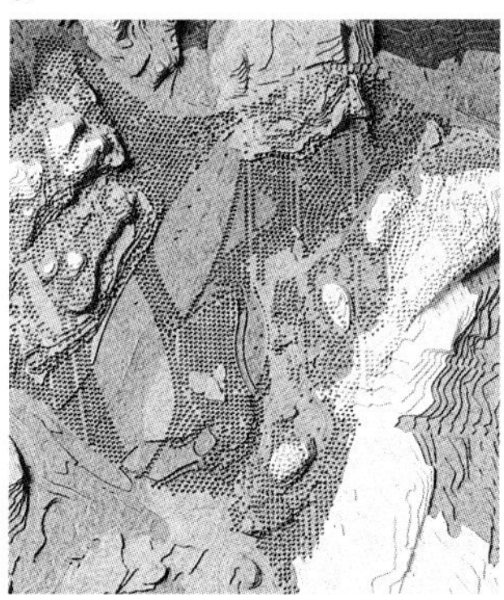

10

11

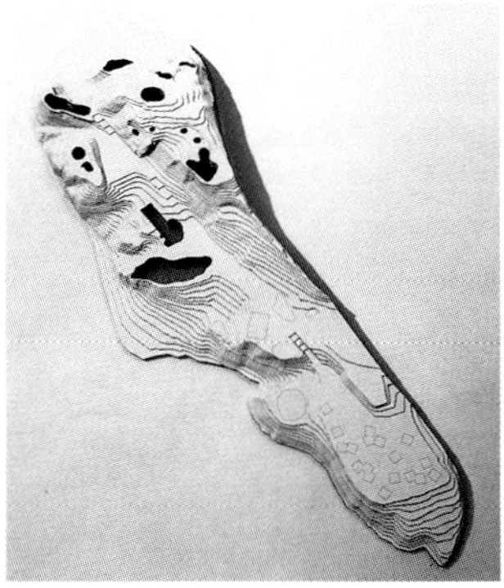
12

13

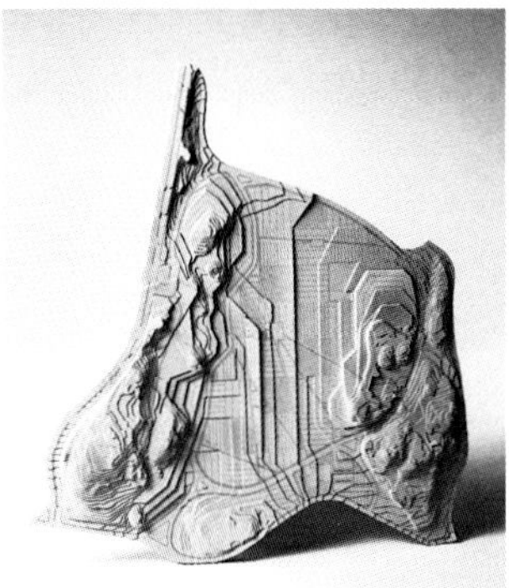
14

15

16

17

18

19

20

21

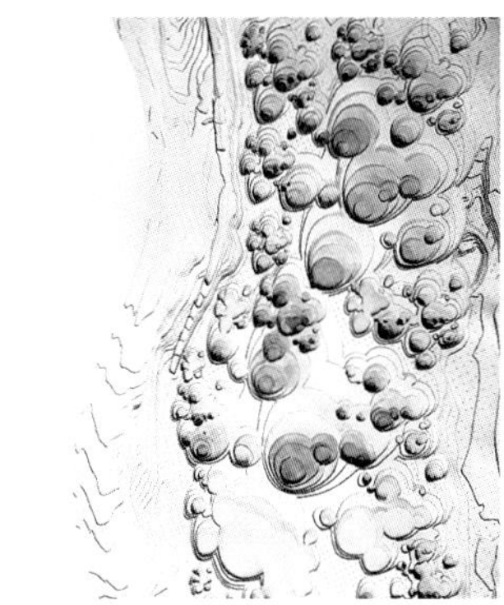
22

Sarah Canepa (MLA I). Instructor: Jill Desimini

Xinhui Li (MLA I). Instructor: Luis Callejas

Clementine InHye Jang (MLA I). Instructor: Jill Desimini

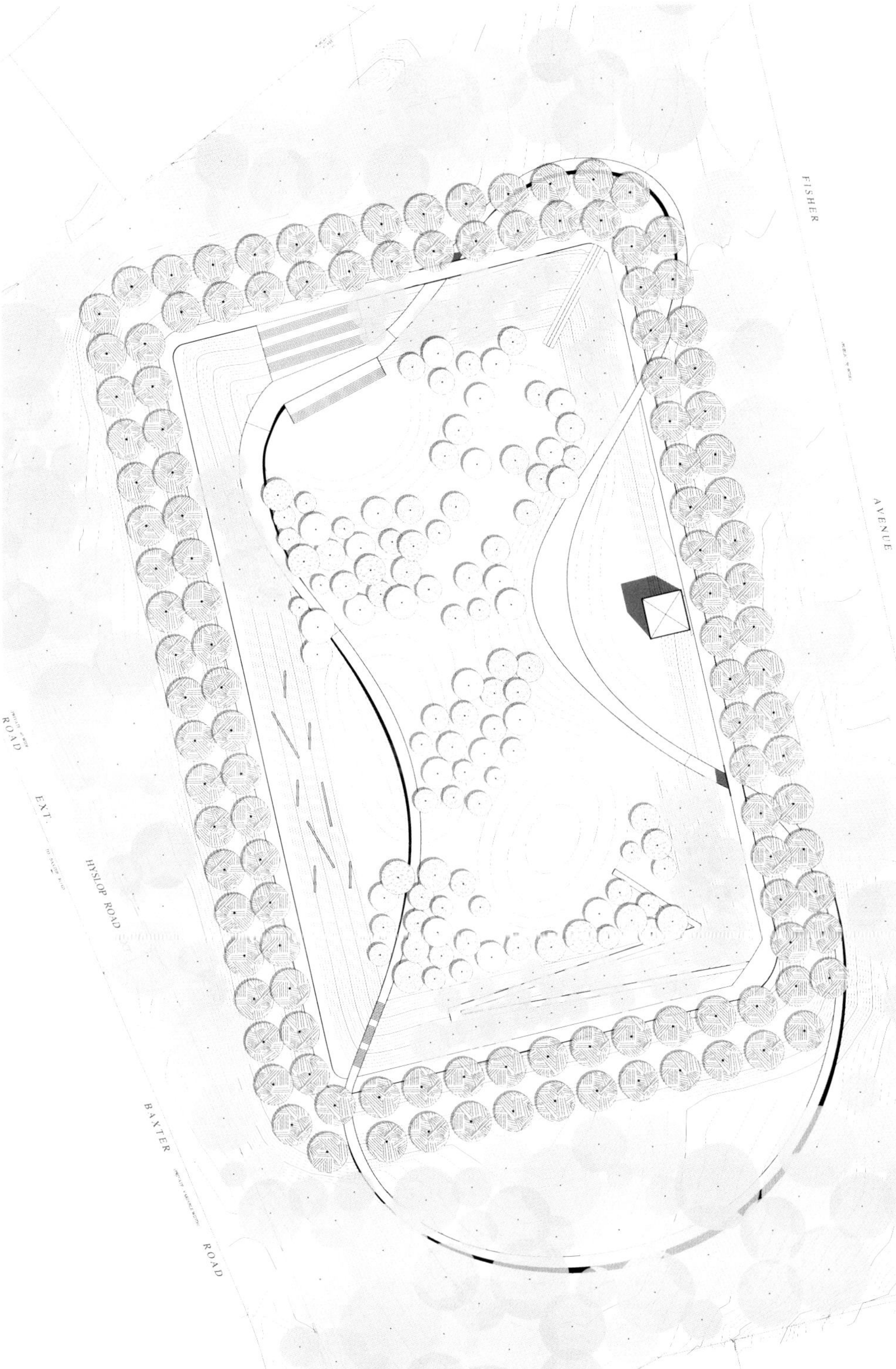

Ambrose Luk (MLA I). Instructor: Jill Desimini

Coordinator
Ann Forsyth
Instructors
Daniel D'Oca
Kathryn Madden
Robert Pietrusko

Urban Planning II

The second-semester core planning studio expanded the topics and methodologies studied in the first-semester core studio to prepare students for the mix of analytical and creative problem-solving needed to address planning issues at the advanced level of the options studios. The studio addressed the following concerns, all of which are currently central to planning: the pattern and development nature of settlement form; the visual and scenic impact of development either at the fringe or in built-up areas; accessibility, walkability, and the relationship between transit and autos; the location and utility of open space, particularly with respect to development; how planning can promote development of places, businesses, and cultural activities; how to interact with and appreciate the perspectives of diverse constituencies; and the respective roles of large-scale concepts (e.g., plans) versus regulation in shaping the built environment.

Erica Blonde (MUP), Patrick Boateng (MUP), Andrew Cantu (MUP), Kathryn Casey (MArch I/MUP), Young Ae Chung (MUP), Owen Deutsch (MUP), Irene Figueroa Ortiz (MUP), Matthew Furman (MUP), Jonathan Goldman (MUP), Allison Green (MUP), Kevin Gurley (MUP), Mark Heller (MUP), David Henning (MUP), Virginia Keesler (MUP), Jacob Koch (MUP), Ethan Lassiter (MUP), Joyce Lee (MUP), Zachery LeMel (MUP), Maynard Leon (MArch I AP/MUP), Joshua Levitt (MUP), Yani Li (MUP), Yang Mao (MUP), My Tam Nguyen (MUP), Ning Pei (MUP), Martha Pym (MUP), Jeenal Sawla (MUP), Margaret Scott (MUP), Jonathan Springfield (MUP), Aldarsaikhan Tuvshinbat (MUP), Sofia Viguri Gomez (MUP), Robert Wellburn (MUP), Samuel Wright (MUP), and Heidi Youngha Cho (MAUD/MUP).

"This Is Chelsea"
01 Local Industry
02 St. Luke's Church Chelsea Collaborative
03 My Chelsea
04 Presentation to Community

01

02

03

04

PRODUCE
WIC CHECKS

CHELSEA CLOCK

Chelsea Community Feedback
Retroalimentación
Come have a say
in Chelsea's future!

MY
MI CHELSEA!

MY
MI CHELSEA!
CHELSEA
LOVES
YOU

MY
MI CHELSEA!

"We want to evolve from 'Chelsea is a great place to be from' toward 'Chelsea is a great place to be.'"

From Left: Owen Deutsch (MUP), Jonathan Goldman (MUP), Allison Green (MUP), Kevin Gurley (MUP), Zachery LeMel (MUP), My Tam Nguyen (MUP), Ning Pei (MUP), Jeenal Sawla (MUP). "This Is Chelsea." Workshop Presentation. Engage children and gather feedback from them while drawing; Andrew Cantu (MUP), Allison Green (MUP), Kevin Gurley (MUP), Margaret Scott (MUP). "The Neighborhood Developers." Participation Workshop

AFFORDABLE HOUSING FOR DISABLED
· higher build-up
· commercial on 1st floor.
· Parking problem.
NEI
NO more people! They can come to workshop, but they should LEAVE!!
· Skate parks for teens!
· MORE FOOD FOR POOR PEOPLE — farma markets are expensive

PLATFORM 7

food incubator
tech incubator
flexible space
HUB Chelsea

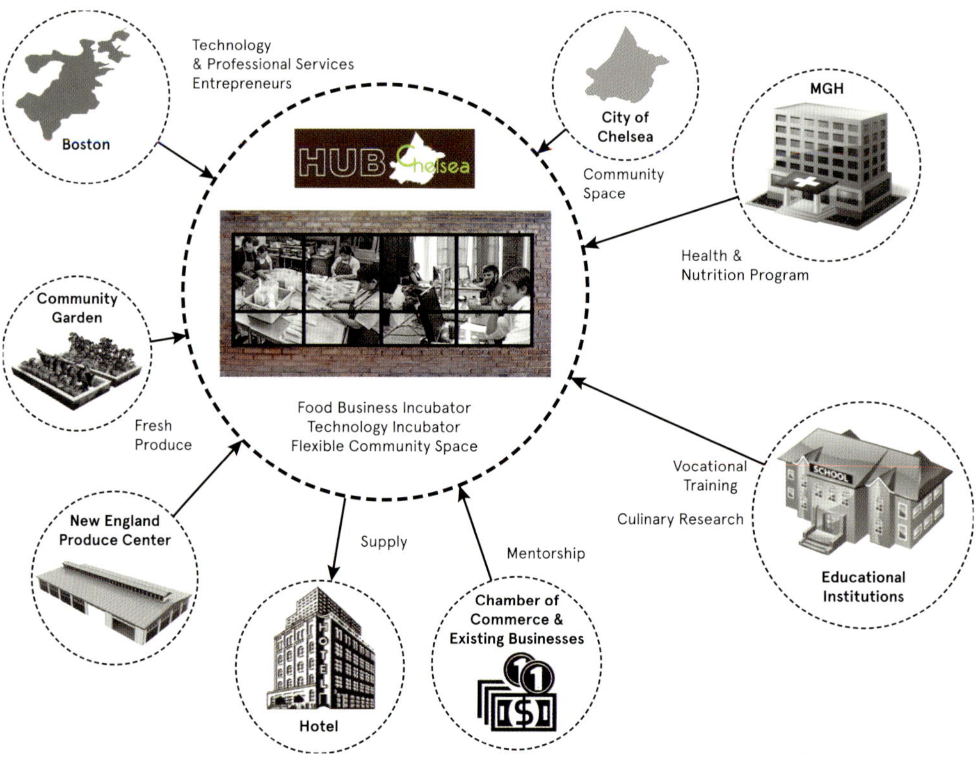

Boston
Technology
& Professional Services
Entrepreneurs
City of Chelsea
Community Space
MGH
Health & Nutrition Program
HUB Chelsea
Community Garden
Fresh Produce
Food Business Incubator
Technology Incubator
Flexible Community Space
Vocational Training
Culinary Research
Educational Institutions
New England Produce Center
Supply
Hotel
Mentorship
Chamber of Commerce & Existing Businesses

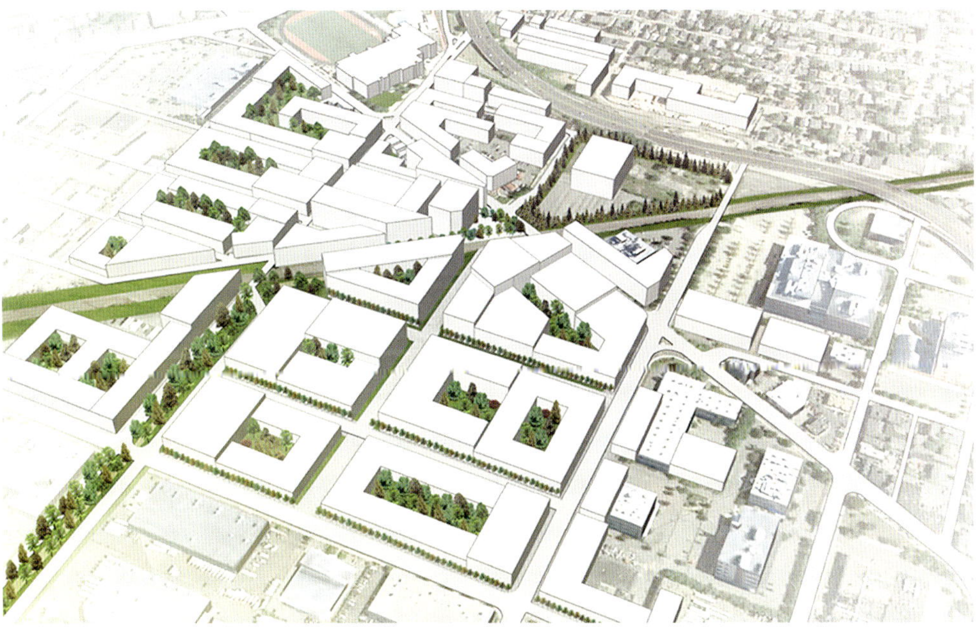

From Top, Clockwise: Erica Blonde (MUP), Patrick Boateng (MUP), Andrew Cantu (MUP), Kathryn Casey (MArch I/MUP), Young Ae Chung (MUP), Owen Deutsch (MUP), Irene Figueroa Ortiz (MUP), Matthew Furman (MUP), Jonathan Goldman (MUP), Allison Green (MUP), Kevin Gurley (MUP), Mark Heller (MUP), David Henning (MUP), Virginia Keesler (MUP), Jacob Koch (MUP), Ethan Lassiter (MUP), Joyce Lee (MUP), Zachery LeMel (MUP), Maynard Leon (MArch I AP/MUP), Joshua Levitt (MUP), Yani Li (MUP), Yang Mao (MUP), My Tam Nguyen (MUP), Ning Pei (MUP), Martha Pym (MUP), Jeenal Sawla (MUP), Margaret Scott (MUP), Jonathan Springfield (MUP), Aldarsaikhan Tuvshinbat (MUP), Sofia Viguri Gomez (MUP), Robert Wellburn (MUP), Samuel Wright (MUP), Heidi Youngha Cho (MAUD/MUP). "Connect Chelsea: Three Visions for a Gateway City." Massing Study of Potential Buildout of the West Chelsea Neighborhood at Full Allowable FAR; Hub Chelsea Relationships; Envisioning Hub Chelsea; Form-Based Code Recommendations

Lecture: Jonathan Sergison and Stephen Bates
On Continuity
March 25, 2014

SB: "To focus teaching on the act or art of inhabitation is appropriate, because it holds the essential in architecture. It forms the basis of urbanity and a background atmosphere of living, of possible happiness and comfort. It has codes and conventions that need to be learned and understood, and then later challenged, intelligently.

[...] It is an architecture of the center ground. From the scale of the house in the city center to the strategy plan of the urban hinterland. Victim of recession, mantle of economic recovery, tool of political maneuvering. Always subject to the vagaries of the local situation, protective neighbors, outdated planning policy, and the unending amount of regulation. But amidst all that is the built space—the room, the wall, the space between.

[...] These have a more stabilizing underlying character, and represent the components to be utilized in those never-ending questions. What should the character of this room be? How should it feel? How do we form a window? How do we use the ground floor? How do we renew our thinking about the collective? To work out how our building should face the city, to expresses the material, and then beyond the building itself, beyond its texture, weight, and scale, to reinforce its representational role, making a coherent language of construction.

This remains the challenge and forms the basis of an education, a journey toward personal artistic identity and social responsibility. I like [Luigi] Snozzi's reply to the question about the responsibility of an architect: that it is to replace the value of the land in which he or she is intervening. To first recognize what that value is needs guidance and study."

"[...] I think it's interesting to seek credible building types, which make a contemporary union between dwelling and the urban condition. The seeking of a relationship between use and space is uncommon in school or practice, beyond a functional discussion. And I feel that this needs to be addressed. I identify with Aldo Rossi's observation that form persists and comes to preside over a built work, in a world where functions continually become modified."

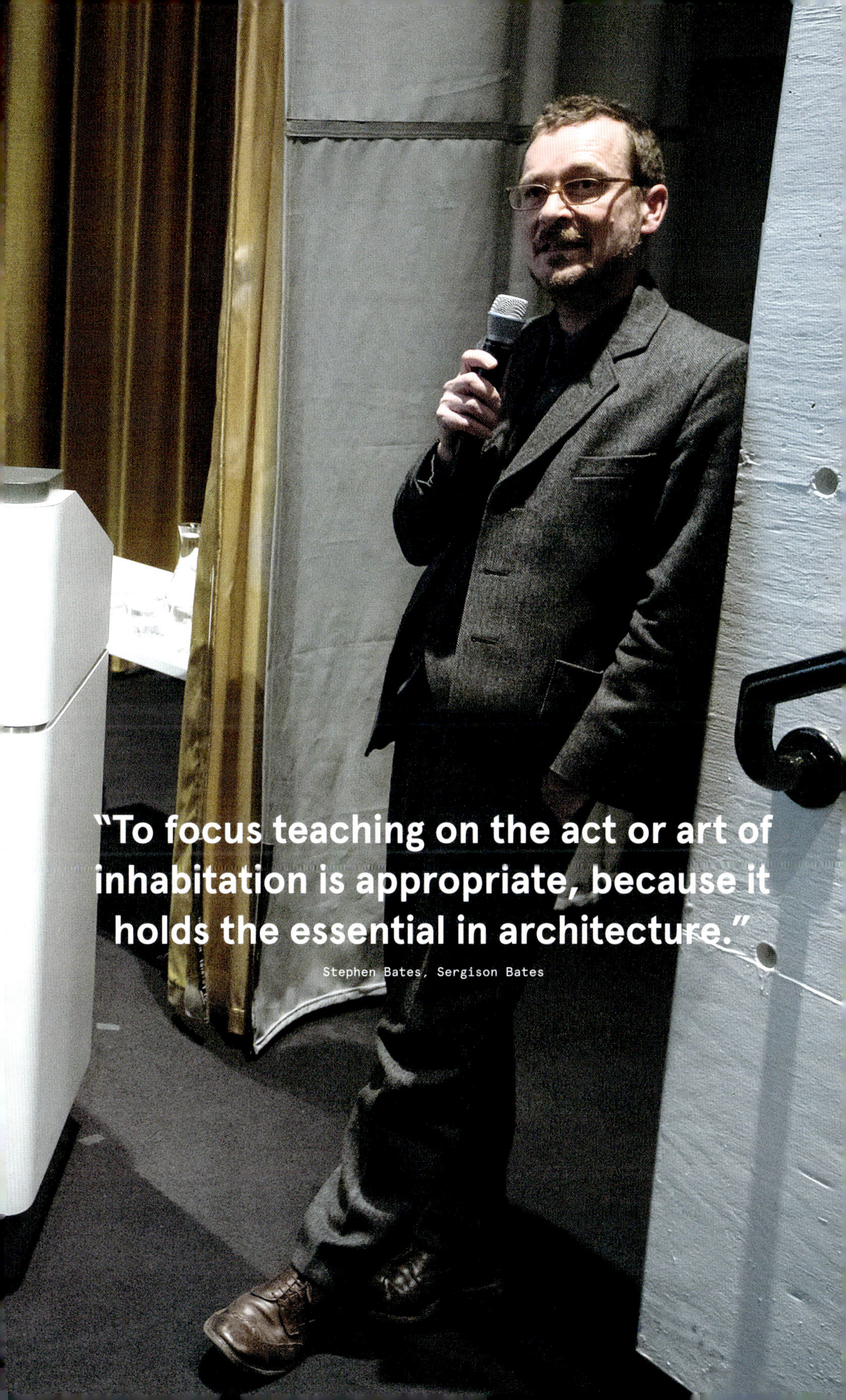

"To focus teaching on the act or art of inhabitation is appropriate, because it holds the essential in architecture."

Stephen Bates, Sergison Bates

Architecture III

Coordinators
Iñaki Abalos
Eric Höweler
Instructors
Vincent Bandy
Danielle Etzler
Mariana Ibañez
Maryann Thompson

Integration was the agenda for the third-semester architecture design studio. Architecture is fundamentally a part-to-whole problem, involving the complex synthesis of building components, systems, and processes. Structural systems, envelope design, and environmental and thermodynamic processes were systematically addressed in the development of a single project during the course of the semester. The building type consisted of a multi-program urban building, requiring careful consideration of access and exchanges (circulatory, visual, and energy) among programs.

01 Raffy Mardirossian (MArch I AP)
02 Frederick Kim (MArch I)
03 Ping Wang (MArch I)
04 Giancarlo Montano (MArch I)
05 Abigail Chang (MArch I)
06 Chris Soohoo (MArch I)
07 Josh Feldman (MArch I)
08 Frederick Kim (MArch I)
09 Bennett Gale (MArch I)
10 Ping Wang (MArch I)
11 Jyri Eskola (MArch I AP)
12 Chris Soohoo (MArch I)
13 Ali Karimi (MArch I)
14 Frederick Kim (MArch I)
15 Abigail Chang (MArch I)
16 Bennett Gale (MArch I)
17 Jyri Eskola (MArch I AP)
18 Wen Wen (MArch I)
19 Frederick Kim (MArch I)
20 Abigail Chang (MArch I)
21 Ping Wang (MArch I)
22 Giancarlo Montano (MArch I)

01

02

03

04

05

06

07

08

09

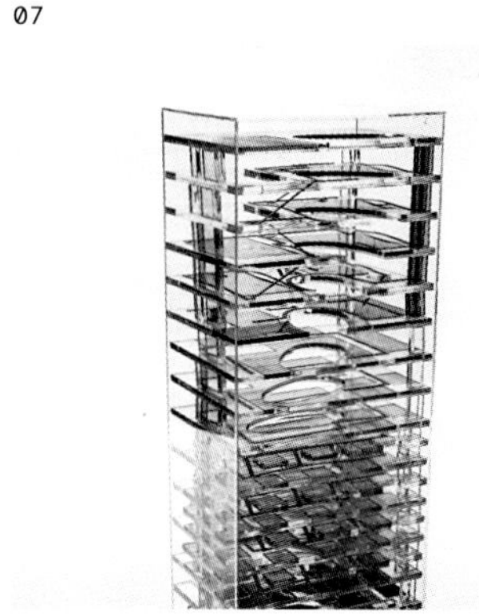

10

11

12

13

14

15

16

17

18

19

20

21

22

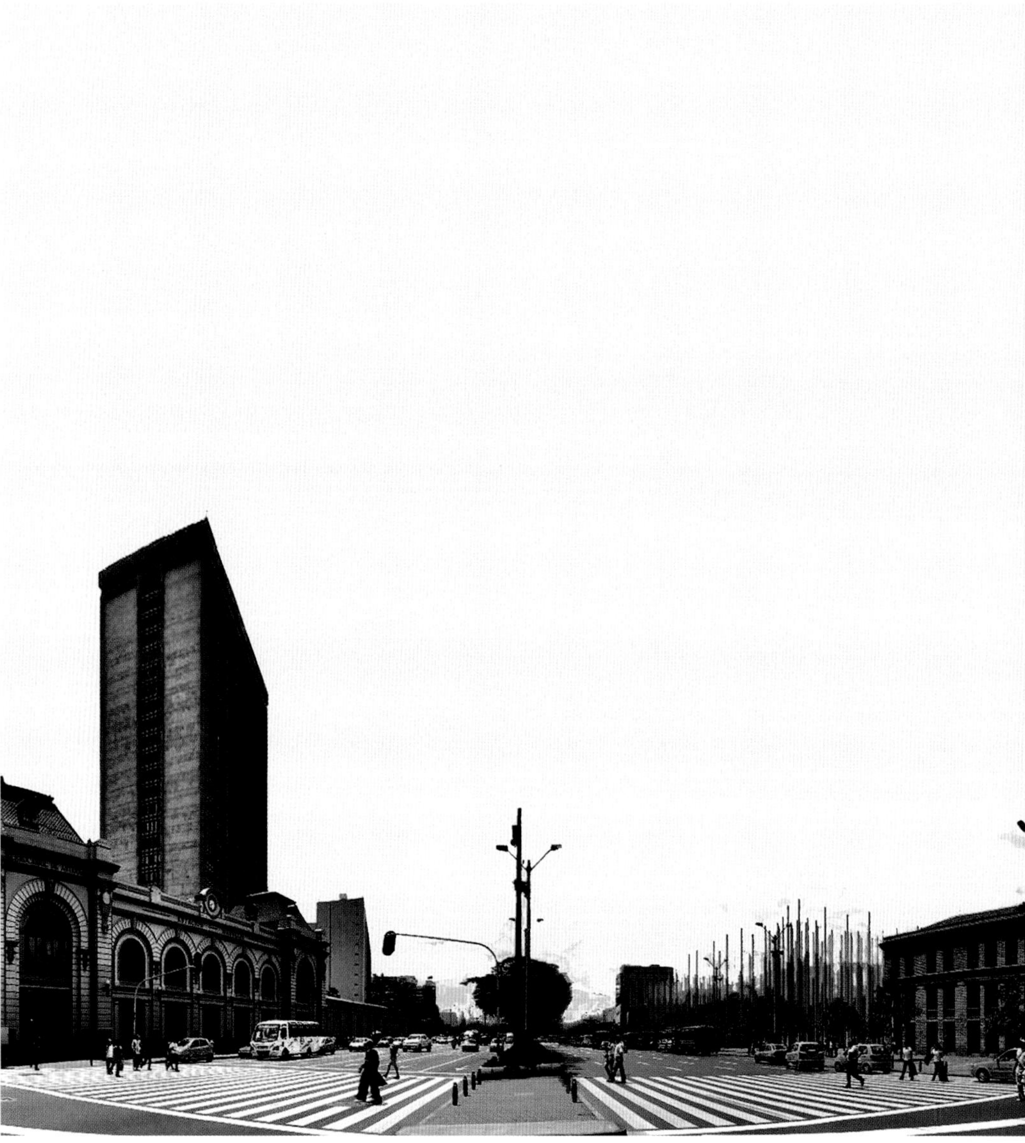

John Kirsimagi (MArch I). Instructor: Danielle Etzler

PLATFORM 7

From Left: Daniel Carlson (MArch I), Instructor: Eric Höweler; Josh Feldman (MArch I), Instructor: Danielle Etzler; Giancarlo Montano (MArch I), Instructor: Mariana Ibañez; Raffy Mardirossian (MArch I AP), Instructor: Eric Höweler; Chris Soohoo (MArch I), Instructor: Mariana Ibañez; Bennett Gale (MArch I), Instructor: Mariana Ibañez

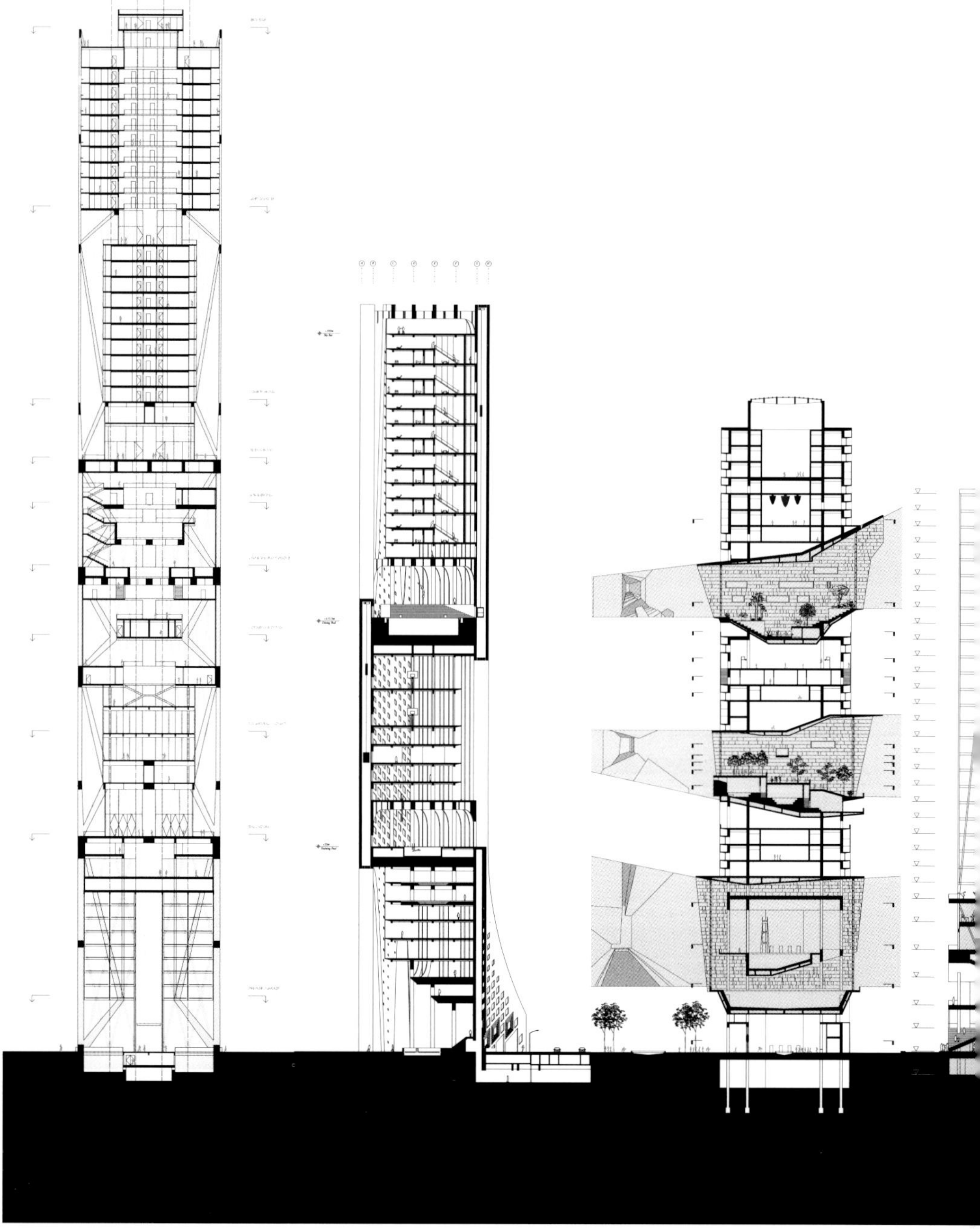

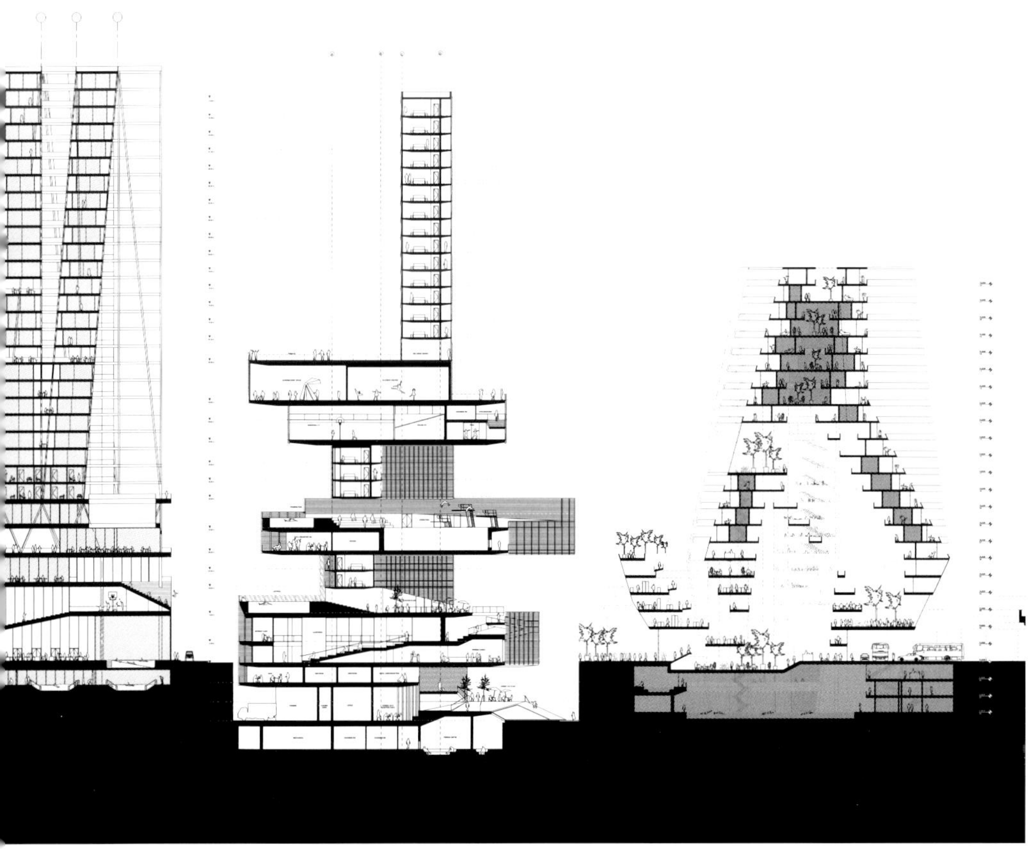

Raffy Mardirossian (MArch I AP). Instructor: Eric Höweler

PLATFORM 7

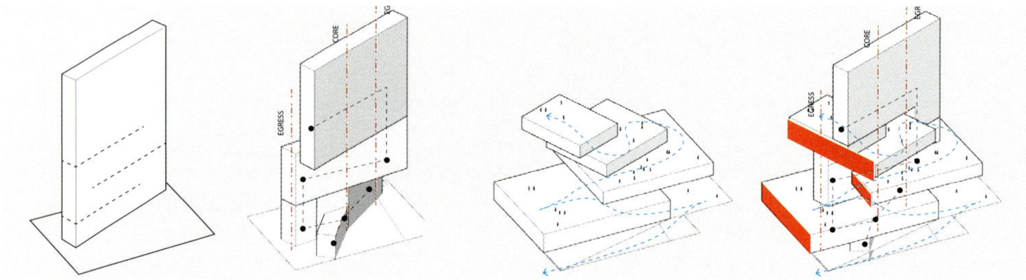

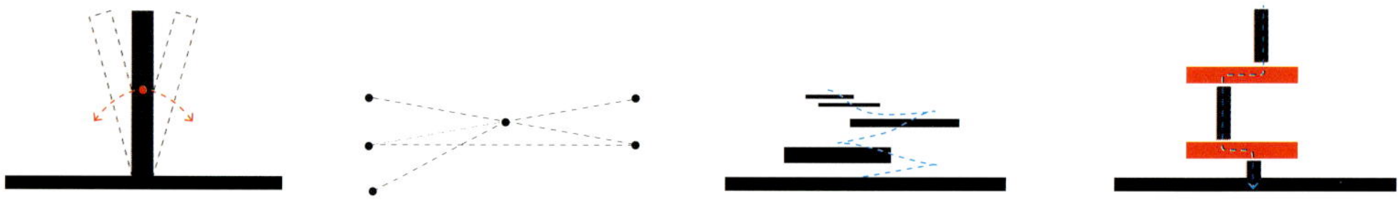

TOWER IS CUT AND FOLDED FOR STO
INTEGRATE PODIUM AND STRUCTURE

PLAN OVERLAP OF FOLDED TOWER

CONTINUITY BETWEEN PODIUM
FRAGMENTS

PODIUM AND TOWER MUTUALLY
SUPPORT EACH OTHER

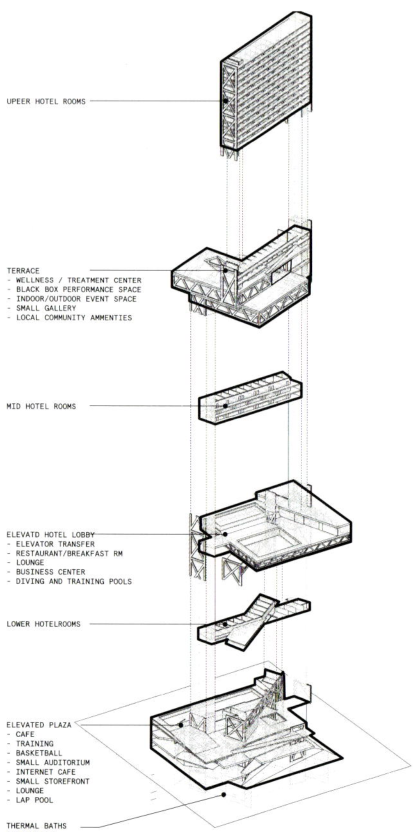

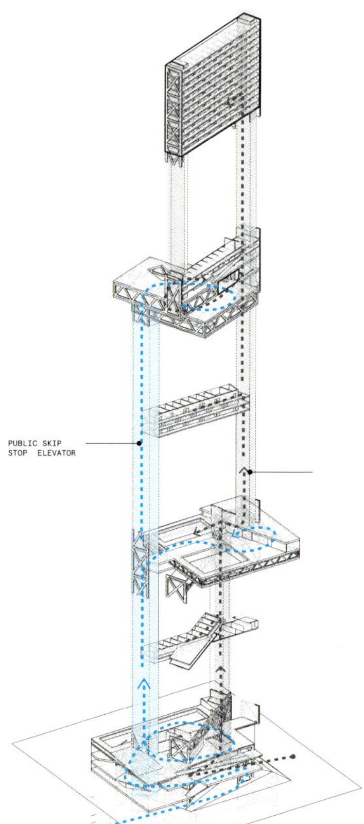

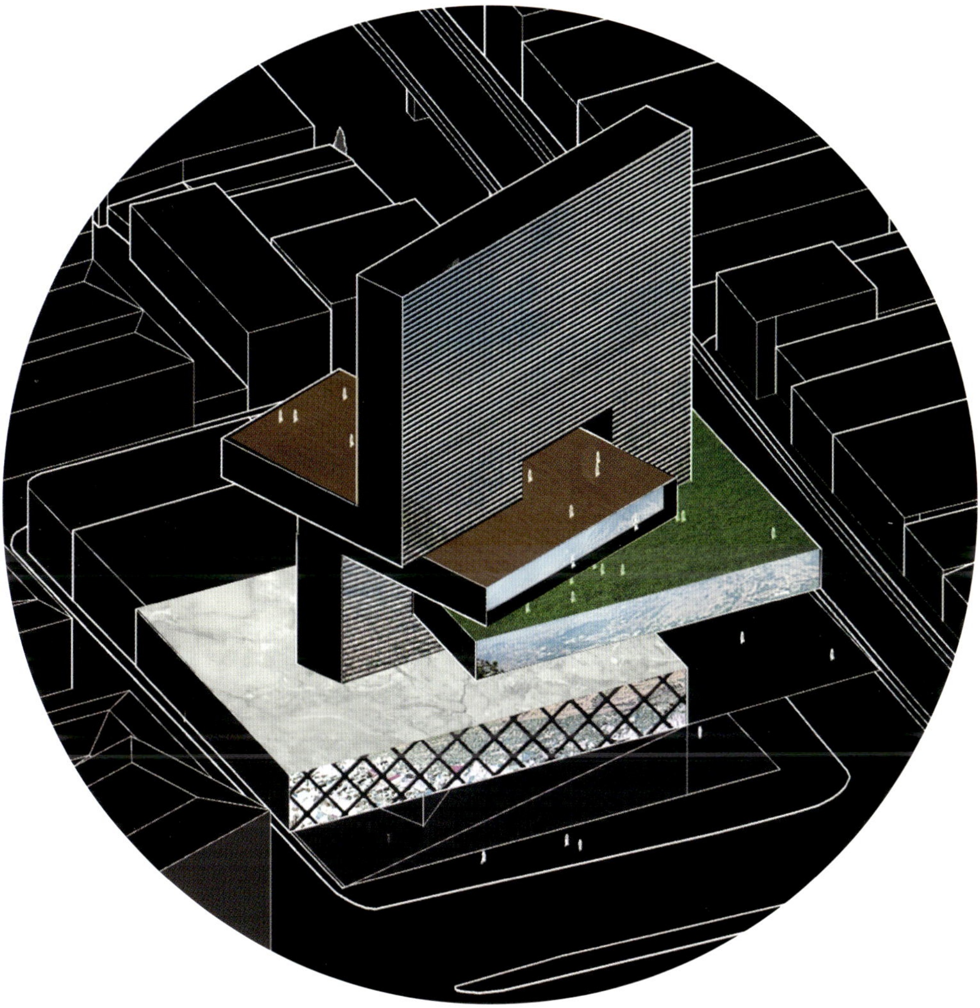

Chris Soohoo (MArch I). Instructor: Mariana Ibañez

Landscape Architecture III

<u>Coordinator</u>
Pierre Bélanger
<u>Instructors</u>
Luis Callejas
Kelly Doran
Rosetta Elkin
Andrea Hansen
Niall Kirkwood
<u>Workshops</u>
Philippe Coignet
Robert Pietrusko

Addressing the inertia of urban planning and the overexertion of civil engineering in the twentieth century, this course focused on the design of large, complex, contaminated brownfield sites with a regional, ecological, and infrastructural outlook. Employing the agency of regional ecology and landscape infrastructure as the dominant drivers of design, the studio developed projective biodynamic and biophysical systems that provided flexible yet directive patterns for future urbanization. Through a series of contemporary mapping methods, field measures, case studies, readings, and design investigations, the course was a series of collaborative exercises leading to a large-scale design project and future scenarios. Precluding conventional forms of urban development such as housing or retail development, the penultimate objective of the course was to explore and articulate the potential effectiveness of broader and longer-range strategies where biophysical systems prefigure as the denominator for reenvisioning public infrastructures and regional urban economies in the future.

PLATFORM 7

01-04:
Peichen Hao (MLA I)
Jennifer Saura (MUP/MLA I)
Elizabeth Wu (MLA I AP)
05 Ian Brennick (MLA I)
Bingjie Shi (MAUD/MLA I AP)
Sara Zewde (MLA I)
06 Paloma Garcia Simon (MLA I)
Yi Lun Yang (MLA I)
Hyosun Yoon (MLA I AP)
07-09:
Lisa Caplan (MLA I)
Michael Keller
(MAUD/MLA I AP)
Wenling Li (MLA II)
10 Siwei Gou (MLA I AP)
Lara Mehling (MLA I)
Nina Phinouwong (MUP/MLA I)
11 Hillary Archer (MLA I)
Timothy Wei (MLA I)
Emily Wettstein
(MArch I/MLA I AP)
12,15,18,21:
Xiaoran Du (MLA I AP)
Leo Miller (MLA I)
Sarah Winston (MUP/MLA I)
13 Weimao Kong (MLA I AP)
Zannah Matson (MLA I)
14 Radhya Adityavarman
(MLA II)
Vanessa Moon (MUP/MLA I AP)
Han Yang (MLA I)
16 Marissa Angell (MLA I)
Bradley Howe (MLA I)
Sonja Vangjeli (MLA I AP)
17 Shahab Al Bahar (MLA I AP)
Sherry Chen (MLA I)
Dima Rachid (MLA II)
19 Joseph Bivona (MLA II)
Danika Cooper
(MDes/MLA I AP)
Michelle Franco (MLA I)
20 Rebekah Armstrong (MLA I)
Zheming Cai (MLA II)
Hector Tarrido-Picart
(MAUD/MLA I AP)

01

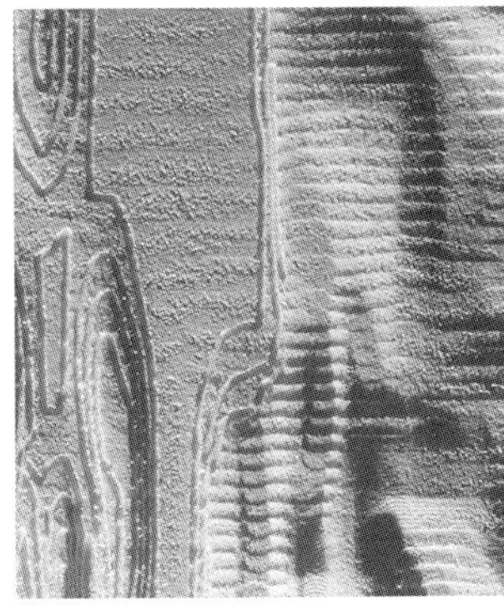
02

03

04

05

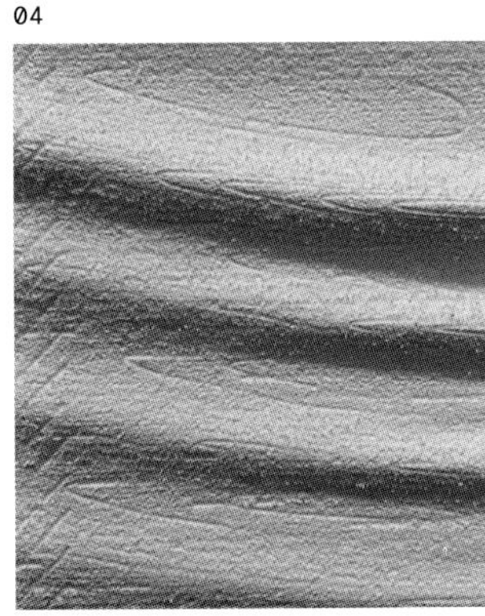
06

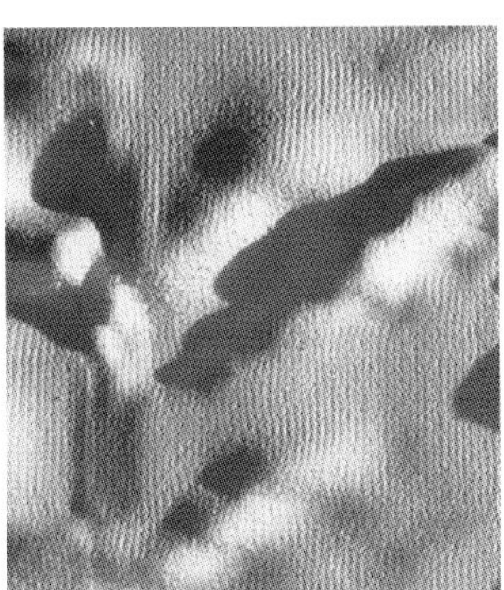
07

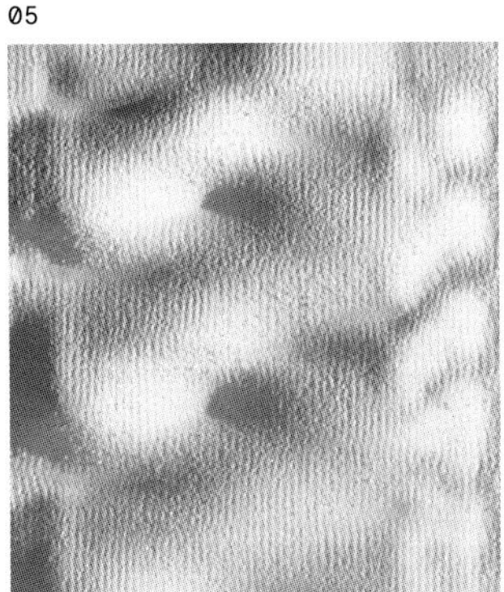
08

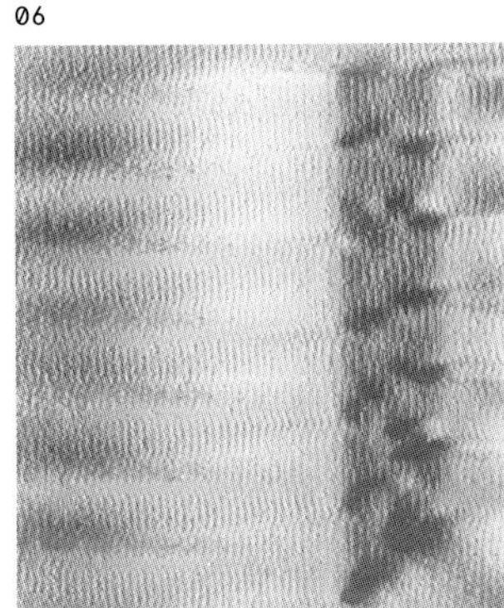
09

10

11

12

13

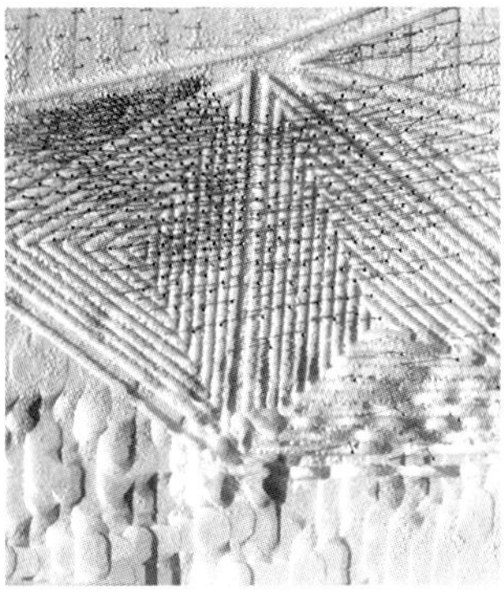
14

15

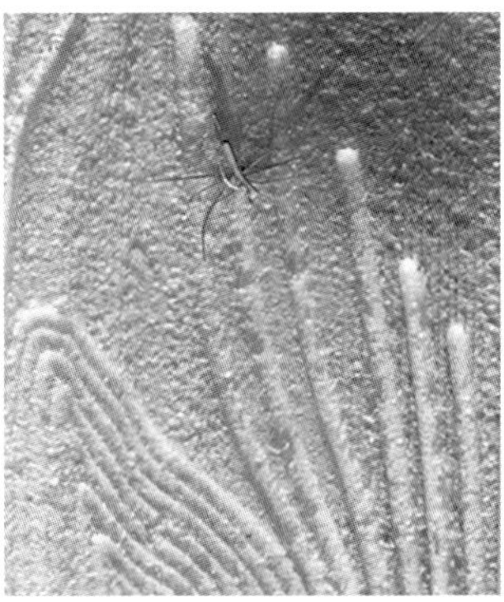
16

17

18

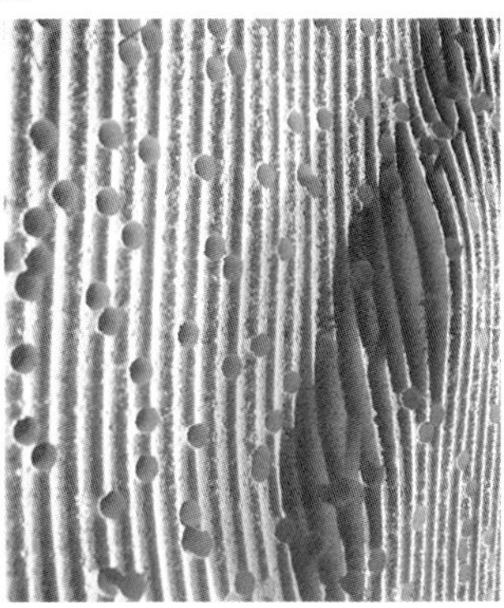
19

20

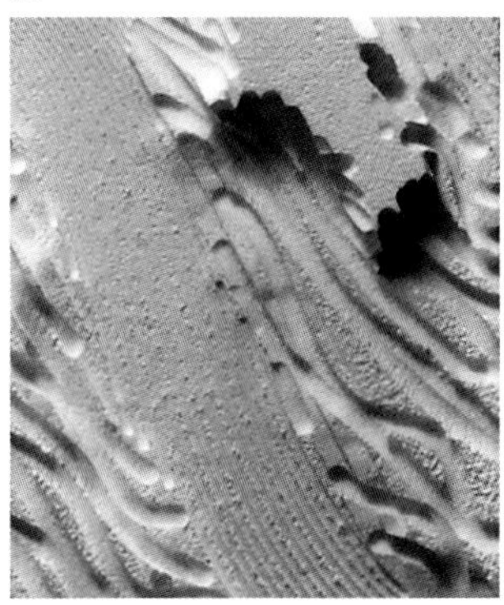
21

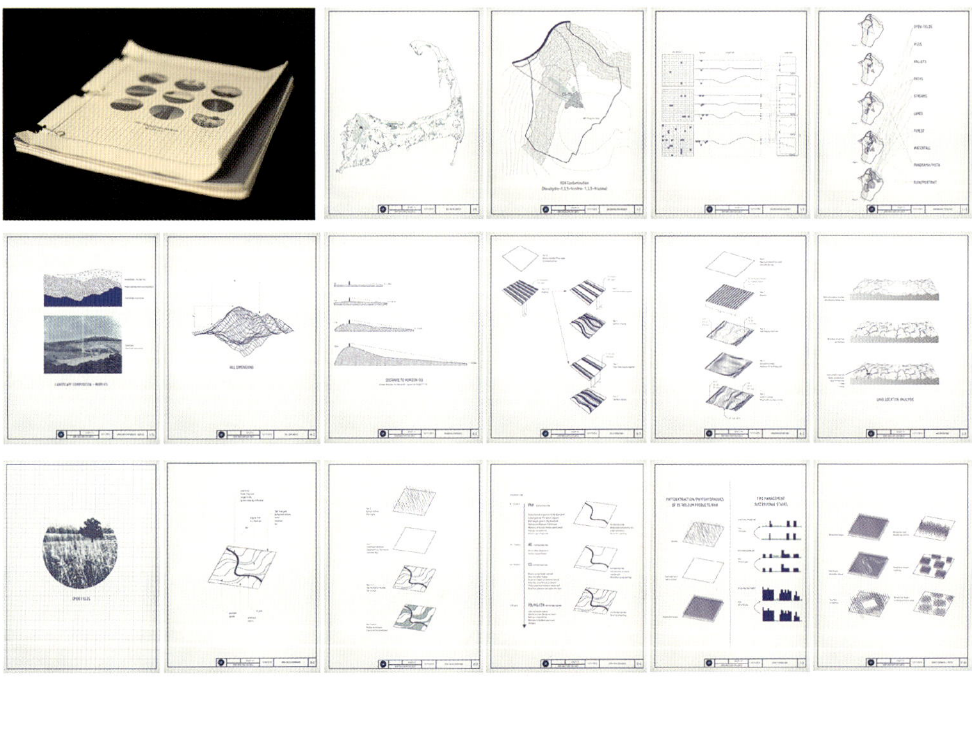

Stephanie Hsia (MLA I), Aliza Sovani (MLA I AP), and Vi Vu (MLA I). "The Operative Reveal"
Instructor: Andrea Hansen

T BASE
CAPE COD

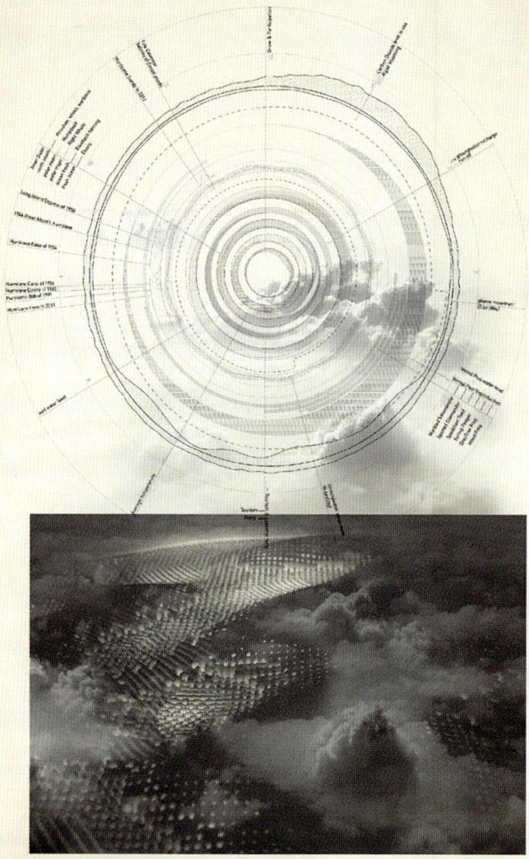

CIVIL LIGHTS: From an aerial perspective, night lights indicate densities of human settlement. Vernal occupation adopts the notion of nocturnal inhabitation, terrestrial-aquarian half-lives, and on/off switch circuit boards. A seasonal round allows for coordination.

3,000 meter vantage

Siwei Gou (MLA I AP), Lara Mehling (MLA I), and Nina Phinouwong (MUP/MLA I). "Vernal Occupation"
Instructor: Pierre Bélanger

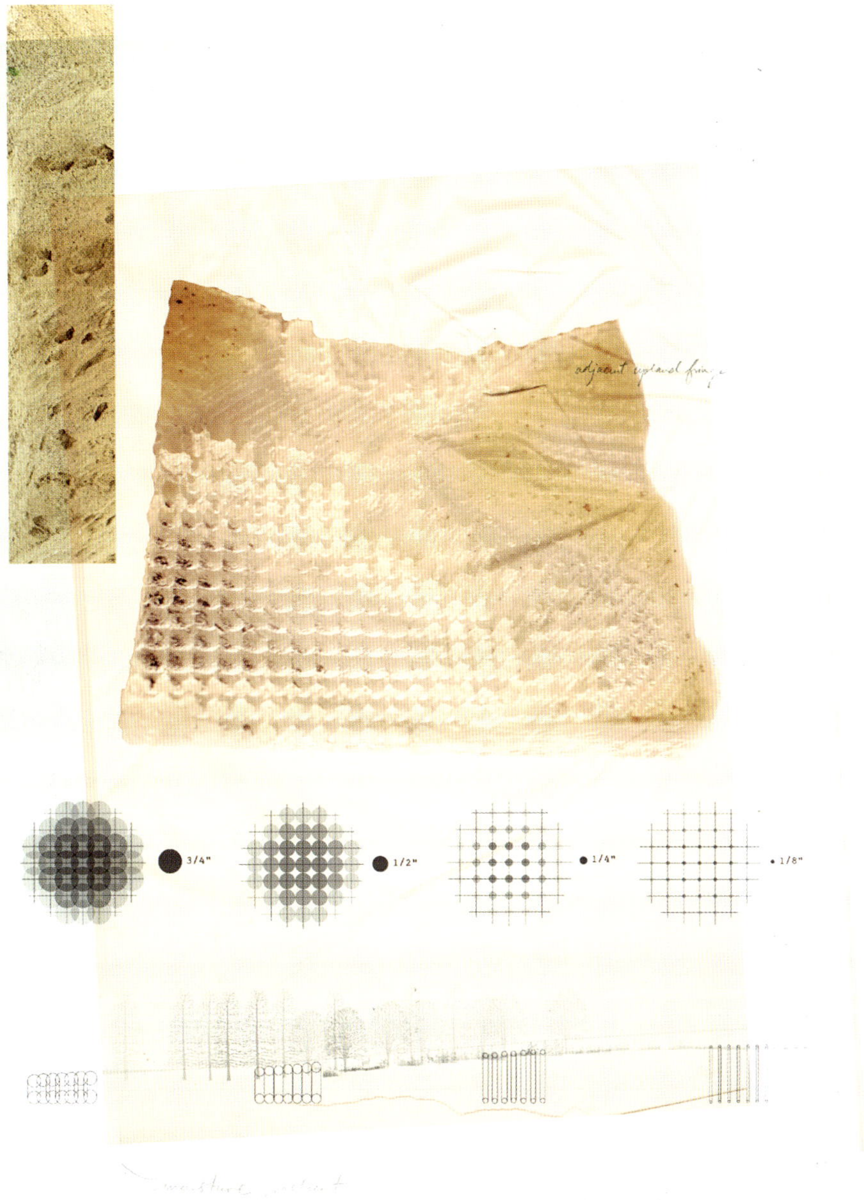

TERRESTRIAL POROSITY: Water availability decreases in the adjacent upland fringes of a vernal pool. The groundwater lens becomes less palpable with higher elevations and the soil conditions drier. Sandy substrate supports higher levels of compaction while the nutrient-rich basins remain active as zones of carbon exchange.

5.0 meter vantage

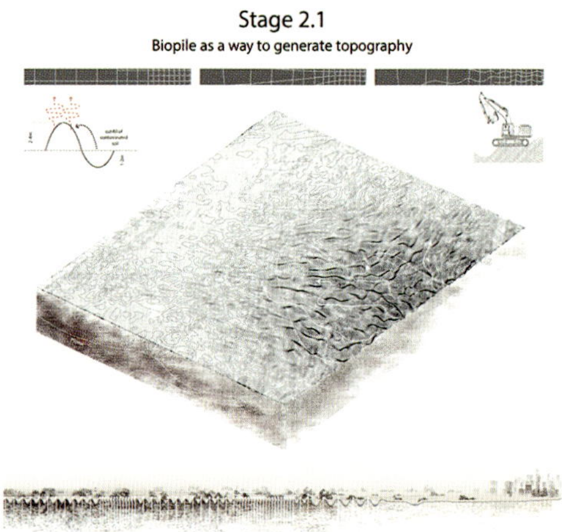

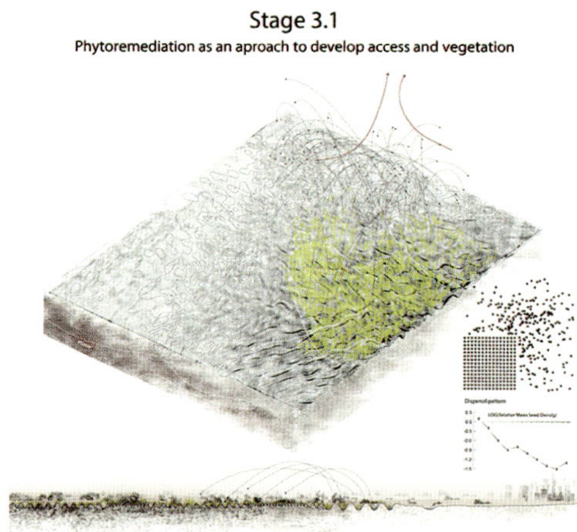

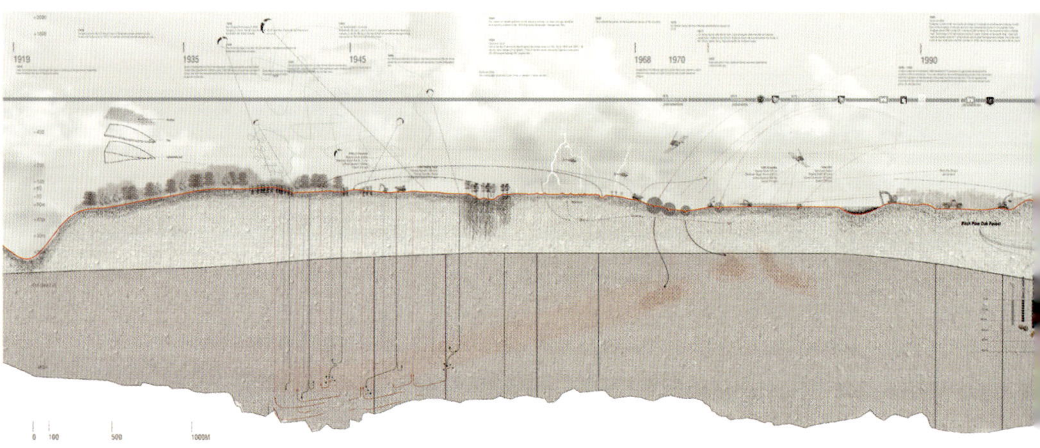

From Top: Jordan Boan (MLA I AP) and Yinjia Gong (MLA I AP). Instructor: Luis Callejas;
Sourav Biswas (MLA I AP), Xinjun Gu (MLA I AP), and McKenna McKetty (MLA I)
Instructor: Luis Callejas

Stage 1.3

Monitoring as to complete remediation of MMR

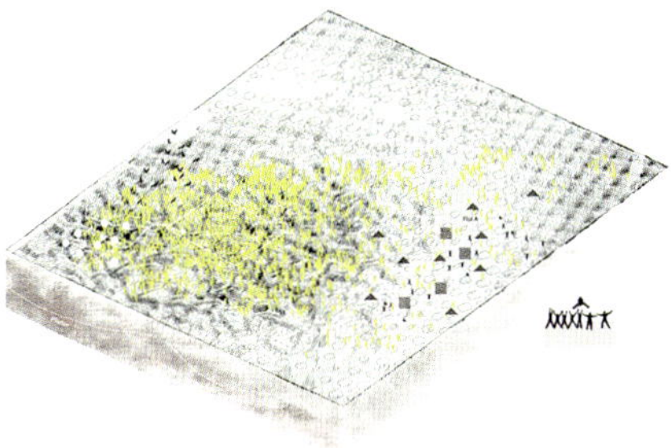

Stage 3.3

Phytoremediation as a dynamic and continues process

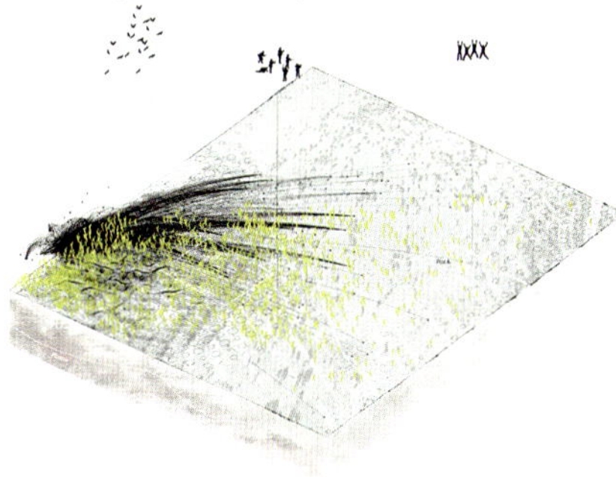

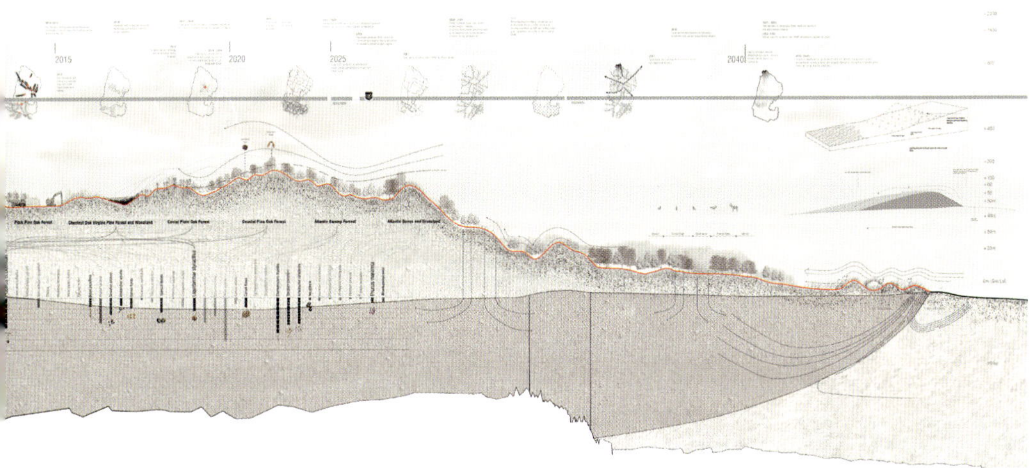

GSD Talks: Michael Hays, Erika Naginski, and Pier Vittorio Aureli
On the Legacy of Manfredo Tafuri
February 27, 2014

PVA: It's very difficult to hide the fact that the work of Tafuri has been one of the major influences on my way of approaching architecture. I encountered his work when I was in high school—I think I was sixteen or seventeen. I read his book on contemporary architecture, which was part of a large series on the history of architecture, and through Tafuri, Francesco Dal Co actually wrote the last volume of this series, which was on contemporary architecture, basically twentieth-century architecture. I was really shocked because until then I thought architecture was about buildings, and of course reading such a historically visionary outlook on modern and contemporary architecture was a revelation. At that time I was also very much politically involved, which was something very normal in Italy. And for me, architecture was the most remote position from engaging with politics because it was a very constrained profession. It's the most expensive "art," and always needs a client and financial support. So I considered architecture as the last place to be critical within the kind of present condition, and reading Tafuri I realized that on the contrary, architecture not as a design problem but really as a form of knowledge was perhaps one of the most precise and comprehensive ways to analyze the way in which the city and its architecture were instrumentalized to govern society and actualize its condition.

PVA: His lectures were incredibly powerful, and with very simple words and concepts displayed the specific historical moments where architecture changed,

"...architecture not as a design problem but really as a form of knowledge was perhaps one of the most precise and comprehensive ways to analyze the way in which the city and its architecture were

not only in terms of new forms or new projects but in terms of the way architecture is considered. Why Tafuri was obsessed by this very short period, the very late fifteenth century or beginning of the sixteenth century—well, it is the moment in which architecture becomes a profession. I mean, before let's say Bramante, of course there is a discourse on architecture. Alberti has in very radical terms established the basis for such a discourse, but until Bramante there are not yet fully professional architects. Bramante, Sangallo—

EN: Sangallo is the architect's architect.

PVA: Exactly. They're really architects that make architecture a profession, and that's why for Tafuri this period is foundational, because architecture—not only as a discipline but also as a practice at the service of specific forms of power or specific interests—becomes an instrumental operative knowledge, whose influence would last until modernity. So for Tafuri, the Renaissance was not to retire into some kind of Golden Age of architecture, but to really analyze the roots of the problem, which was this junction, the gap that always exists between architecture as a project and what at the end architecture can really affect and eventually change.

Architecture IV

<u>Coordinators</u>
Florian Idenburg
Carles Muro
<u>Instructors</u>
Eric Höweler
Timothy Hyde
Ingeborg Rocker
Spela Videcnik

Cities are more than simply an assemblage of buildings. Through time and occupation, these orchestrations of matter can grow into dynamic social ecologies. Architecture in the city is the "temporary" outcome of a continuous dialogue between individual or semicollective aspirations and our collective "civic" positions and convictions. A sense of the civic can be achieved through the careful creation of a multilayered tissue that organizes scales, densities, programs, typologies, relations, etc. Operating on the city requires an understanding of the workings of these mechanisms and how they interrelate. The work of the studio constituted a unique piece of urban fabric in New York City, understood and realized as a relational structure. The lens through which this relational structure was negotiated was the individual dwelling unit. The unit was understood as the "currency" that allows a city to establish more collective functions, such as transportation, parks, and infrastructure.

01 Lauren McClellan (MArch I)
Patrick Mayfield
(MArch I AP)
02 Gregory Logan (MArch I)
Jing Ng (MArch I)
Emma Silverblatt (MArch I)
Lance Smith (MArch I)
03 Paruyr Matevosyan
(MArch I AP)
04 Ping Wang (MArch I)
05 Gregory Logan (MArch I)
Jing Ng (MArch I)
Emma Silverblatt (MArch I
Lance Smith (MArch I)
06 Majda Al Marzouqi (MArch I)
Arion Kocani (MArch I)
Royce Perez (MArch I AP)
07 Iman Fayyad (MArch I)
Giancarlo Montano (MArch I)
Chong Ying Pai (MArch I AP)
Jonathan Rieke (MArch I)
08 Aaron Menninga (MArch I)
Yufeng Zheng (MArch I AP)
09 Whitney Hansley (MArch I)
10 Patrick Burke (MArch I AP)
Sonya Chao (MArch I)
Jaewoo Chon (MArch I AP)
Justin Kollar (MArch I AP)
11 Yu Chen (MArch I)
Yi Li (MArch I AP)
Raffy Mardirossian
(MArch I AP)
12 Frankie Au (MArch I)
Eliana Dotan (MArch I)
Patrick Herron (MArch I)
Elizabeth Pipal (MArch I)
13 Frederick Kim (MArch I)
14 Raffy Mardirossian
(MArch I AP)
15 Lauren McClellan (MArch I)
Patrick Mayfield
(MArch I AP)
16 Paruyr Matevosyan
(MArch I AP)
17 Ali Karimi (MArch I)
18 Iman Fayyad (MArch I)
Giancarlo Montano (MArch I)
Chong Ying Pai (MArch I AP)
Jonathan Rieke (MArch I)
19 Frankie Au (MArch I)
Eliana Dotan (MArch I)
Patrick Herron (MArch I)
Elizabeth Pipal (MArch I)
20 Jonathan Rieke (MArch I)

01

02

03

04

05

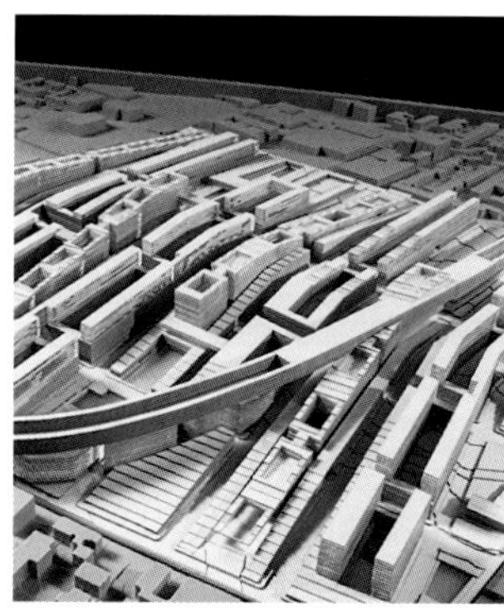
06

07

08

09

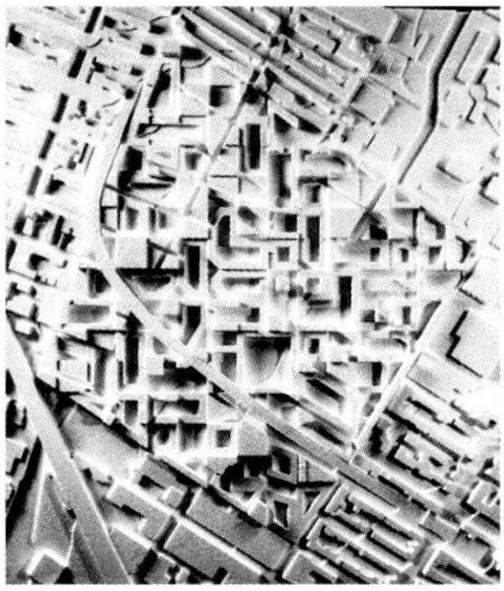

10

11

12

13

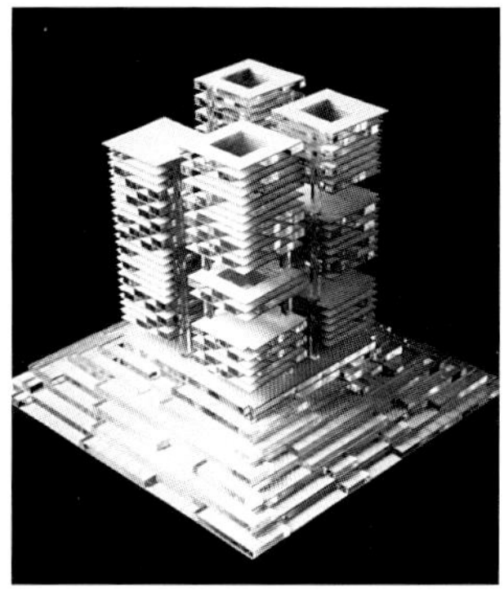

14

15

16

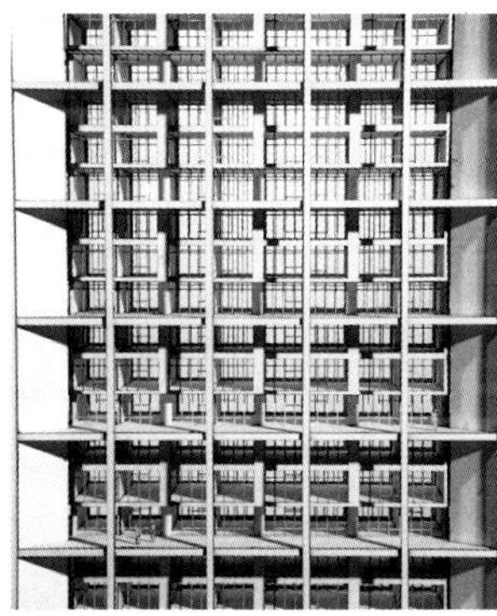

17

18

19

20

Aaron Menninga (MArch I) and Yufeng Zheng (MArch I AP). Instructor: Spela Videcnik

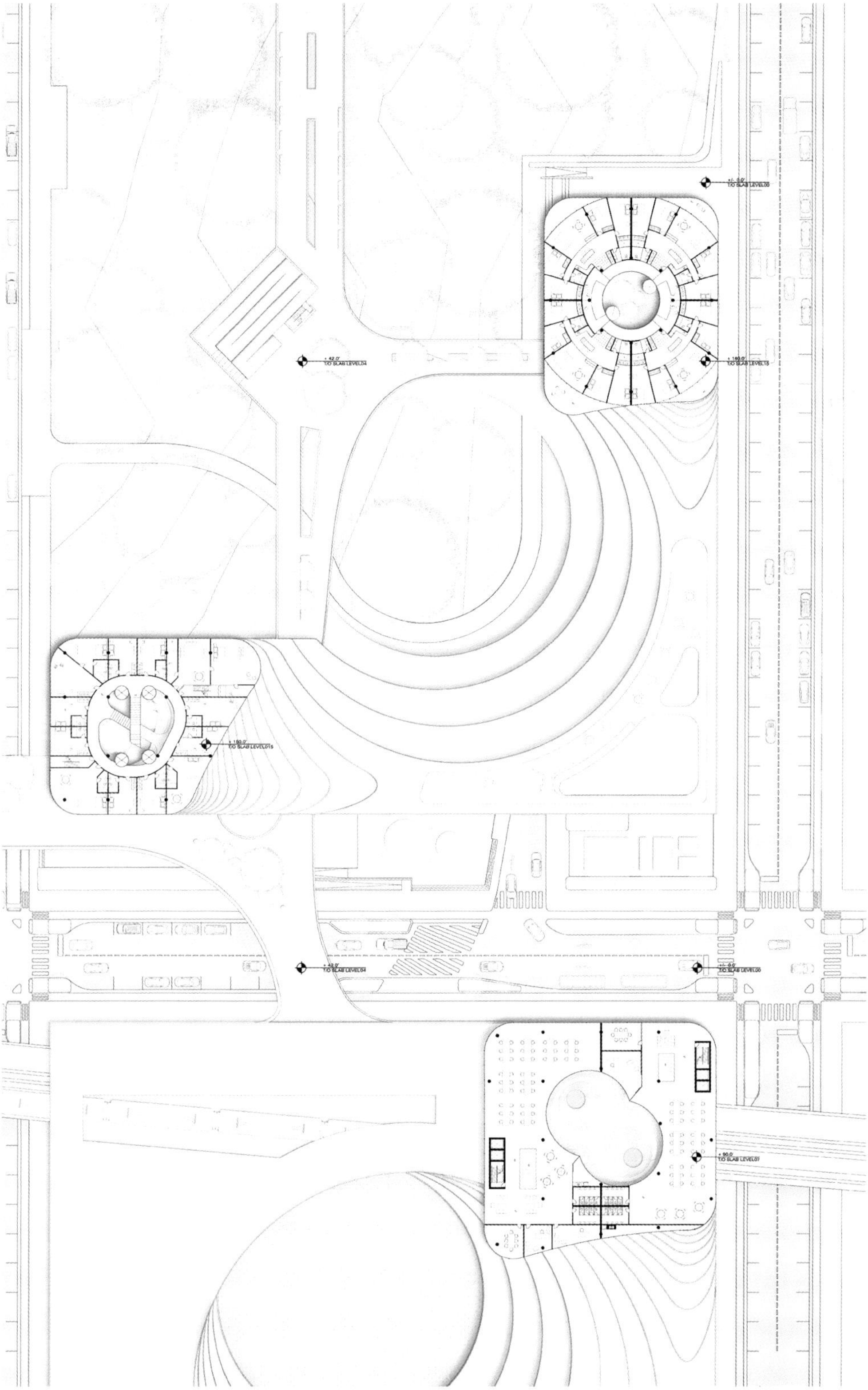
+/- 0.0'
T/O SLAB LEVEL00
+ 42.0'
T/O SLAB LEVEL04
+ 180.0'
T/O SLAB LEVEL15
+ 180.0'
T/O SLAB LEVEL015
+ 42.0'
T/O SLAB LEVEL04
+/- 0.0'
T/O SLAB LEVEL00
+ 90.0'
T/O SLAB LEVEL07

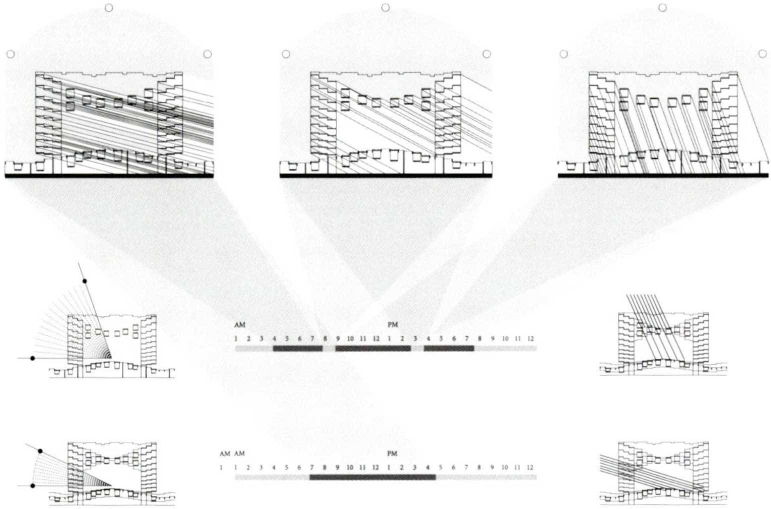

Jyri Eskola (MArch I AP) and Jee Hyung Park (MArch I). Instructor: Spela Videcnik

Aaron Menninga (MArch I) and Yufeng Zheng (MArch I AP). Instructor: Spela Videcnik. From Top: Building surfaces are responsive to solar angles; additional program creates a winter solar corridor; elevated public corridor traces and connects solar corridor; total FAR of 4.7 while ground plane remains preserved

01 Brett Keese (MArch I/MLA I AP)
Hyeyun Jung (MArch I)
Paruyr Matevosyan (MArch I AP)
Chun Ting Tsai (MArch I)
Instructor: Florian Idenburg
02 Josh Feldman (MArch I)
Arianna Galan Montas (MArch I)
Insu Kim (MArch I)
Yi Ren (MArch I)
Instructor: Eric Höweler
03 Lauren McClellan (MArch I)
Aaron Menninga (MArch I)
Patrick Mayfield (MArch I AP)
Yufeng Zheng (MArch I AP)
Instructor: Spela Videcnik
04 Yu Chen (MArch I)
Yi Li (MArch I AP)
Raffy Mardirossian (MArch I AP)
Instructor: Spela Videcnik
05 Gregory Logan (MArch I)
Jing Ng (MArch I)
Emma Silverblatt (MArch I)
Lance Smith (MArch I)
Instructor: Timothy Hyde
06 Daniela Leon (MArch I AP)
Sicong Ma (MArch I)
Ivan Ruhle (MArch I)
Instructor: Florian Idenburg
07 Clare Adrien (MArch I)
Patrick Baudin (MArch I)
Wen Wen (MArch I)
Dana Wu (MArch I)
Instructor: Timothy Hyde
08 Iman Fayyad (MArch I)
Giancarlo Montano (MArch I)
Chong Ying Pai (MArch I AP)
Jonathan Rieke (MArch I)
Instructor: Ingeborg Rocker
09 Ali Karimi (MArch I)
Xuanyi Nie (MArch I)
Adelene Tan (MArch I)
Alex Timmer (MArch I)
Instructor: Florian Idenburg
10 Majda Al Marzouqi (MArch I)
Arion Kocani (MArch I)
Royce Perez (MArch I AP)
Instructor: Ingeborg Rocker

01

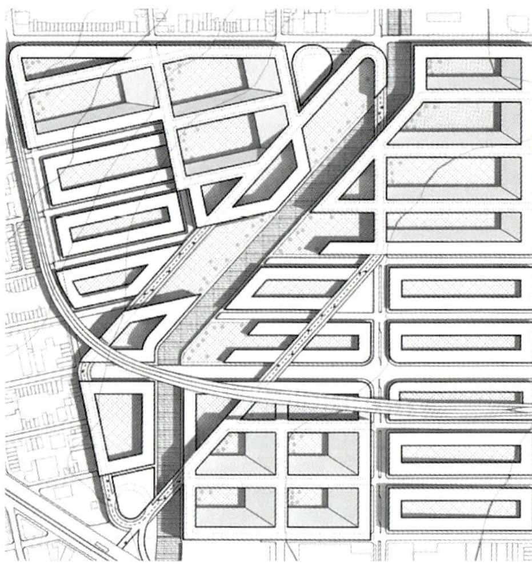
02

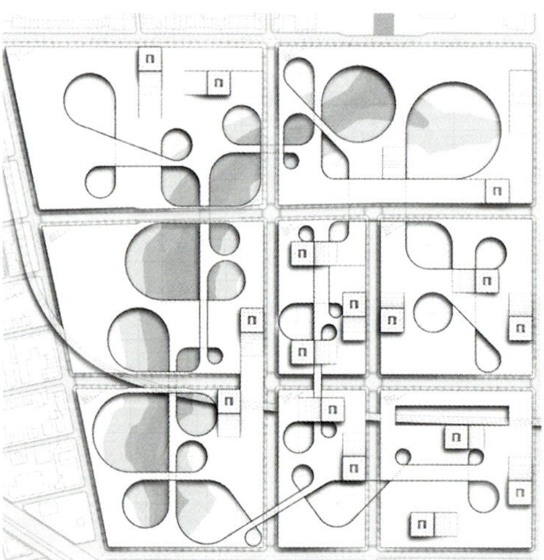
03

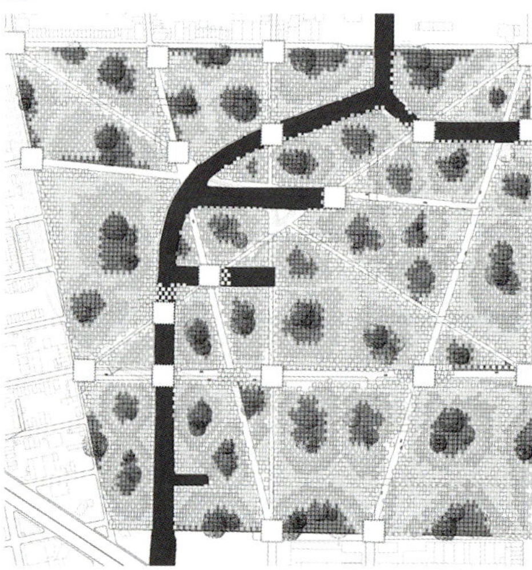
04

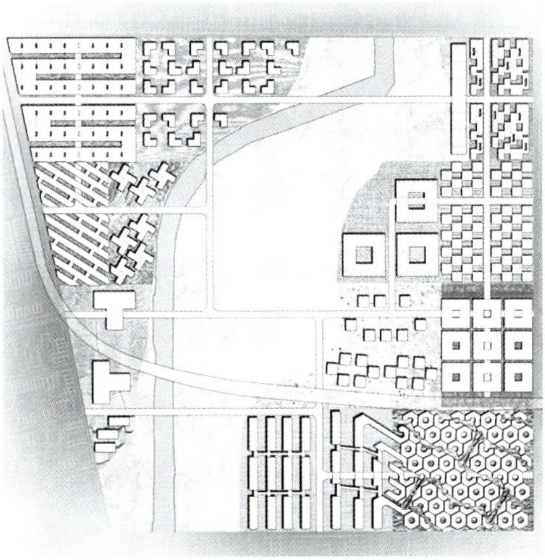

05

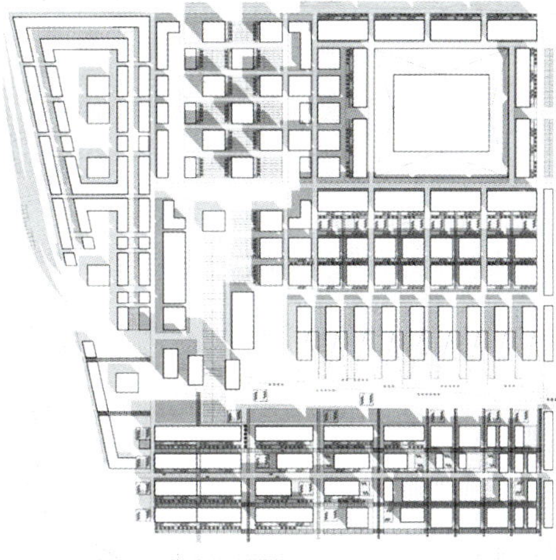

06

07

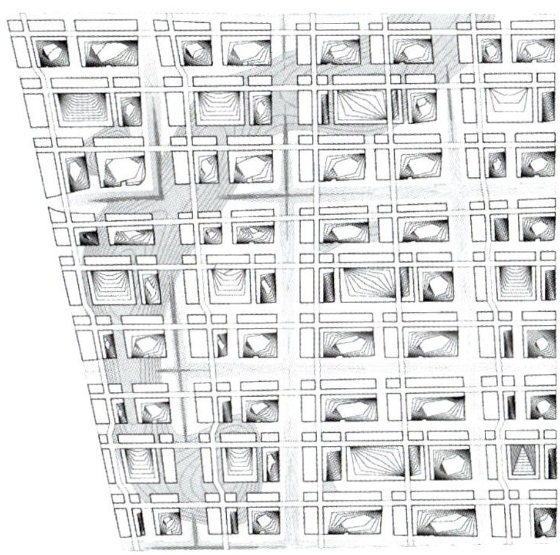

08

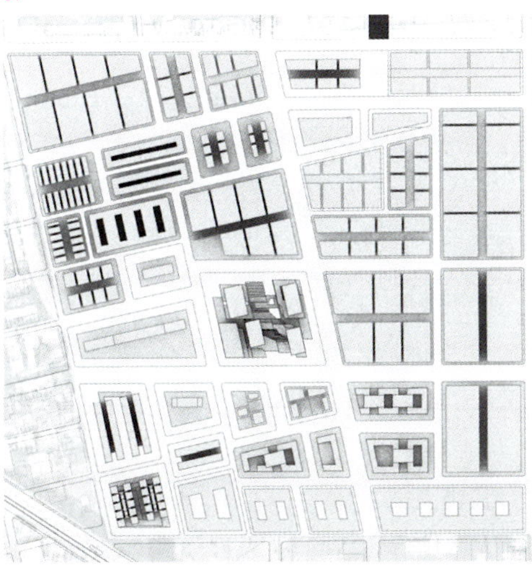

09

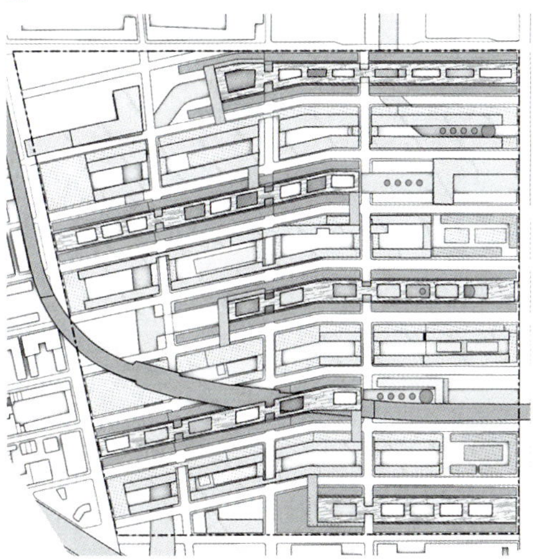

10

Jaewoo Chon (MArch I AP). Instructor: Timothy Hyde
From Left: "Off-Shoot City"; "Field of Unfulfilled Voids"

PLATFORM 7

Frankie Au (MArch I)
Eliana Dotan (MArch I)
Patrick Herron (MArch I)
Elizabeth Pipal (MArch I)
Instructor: Carles Muro

01 The mat is perforated where paths of mobility pass through it.
02 Housing stitches the residual space in the plan – it builds a mat.
03 Parking is situated between commercial space, out of view from piazzas.
04 Buildings are higher toward the center of the site and lower at the periphery.
05 All housing must have two distinct points of access.
06 Mat building bleeds into existing city fabric by appropriating courtyard dimension from existing block.
07 Subway station entry must be continuous with a pedestrian path.
08 Bays are organized to create courtyards.
09 Each plaza is anchored by a cultural facility and is fronted by commercial.
10 Housing bays will measure 20 x 45 feet.
11 The mat building will recess incrementally by offsets of 20 feet around commercial piazzas and 10 feet around housing courtyards.
12 Identify potential piazzas in spaces framed by three industrial buildings Maintain the walls around piazzas; demolish others.
13 No vehicular road may wrap a single building.
14 Housing will include a new level of pedestrian networks.
15 Edge is negotiated through material – transitions are negotiated by moving between new reflective surfaces and existing masonry.
16 There must not be any dead-end roads.
17 Mat building recessions are inverted to allow for passage over the canal where it crosses the mat.
18 Edge is negotiated through program – the mat grows by responding to its environment through program.
19 There must be an occurance of green space at minimum 200-foot intervals on pedestrian paths.
20 Canal is diverted such that it becomes adjacent to piazzas.

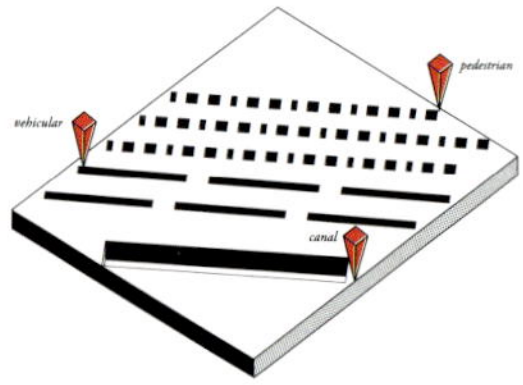

01

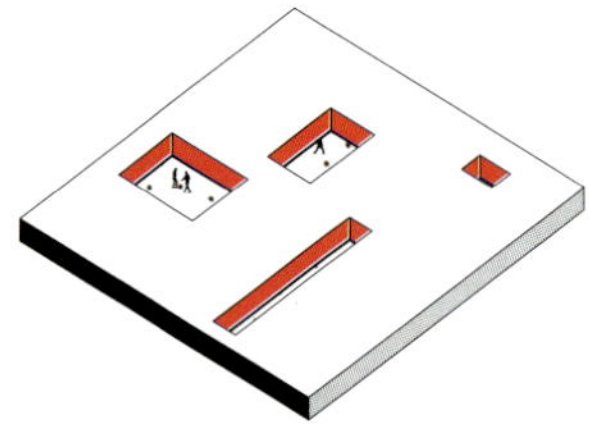

02

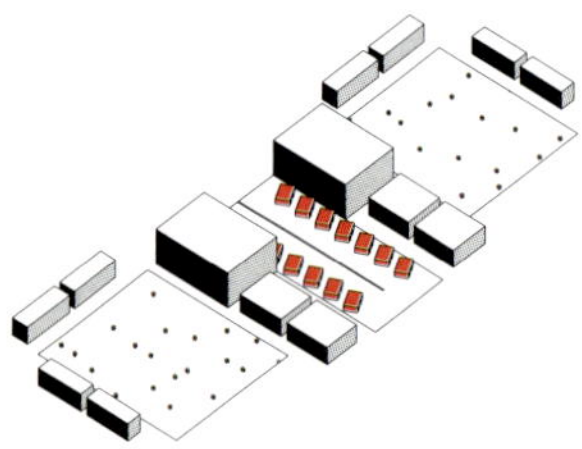

03

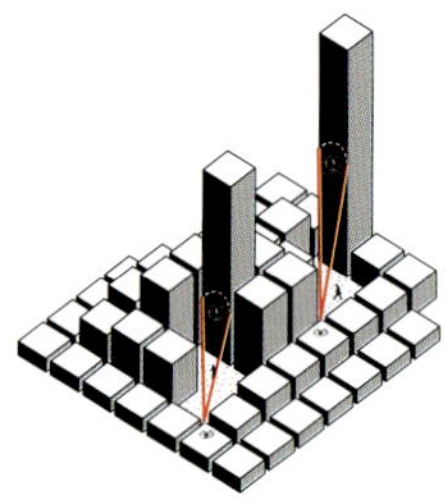

04

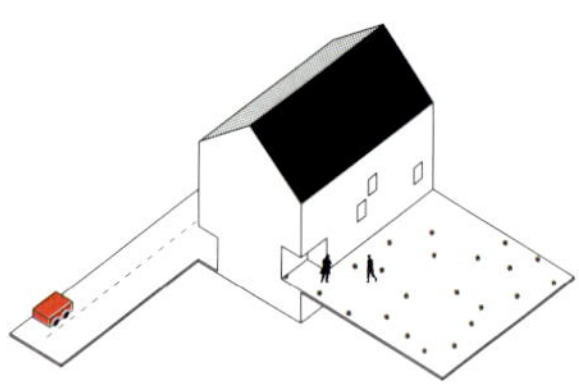

05

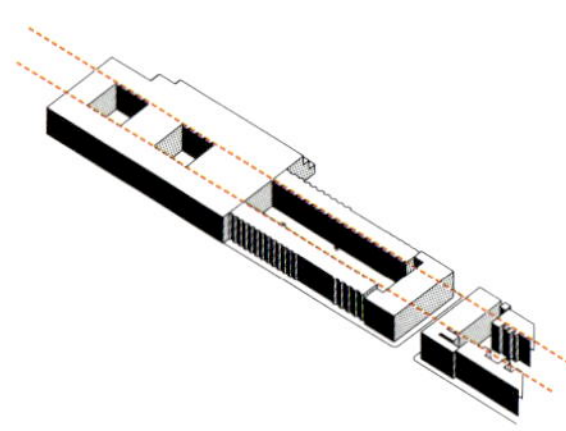

06

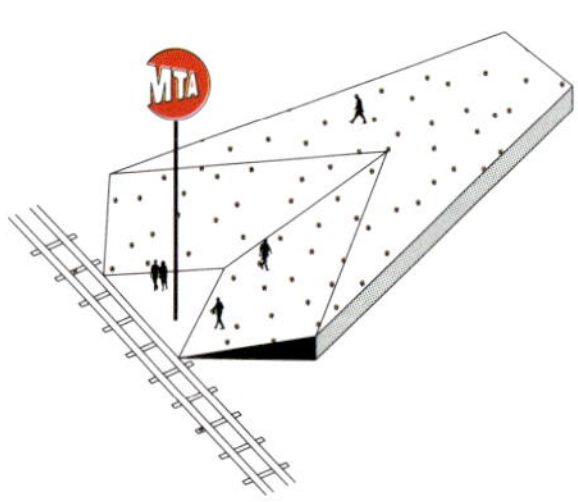

07

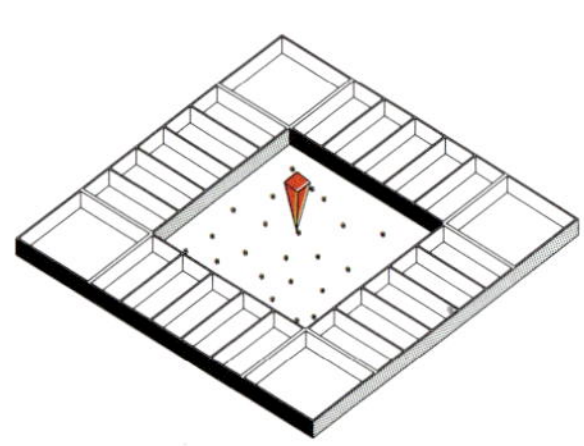

08

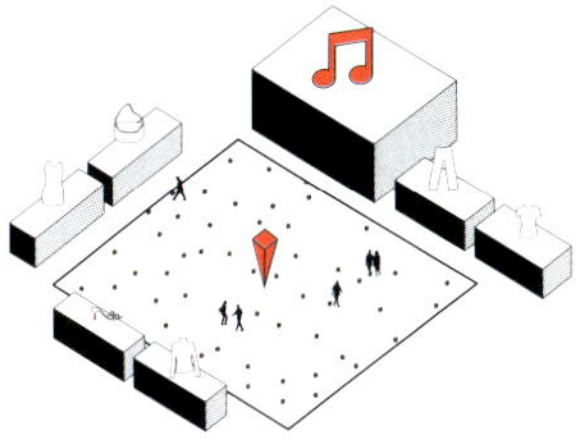

09

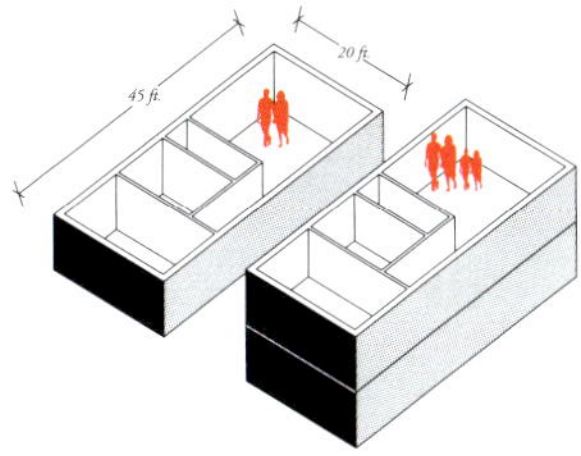

10

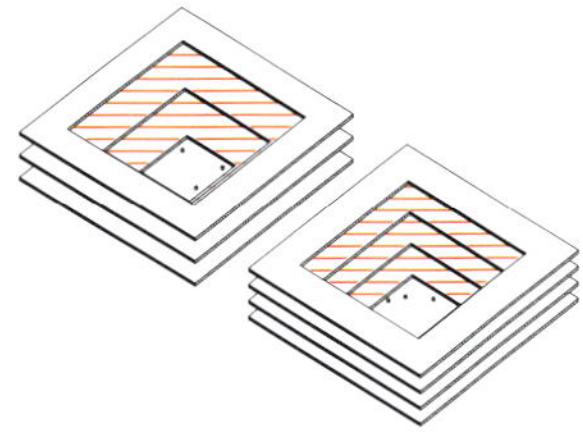

11

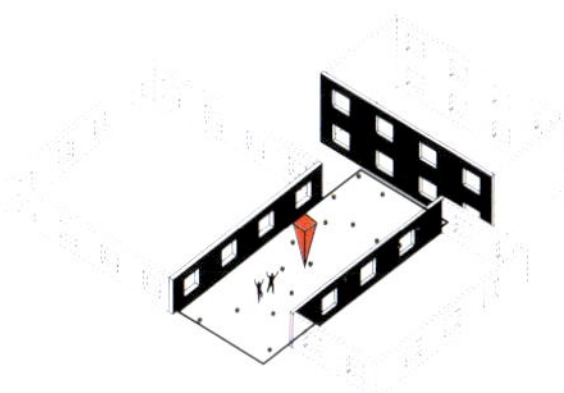

12

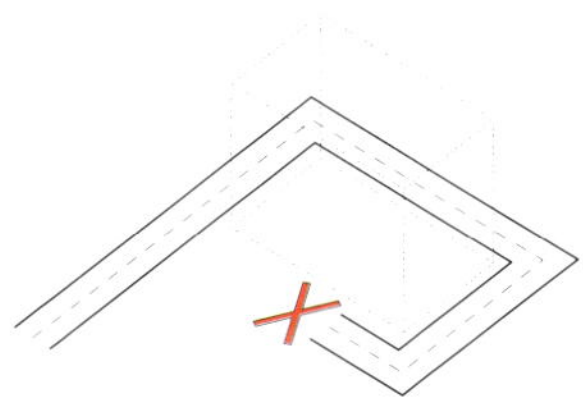

13

14

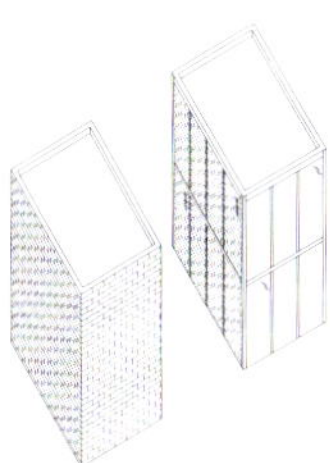

15

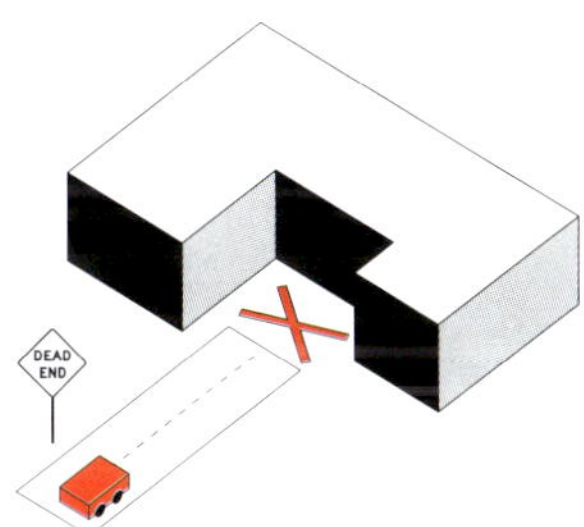

16

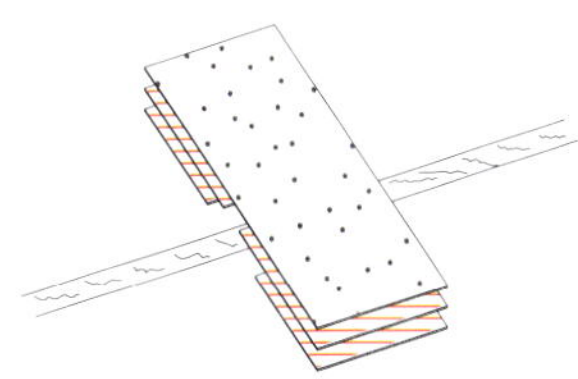

17

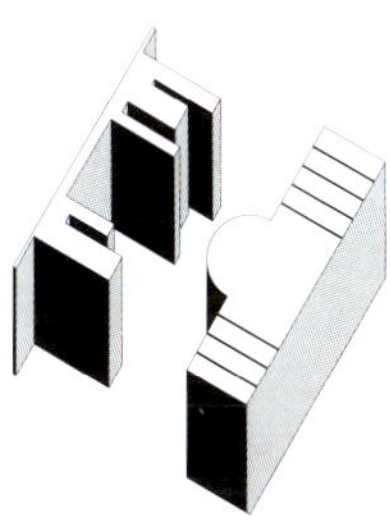

18

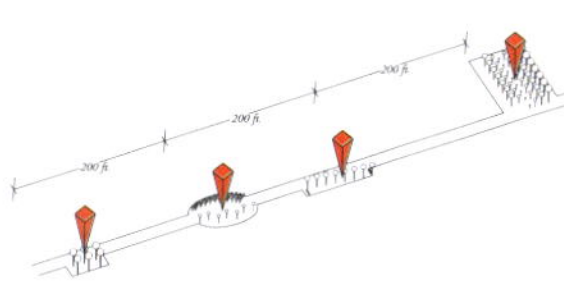

19

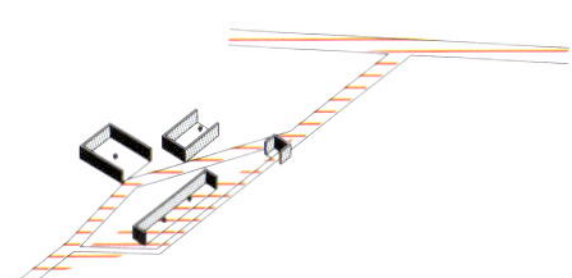

20

Chong Ying Pai (MArch I AP). Instructor: Ingeborg Rocker

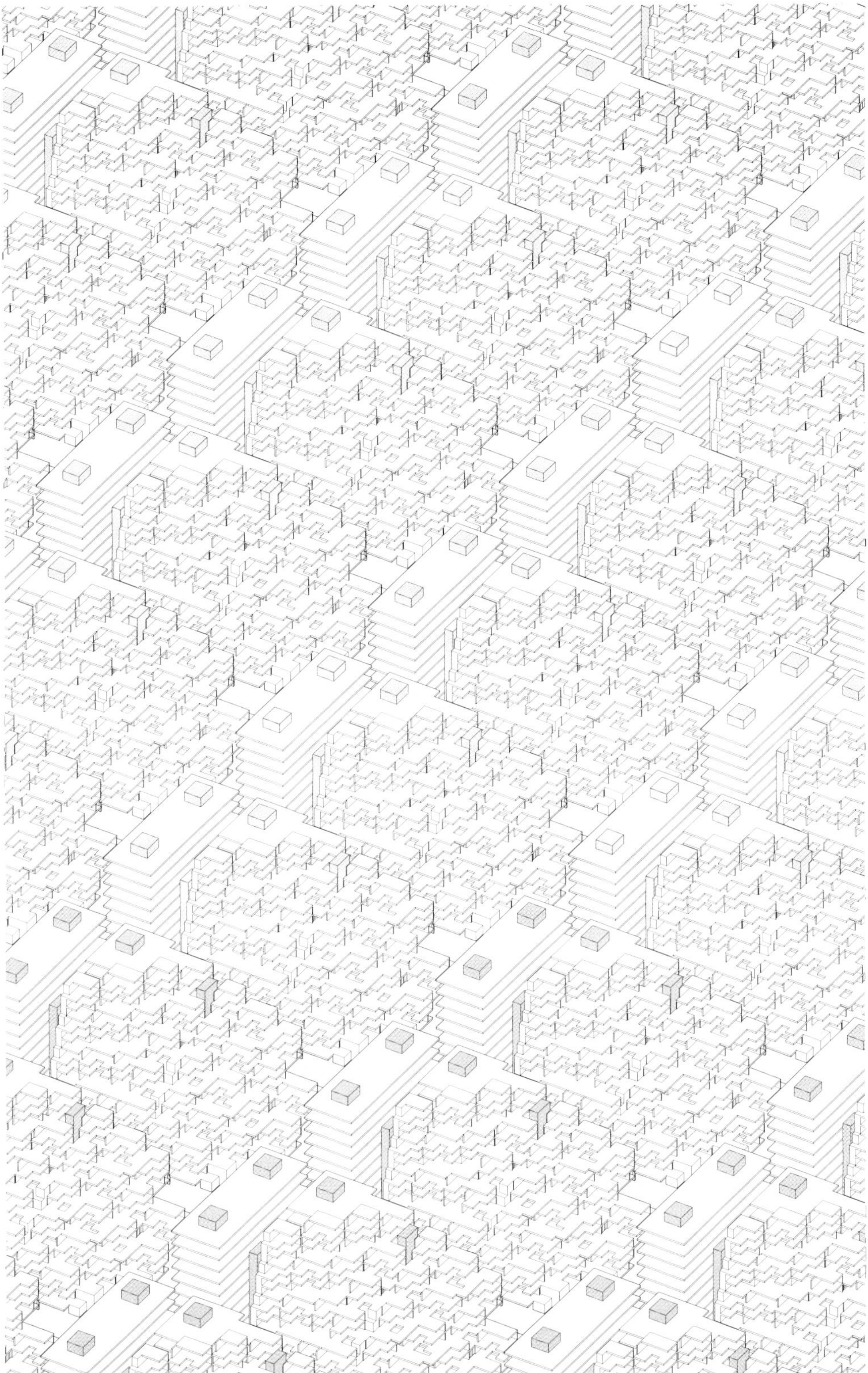

Landscape Architecture IV

<u>Coordinators</u>
David Mah
Chris Reed
<u>Instructors</u>
Leire Asensio Villoria
Silvia Benedito
Leena Cho
Sergio Lopez-Pineiro
<u>Workshops</u>
Zaneta Hong
Enriqueta Llabres-Valls
Eduardo Rico Carranza

This studio focused on the development of urban form as driven by ecology and environmental dynamics. The studio introduced students to methods and representational techniques for describing urban form and the underlying ecologies that might be invoked to shape the urban fabric. Representational strategies began with mapping and diagramming larger ecological processes and dynamics on an urban brownfield site, and then focused on the description of built form, urban infrastructure, and the relationships between the city and its reconstituted riverine setting.

01 Shahab Al Bahar (MLA I AP)
Rituparna Simlai (MLA I AP)
02 Ken Chongsuwat (MLA I)
Peichen Hao (MLA I)
03 Eri Yamagata (MLA I)
Yi Lun Yang (MLA I)
04 Elizabeth Wu (MLA I AP)
Tzyy-Haur Yeh
(MArch I/MLA I AP)
05 Christina Geros
(MAUD/MLA I AP)
Craig Reschke (MLA I AP)
06 Xinjun Gu (MLA I AP)
Han Yang (MLA I)
07 Weimao Kong (MLA I AP)
Bingjie Shi (MAUD/MLA I AP)
08 Nina Phinouwong (MUP/MLA I)
Emily Wettstein
(MArch I/MLA I AP)
09 McKenna McKetty (MLA I)
Timothy Wei (MLA I)
10 Sourav Biswas (MLA I AP)
Flavio Sciaraffia
(MLA I AP)
11 Xiaoran Du (MLA I AP)
Yue Shi (MLA I AP)

01

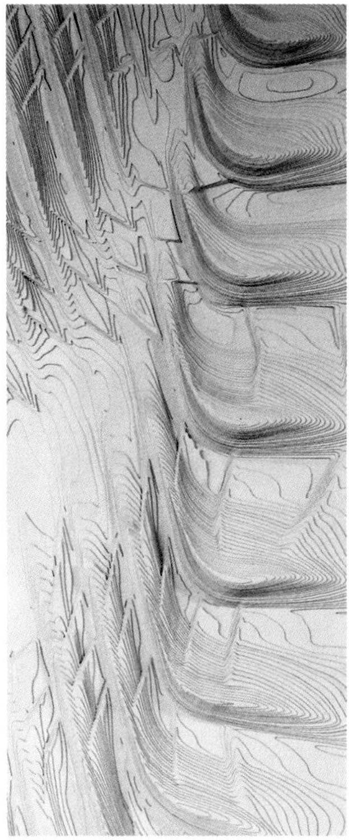

02

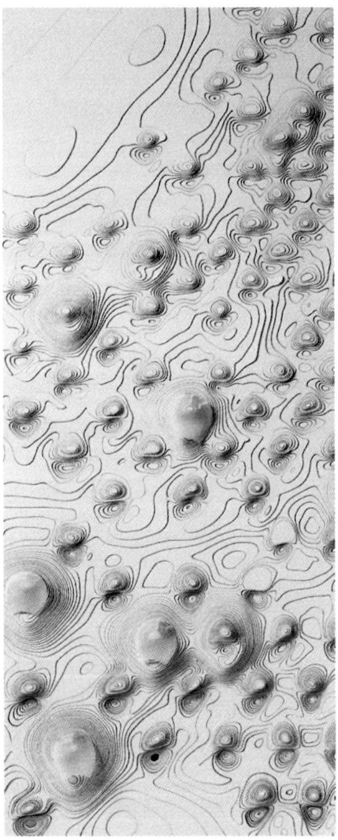

03

04

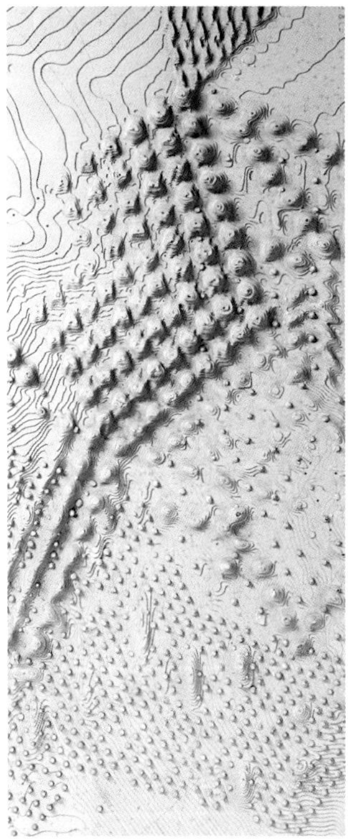

05

06

07

08

09

10

11

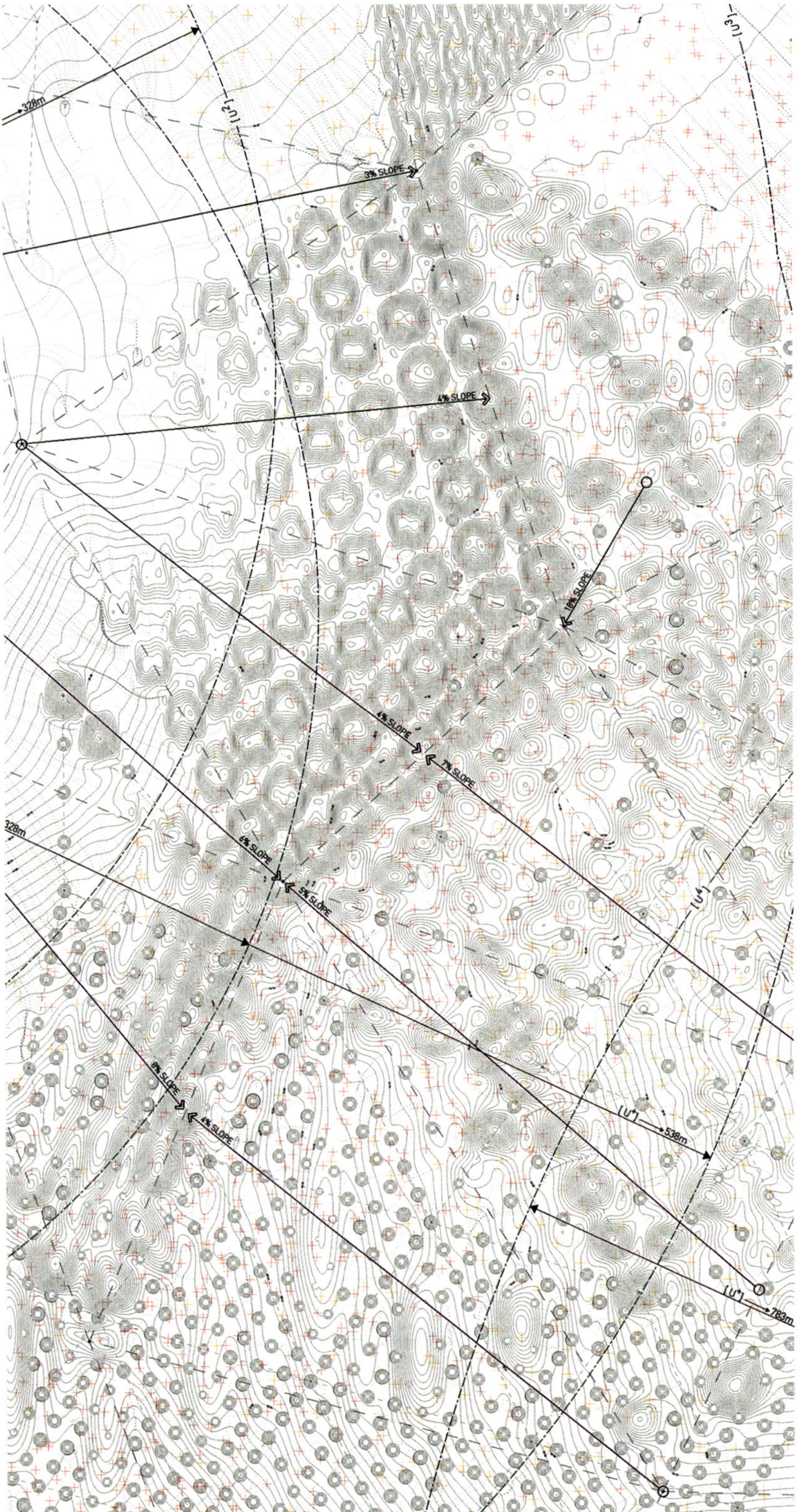
328m
3% SLOPE
4% SLOPE
18% SLOPE
4% SLOPE
7% SLOPE
328m
6% SLOPE
5% SLOPE
8% SLOPE
4% SLOPE
538m
783m

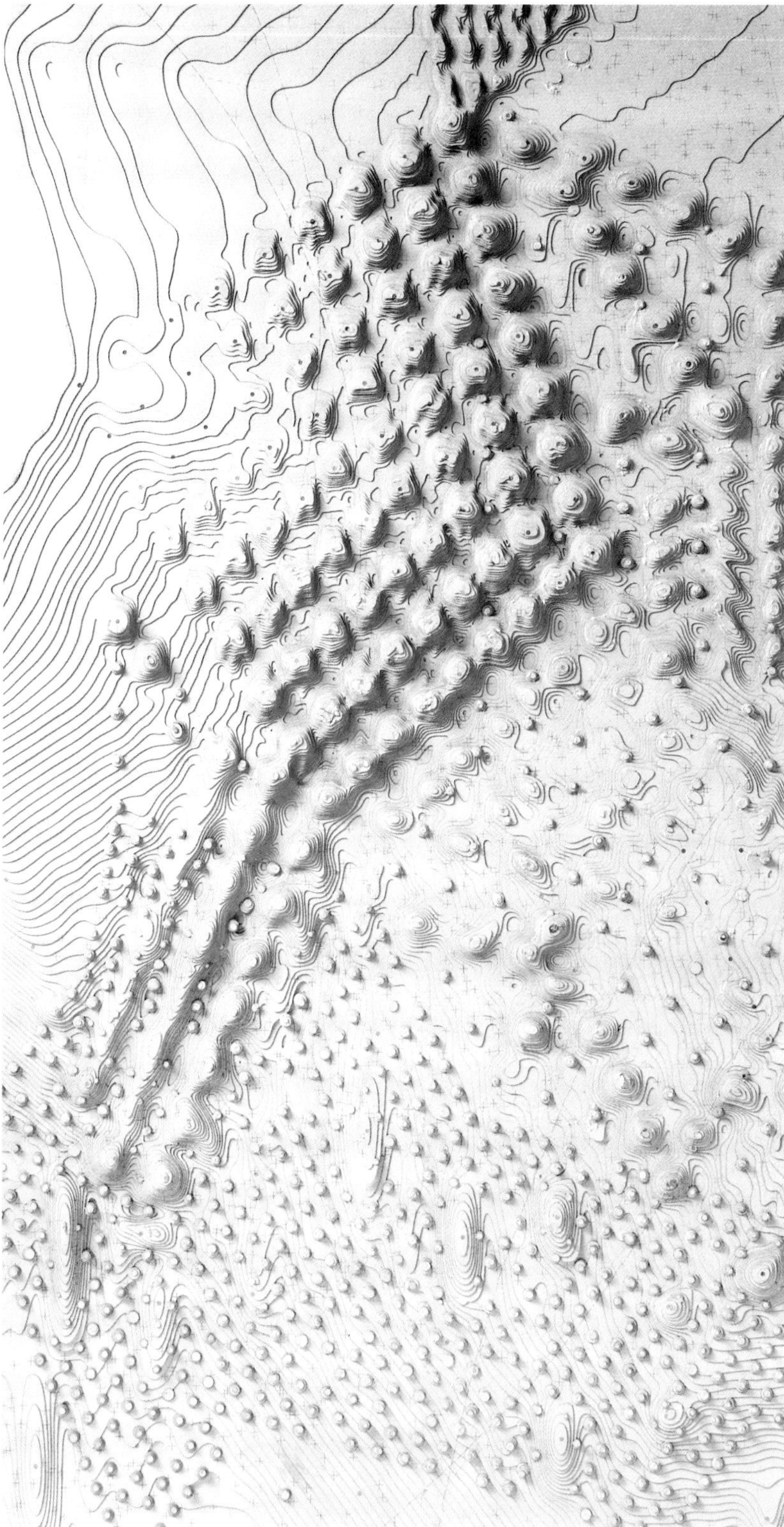

Christina Geros (MAUD/MLA I AP) and Craig Reschke (MLA I AP). Instructor: Leire Asensio Villoria
"[on] Edge: Equiposed Forces of Stability and Flux along Fragile Coastal Conditions"

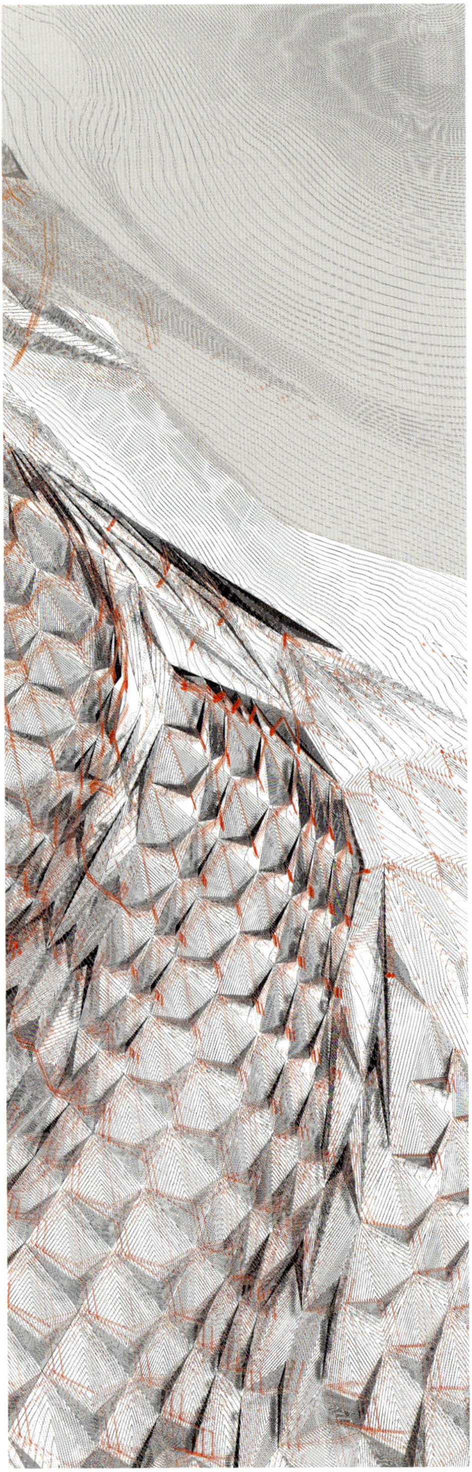

Shahab Al Bahar (MLA I AP)
Rituparna Simlai (MLA I AP)
Instructor: Leire Asensio Villoria

Christina Geros (MAUD/MLA I AP)
Craig Reschke (MLA I AP)
Instructor: Leire Asensio Villoria

Hector Tarrido-Picart (MAUD/MLA I AP)
Sara Zewde (MLA I)
Instructor: Sergio Lopez-Pineiro

Ken Chongsuwat (MLA I)
Peichen Hao (MLA I)
Instructor: David Mah

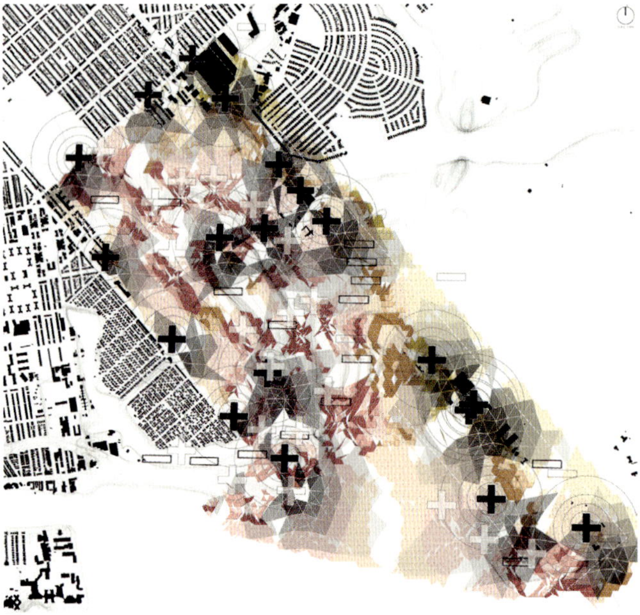

Christina Geros (MAUD/MLA I AP) and Craig Reschke (MLA I AP). "[on] Edge: Equiposed Forces of Stability and Flux along Fragile Coastal Conditions"
Instructor: Leire Asensio Villoria

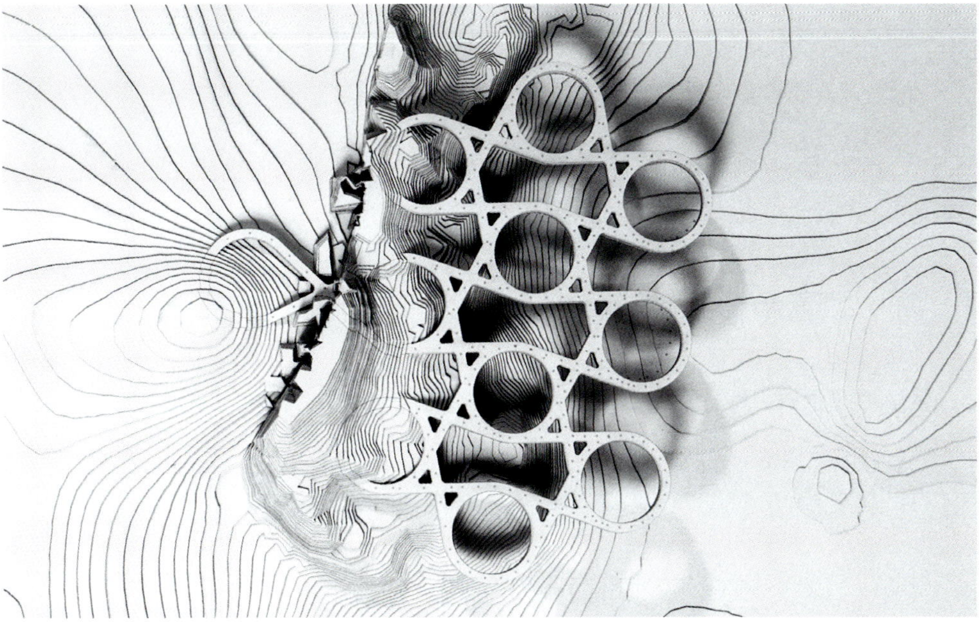

From Top: Vi Vu (MLA I) and Sarah Winston (MLA I). "A Delirious Story: Urban Tale of the Ecological Fantastic" Instructor: David Mah
Hector Tarrido-Picart (MAUD/MLA I AP)and Sara Zewde (MLA I). "Niebla"
Instructor: Sergio Lopez-Pineiro

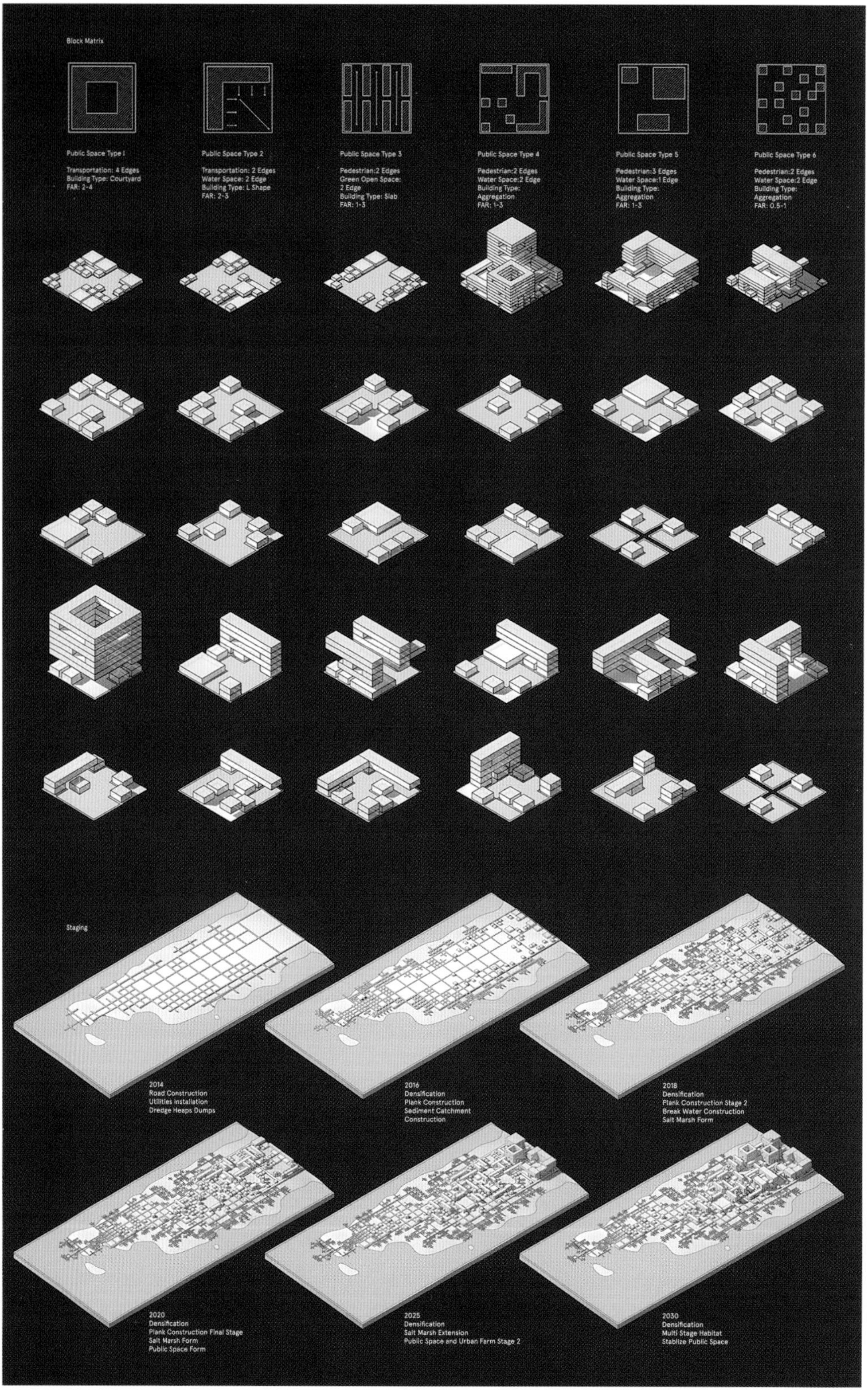
Block Matrix
Public Space Type I
Transportation: 4 Edges
Building Type: Courtyard
FAR: 2-4
Public Space Type 2
Transportation: 2 Edges
Water Space: 2 Edge
Building Type: L Shape
FAR: 2-3
Public Space Type 3
Pedestrian:2 Edges
Green Open Space:
2 Edge
Building Type: Slab
FAR: 1-3
Public Space Type 4
Pedestrian:2 Edges
Water Space:2 Edge
Building Type:
Aggregation
FAR: 1-3
Public Space Type 5
Pedestrian:3 Edges
Water Space:1 Edge
Building Type:
Aggregation
FAR: 1-3
Public Space Type 6
Pedestrian:2 Edges
Water Space:2 Edge
Building Type:
Aggregation
FAR: 0.5-1
Staging
2014
Road Construction
Utilities Installation
Dredge Heaps Dumps
2016
Densification
Plank Construction
Sediment Catchment
Construction
2018
Densification
Plank Construction Stage 2
Break Water Construction
Salt Marsh Form
2020
Densification
Plank Construction Final Stage
Salt Marsh Form
Public Space Form
2025
Densification
Salt Marsh Extension
Public Space and Urban Farm Stage 2
2030
Densification
Multi Stage Habitat
Stablize Public Space

Rui Qian (MLA I AP), Yujun Yin (MArch II/MLA I AP). "The Fluctuated Urban Framework"
Instructor: David Mah
The urban grid circulation system operates as an ecological infrastructure to accommodate the collection and circulation of urban gray-water canals, flood corridors, or tidal canals/swales. As the grid is not isotropic and integrates a number of changing scales, the developments that can be accommodated in various areas of the overall grid are limited and controlled.

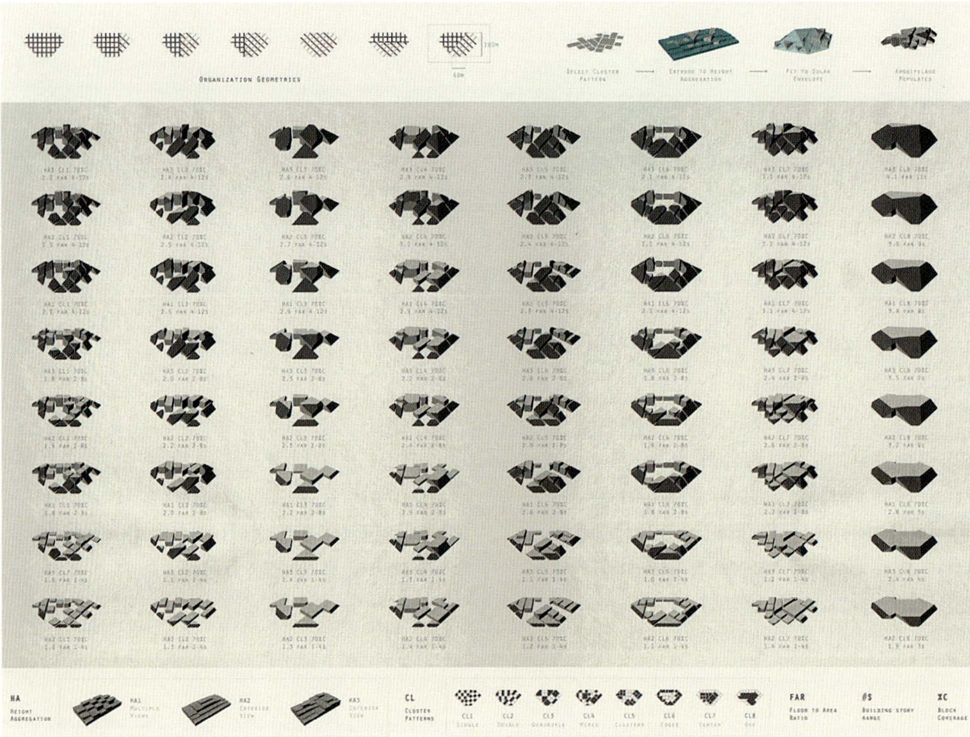

McKenna McKetty (MLA I) and Timothy Wei (MLA I). "From Heat Island to Microclimate Archipelago"
Instructor: David Mah
A menu of microclimate archipelago blocks denotes various combinations of densities and organization patterns.

From Top: Hector Tarrido-Picart (MAUD/MLA I AP) and Sara Zewde (MLA I). "Niebla"
Instructor: Sergio Lopez-Pineiro
Elizabeth Wu (MLA I AP) and Tzyy-Haur Yeh (MArch I/MLA I AP). "Liminal Mosaics"
Instructor: Leire Asensio Villoria

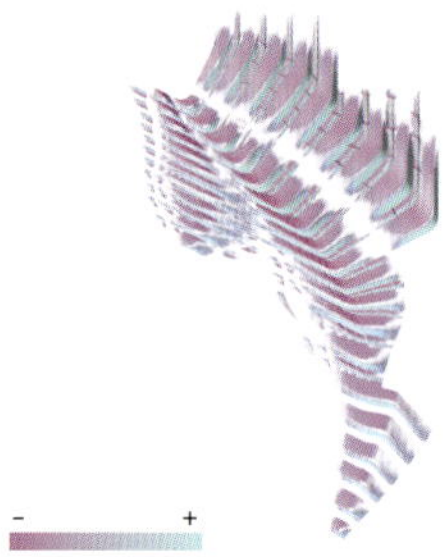

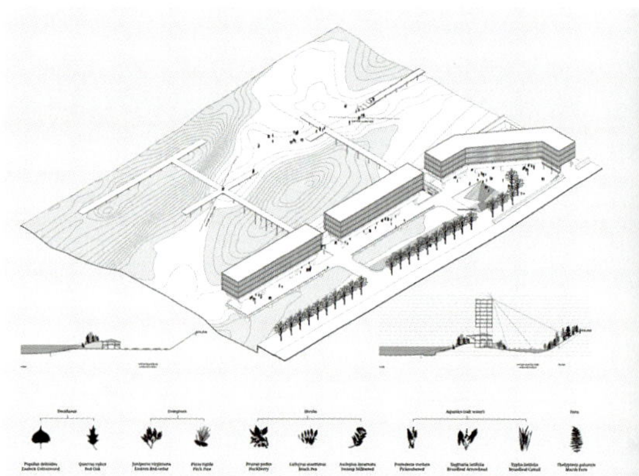

Ken Chongsuwat (MLA I) and Peichen Hao (MLA I)
"Orographic Hills"
Instructor: David Mah
By envisioning a novel landscape framework that allows urbanization and public spaces to integrate seamlessly, landform operations become the main structural system. Shaped to take advantage of the wind direction and moisture collection, they produce suitable and sustainable microclimates throughout the year.

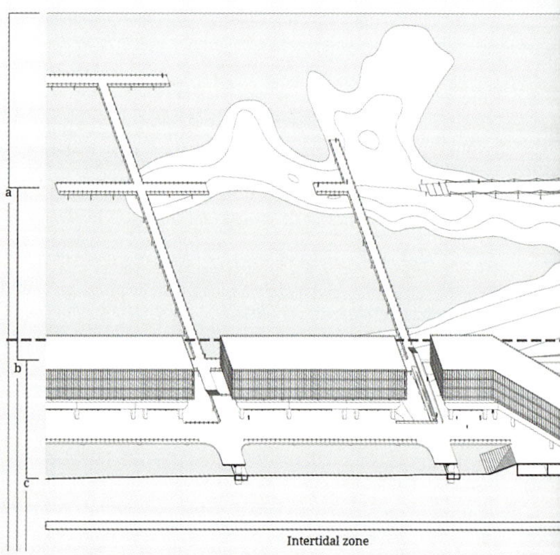

Left: Yinjia Gong (MLA I AP) and
Siwei Gou(MLA I AP)
"Thermal Intelligence"
Instructor: Leena Cho

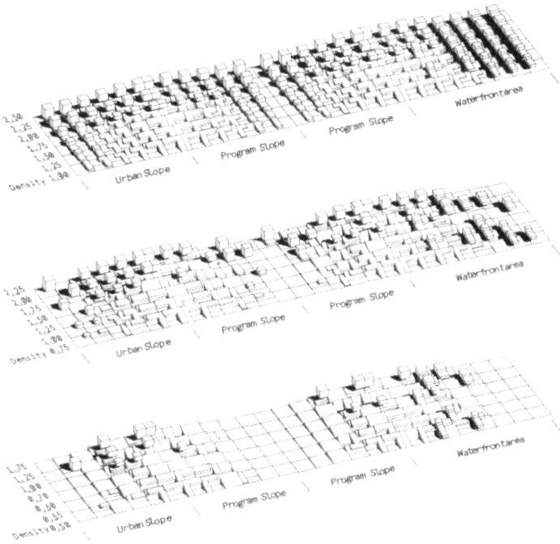

Building Formation

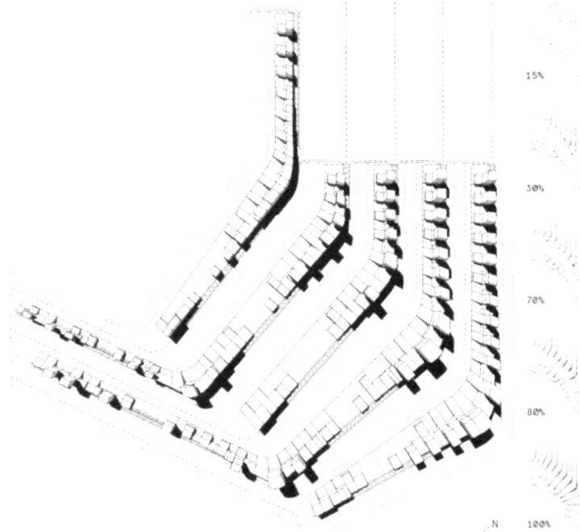

Building Density

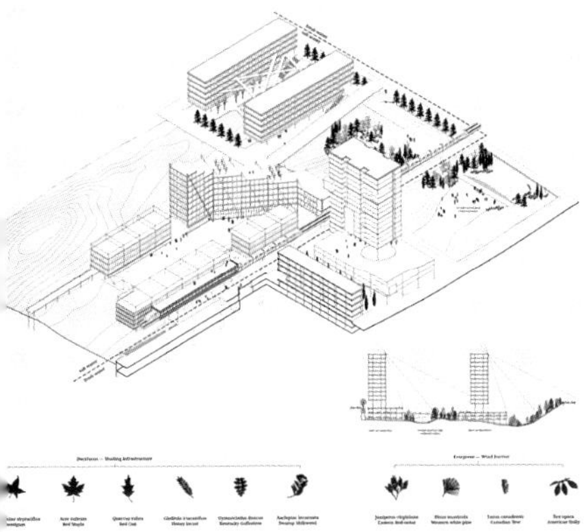

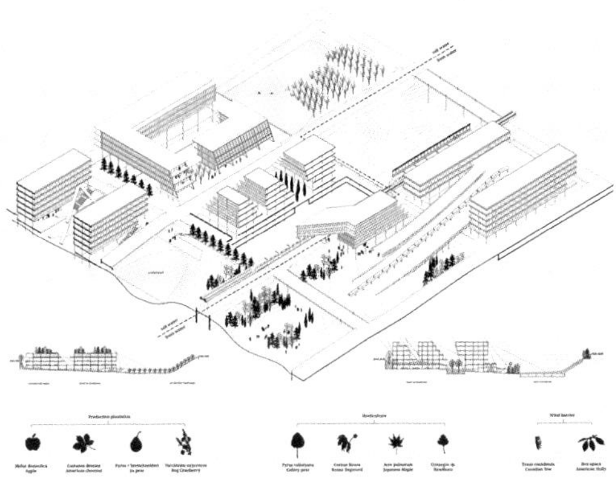

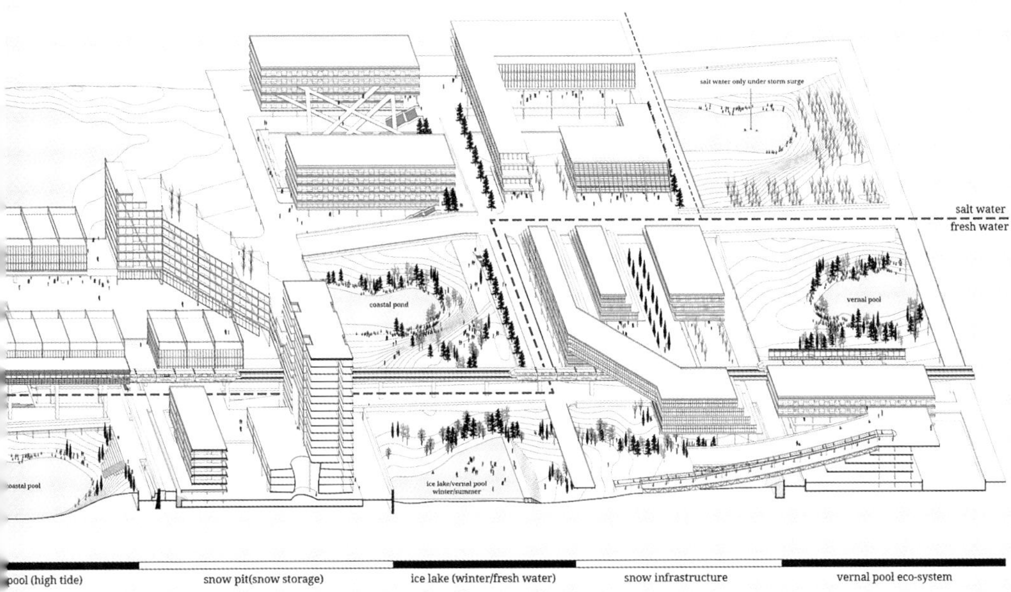

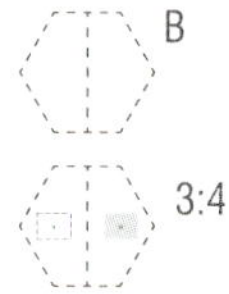

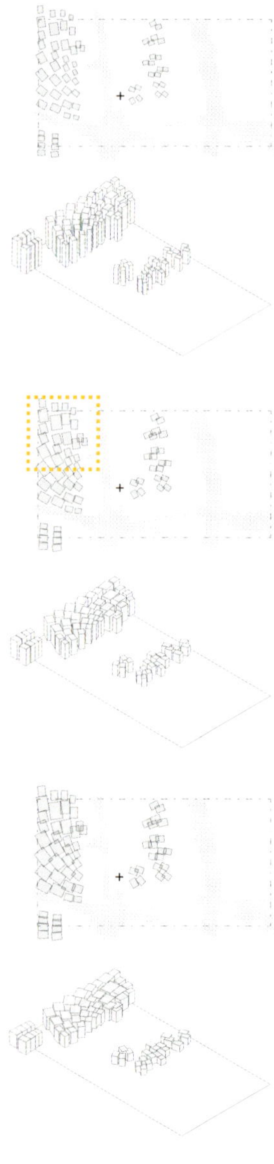

Elizabeth Wu (MLA I AP) and Tzyy-Haur Yeh (MArch I/MLA I AP)
"Liminal Mosaics"
Instructor: Leire Asensio Villoria
The physical space is redistributed through a systematic parcelization of land based on a hydrological context. Programmatic adjacencies and ecological functions encourage a patchwork of urban density gradients in lieu of a typically striated fabric.

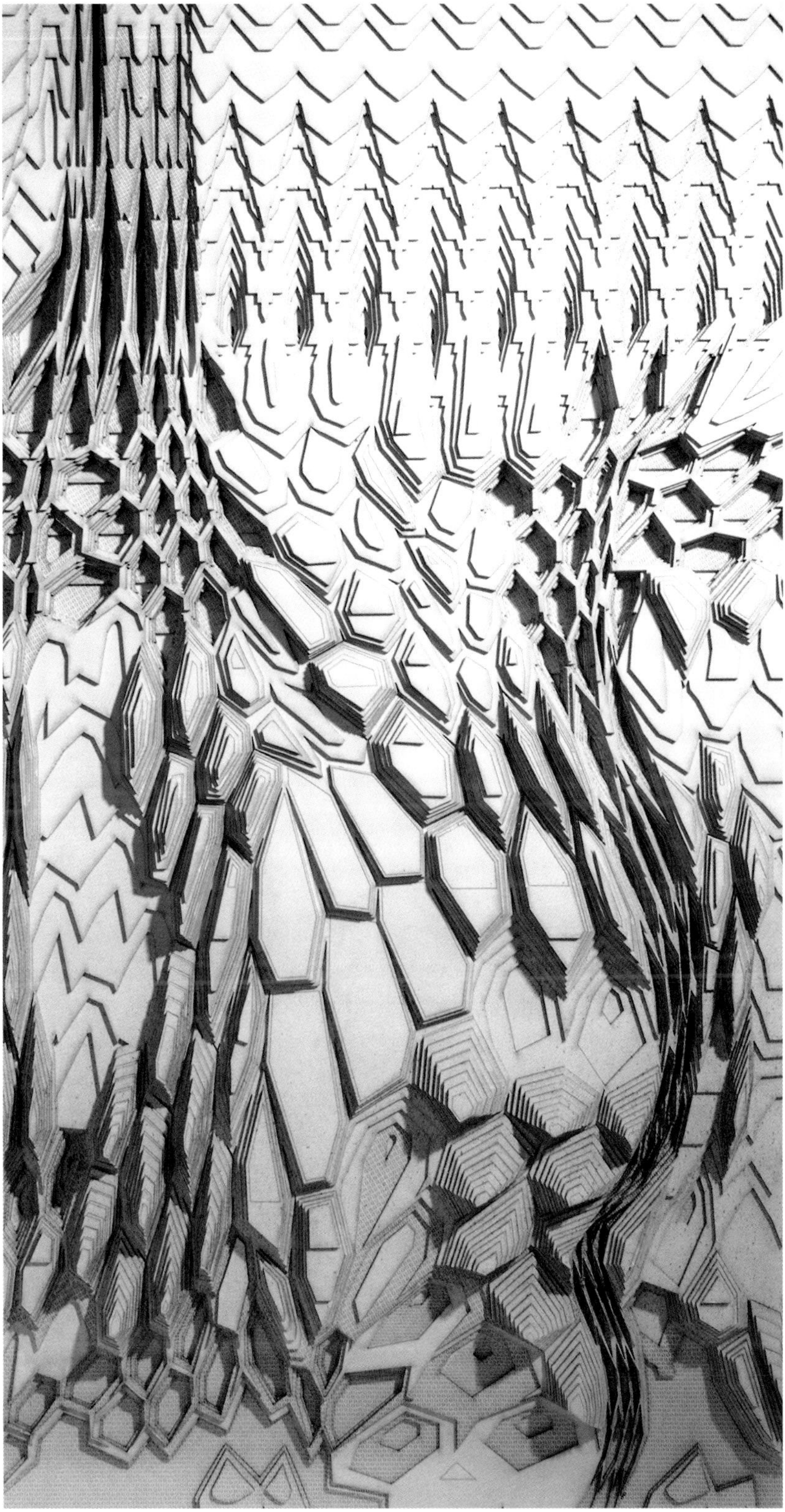

"What value does architecture provide to society?"

Michael Murphy, MASS Design Group

Open House Lecture:
Michael Murphy and Alan Ricks of MASS Design Group
Open House Lecture
April 4, 2014

MM: [...] "About the time when we were finishing [school], this was a headline in the *New York Times*: 'Want a job? Go to college and don't major in architecture.'

[...] Further down in that same article in the *Times* was this: 'Architecture majors are still more likely to be unemployed than English Literature graduates.'

[...] This brings up a challenge that we were going through in the discipline of architecture and design, which is this notion of value. What value does architecture provide to society? And as architects ebb and flow with their careers, when the economy tanks and they lose their work, we have to ask this question in a myriad of different ways to see what is the value we provide to society, and how can we articulate that in a different way?"

[...] "While here at school, when we looked at another discipline, that of health, we saw that the same kind of discussions of value to volume were happening there." [...]

"And so this notion that we as architects have direct effects on people's lives is very real [...] If buildings are making us sick, can they also make us better? Can they make us healthier?" [...]

AR: [...] "We learned that the construc-

Clayton Strange-Lee (MAUD) and Long Zuo (MAUD). "Simultaneous City"
Instructor: Felipe Correa

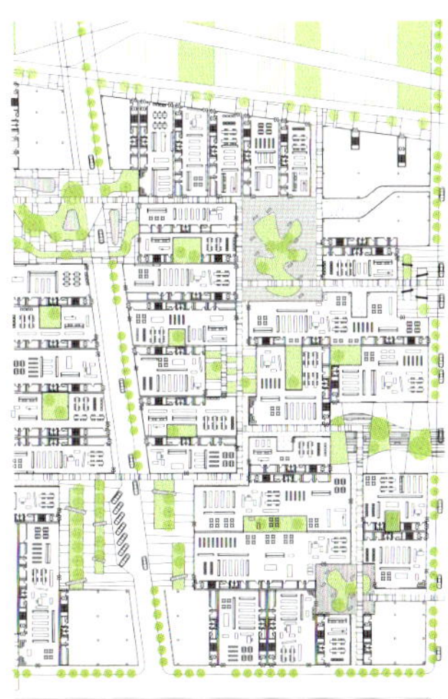

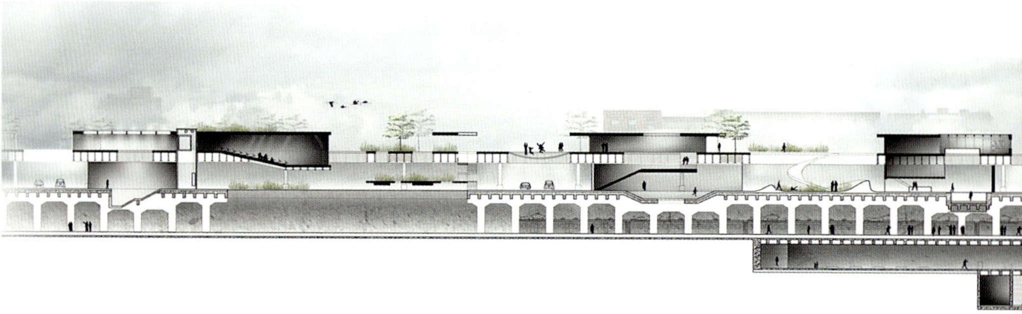

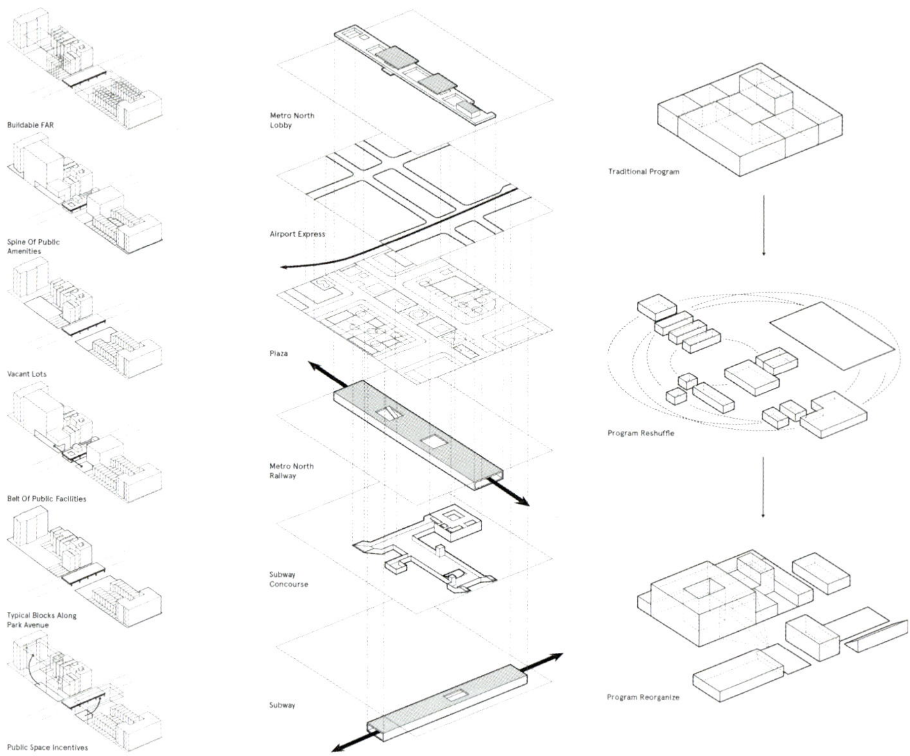

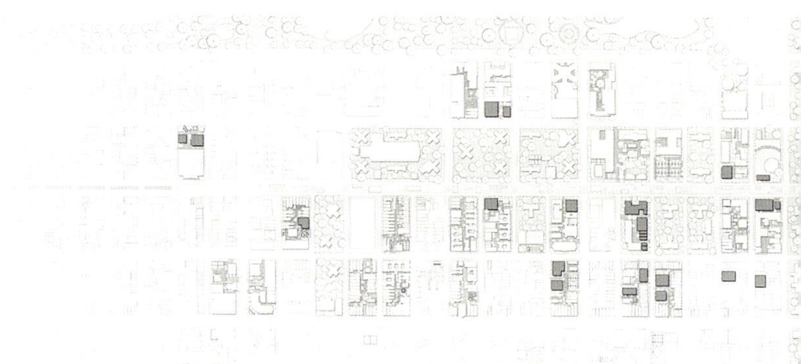

Wei Lin (MAUD) and Janice Tung (MLAUD). "Park Ave 2"
Instructor: Felipe Correa

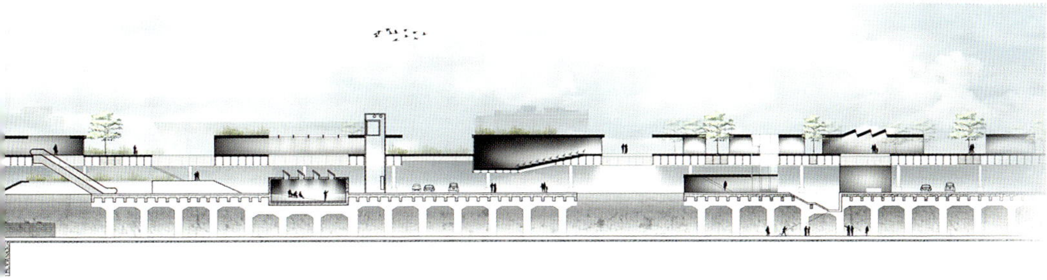

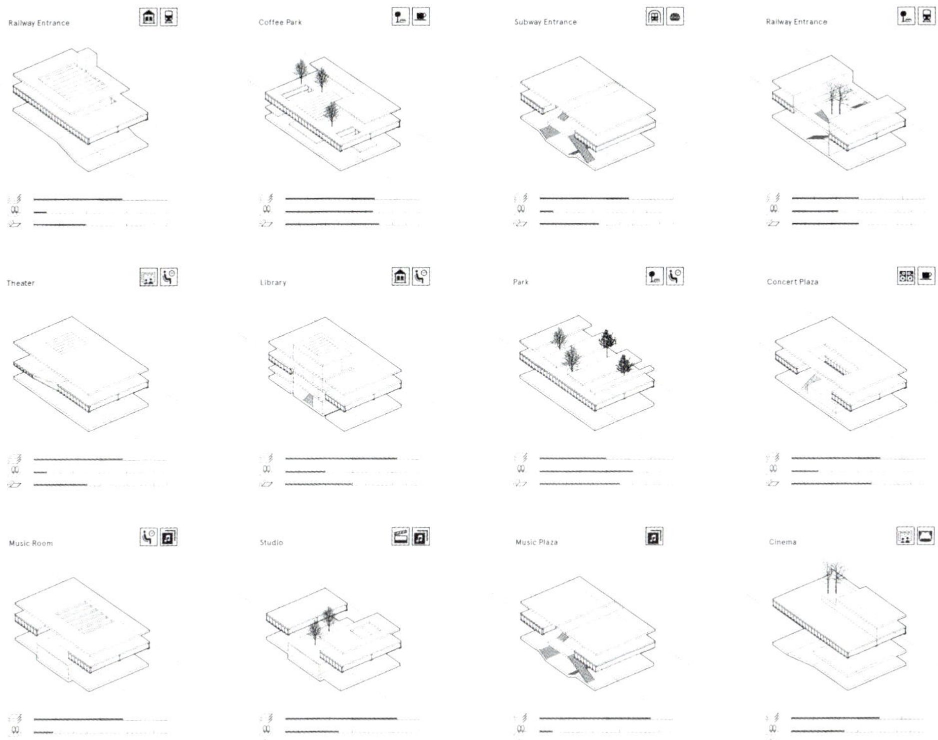
Railway Entrance
Coffee Park
Subway Entrance
Railway Entrance
Theater
Library
Park
Concert Plaza
Music Room
Studio
Music Plaza
Cinema

Wei Lin (MAUD) and Janice Tung (MLAUD). "Park Ave 2"
Instructor: Felipe Correa

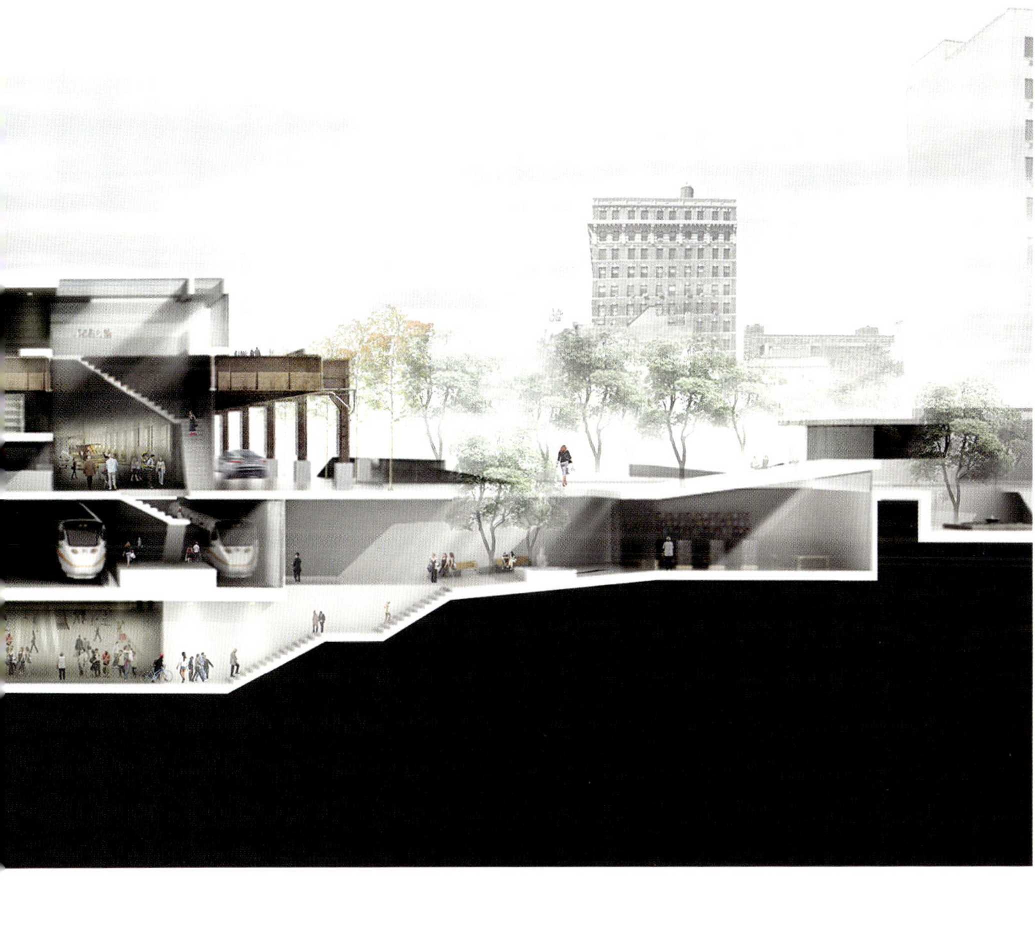

Final review for the option studio led by Achim Menges

This third installation of "Unfinished Work" broadened the research and design interests developed in the last two studio sessions. In the first studio, students addressed the question of knowledge space, and how such spaces facilitate the generation and dissemination of information. For the second studio, we looked at the relationship between architecture and emerging modes of production. Drawing from experiences in technology companies, professional service firms, communications agencies, and other practice-based organizations, this studio researched and explored how changing ideas about work alter the demands and performance of space. Our site was in Amsterdam, and our focus was to establish a hub for entrepreneurial innovation, as a prototype that can be absorbed within the local urban community and repeated in other cities. This new prototype of a think-tank was designed to allow multiple businesses to be involved in joint ventures; provided practical tools for researchers in their attendant challenges; and housed a public city database that expands on the digital archive to create a gallery of "visual complexity" that makes legible the cities' dynamic workings. In this studio, we explored these shifting ideas and determined how architecture can respond to facilitate innovative entrepreneurship and urban prosperity. It will be our business in the future, but for now it is unfinished work.

Unfinished Work III

Ben Van Berkel
Imola Berczi

Sunggi Park (MArch I AP). "Speculative Research on the Music Industry's Transformation"

Ciro Najle
Hanif Kara

Borrominations, or the Auratic Dome

Thousands of lives sharing their lack of reciprocity and involvement under a single roof: this seems to be the way public space functions today. The ancient notion of "people" rapidly loses its meaning in favor of "networks," and the modern notion of a crowd has lost all of its former heroic effervescence and the qualitative power of quantity. The masses have simultaneously lost historical significance and at the same time have opened up to new forms of what constitutes the public. Contemporary architecture is faced with the challenge of turning indifference into a new form of aura by engaging its archaic power of congregation at a radically new, non-sacred level. The studio took on this challenge by engaging architectures whose elusive and poignant sensibility, often regarded as capricious, delirious, ignorant, or plainly malignant, were able to construct forms of aura that could project themselves to the future and persist in time. Borrominations explored the work of Francesco Borromini (1599–1667) at San Carlo alle Quatro Fontane, Rome, with the purpose of using its formal and organizational machinery—complex spatial totalities constructed as if they were indivisible figures—as a series of primitives for further differentiation. San Carlino was adopted as a model and differentiated to imagine new forms of public space, "where the city itself will be held in a state of suspended animation."

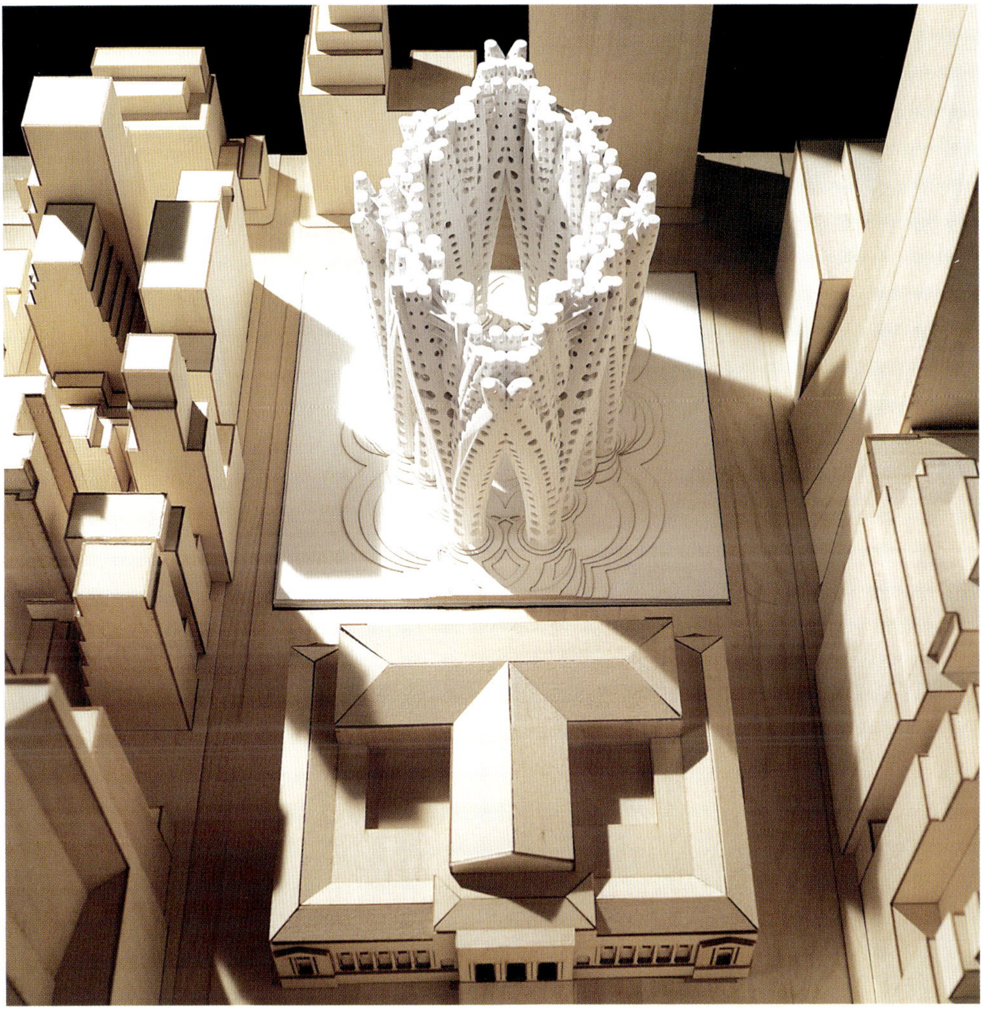

Ben Burdick (MArch I). "Social Circles: Clustering the Club and the Crowd"
Physical Model on Bryant Park Site

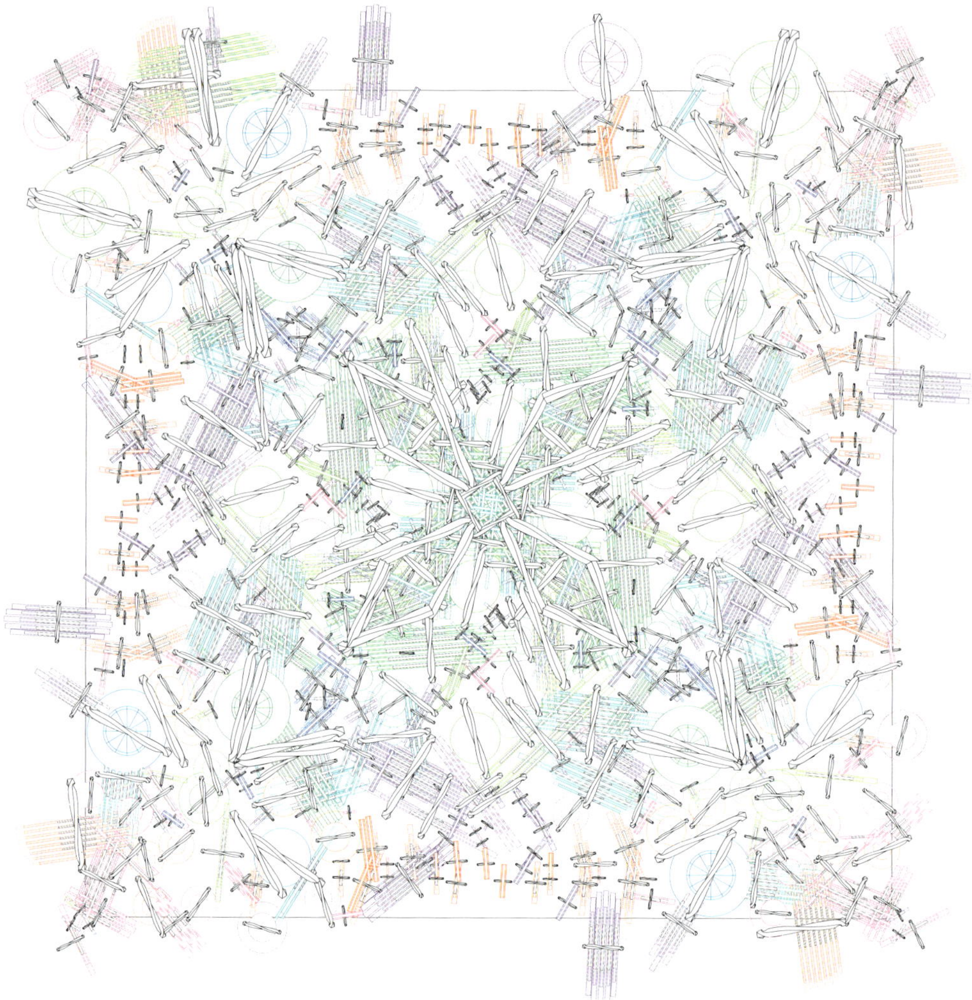

Thena Tak (MArch II), "Babylonian Slowness: Curly Strolls, Twisted Arches, Hanging Swings and Flower Power" Plan

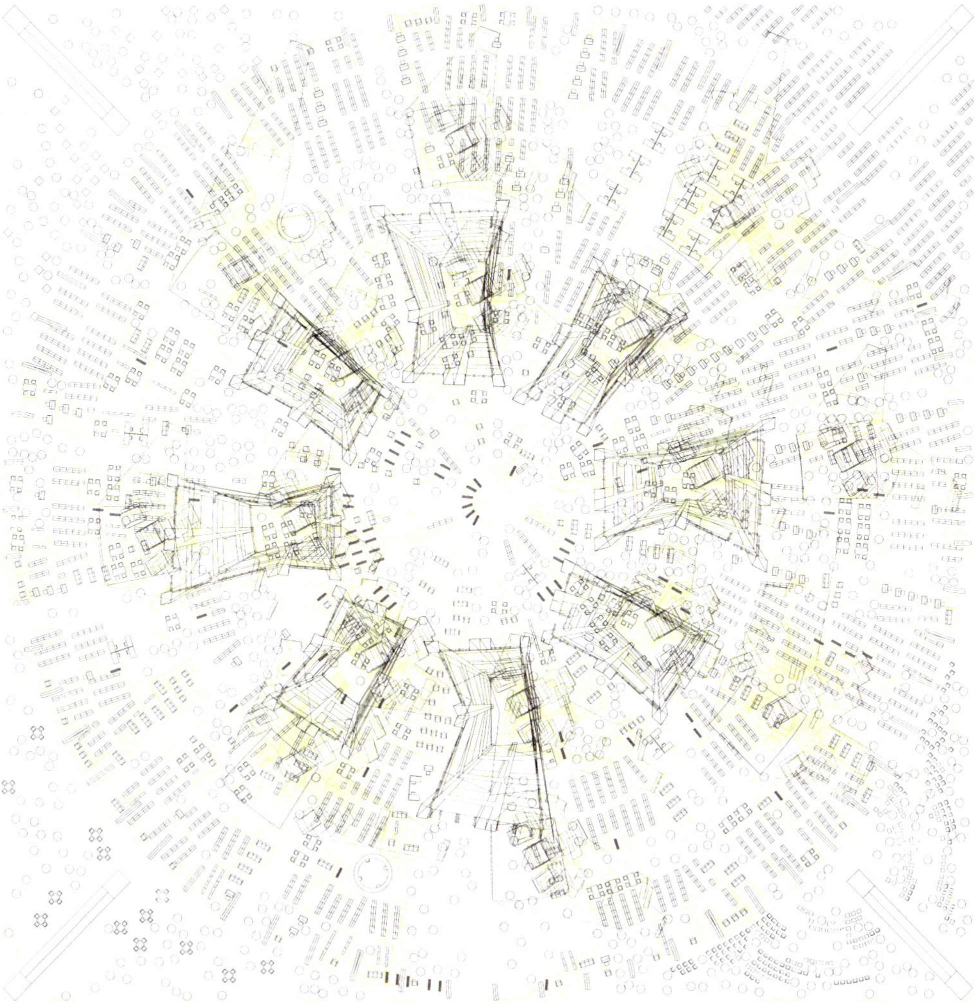

See Jia Ho (MArch I), “Field of Windows: Library Urbanism” Plan

Tristan McGuire (MArch II), "Isolation and Atmosphere: The Double Life of Public Intimacy" Physical Model

Thena Tak (MArch II), "Babylonian Slowness: Curly Strolls, Twisted Arches, Hanging Swings and Flower Power" Physical Model

Patrik Schumacher
Marc Fornes

Parametric Semiology: High-Performance Architecture for Apple, Google, and Facebook

All problems of society are problems of communication. Especially within post-Fordist network society, total social productivity increases with the density of communication. High-performance organizations are thus marked by a high intensity of communication. The life process of society is a communication process that is structured by a rich panoply of communicative situations. The built environment stabilizes this matrix of institutions and makes it legible. The project aimed to design a corporate campus as a coherent spatio-morphological system of signification. High-performance creative organization such as Apple, Google, or Facebook entail a sufficiently large and complex matrix of social institutions and specific communicative situations to enable the design of a rich architectural language. The designed Apple, Google, or Facebook campus should be an information-rich, densely articulated environment that orders and encodes the manifold social interactions to be expected and thus facilitates orientation and communication. As a morphological/tectonic a priori, the studio worked with the combination of shell and tensile structures to create intricately differentiated, layered fields. Patterns of communicative interaction were modeled via programmed agents that respond to the coded environmental clues. The implication is that architecture can enter the digital model (design medium) and thus becomes the object of cumulative design elaboration.

01

02

01,10:
Felix Luong (MArch II)
John Morrison (MArch II)
Joseph Ross (MArch II)

02,04,07:
Conor Coghlan (MArch II)
Shaoliang Hua (MArch II)

03,10:
Christopher Esper (MArch I AP)
Weishun Xu (MArch I AP)

05:
Alessandro Boccacci (MAUD)
Mark Eichler (MArch II)

06,08:
Jie Xie (MArch II)
Juan Yactayo (MArch I AP)

03

04

05

06

07

08

09

10

"All problems of society are problems of communication. Especially within post-Fordist network society, total social productivity increases with the density of communication."

Conor Coghlan (MArch II)and Shaoliang Hua (MArch II). "Active Gridshell"

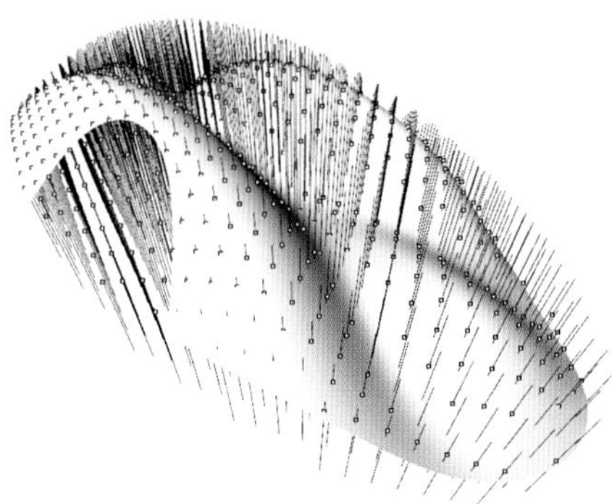

Alessandro Boccacci (MAUD)and Mark Eichler (MArch II). "Catenary Field"

This studio focused on the new wave of urbanization of medium-scale cities in China characterized by large infrastructure expansion, interest in sustainable urban development, and needed improvements in the quality of life. Two such cities, Qingdao and Yiwu, different in nature and climate, are planning new urban developments around strategically located high-speed train stations. These case studies gave us the opportunity to rethink, from a typological and thermodynamic perspective, the three main facts of Chinese urban developments: high-speed train stations, central business districts, and megaplots. The hypothesis tested was based on alternative prototypes that instead of segregating the three activities explore the potential impact of mixed-use conglomerates in both improving the quality of public life and establishing new ways to relate form, program, energy, matter, and the human body—what we call a new "thermodynamic materialism." The defense of a new thermodynamic materialism concentrates on the field of design processes and a return to an integrated view of architecture that combines, with the utmost syncretism, all of the materials, visible and invisible, that make up the experience of architecture and the city. Form, body, natural elements, material, program, time, and beauty are some of the basic categories of a system woven around the word "materialism."

Thermodynamic Materialism Applied to Dense Urban Conglomerates, Two Chinese Case Studies

Iñaki Abalos
Matthias Schuler

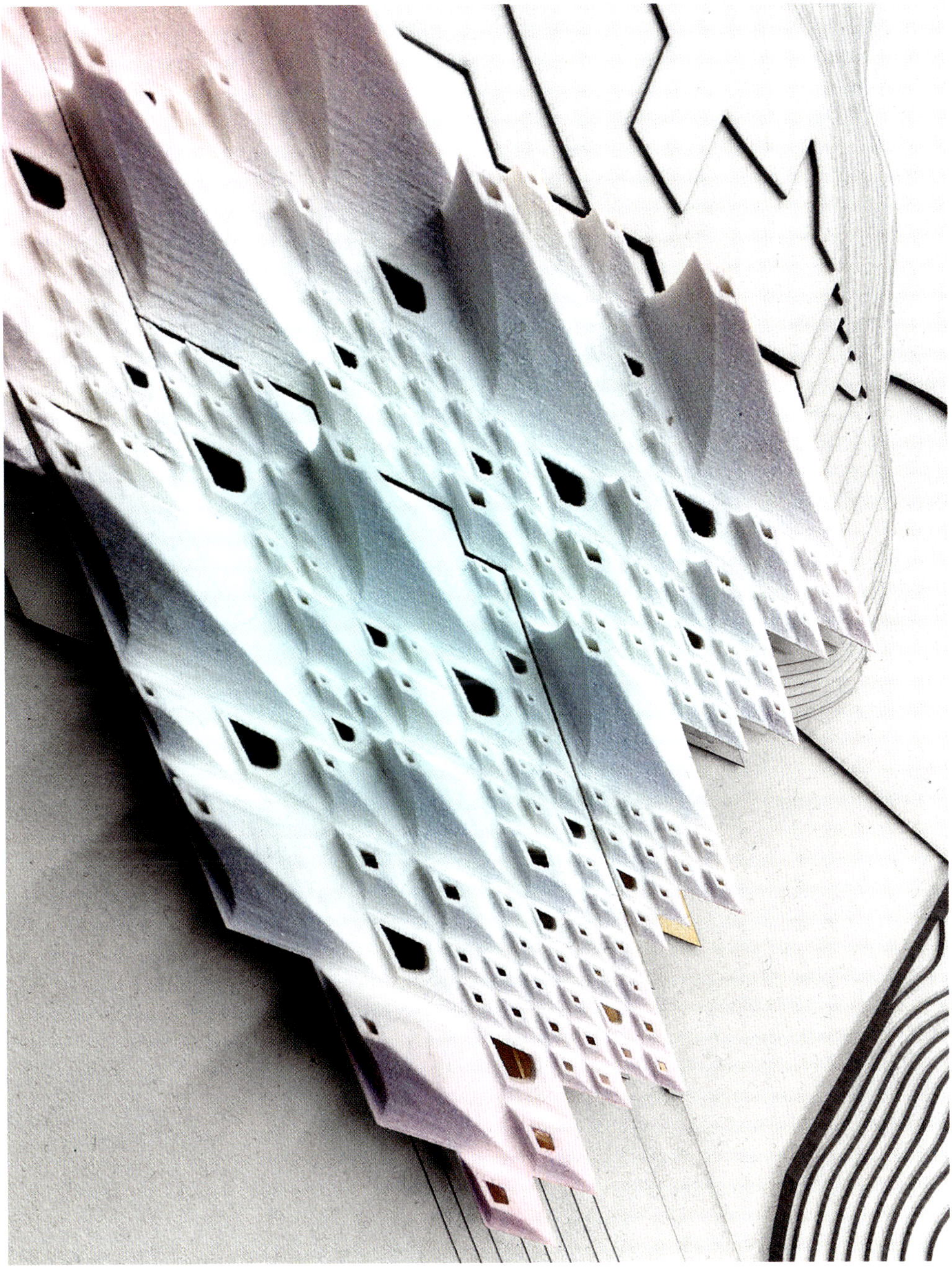

Hao Chen (MAUD)

PLATFORM 7

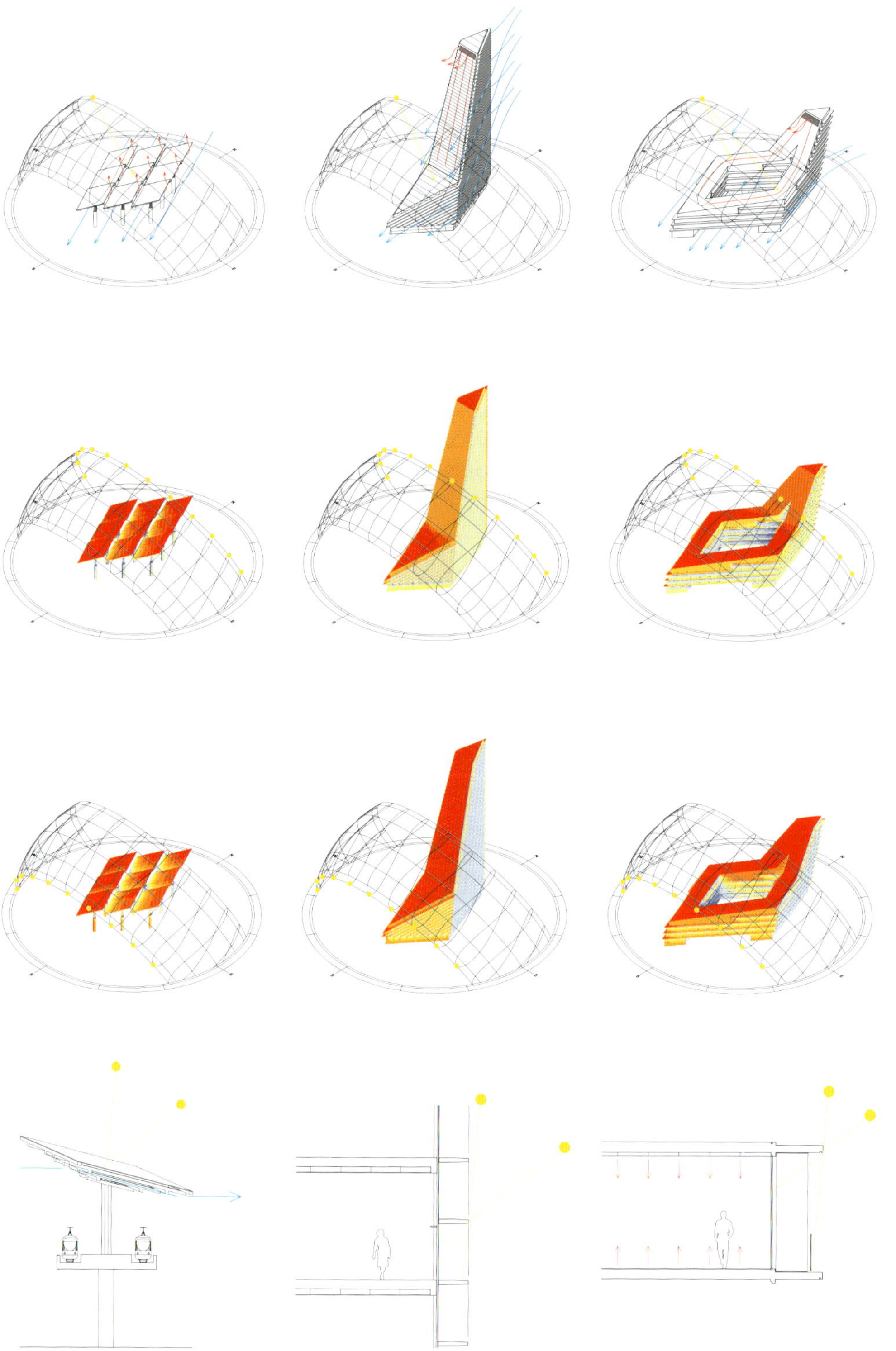

01 02 03

Jose Ramon Sierra Gomez de Leon (MArch II)
01 Station Typology
02 Tower Typology
03 Block Typology

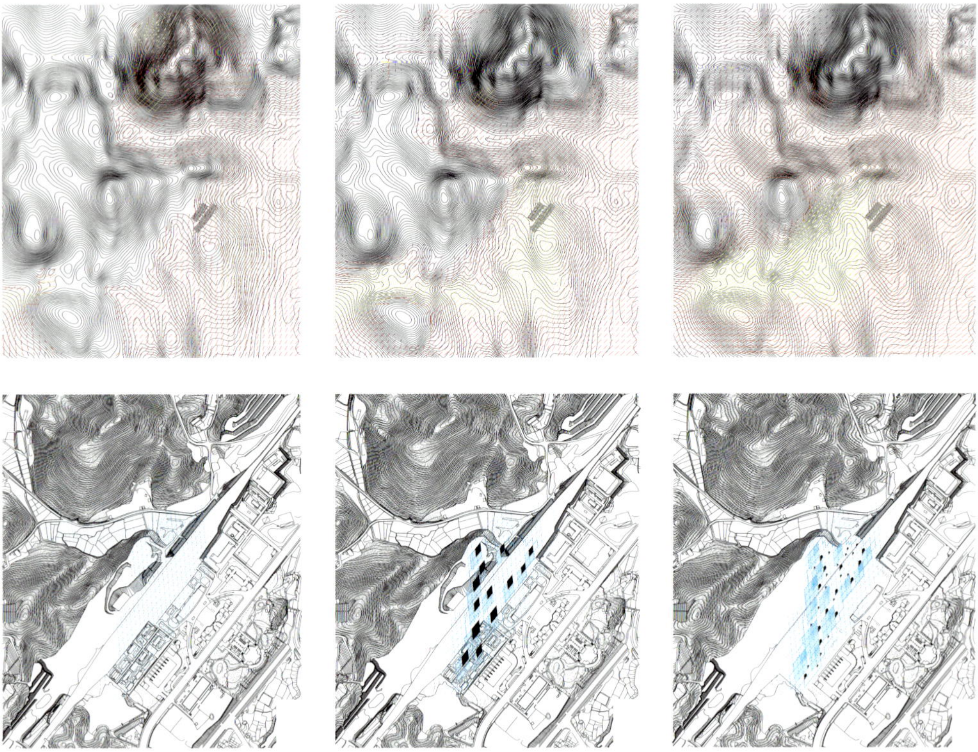

Hao Chen (MAUD)

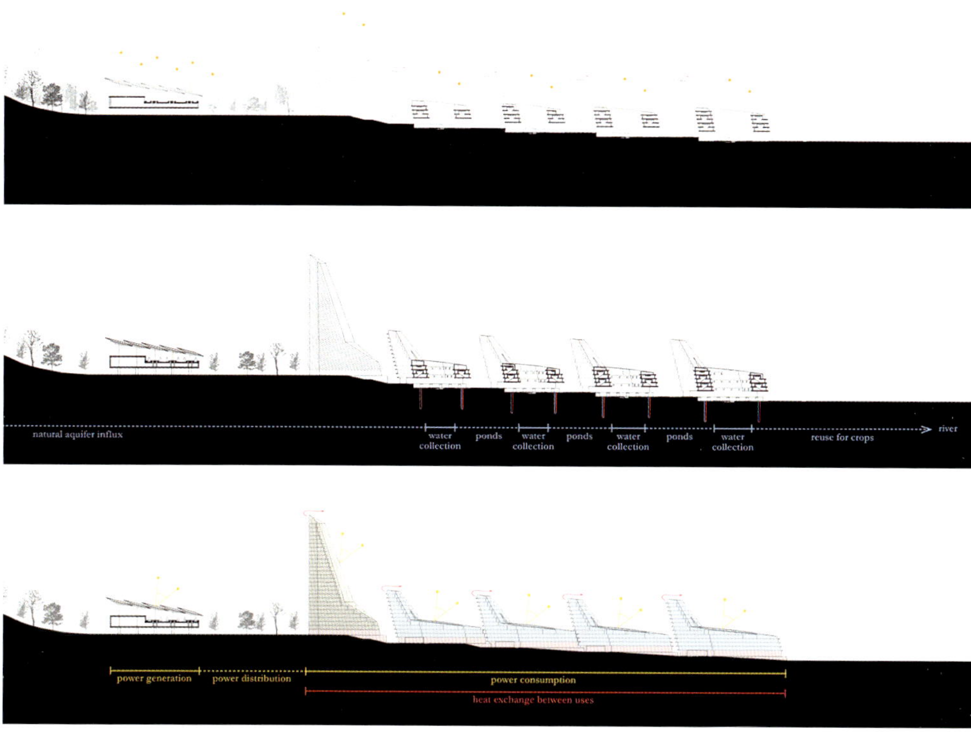

Jose Ramon Sierra Gomez de Leon (MArch II)

Lecture: Silvia Gmür
A Hospital Is a House For a Man
March 3, 2014

"[...] While the hospital should make the patient feel respected as an individual and respond to his personal needs, hospital architecture is generally an expression of the power of the healthcare industry, with the patient at its mercy. The current trend to integrate shopping centers into hospital structures reinforces the status of the patient as a consumer, and misunderstands the concept of urban integration."

"[...] The purpose of my lecture is not to teach you how to build good hospitals but to convince you to do whatever you do as an architect with intensity, curiosity, and the urge to understand what you are doing and why. To realize a project is to open yourself to the pleasure of constructing thoughts. If you discover and live this conviction, you will be a very happy architect. For all your life, you are going to have a dialogue with yourself, asking questions in order to make decisions. So make sure that your horizon is wide and open. The quality of the question is more important than the answer, [...] three architectural themes are of great importance for our philosophy and our work: the typology as the expression of structural and formal order, the unity that is the goal we search in every project, the light — the light is the maker of space, [...] you might expect that I will speak about functionality and efficiency concerning hospital planning. I think that these topics are results, not starting points. Form is much more durable than function. Developing the appropriate typology and structure will guarantee the flexibility and efficiency of function."

"[...] The aim was to search for the essence, the indispensable parts of a room. These are, in my opinion, the unity and the light. The unity defines the structure, the form, the architectural order, the material, and the serving elements of the room. The way you let light enter in your room defines its expression, its atmosphere, and is closely related to the form of the room."

"[...] The result is indeed a quiet room with boundaries determined by the vegetation and the landscape. Being radical in its elements, it diffuses an extremely poetic atmosphere. It leaves space for your imagination because of its abstraction. Abstraction is the inner synthesis of form. [...] The patient room must be his shelter, the space where he feels protected, intimate. It is a small room, but each activity should find its place: a zone for the bed, a place for a table, a space for a chair near the window. The room must be a unity, and its light corresponds to the room. The light needs a space to be transformed into a softer light. After speaking about the room, let us now speak about the society of rooms. The plan is a society of rooms [...] the question of type and typology are of great importance for hospital design. The type is conceptual. It is a regulating principle that determines how a series of elements connected in precise relationships form a specific structure. The typology is a promise of order, and order is a promise of beauty."

"To realize a project is to open yourself to the pleasure of constructing thoughts. If you discover and live this conviction, you will be a very happy architect. For all your life, you are going to have a dialogue with yourself, asking questions in order to make decisions."

Halfway between the socially responsive discourse of programmatic indeterminacy and the alleged futility of form giving, we explored architecture's critical return to form. Our interest in the topic of form is neither aesthetic nor ideological. Contrary to the notion of shape—with which it is often confused—form is a syntactic, procedural, and increasingly technical problem. In this studio we explored the seminal thesis of architecture as a complex interplay of desire and automatic writing. Architecture depends on achieving a practical and theoretical balance between real and imaginary variables: real variables depend on empirical knowledge of a given type, site, and program; imaginary variables depend on the equally important—though far less intuitive—properties of indexical modeling. The two parts of the equation need one another to fulfill themselves: without the imaginary part, the type withers into predictability and repetition; without the real part, it becomes self-fulfilling and ultimately irrelevant. We figured out fresh ways in which a formal analytic model, otherwise known as a seed, might correlate to a building type's functional organization, program, and material structure. Using our trademark combination of seed bank, user manual, and real-life brief, we developed the two parts of the process in tandem. When both parts were sufficiently developed, we devised proposals for a 40,000-seat football stadium currently planned for the Old Oak regeneration area of West London.

Real and Imaginary Variables (Final): Global Arenas

George L. Legendre

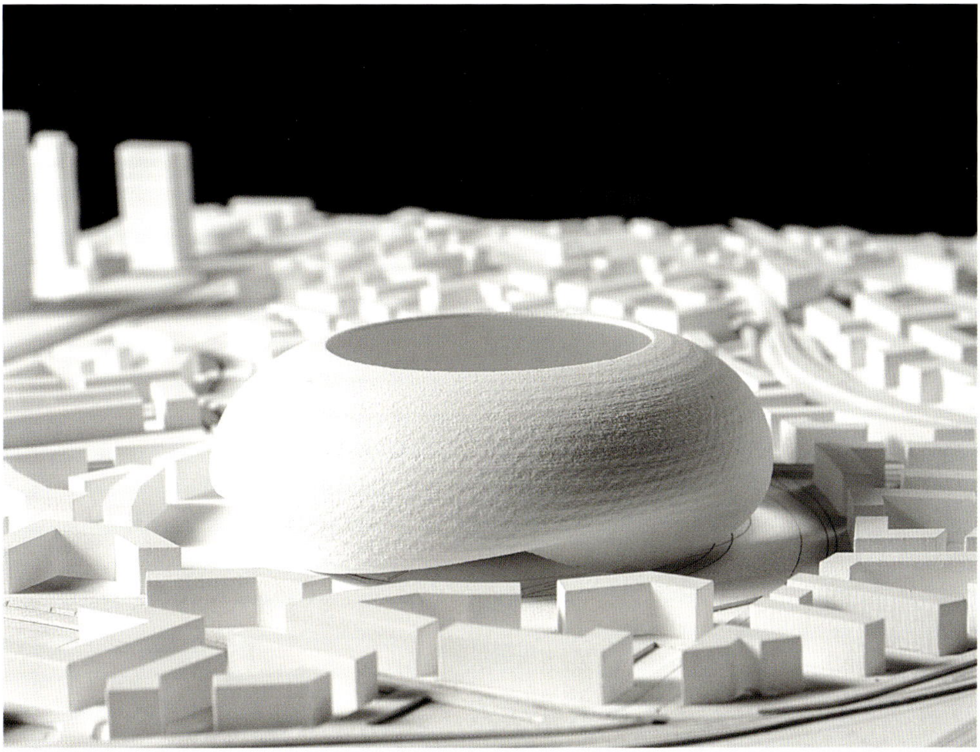

Jeonghyun Kim (MArch II) and Julia Michalski (MArch II)
"The Lifted Eccentric Skirt: Centralized Modulation"

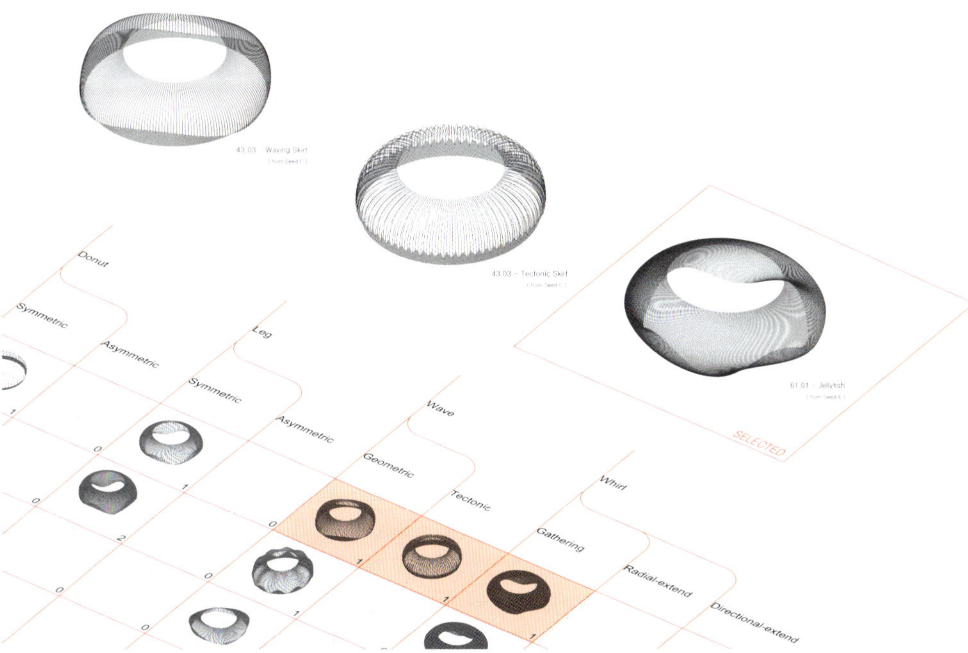

$\Lambda := \frac{0}{4}\cdot\pi$ $\Lambda := \frac{1}{4}\cdot\pi$ $\Lambda := \frac{3}{4}\cdot\pi$

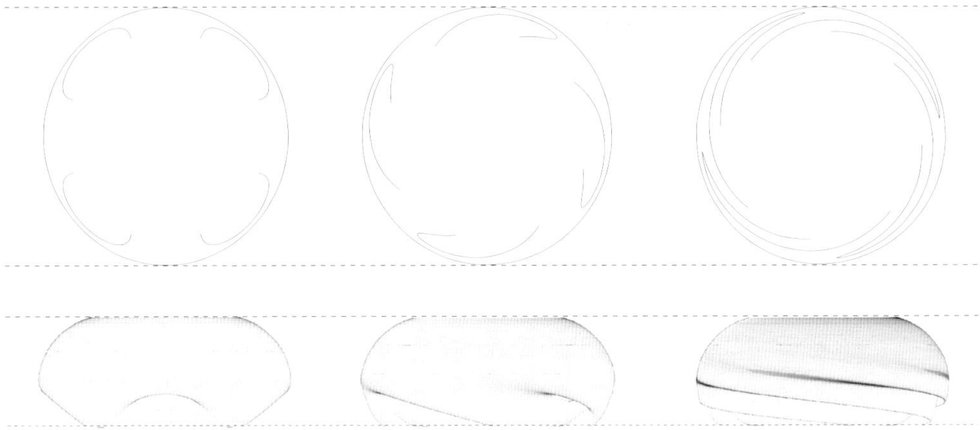

$DEF_{in,jn} := \sin\left(4\cdot\pi\frac{in}{endI}+\frac{\pi}{2}\right)\cdot\left[\left(\frac{jn}{endJ}\right)^4\right]\cdot\Omega s$

$DEF_{in,jn} := \sin\left(6\cdot\pi\frac{in}{endI}+\frac{\pi}{2}\right)\cdot\left[\left(\frac{jn}{endJ}\right)^4\right]\cdot\Omega s$

$DEF_{in,jn} := \sin\left(8\cdot\pi\frac{in}{endI}+\frac{\pi}{2}\right)\cdot\left[\left(\frac{jn}{endJ}\right)^4\right]\cdot\Omega s$

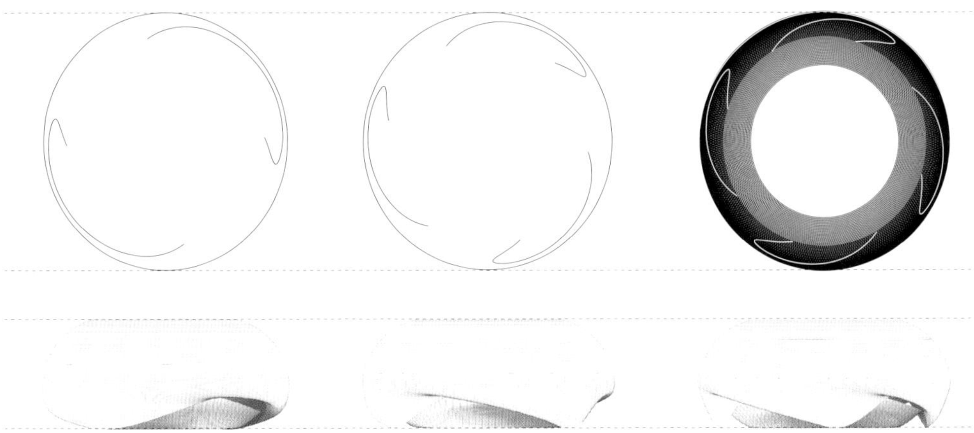

$DEF_{in,jn} := \sin\left(10\cdot\pi\frac{in}{endI}+\frac{\pi}{2}\right)\cdot\left[\left(\frac{jn}{endJ}\right)^4\right]\cdot\Omega s$

$DEF_{in,jn} := \sin\left(16\cdot\pi\frac{in}{endI}+\frac{\pi}{2}\right)\cdot\left[\left(\frac{jn}{endJ}\right)^4\right]\cdot\Omega s$

$DEF_{in,jn} := \sin\left(32\cdot\pi\frac{in}{endI}+\frac{\pi}{2}\right)\cdot\left[\left(\frac{jn}{endJ}\right)^4\right]\cdot\Omega s$

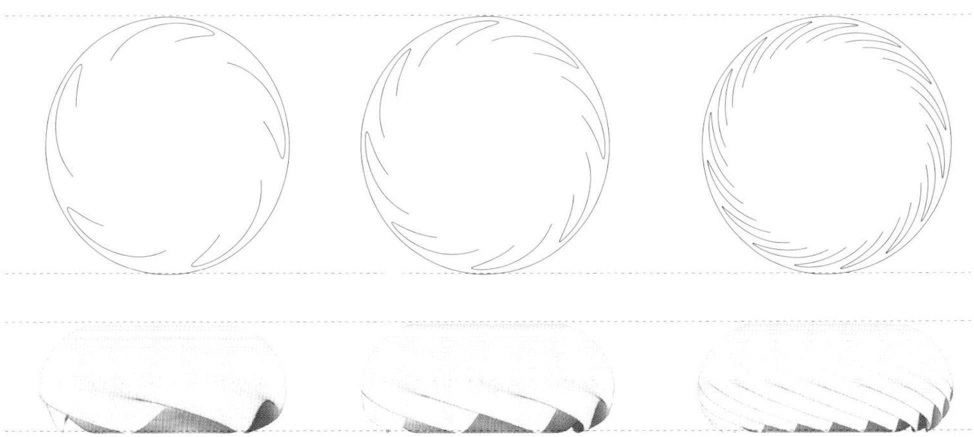

endI := 64
in := 0,1..endI

endJ := 32
jn := 0,1..endJ

_BOWL...............................
_Max height heightB := 21
_Radius Ra := 80
_Global scale scaleBX := 1 scaleBY := 1
_Elev humps δh := 8
_Hump inflection infB := 4
_Filletted Outline
_Top β := 160
_Btm η := 1
_Btm(adjustment) σx := −0.25 σy := −0.1

_PITCH...............................
_Width pitchW := 68
_Length pitchW · scalePX := 68
_Aspect ratio scalePX := 1 scalePY := 1

_SPHERICAL ENVELOPE...................
_Height heightW := 28
_Scale scaleEX := 2.4 scaleEY := 2.4
_Setback from bowl (%) sbx := 0 sby := 0
_Lower outline Ωs := 11
_Edges filletting factor
_lower ι := 100
_upper κ := 80
_upper deform εz := 0
_Excentricity $\Lambda := \frac{1}{4} \cdot \pi$

$$DEF_{in,jn} := \sin\left(8 \cdot \pi \frac{in}{endI} + \frac{\pi}{2}\right) \cdot \left[\left(\frac{jn}{endJ}\right)^4\right] \cdot \Omega s$$

$$\xi := \frac{20}{10} \quad \xi 2 := \frac{9}{10} \quad \varphi := \frac{5}{10} \quad \Theta := \frac{2}{10} \quad \Lambda 2 := \frac{1}{10} \quad \psi := \frac{0.3}{\iota}$$

$$\Phi a_{in,jn} := \left[a\sin\left[\sin\left(\frac{in}{endI} \cdot \kappa\pi\right)\right] \cdot \frac{2}{\pi}\right] \quad Gx_{in,jn} := \left[1 + \left(\Phi a_{in,jn}\right)^{\varepsilon z} \cdot \psi \cdot \frac{jn}{endJ}\right]$$

$$envX_{in,jn} := \left(\cos\left(\frac{in}{endI} \cdot \xi\pi + \frac{jn}{endJ} \Lambda \cdot \pi\right) \cdot \sin\left(\frac{jn}{endJ} \cdot \varphi\pi + \pi\Theta\right) \cdot Ra \cdot Gx_{in,jn} \cdot \frac{scalePX}{2}\right) \cdot scaleEX \cdot (1 + sbx)$$

$$envY_{in,jn} := \left(\sin\left(\frac{in}{endI} \cdot \xi\pi + \frac{jn}{endJ} \Lambda \cdot \pi\right) \cdot \sin\left(\frac{jn}{endJ} \cdot \varphi\pi + \pi\Theta\right) \cdot Ra \cdot Gx_{in,jn} \cdot \frac{scalePY}{2}\right) \cdot scaleEY \cdot (1 + sby)$$

$$envZ_{in,jn} := \left(\cos\left(\frac{jn}{endJ} \cdot \xi 2\pi + \Lambda 2\pi\right) \cdot heightW + DEF_{in,jn}\right) + heightW + \max(DEF)$$

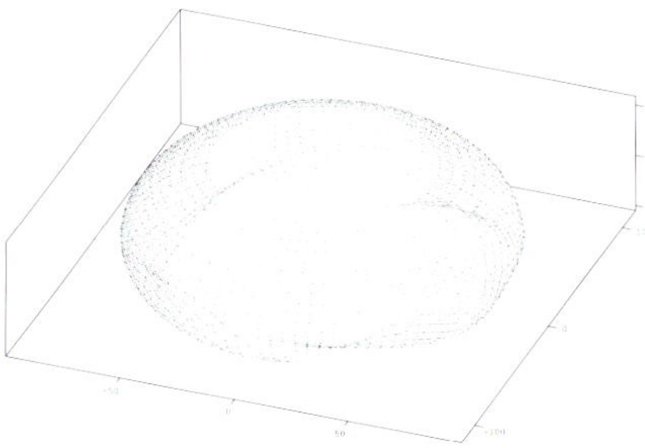

(bowlX,bowlY,tiers), (pitchX,pitchY,pitchZ),(envX,envY,envZ)

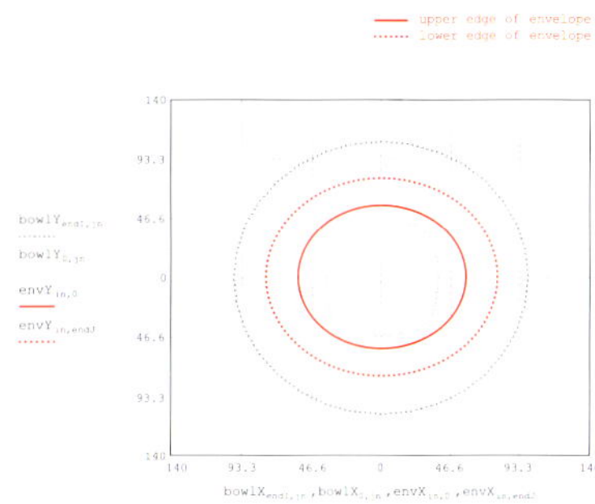

Jeonghyun Kim (MArch II) and Julia Michalski (MArch II)
"The Lifted Eccentric Skirt: Centralized Modulation" XY-Plan Section

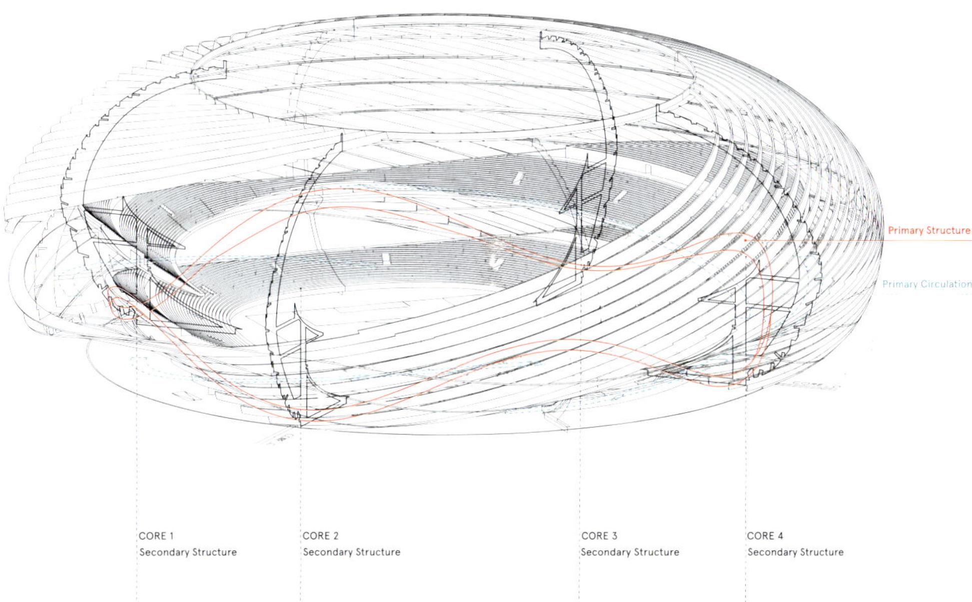

01-03:
Zunheng Lai (MArch I AP)
Weishun Xu (MArch I AP)
Tim Zeitler (MArch I)

04-05:
Chase Pitner (MArch II)
Catherine Soderberg (MArch II)

06:
Jeonghyun Kim (MArch II)
Julia Michalski (MArch II)

07-09:
Lily Wubeshet (MArch I)
Xiang Chang (MArch II)

01

02

03

04

07

05

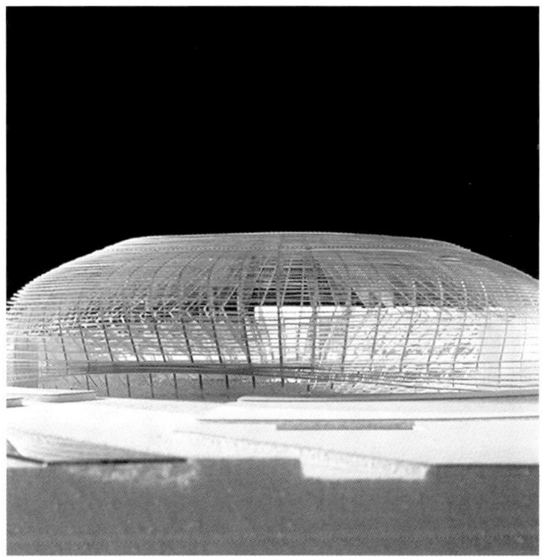

08

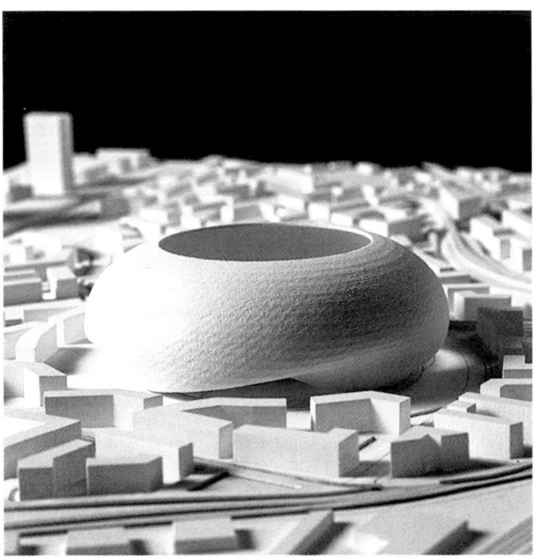

06

09

The Continuous City, characterized by clearly delineated urban spaces of streets, squares, and boulevards, was a dominant concept of urban form until the end of the nineteenth century. Within this model, every building is integrated into the street. Architecture recedes into the background, and building type is subjugated to the larger urban form, with the exception of municipal and national centers, which are excluded from this system. The Discontinuous City, propagated by opening up the enclosed block at the beginning of the twentieth century, is the opposite of the Continuous City; here buildings liberate themselves from the urban fabric. Within this model, every building is an autonomous object independently displayed—a privilege previously reserved for churches, town halls, and palaces. Buildings have greater freedom in type and are not subordinate to the form constituted by urban space. The studio investigated the intersection of these two urban models through the design of a small- to medium-scale building situated on a new pedestrian street in the Design District of Miami. Rather than viewing the Continuous City and the Discontinuous City as mutually exclusive models, the studio investigated a hybrid between the two as an opportunity to promote an alternative form of collectivity through the aggregation of singular and semi-detached buildings.

La Strada Novissima: Continuous City versus Discontinuous City

Sharon Johnston
Mark Lee

Nelson Byun (MArch II)

Joan Tom (MArch I)

Manuel Maibach (ETH Exchange Program)

Rem Koolhaas
Stephan Trüby
AMO

Rotterdam Study-Abroad Studio Option: Elements of Architecture

Following two semesters of work by GSD students on architectural elements—the door, the floor, the ceiling, the roof, the façade, etc.—the Fall 2013 Rotterdam Studio, composed of a new generation of students, was the final and most intensive phase of research, content production, editing, and concept design for the exhibition "Elements of Architecture" at the 2014 Venice Biennale of Architecture. The studio was a masterclass in real exhibition making, encompassing the full range of creative endeavor: it required academic rigor and original research—many of the elements, like the balcony, have not been properly theorized in architectural history; it required spatial invention and hands-on testing for the development of the exhibition's design; it required editorial and rhetorical precision for the expression of new-found architectural knowledge in the form of the exhibition catalogue; and it required diplomatic creativity and organization for a complex production taking place on an international stage. The new students who worked in Rotterdam in the Fall were paired with former GSD students who took the studio last year. Former students and new students collaborated on the enormous amount of work that had to be achieved during the semester, ensuring the continuity of this important new body of knowledge.

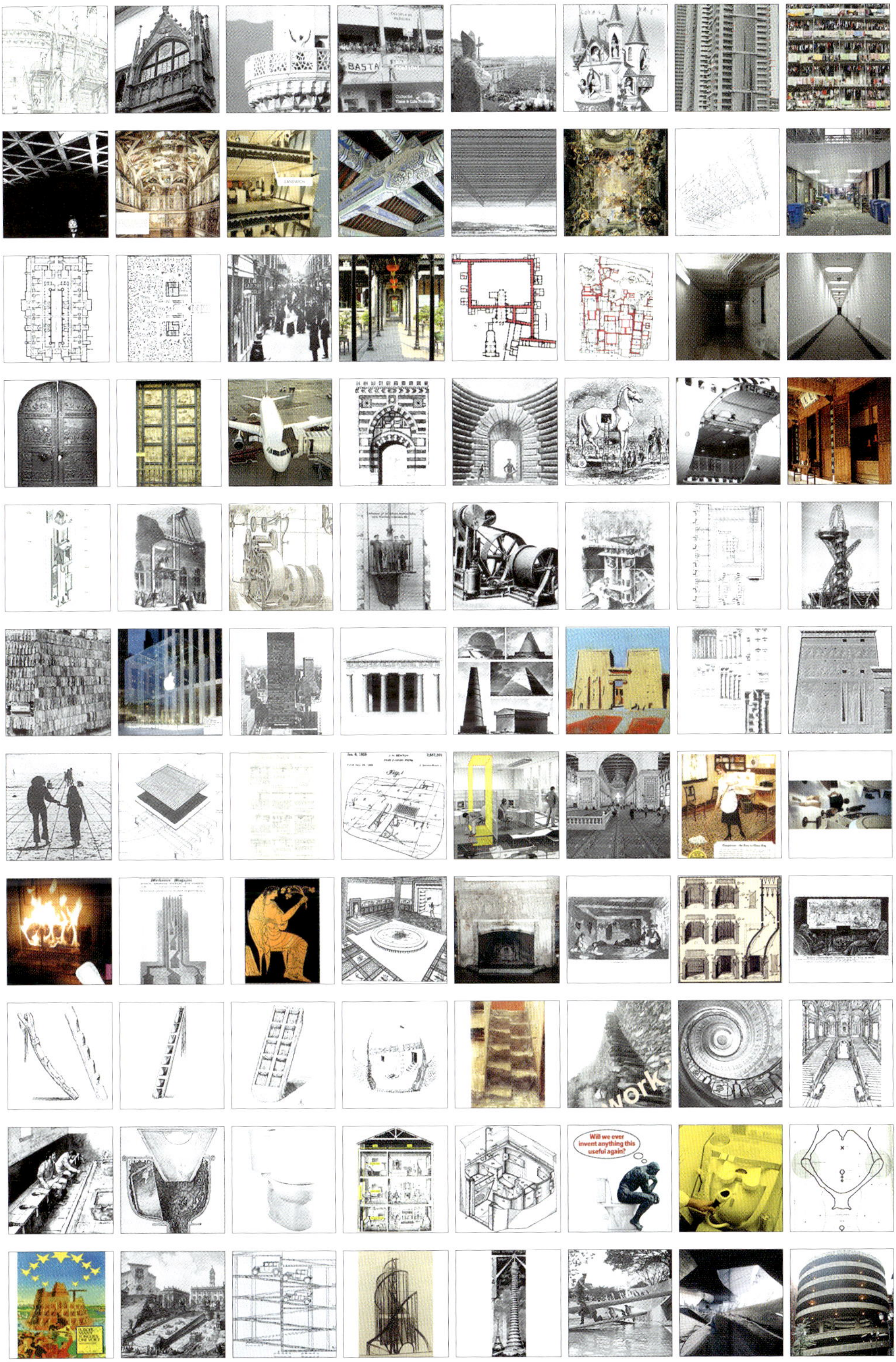
BASTA
Will we ever invent anything this useful again?
work

balcony
ceiling
corridor
door
elevator
facade
floor
hearth
stair
toilet
ramp
FORMAL VARIATIONS
la Biennale

Bookshop

Jonathan Sergison
Stephen Bates

High-Rise High-Density

We are interested in questions of housing in the city and, in this instance, in how an American typology—the high-rise, multi-story apartment building—can be reappraised and applied to an existing urban situation as a strategy of densification and consolidation. The semester was structured around four components that resulted in an overall understanding of the questions that the theme demanded. To begin with, each student was required to study existing examples of that building type. Working in Boston, we selected sites to develop multi-story building proposals that had to be sensitive to their context, and students were asked to make an argument for how they could be reasonably situated in the city. Later in the semester, we invited them to consider the nature of the public spaces in their building, how the building met the city, and how the common parts were organized. Ideas for apartments had to be developed anticipating how they could be inhabited. The final component of the work required students to develop a concept for the façade and to consider the building's material language.

Bicen Yue (MArch II)

"How can the American typology of the high-rise, multi-story apartment building be reappraised and applied to an existing urban situation as a strategy?"

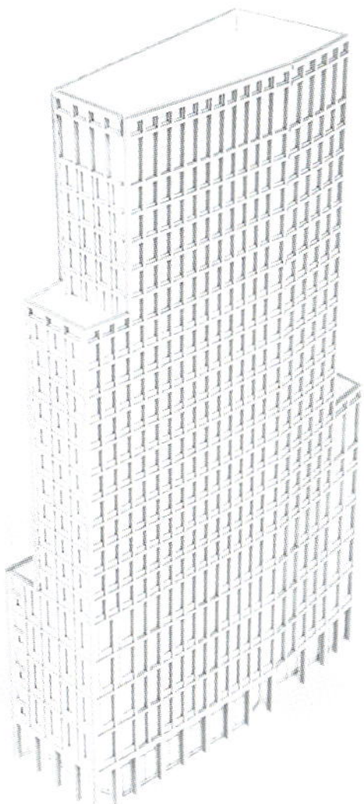

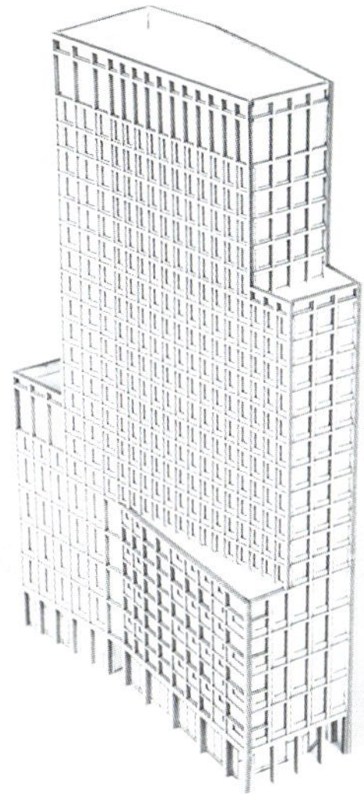

From Top Right, Clockwise: Seungho Park (MArch II); Lauren Bordes (MArch I); Lauren Bordes (MArch I)

Michel Desvigne
Inessa Hansch

Caen Island: Public Space

Caen is a city of 100,000 inhabitants situated in Normandy, France. The Caen Presque Ile, an industrial peninsula defined by canals and rivers, is in the midst of a massive urban transformation. At the tip of this peninsula, in the center of downtown, we find the "Ile de Caen," or Caen Island, a territory of 12 hectares. Approximately 5 hectares of public space on the Ile de Caen will be designed and built in the near future. This zone was the subject of the studio investigation. The island is an extraordinary prototype that concentrates and miniaturizes an exceptional sampling of urban situations and diverse typologies of public space—esplanade, plaza, quay, courtyard, parvis, roads, gardens, and large meadows. The project brief alternated between two points of view, architecture and landscape architecture. This exchange was required as a confluence of competencies was needed to develop the matrix of spatial composition and also to imagine how certain constructed elements constitute nodes of intensity that orient and animate the larger public landscape. The studio mimicked the actual situation: the program, the phases, the rhythms, and the supporting documents demanded of participants were dictated by the rigorous needs of the client. Each student specialized in a different area of focus, studying either a specific site or design typology.

PATCH
MEANDER
PATH
REFLECT.
SINGLES.
EXHIBIT
MEMORIAL
ISLAND
WALL
VIEW

Zi Gu (MLA I)

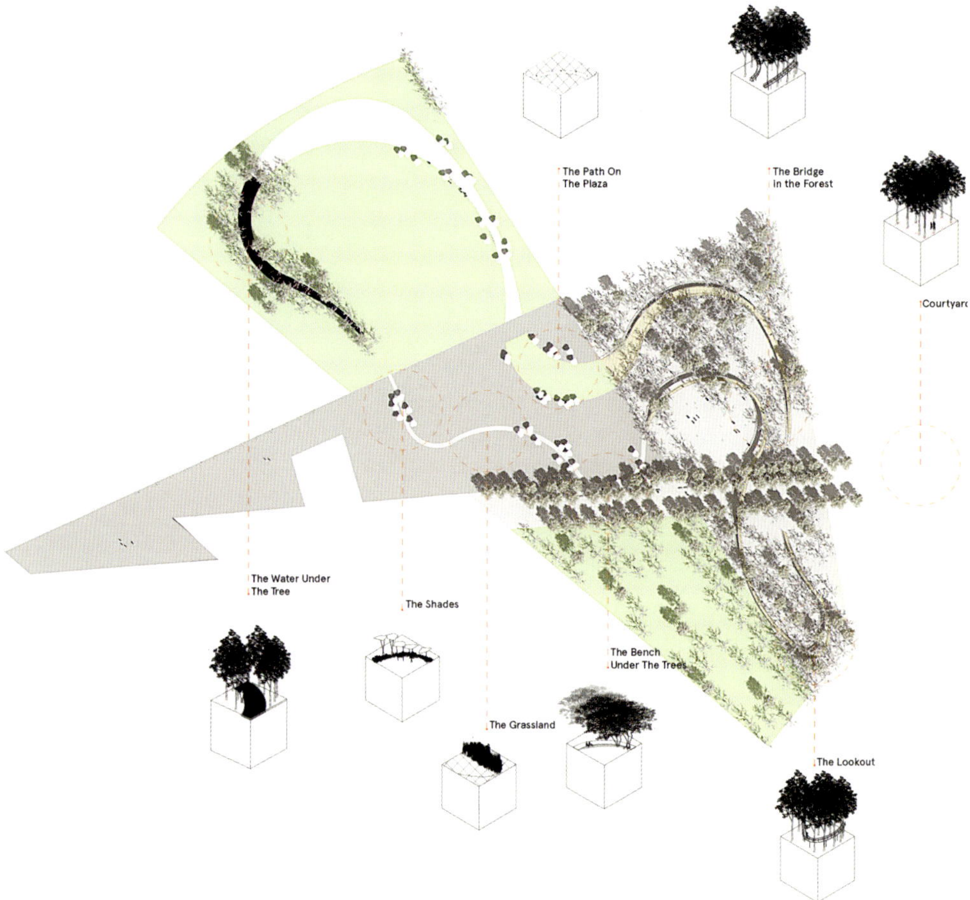

From Top: Zi Gu (MLA I); Yuan Zhu (MLA I AP)

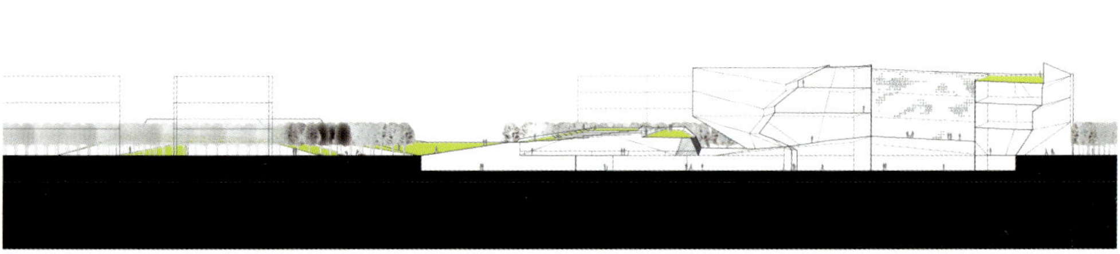

Zi Gu (MLA I)

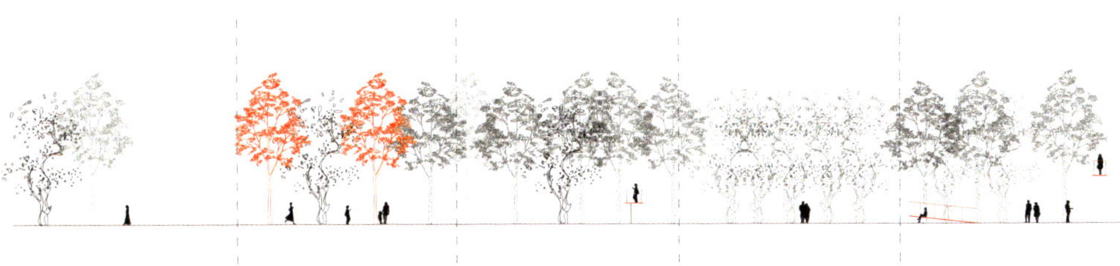

The year 2017 marks three important dates for the City of Montreal: the 150th anniversary of Canadian Confederation, the 375th anniversary of the City of Montreal, and the 50th anniversary of Expo 1967. Expo 1967's "Man and His World International Exhibition" was a magical moment in the history of the city, a recognition of Montreal's importance to the international community. Feats of human ingenuity guided all interventions including the enlargement of the Expo site, Ile Sainte-Hélène in the middle of the St. Lawrence River. Material excavated in building the underground metro system was used to expand the island. Innovative urban, architectural, landscape, graphic, and urban furniture designs were widely celebrated at the time. A new intervention will take place on the island for the 2017 celebrations, recalling traces of the past and the rich history of the site. This studio titled Terre des Hommes 2017 addressed the problematic of creating a gateway to the island and a linear land and bridge promenade over the St. Lawrence River. The studio focused on a multidisciplinary approach, from the city to the object, questioning the true definition of a gateway and a linear public space defined with urban design, architectural components, landscape strategies, and graphic and urban furniture.

From the City to the Object: Terre des Hommes 2017 Toward a New Identity

Renée Daoust
Jane Hutton
Réal Lestage

"...provides both a spatial approach to windows of sky and water, acting as a physical bridge between water and sky."

Dane Carlson (MLA II) and Kyle Irulen (MLA II). "The Oculus"

Symposium: "Waste"
Introduction by Mohsen Mostafavi
April 01, 2014

Panel 1:
Alan Berger, MIT
Rania Ghosn, University of Michigan
Hanif Kara, Engineer AKT II
Ed Eigen, Harvard GSD, Moderator

Panel 2:
Caroline O'Donnell, CODA
Nicholas Anderer, Maialino, Chef
Iñaki Abalos, Abalos+Sentkiewicz, Harvard GSD
Andrew Witt, Gehry Technologies, Moderator

Hanif Kara:
"I think by now we all know that the majority of us are going to be working on existing buildings, or redoing sites that have already been built on."

Nicholas Anderer:
"And if it were the ideal world for them [farmers], they would be able to grow cows that were just basically walking tenderloins of beef, that didn't have any other parts, but that's not the way it is, so you have to buy whole cows, and so we figured out ways in which to both preserve and also to make more flavorful some parts of these animals that maybe were less prized."

Iñaki Abalos:
" [...] The incinerator that originally was there was transformed into a recycling plant. We tried to give it a new face. And that gave way to a wonderful place for the neighbors who were in reality our clients, in this case. So I think that in many ways, recycling is an opportunity to create innovative spaces and new ideas for public space."

"I think that there is an important thing, which is to understand that there is a kind of vernacular Modernist architecture too, when you use these cheap materials. I want to make a loop and come back to the reason to be interested in this. I think it is a crucial aspect because many times we forget that this is also a part of history."

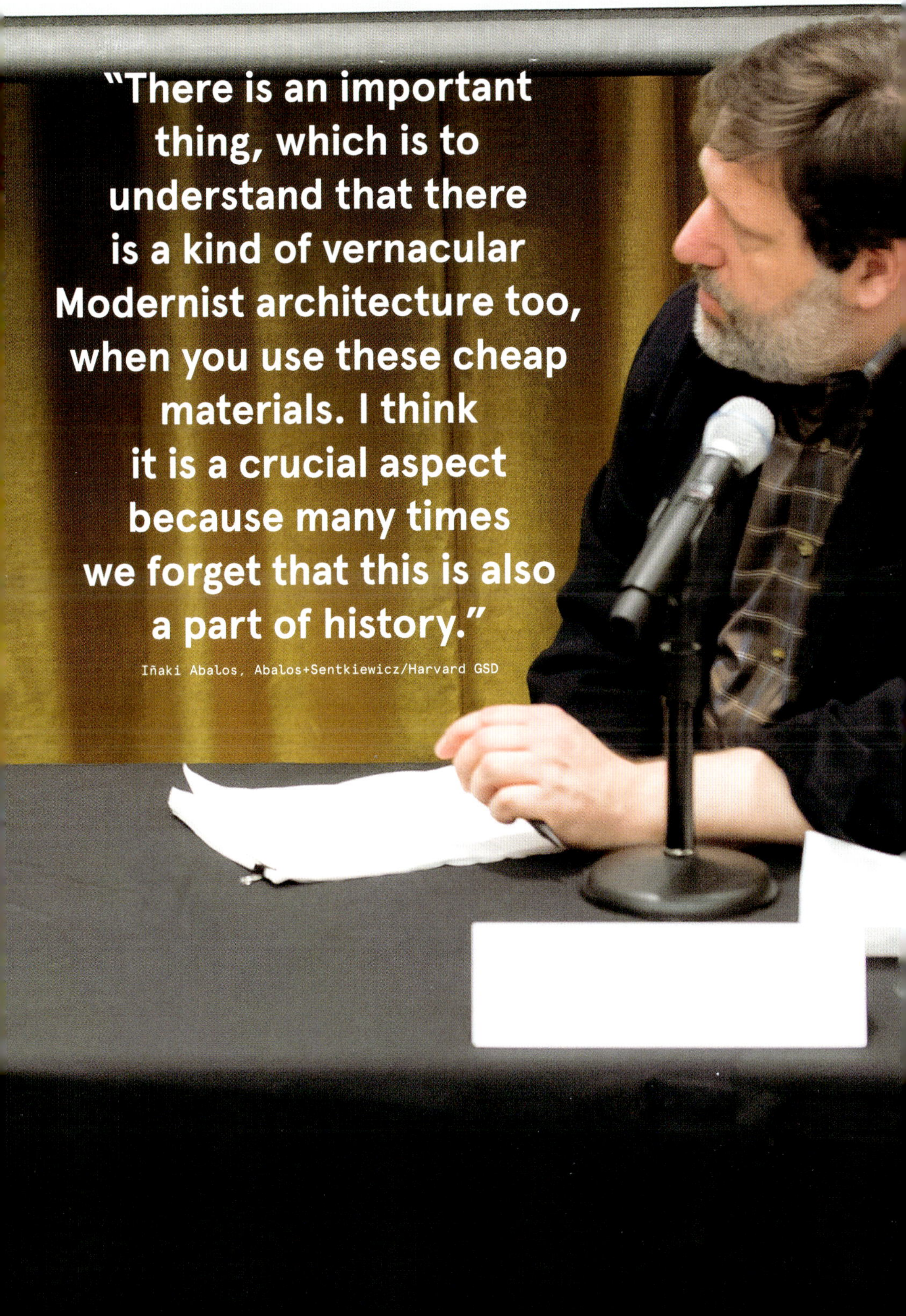

"There is an important thing, which is to understand that there is a kind of vernacular Modernist architecture too, when you use these cheap materials. I think it is a crucial aspect because many times we forget that this is also a part of history."

Iñaki Abalos, Abalos+Sentkiewicz/Harvard GSD

Diane Davis
Jose Castillo

Retrofitting the (Post?) Industrial Metropolis: Housing and Economic Growth in the Mexico City Metropolitan Area and the Bajio Region

Mexico's national authorities are rethinking their housing policy frameworks to connect questions of housing supply and affordability to location as well as to the larger goals of densification, job creation, and economic growth. This studio asked questions about what can and should be done to densify or retrofit urban areas; it evaluated the potential role that new versus existent housing stock (or related infrastructures) can play in this process; and it addressed these concerns in the context of two very different urban contexts, one de-industrializing and the other re-industrializing—thus framing the studio's concern with urban planning and design interventions in the context of larger regional, national, and global economic trends affecting cities in Mexico and elsewhere. The studio focused on two sites: the municipality of Tlalnepantla in the Mexico City Metro Area and the city of Celaya, Guanajuato. By working in these two locations, the studio inquired into the complexities of intertwining housing policies with state and local agendas as well as larger-scale dynamics of investment, industrial development, and job creation.

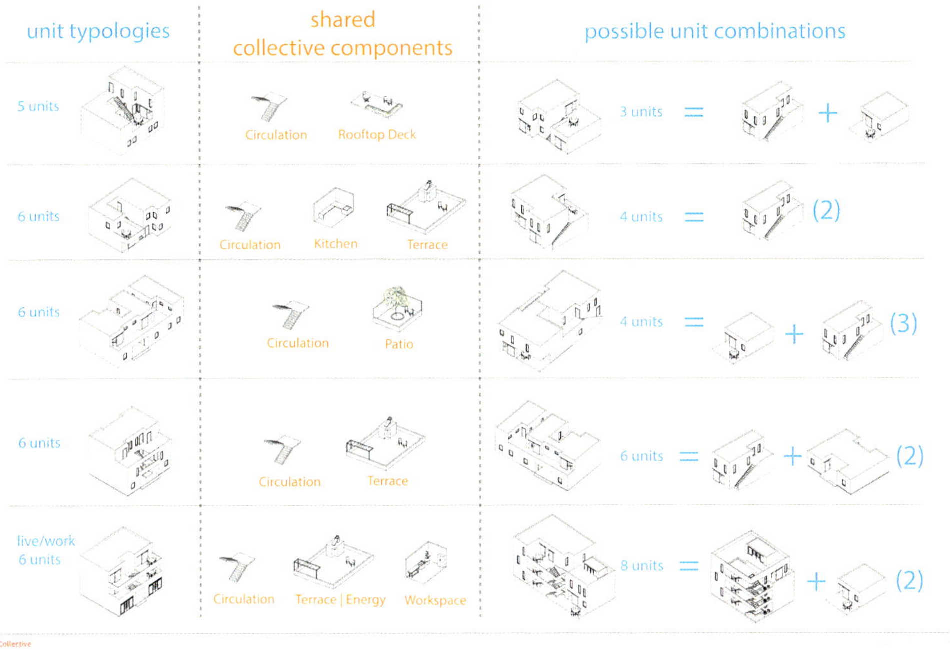

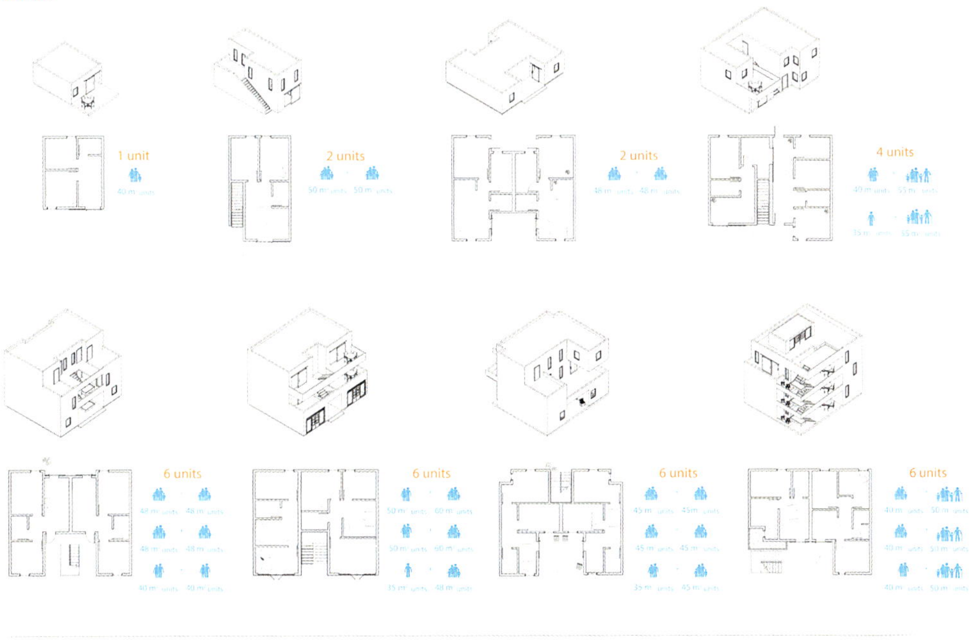

Carly Augustine (MArch II) and Hayrettin Gunc (MAUD). "The Collective"

Peter G. Rowe

Obsolescence and China's Pathways to Redevelopment: The Shekou Industrial District in Shenzhen

A striking aspect of China's recent modernization and urbanization has been a relatively high rate of obsolescence, variously pegged at around thirty years for many built structures. Consequently, as China moves forward, redevelopment and renewal will become an increasingly large part of its developmental agenda. As one of the earliest excursions into modern industrial and urban development since China's historic opening up in 1978, the Shekou Industrial District in Shenzhen, dating from 1979, now confronts areas of moribund and obsolete development at the same time that it is part of the newly developing economic zone of Qinhai. The issue confronted in the studio was how should the industrial district comport itself and be reconfigured to best leverage the obsolescence of the plant and other facilities and ongoing new development. To date, when considering redevelopment, those in China have pursued several strategies, including: outright conservation and reuse, demolition with or without selective renewal, deployment of so-called creative districts, retrofitting for reuse, and new building reinterpreted according to some version of past practice. In scope, the studio included overall planning proposals for all or part of the study area, more specific urban design proposals for particular redevelopment opportunities within the area, and urban-architectural proposals for specific building-scale projects, including incorporation of the reuse of older, disused facilities.

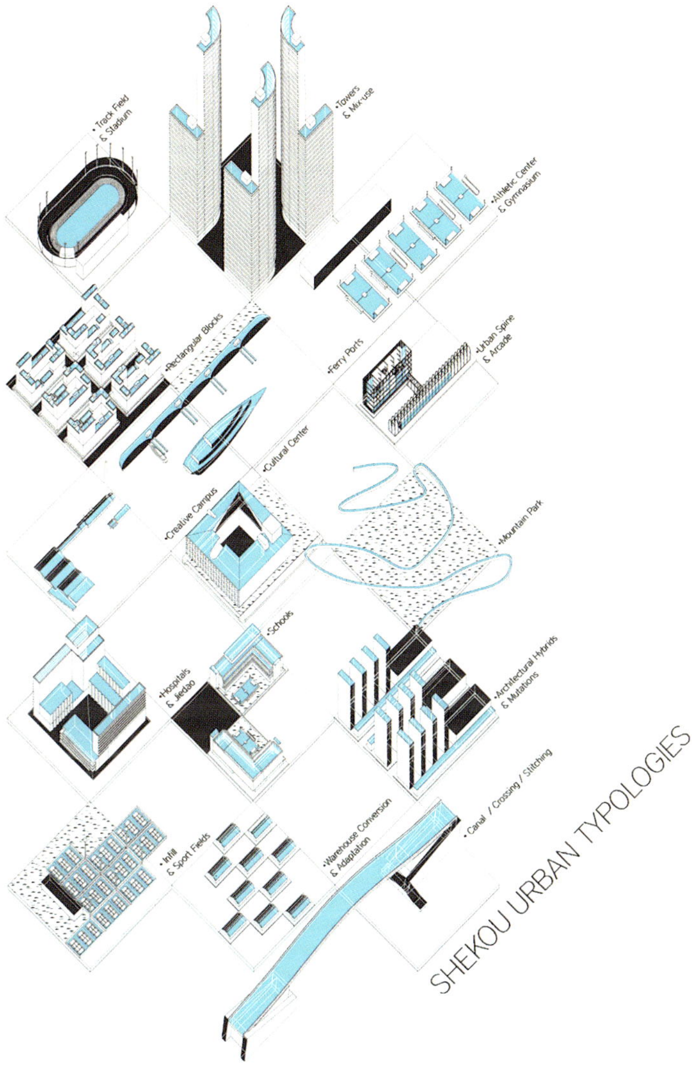

Thien Nguyen (MAUD) and Orcun Tonyali (MAUD)
"Permanence, Temporality, Shekou and the Pearl River Delta Region"

"A striking aspect of China's recent modernization and urbanization has been a relatively high rate of obsolescence."

Alejandro Lara (MAUD), Jiaqi Wang (MAUD), Wenxin Ye (MAUD), and Long Zuo (MAUD)
"Shekou-Dethematization of the Modern City: Generic vs. Organic"

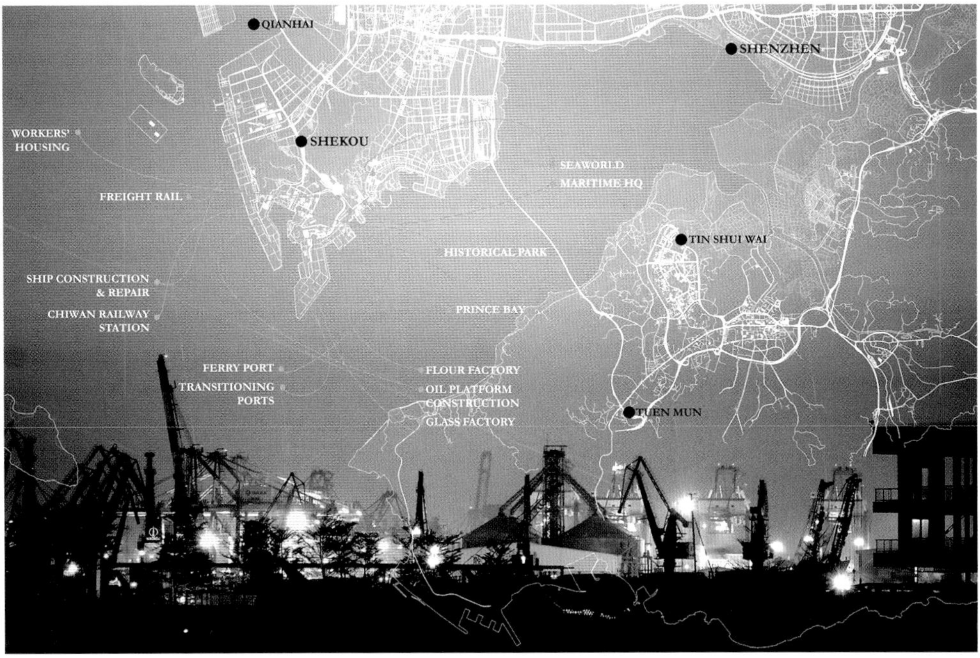

Thien Nguyen (MAUD) and Orcun Tonyali (MAUD)
"Permanence, Temporality, Shekou and the Pearl River Delta Region"

Alejandro Lara (MAUD), Jiaqi Wang (MAUD), Wenxin Ye (MAUD), and Long Zuo (MAUD)
"Shekou-Dethematization of the Modern City: Generic vs. Organic"

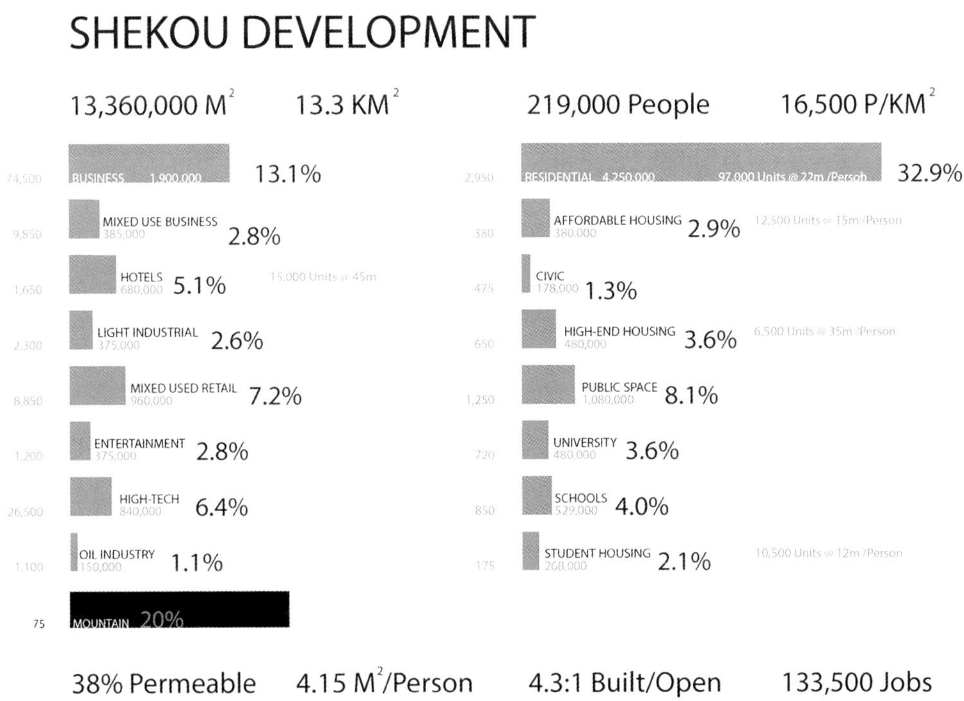

Thien Nguyen (MAUD)and Orcun Tonyali (MAUD)
"Permanence, Temporality, Shekou and the Pearl River Delta Region"

A: Different Housing Typologies Provide a Mixture of Units
B: A+Express C: Civic Programs Such as Museums, Libraries, Schools, and Hospitals Are Scattered across the Cities D: Blocks Are Flexible for a Variety of Uses, Promoting Different Characters and Engagement with the City E: Canals as Infrastructure F: Ferry, Harbor, Marina, Boardwalk, Promenade, Boathouse, and Docks G: Event Stadium Anchors One End of the Axis

Thien Nguyen (MAUD) and Orcun Tonyali (MAUD)
"Permanence, Temporality, Shekou and the Pearl River Delta Region"

"Consequently, redevelopment and renewal will become an increasingly large part of China's developmental agenda."

Joan Busquets
Pablo Perez Ramos

Barcelona's Grids: In Search of New Paradigms

The construction of modern Barcelona can be seen as a laboratory of urban projects and planning strategies. This process spanning two centuries features a series of innovative experiments that correspond to different scales and explain the complexity involved in constructing such a singular capital city. In this process, many of the city's developments were based on regular forms of urban organization, principally grid forms. The clear contrast between two forms of urban grids stands out in particular. The first corresponds to the large scale, with Cerdà's project of 1859 "to Extend the city across the Plain," which used a regular isotropic grid with city blocks of 113 meters, laid out according to the lines of the coast and the Collserola hill range. At the same time, a series of grid projects at a smaller scale were implemented beyond Cerdà's scope, in neighborhoods such as Gràcia, Sant Andreu, and Poble Sec. The studio hypothesis was to verify the capacity for transformation, based on initial models seen as designs that allow constant reinterpretation according to programmatic needs and capable of offering multiple urban forms. At the same time, it set out to discover emerging forms of networks that can enhance the morphological reading of this contrast in urban grids, producing an urban project that also manages the territorial scale with a view to achieving more lasting, sustainable projects and strategies.

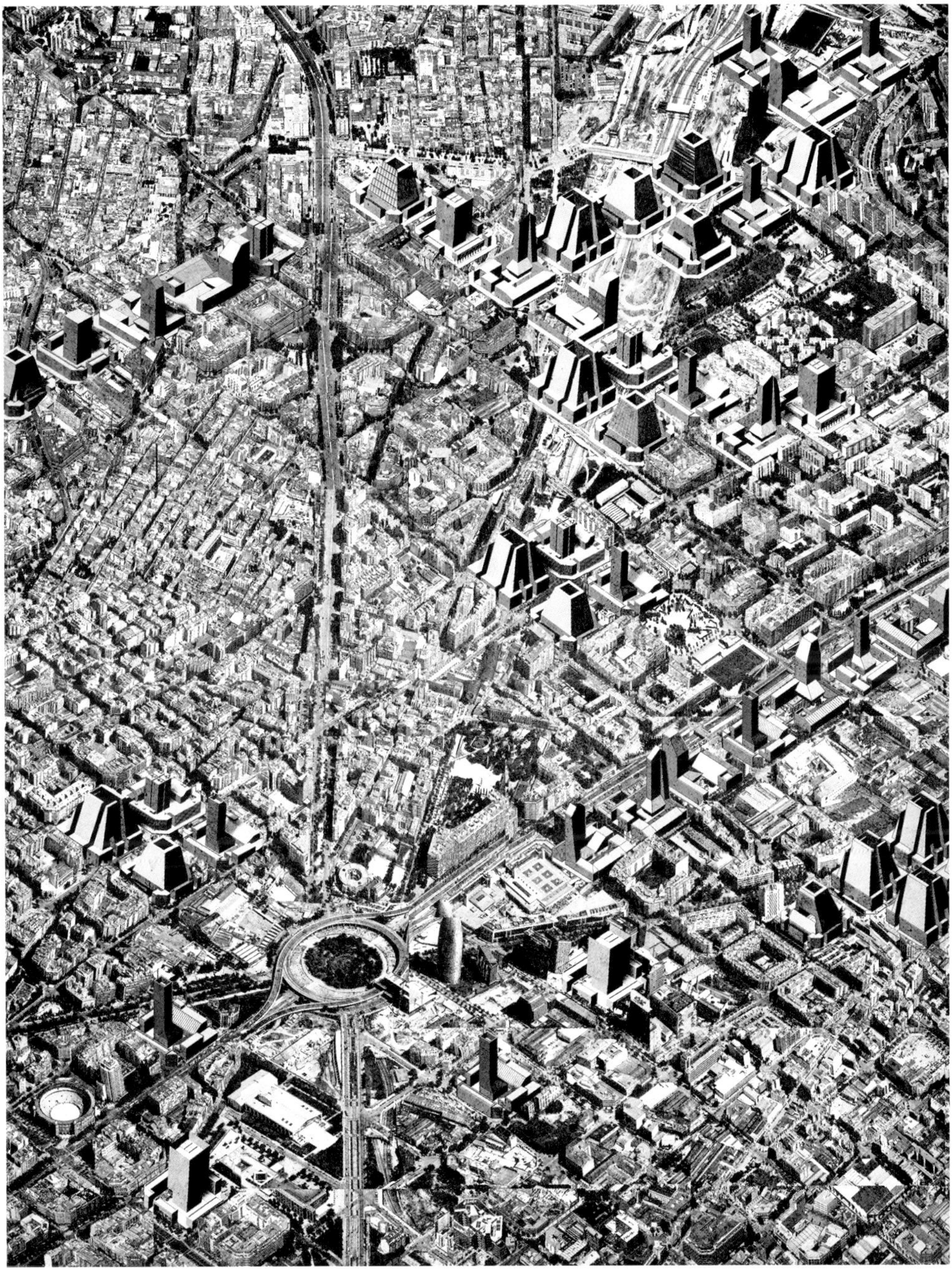

Jose Alexandro Medina (MAUD)

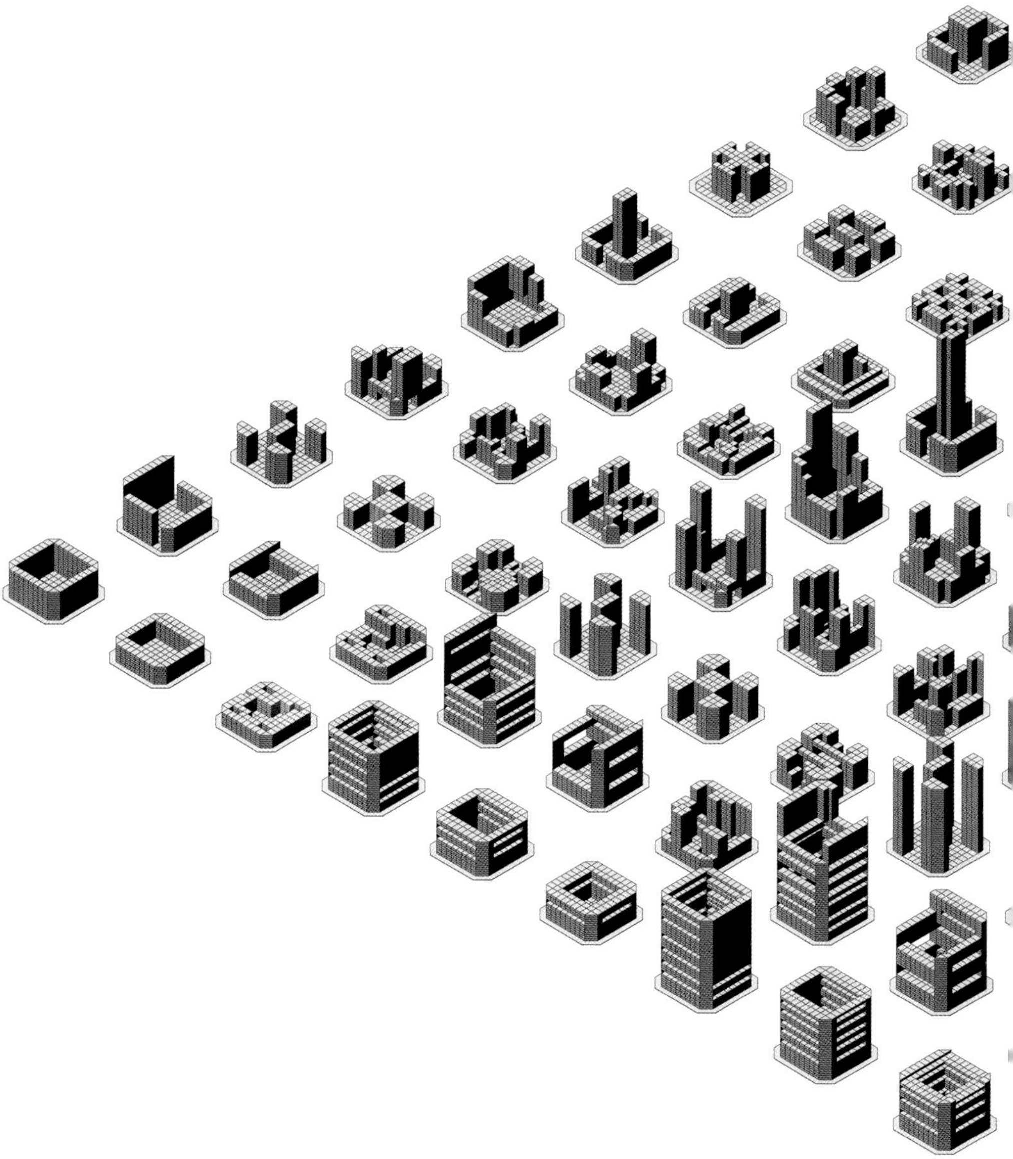

Jose Alexandro Medina (MAUD)

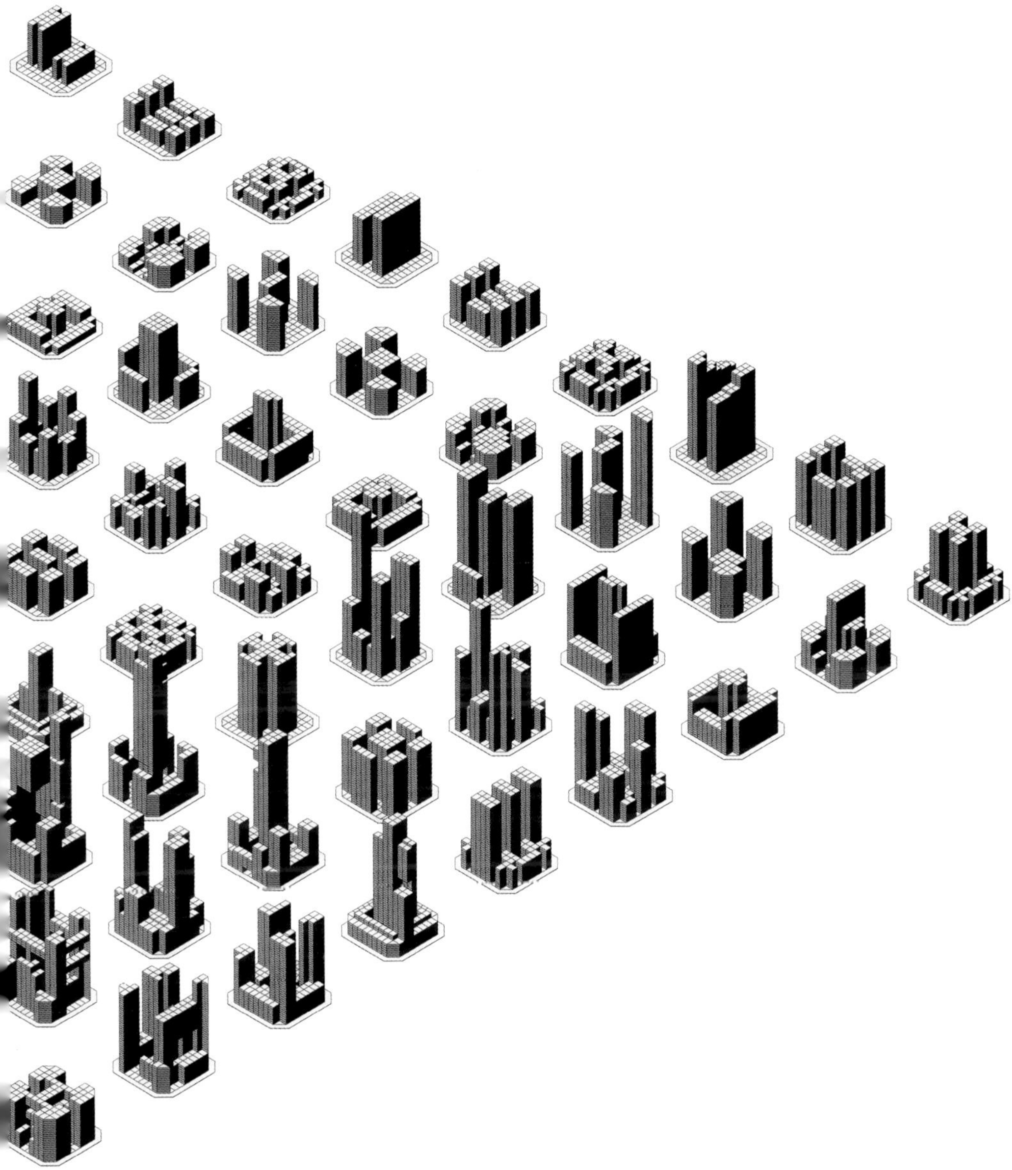

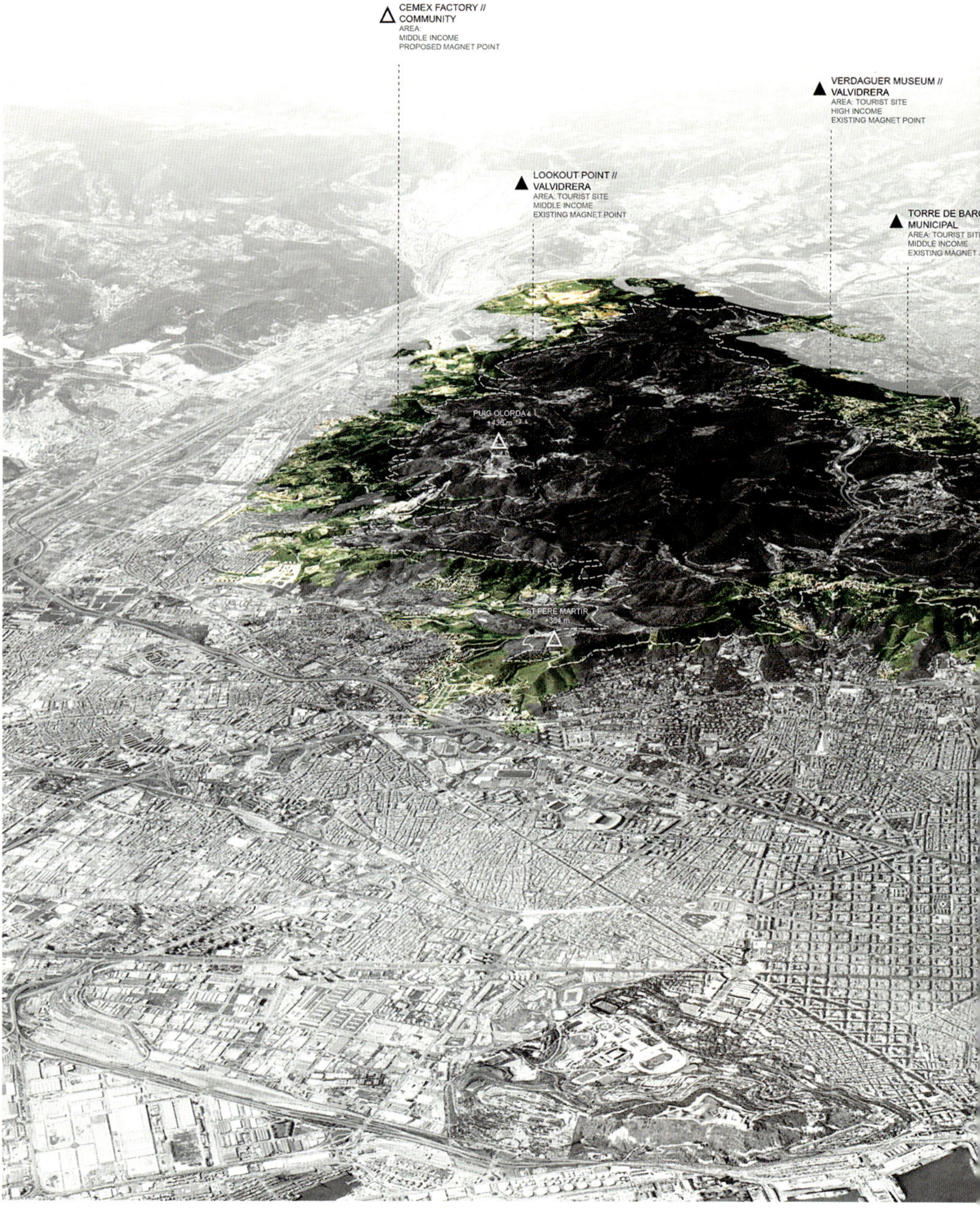

<u>Angela Clubb</u> (MUP), <u>Daniel Toole</u> (MAUD), <u>Won Joon Seol</u> (MLA I AP/MLAUD)

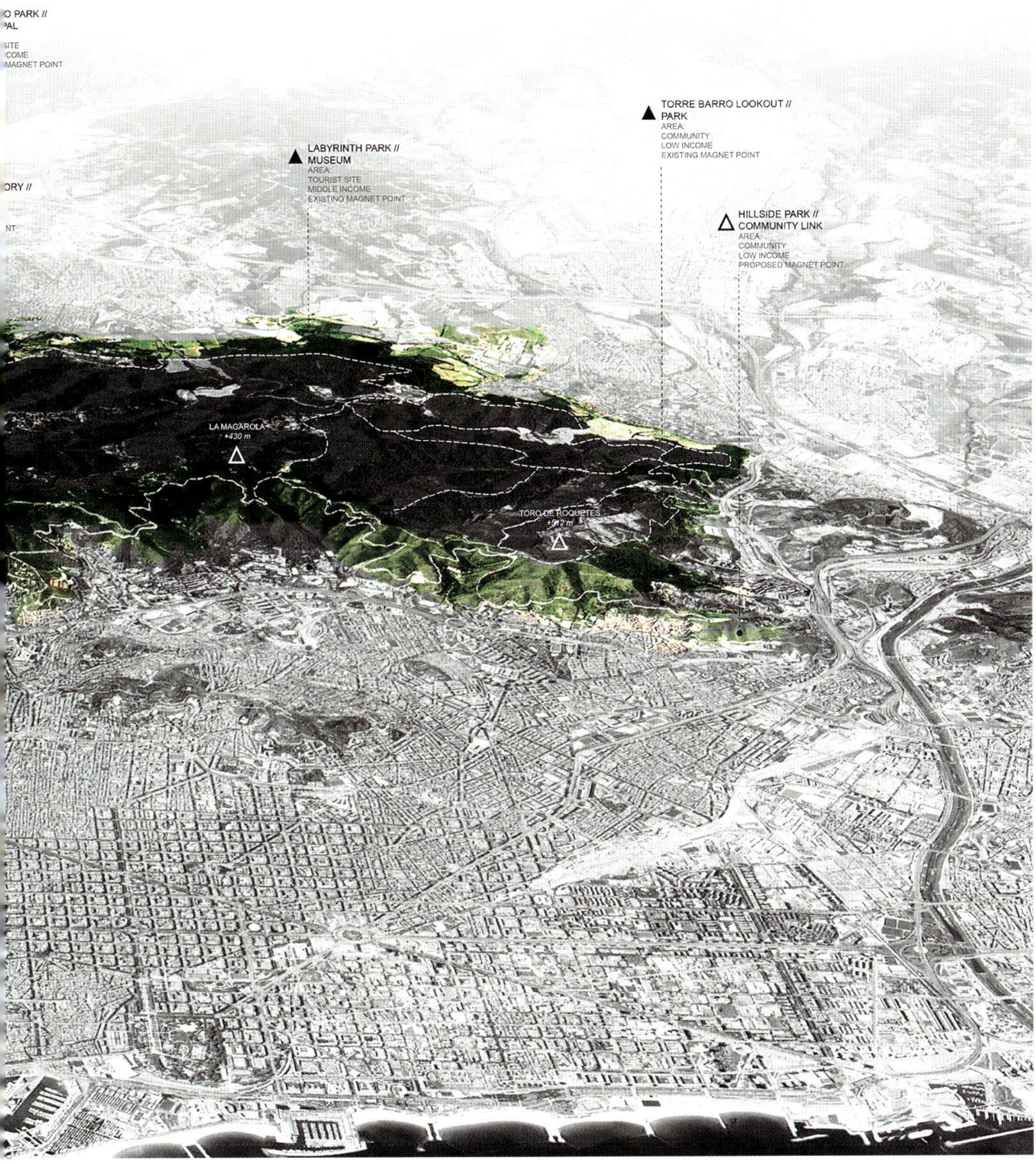
LABYRINTH PARK //
MUSEUM
AREA:
TOURIST SITE
MIDDLE INCOME
EXISTING MAGNET POINT
TORRE BARRO LOOKOUT //
PARK
AREA:
COMMUNITY
LOW INCOME
EXISTING MAGNET POINT
HILLSIDE PARK //
COMMUNITY LINK
AREA:
COMMUNITY
LOW INCOME
PROPOSED MAGNET POINT
LA MAGAROLA
+430 m
TORO DE ROQUETES

Alimentary is defined as relating to nourishment or nutrition—furnishing sustenance or maintenance. Food is a fundamental requirement of human life and a universal experience that transcends cultural and temporal boundaries. Within this topic of food, this studio looked at a number of specific issues extensively through research. Rather than addressing one site or one program, each person addressed a particular area of research that would become a uniquely individual design project under the umbrella topic of food. This included projects that address global issues of food shortage, diversity, waste, and sustainability through typologies such as the super farm, food bank, corn city, food ark, compost center, or waste-to-energy plant. Typologies that are defined by mobility such as the drive-in, food trucks, and supermarkets can be reassessed considering future models of urbanism and transportation, while issues of iconicity and identity can be tackled through the food and beverage company headquarters, food theme park, winery, brewery, and distillery. Reconceptualizing the kitchen and dining room through historical and technological changes can create new housing and collective consumption typologies, while innovations in food science such as the 3D printer or molecular gastronomy can redefine how food is produced and how the programs associated with it can evolve.

Alimentary Design

Shohei Shigematsu
Christine Cheng

Wesley Ho (MArch I). "Fish Revolution"

Achim Menges

Material Performance: Fibrous Tectonics

Advances in the conception of materiality and the technologies of materialization have always been a catalyst for design innovation in architecture. Today, technological advancements across multiple disciplines suggest a profound transformation of the way the future built environment will be conceived, designed, and materialized. As design computation is no longer limited to the binary realm of the digital, it can be perceived as an intense interface to the more complex domain of the physical. A new understanding of the material in architecture is beginning to arise, forging new alliances between the fields of design, engineering, and natural sciences, and leading to multidisciplinary and multifaceted material cultures in architecture. The studio explored the notion of material performance—its manifold and deep interrelations with technology, biology, and culture as a central field of architectural inquiry. It sought to trace the emergence of new material cultures within the context of the ever-accelerating integrative technologies of design computation and robotic fabrication, with a particular focus on advanced fiber composite materials. Students were introduced to a design approach that bridges the cultural as well as technical dimension of fibrous materials in architecture and the repertoire of material organization in nature.

Georgios-Spyridon Athanasopoulos (MAUD) and Brian Chu (MArch II). “Embedded Fiber Structures”

Zunheng Lai (MArch I AP)
Jun Wang (MArch I AP)
01 2.5D Technique Study: Hexagon_Aperture Frameless
04 3D Morphology Prototype: Vertical Landing Hybrid Frame
07 2.5D Technique Study: Triangle Flexible Frame
09 3D Morphology Prototype: Vertical Landing Hybrid Frame
10 2.5D Technique Study: Hexagon Aperture Frameless
11 3D Morphology Prototype: Vertical Landing Hybrid Frame
15 2.5D Technique Study: Hexagon_Aperture Frameless
16 3D Morphology Prototype: Vertical Landing Hybrid Frame
21 3D Morphology Prototype: Vertical Landing Hybrid Frame

Kevin Hinz (MArch I)
Alexander Jacobson (MArch I)
Thena Tak (MArch II)
02 Aperture Development, Hedge Hog
03 Surface Development, Red Fox
08 Aperture Development, Hedge Hog
13 Surface Development, Toucan
18 Armature Development, Phoenix, Detail
19 Armature Development, Phoenix, Detail

Georgios-Spyridon Athanasopoulos (MAUD)
Brian Chu (MArch II)
05 Multiple Layered Fibers
06 Embedded Component
12 Horizontal Winding, Span
14 Embedded Component
17 Horizontal Winding, Span
20 Multiple Layered Fibers

01

02

03

04

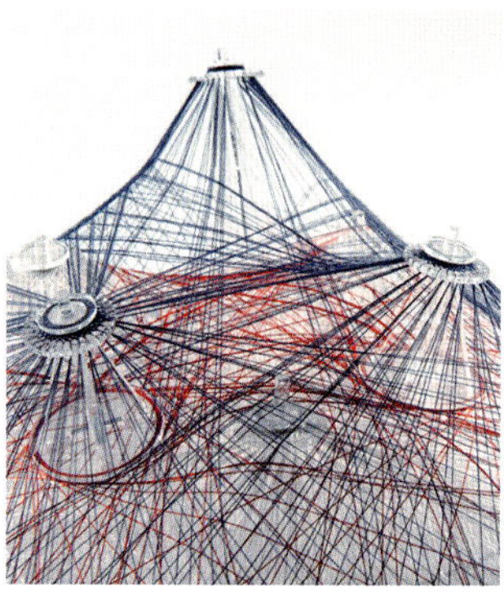
05

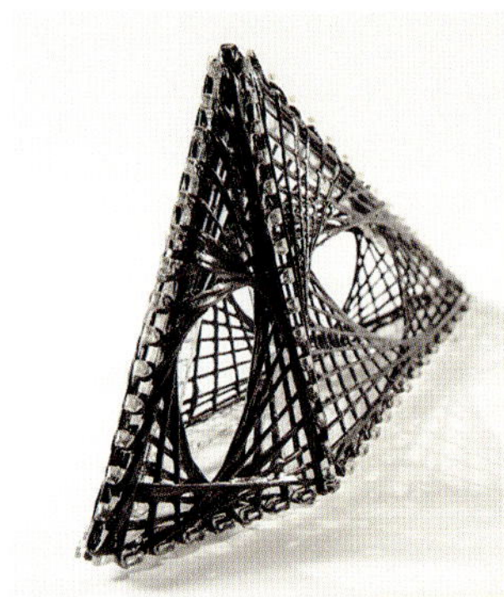
06

07

08

09

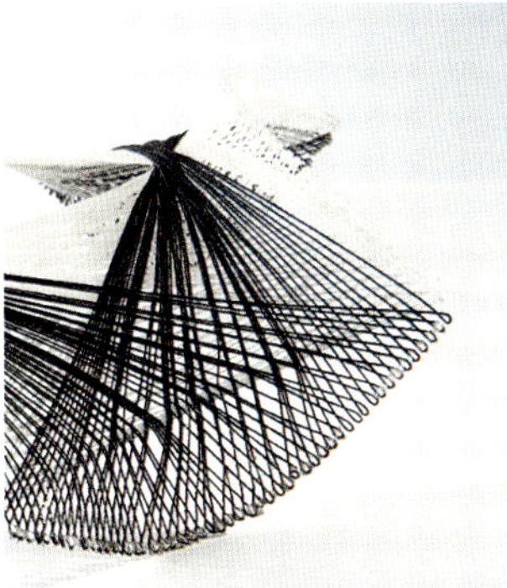
10

11

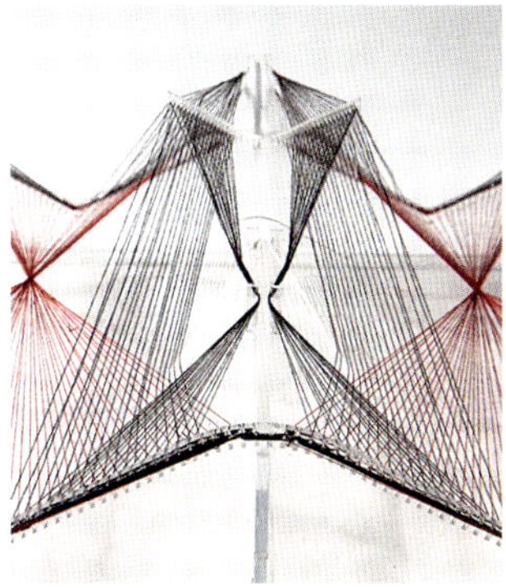
12

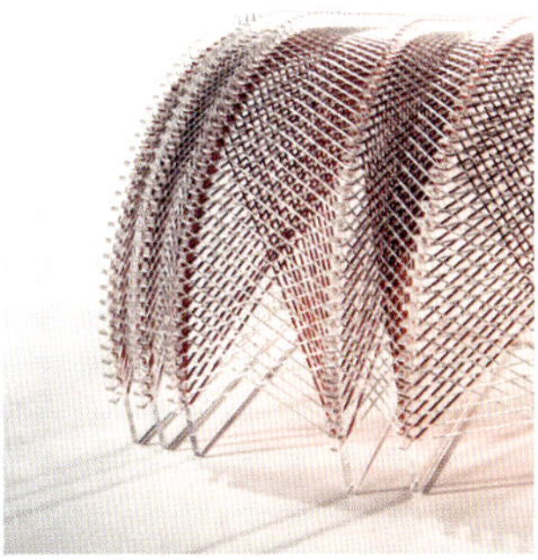
13

14

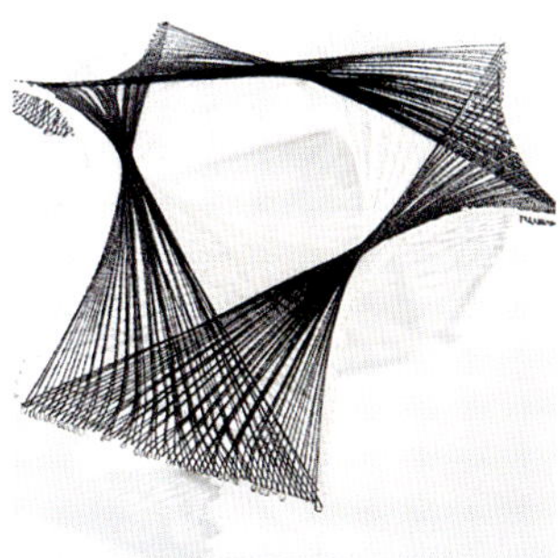
15

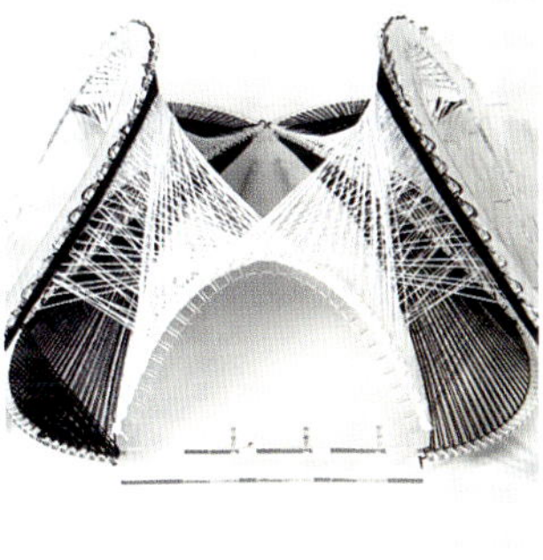
16

17

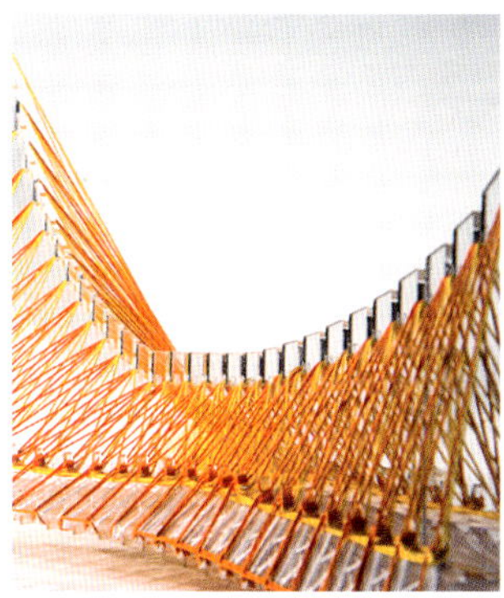
18

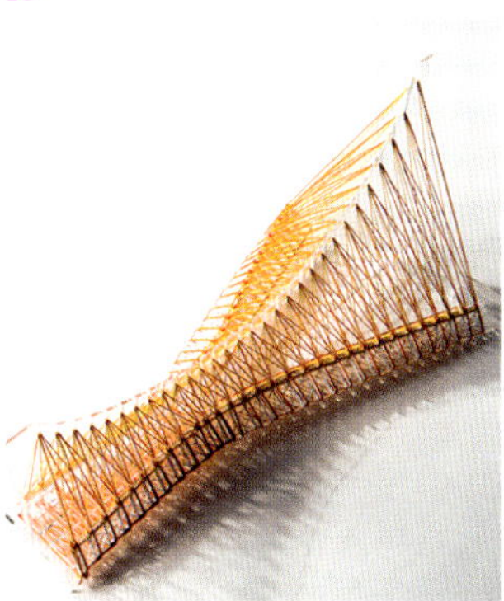
19

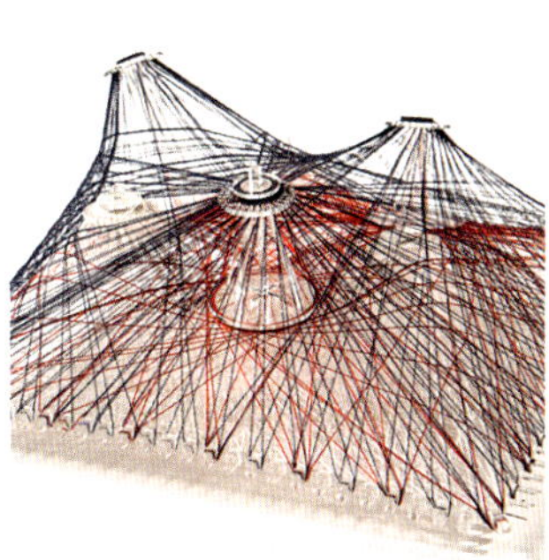
20

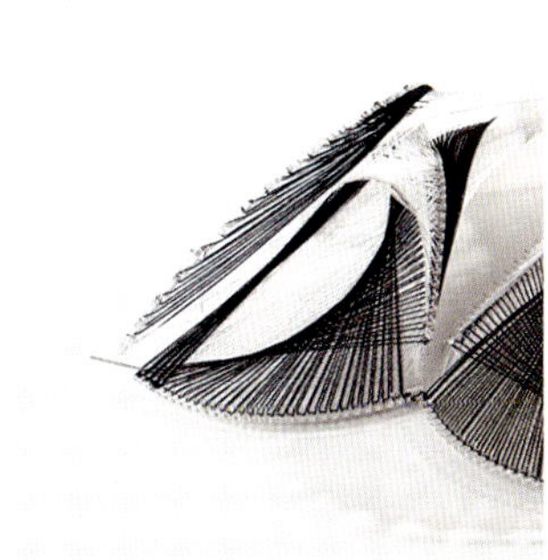
21

INPUTS

cvrA: drive curves
permA: perimeter curv (tentative)
snail: limit loop length
q: ?
div: evaluation parameter for crvA
input: upper limit for link modifier
r: evaluation variable, application of aa

VARIABLES

```
(a)    where: a=((Math.Abs(Ept.X)-Math.Abs(Spt.X))/div);
(aa)   modifier for line[pt1,pt2]
       where: aa1=(a*1.5);
(aa1)  where: b=Math.Abs(a*0.5);
       loop modified variable, dummy for (aa)
(b)    where: b=Math.Abs(a*0.5);
(bb)   where: bb=c+(0.05*(i));
       NOTE: this expression offers high degree of change
(c)    dummy variable, initially 0
       when: bb=c+(0.05*(i));
       where c is initially set to zero
       (i) is used to step the change

       formula: formula=Math.Sin(aa1);
       an expression used to change aa in relationship to a
```

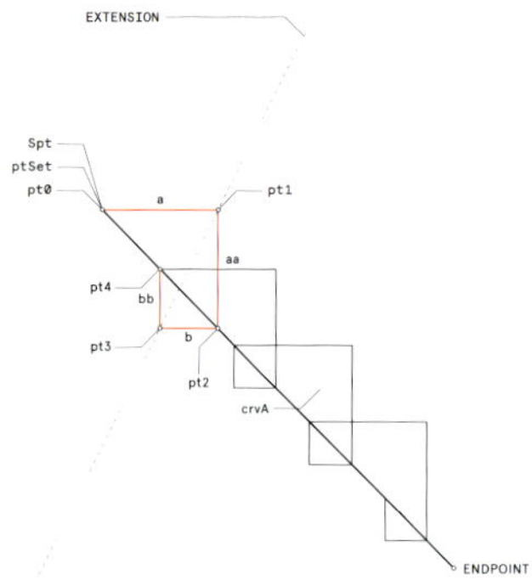


```
set new point to old point
    move new point an increment
        relative to input crv
    get ptl, add pt to output list

set new point to old point
    move new point an increment
        relative to input first fiber
    get pt2

set new point to old point
    move new point an increment
        relative to input first fiber
    get pt3

set new point to old point
    move new point an increment
        relative to second and third fibers
    get pt4
create line[pt3,pt1]
modify changing variable
reset loop
```

2D LINK SET:
All Set Points Planar

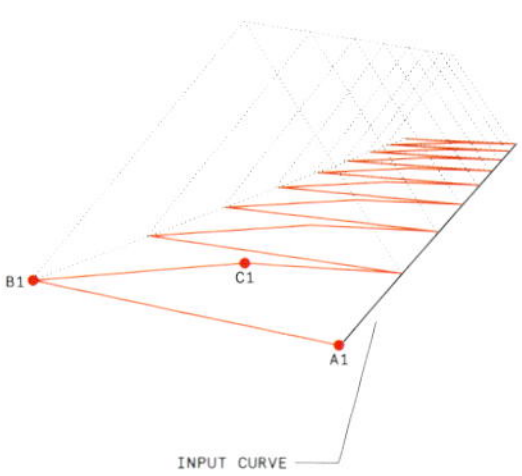

3D LINK SET:
Set Point "C" Transforms In Z-Axis

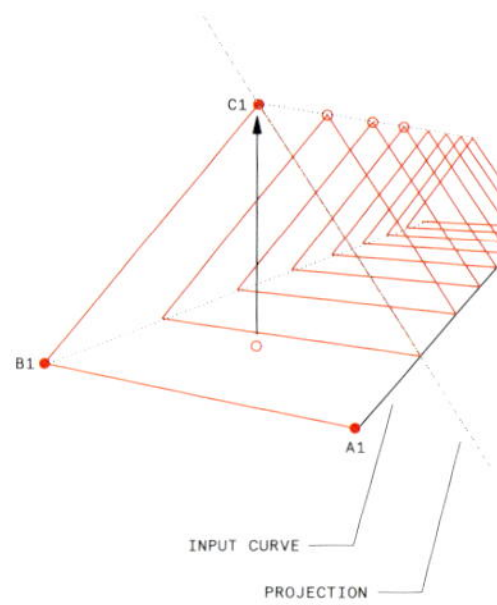

3D LINK SET:
Set Point "C" Transforms In XYZ-Axis

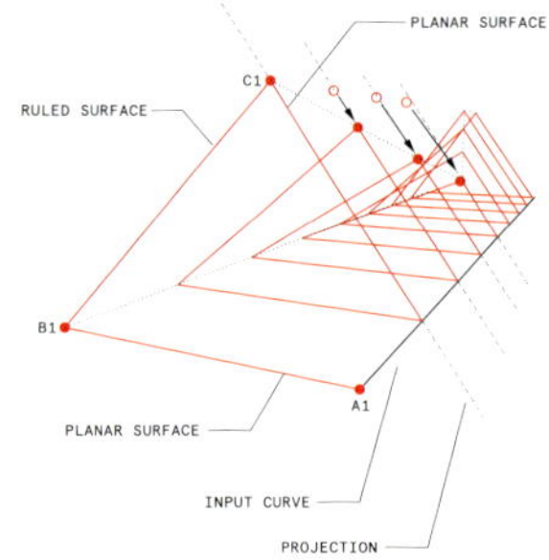

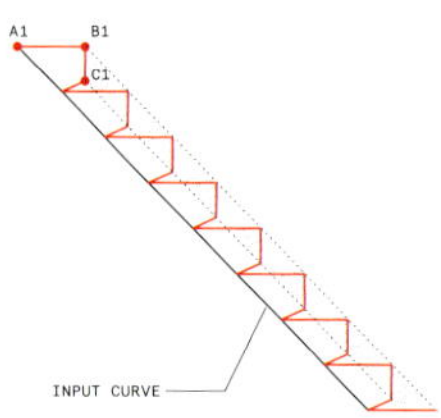

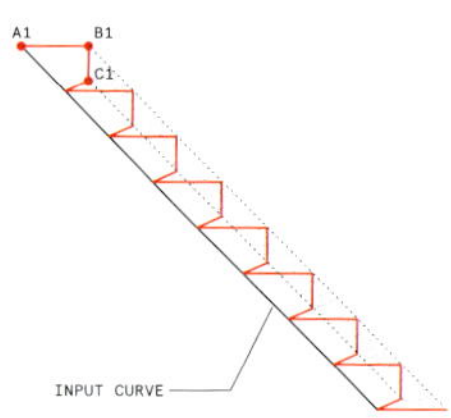

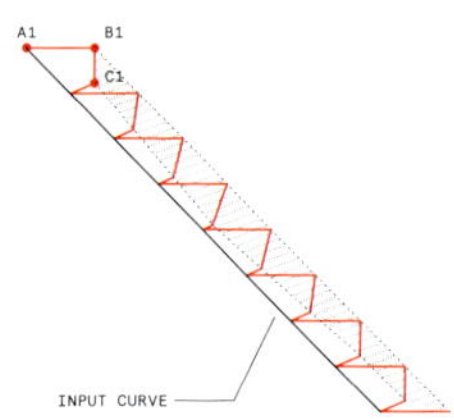

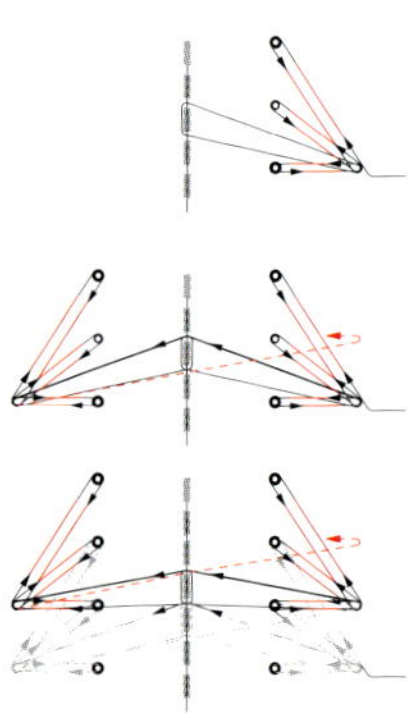

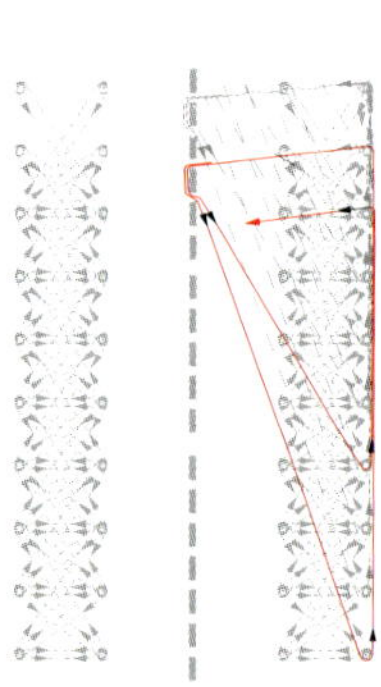

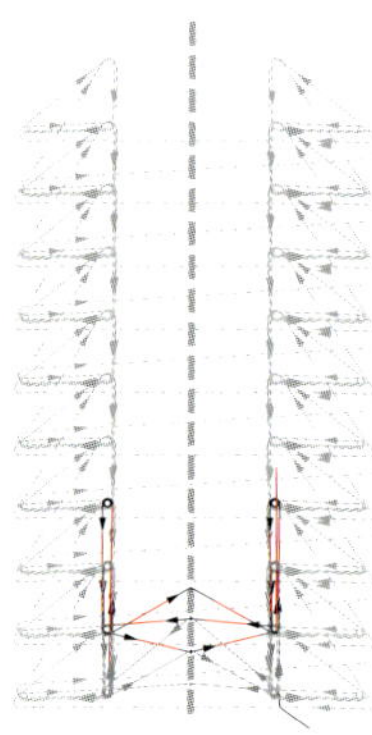

Kevin Hinz (MArch I), Alexander Jacobson (MArch I), and Thena Tak (MArch II). "Surface Tectonics"

Currently, when considering the nature of architecture, it is problematic to simply define it as an "artifact" or "artificial environment" that is conceived and constructed for people. From such a limited point of view, we'll find it impossible to resolve any of the widespread problems that face us today. Instead, isn't it necessary that we consider architecture from a broader perspective? Rather than limiting our understanding of architecture as an "environment for people," we need to foster a broad awareness of contemporary issues that incorporates all aspects of our surroundings. Thinking beyond the scale and implications of the conventional artificial environments that we find in buildings, landscapes, or urban designs, we considered an expanded notion of architecture that meets the demands of today's society.

Another Nature

Junya Ishigami

Jiasi Tan (MAUD)

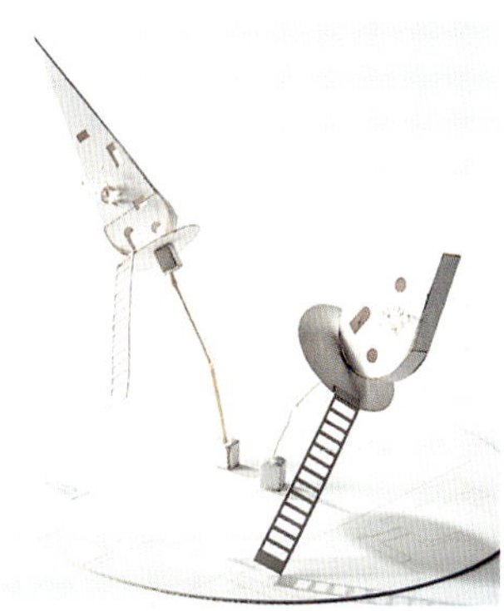

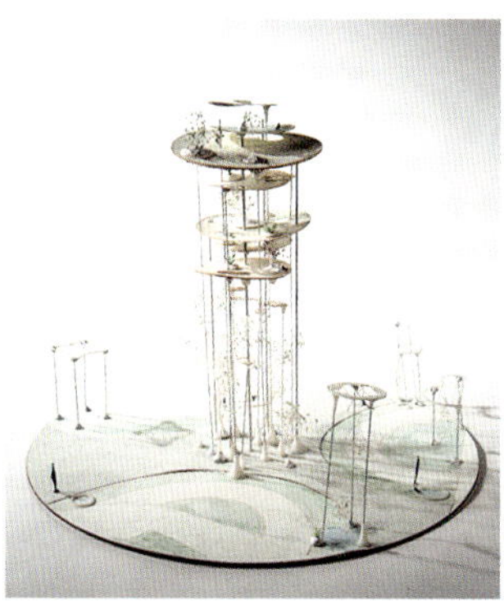

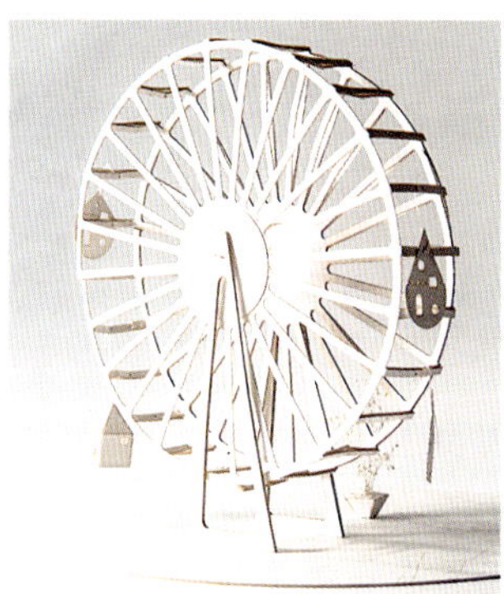

From Top Left, Clockwise: Matthew Montry (MArch II); Patricia Semmler (MArch I); Yun Fu (MArch I AP)

Lecture: Manuel Castells
The Space of Autonomy: Cyberspace and Urban Space in Networked Social Movements
February 18, 2014

"Social movements are emotional movements that are shared collectively and become a collective action through a process of communication between the different subjects. And so their forms of communication, organization, and action depend on the culture, technology, and institutional environment of its particular society, and its particular spatial context. Indeed, social change is inseparable from spatial change. They go together. They interact. They are specific, but they go together. In fact the urban form, all urban form, results from the relentless interaction between the reproduction of this spatial urban form by the institutionalized interest, and by the resistance and alternative project, and counteraction by people, citizens who don't feel represented, who do not feel included in this automatic reproduction of the urban structures. So the urban form is urban structure and urban social movements interacting with each other. This has been my research agenda for all of my life."

"[...] The occupation of urban space— squares, streets, buildings— is a fundamental expression of the movements everywhere. Remember the old revolutionary tradition of the barricades? You enclose yourself behind the barricade. That has no military or defensive use. On the contrary, you become the target. They attack you exactly where you are. The issue is that by being in the barricades, without explicit ideological statement of program, you define an in and an out. You define whoever is with us is here, and the others, please join. And it's an exemplary action to rebuild an alternative space around alternative values, and to feel the communal connection within the barricades as a way to oppose the formal institutions, which are spaces of exclusion, in terms of citizen rights. Moreover it's also in urban terms the claiming of public space. The most important issue in urbanity today, in my opinion, is creating spontaneous interaction, social life, and fighting fear. It's creating instant public space, which is exactly the key issue in all of the speculative processes of urban development."

"[...] 'Space is the material support of time sharing social practices.' Space is the material support of simultaneity. Now of course, throughout history most of this simultaneity depended on contiguity, on being together. That's why cities were created. And with the acceleration of technology, a new space emerged in which simultaneity or chosen time would not depend on contiguity but on connectedness embedded in the flows, a space of communication. And therefore my point was that there are places based on simultaneity through contiguity, and space flows in which simultaneity is based on communication networks. Originally for me, the space of places was the space of experience. And the space of flows was the space of power. It turns out that there is power and counterpower in both forms of space. The critical point then is that to actually enact social change, any actor of social change has to connect the counterpower in the space of places with the counterpower in the space of flows. And that's exactly what these movements are doing. By claiming the public space for citizens, they need to construct a new form of space, a space of autonomy. The space of autonomy where the space of flows as well as the space of places meet with the mental maps that people elaborate to reinvent the institutions that run our lives."

"...any actor of social change has to connect the counterpower in the space of places with the counterpower in the space of flows."

The studio explored the architectural means by which a public space could be configured to support a variety of specific urban functions while encouraging a multiplicity of unspecified social interactions. By relocating a library and a bus station, the studio aimed to reorganize the activities in Beyazit Square, one of the oldest, vital, but more chaotic public spaces in the historic center of Istanbul. In the history of the city, Beyazit Square has moved from a highly formalized space associated with decorum of empire to a more loosely delineated void between highly differentiated activities. Through this transformation, the square has been the subject of periodic rehabilitation attempts, all partially or poorly executed. Today, the synergetic interaction between a wide range of uses, cultures, and architectural typologies (from mat buildings to free-standing objects) is one of the key generators of the square's livelihood despite its practical problems and uninspiring surfaces. The studio focused on the design of the square's façades, the ground surface, and the covers over some of its passages. In the interplay between ground frontage, reflected ceiling, and façade relief, the studio hoped to uncover the possibilities of overdetermination of surfaces and underdetermination of spaces. This contrast between intense edges and open spaces was meant to inspire rather than dictate public activity.

Meydan: Designing the Surfaces of Public Space around Beyazit Square, Istanbul

A. Hashim Sarkis
Erkin Özay

Jose Mayoral Moratilla (MArch II) and Kevin Murray (MArch I)

From Top: Jose Mayoral Moratilla (MArch II) and Kevin Murray (MArch I); Linda Zhang (MArch I AP) and Emily Kappes (MArch I AP)

In recent years our studio explored the iconography and scenography of the American landscape by separate studies of Frederick Law Olmsted's Central Park in New York and Henry Thoreau's Walden in Concord, Massachusetts. This year we invited students to revisit both Central Park and Walden as a parallel project provoking a new synthesis and cross-fertilization between urbanity and nature. We studied and drew upon an illustrious potpourri of dissonant cultural influences, including the musical scores of Charles Ives and the film Walden by experimental filmmaker Jonas Mekas, shot during 1964–1968. Additional inspiration came from land artist Robert Smithson, who observed that Olmsted actually made ponds, unlike Thoreau who just conceptualized them. Finally, we drew from Rem Koolhaas, who recently rediscovered the countryside as the latest big thing. He had earlier described Central Park in *Delirious New York: A Retroactive Manifesto for Manhattan* as "a taxidermic preservation of nature that exhibits forever the drama of culture, outdistancing nature: a synthetic Arcadian carpet, grafted onto grid" and in his essay "Junkspace" envisioned a "parallel Walden of enhanced air, water, wood in order to produce hyper-ecology." Students undertook extensive fieldwork both in Walden and Central Park and were invited to design a double vision of site-specific parallel interventions.

Parallel Motion: Walden Pond, Concord Central Park, New York

Eelco Hooftman
Bridget Baines

Cali Pfaff (MLA I)

"New York is my Walden. I mean, you don't have to be in the middle of a forest, a countryside, to be in nature."

Jonas Mekas

Cali Pfaff (MLA I)

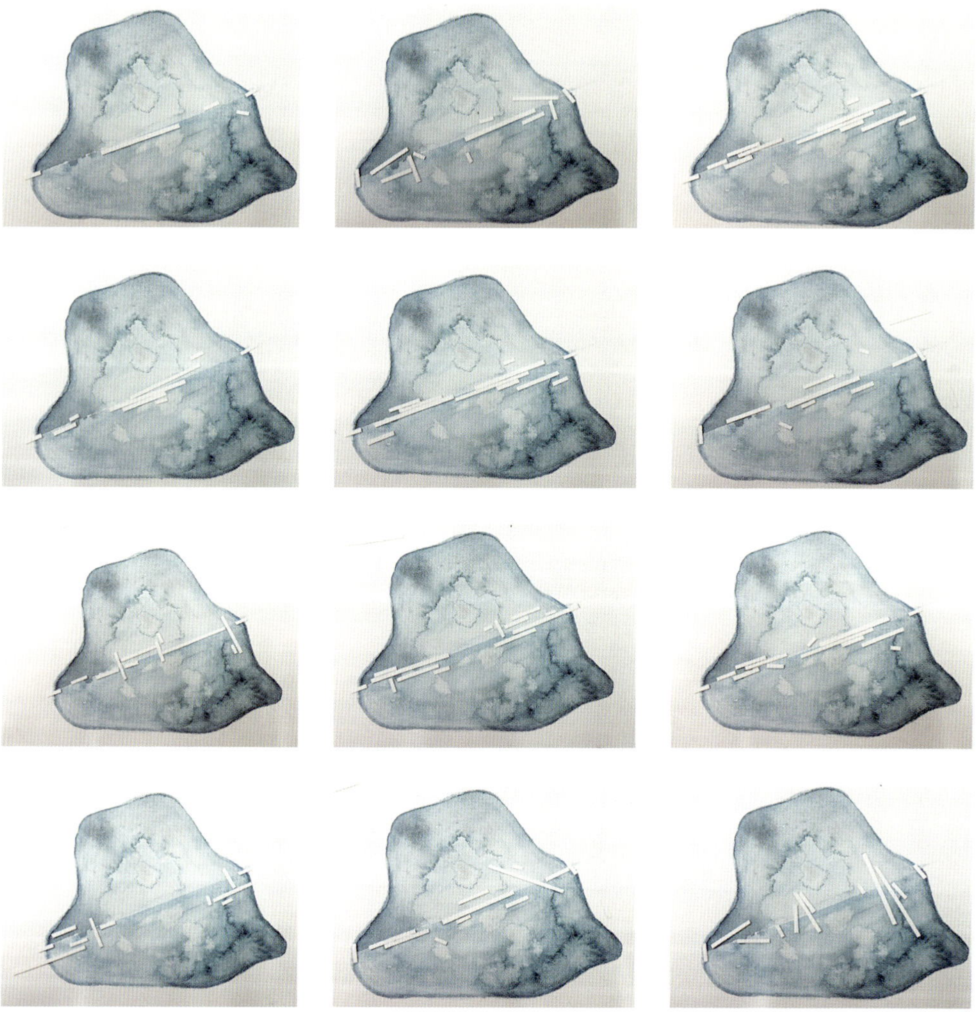

John Tubles (MArch II)

According to the Beijing Master Plan 2004–2020, the metropolitan region will evolve into a polycentric structure, with "two axes, two belts, and multiple centers." The axes run east-west and north-south, crossing at central Beijing. Multiple centers refer to points of density and commercial activity within the broader field of mixed-use urban development. Haidian district is noted for its educational resources and high-tech and scientific research developments, and the official Haidian district plan calls for the expansion of these specialized industries, coupled with residential new towns, and preservation of important open-space and ecological reserves. Nansha River runs through the town of Shangzhuang in the northern part of Haidian district. The studio focused on proposing new patterns for urban development in the area, starting from the concept of negative planning. The class used ecological infrastructure as an organizing system for the design of urban space. Within this area, environmental challenges include urban flooding, water pollution, and lack of basic services and infrastructure in urban villages. The project proposed the design of a mixed-use and mixed-income settlement along the Nanshahe River, which uses ecological infrastructure as a base on which to develop landscape and architectural forms.

Negative Planning in Nanshahe, Haidian District, Beijing

Kongjian Yu
Adrian Blackwell
Stephen Ervin

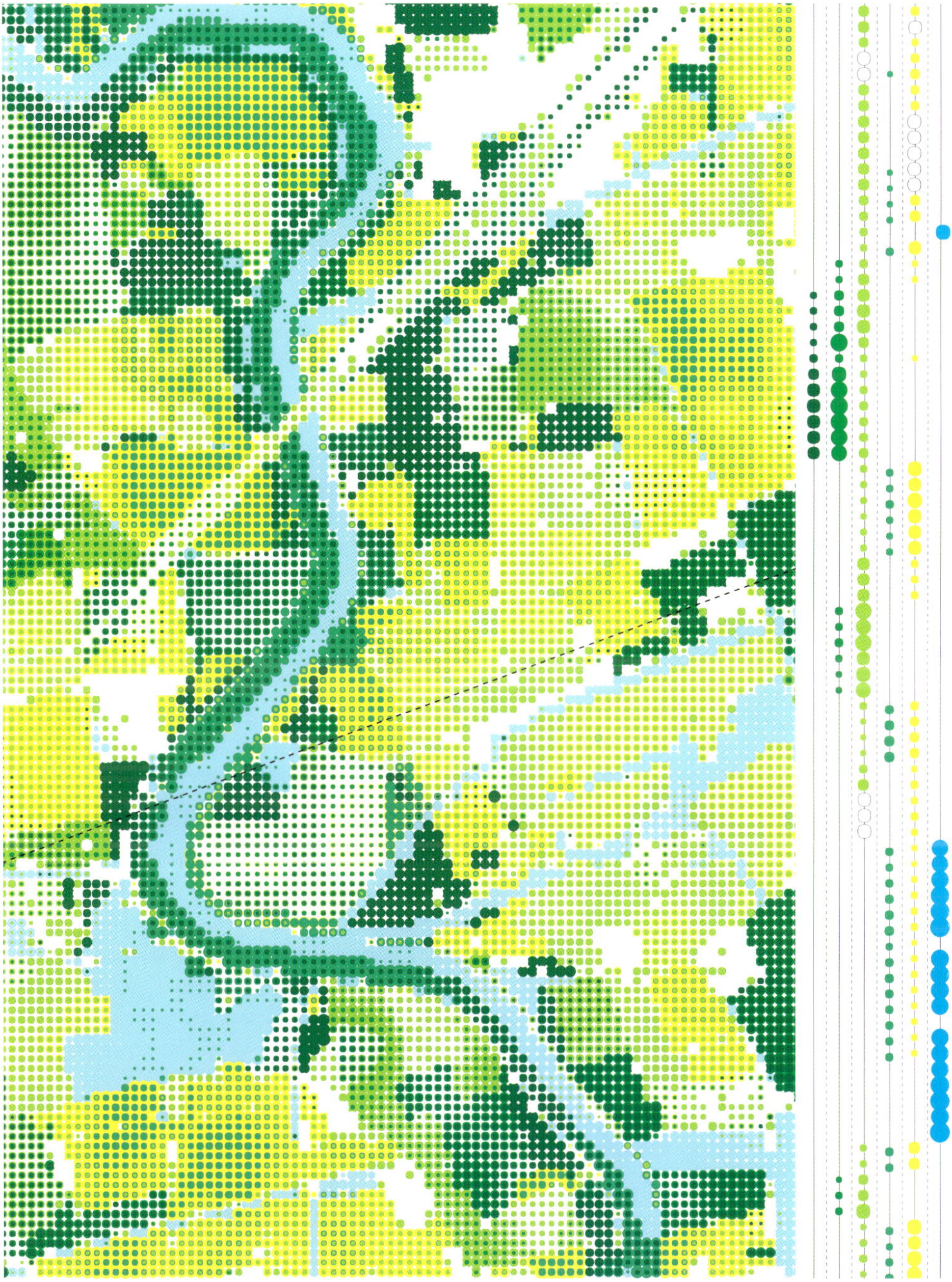

Jisoo Kim (MLA I) and Juan José Reyna Monrreal (MLA I AP). "Articulated Dispersion"

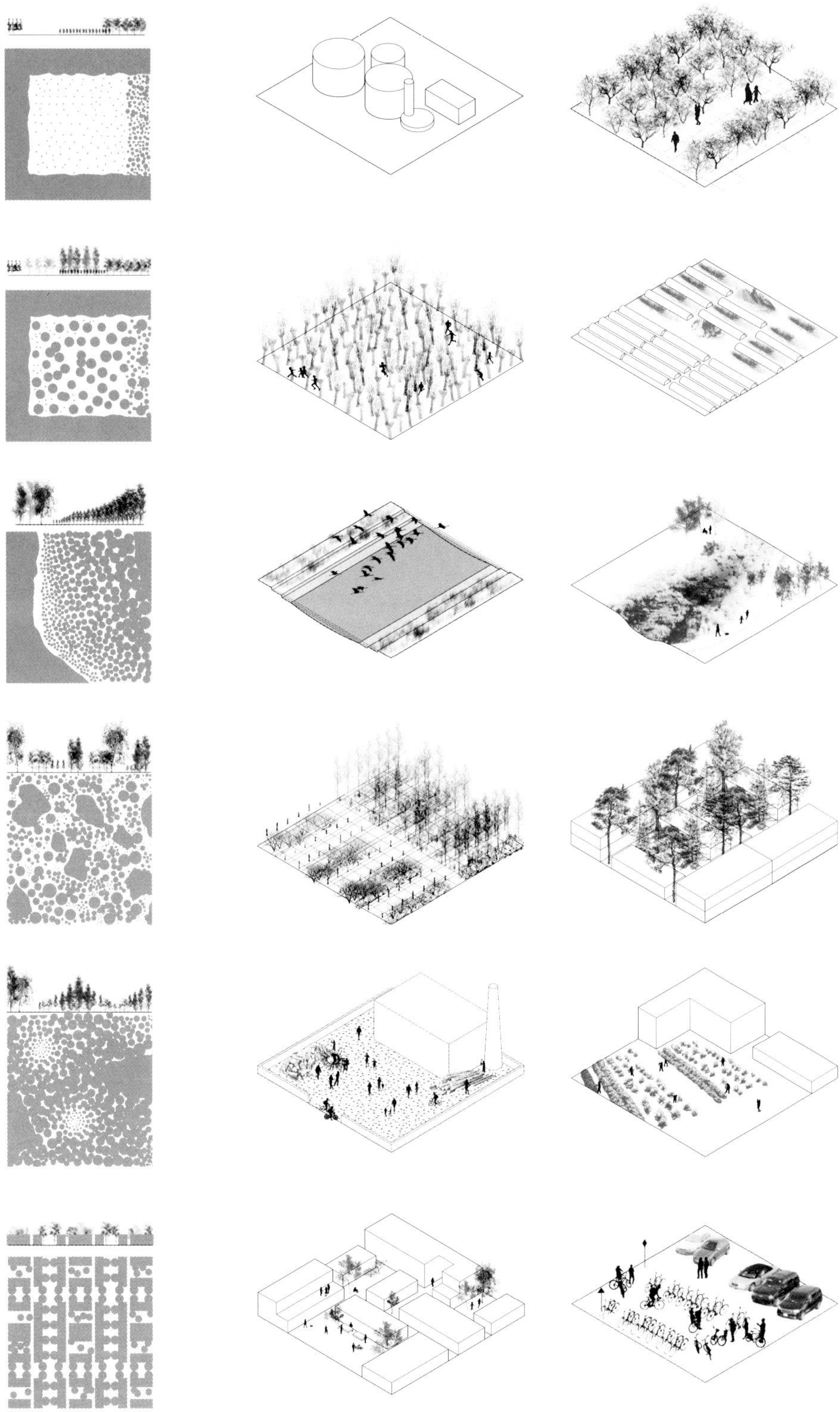

Erin Wythoff (MLA I) and Hannes Zander (MLA II), "From Black to Green"

The studio was premised on two fundamental ambitions: the recuperation of an idea of the city as a project, and the pursuit of alternative forms of urbanization in response to the challenges posed by the developmental city in China. The former treats the project of the city as a cultural and political act, the latter as a strategic project for urbanization, articulated through its architecture, landscape, and infrastructure. Macau was the second city studied by our three-year sponsored design studio in China. One of the defining characteristics of a city within a city-region is the way it frames its identity and competitiveness by emphasizing its difference in relation to other cities. This tendency causes neighboring cities to develop different yet complementary programs at their borders that trigger large daily surges of people across administrative boundaries. The studio was tasked with conceiving a border-crossing facility that acts as a common framework, accommodating housing, work spaces, and other provisions that Macau presently lacks. The studio defined the common framework as an architecture that reifies the idea of the city as a space of coexistence. It acts as a background that accommodates the plurality of city life and is in constant dialogue with its natural environment. It is most poignant when it is experienced and viewed as a whole, as a city—as a collective work of art.

Macau: Cross-Border Cities

Christopher Lee
Simon Whittle

Yun Fu (MArch I AP) and Chen Hao Lin (MArch II). "Collective Border"

Fabiana Alvear (MAUD), Hao Chen (MAUD), Jing Guo (MLA I AP). "Spaces of Exception"

Fabiana Alvear (MAUD), Hao Chen (MAUD), and Jing Guo (MLA I AP). "Spaces of Exception"

Joshua Schecter (MArch I) and Navajeet Kc (MArch I). "Marked Difference Inscribing the City of Parts"

"One of the defining characteristics of a city within a city-region is the way in which it frames its identity and competitiveness by emphasizing its difference in relation to other cities."

Cities cover 2 percent of the world's surface, yet generate 70 percent of the world's waste. Waste is not only trash, it's an intricate mix of social, environmental, and infrastructural outcomes that ensue at distinct scales, but overall waste is the outcome of bad design. The aim of the studio was to direct the problem to the designer's desk, where waste should be designed. Accepting waste as one of the fundamental inadequacies of design provides us with the "problem" for which we need to propose equitable and sustainable solutions. As designers, we attempt to streamline the process and systems by which waste is created, disposed of, and managed at both the human (individual) and urban (community) scales. Can designers improve and reduce the amount of waste? Can waste stimulate our creativity? The Networked Urbanism studio sought to bring interdisciplinary problem solving to the forefront of our work, providing an alternative to the traditional way of designing cities from a bird's-eye view and a single designer's perspective. The studio blended critical theory with hands-on practice, progressive thinking with social engagement, and research with reflection in action.

Networked Urbanism: Urban Waste, Urban Design

Belinda Tato
Jose Luis Vallejo

Scott Liang (MLA I AP), TJ McCourt (MUP), and Ben Scheerbarth (MUP). "Place Pixel"

This course explored the role that the architect/urban designer and urban landscape architect play under contemporary conditions and their capacity as agents of social transformation through design. We value architecture/design not only in itself but for what it produces—the social effects it can cause. We learned to anticipate and pre-define social actions within the public sphere through specific architecture, landscape, and urban design projects. We approached design in terms of its capabilities, going beyond its material or built condition. We looked at how it creates "side effects" for human well-being and how new social dynamics build a third space (porosity) in society where spatial negotiations for change can take place between policymakers and communities, allowing people to be active agents rather than passive viewers. Our tool was public buildings and conditions, with the aim of creating opportunities for social inclusion that can help improve the quality of life and generate economic competitiveness in the urban sphere. We focused on Medellin, Colombia, where public architecture has played a major role in social transformation. Projects engaged and interwove current public policies being developed by Medellin's authorities to create new models of intervention in emergent situations through architecture, urban design, and landscape design.

Medellin: Urban Porosity as Social Infrastructure—A Multidisciplinary Hub for Change

Giancarlo Mazzanti

Akihiro Moriya (MAUD) and Yuwen Tan (MAUD). "Micro Public Hub Hacking the Informal Construction System in Medellin"

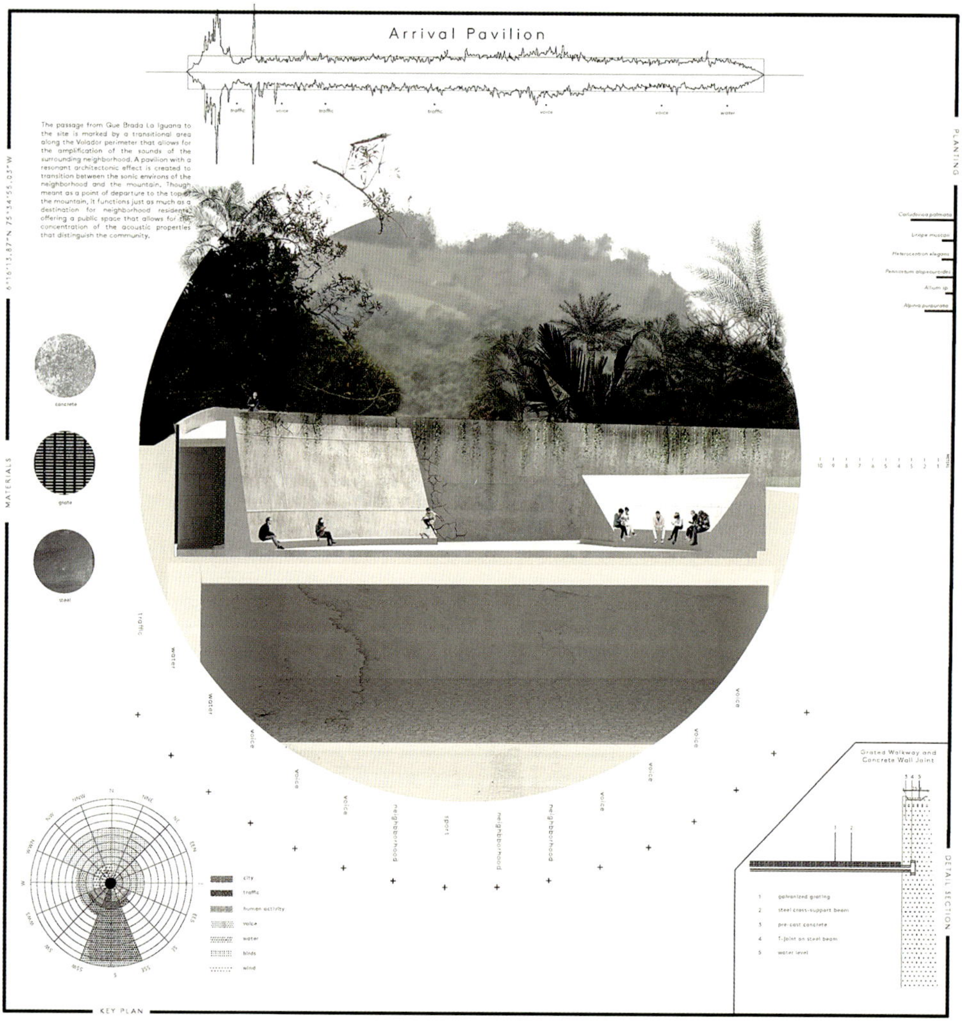

Carolyn Deuschle (MLA I) and Lauren Hamer (MLA I). "Toward a Sonic Landscape"

Intimate Room
Small rooms create spaces for intimate conversation, placing importance on the role and sound of the human voice.
MATERIALS
PLANTING
Vegetated Screen
DETAIL SECTION
KEY PLAN

© Justin Knight, 2013. Niklas Ekstedt cooks for the final review of the option studio led by Shohei Shigematsu and Christy Cheng

The Salvaged Stadium
Yaohua Wang (MArch II)
James Templeton Kelley Prize
Advisor: Preston Scott Cohen

Let's begin with a joke. A man goes into a restaurant and asks the waitress, "Can I have a coffee without milk, please?" The waitress answers, "Sorry, we don't have milk today. Can I give you a coffee without cream?" For me, this is a very interesting moment. It reveals that what you don't get also defines what you do get—the hidden dimension behind the appearance. How could architecture gain this hidden dimension, beyond the physical form?

Here, I offer an option. This option unfolds through a narrative, presented in the form of a comic story. This story is a case study situated in China's hyper-development and top-heavy political climate. It's a story happening in a fictional Chinese city.

The focus of this story is an Olympic stadium. The design appears to meet the need for a building for a one-time blossoming—a national icon showing off the power and leadership of the central government. At the same time, it also hides a slippery future. It's a story about how an Olympic stadium got salvaged. In the end, however, maybe you will find out that this is more than a simple salvation.

There is an old Chinese phrase that means being "fish on somebody's chopping block." It is used to describe a passive situation

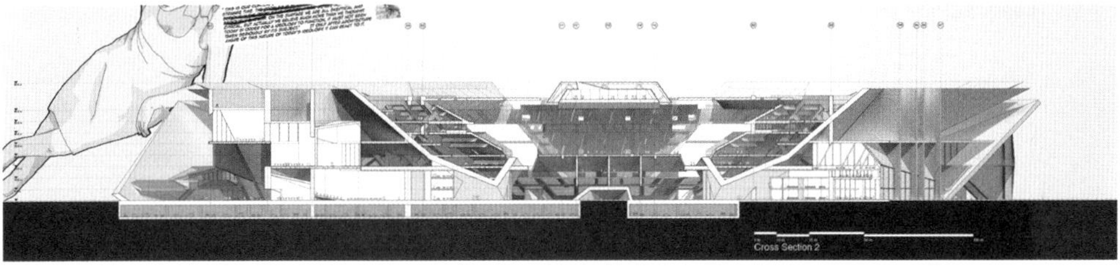

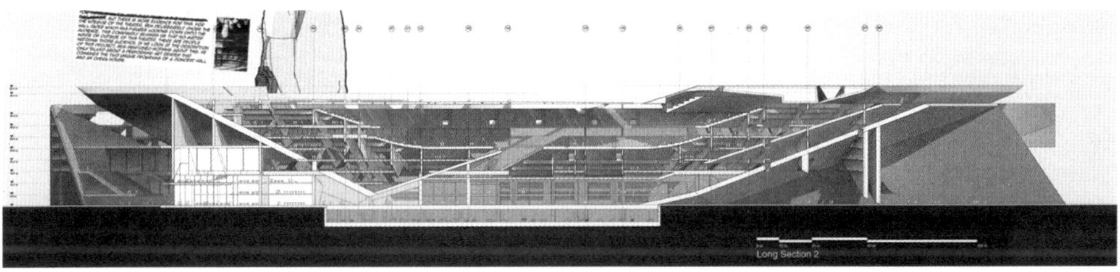

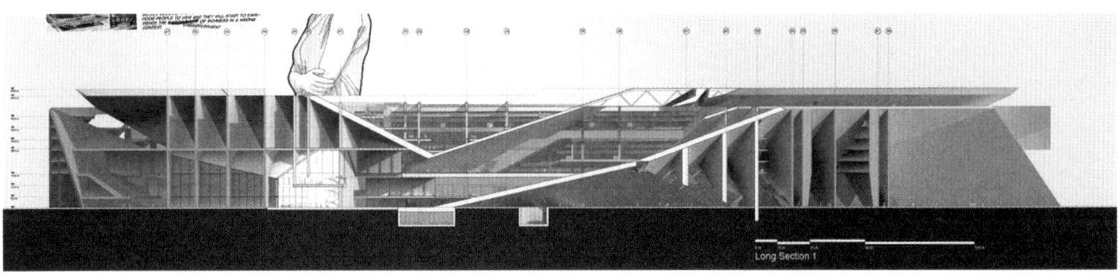

that you might find yourself in. Unfortunately, before the people with real power, we architects often find ourselves in this kind of situation. So when you are just a fish, you better be a little bit slippery. Be aware of your situation, and then find a way to make a comeback.

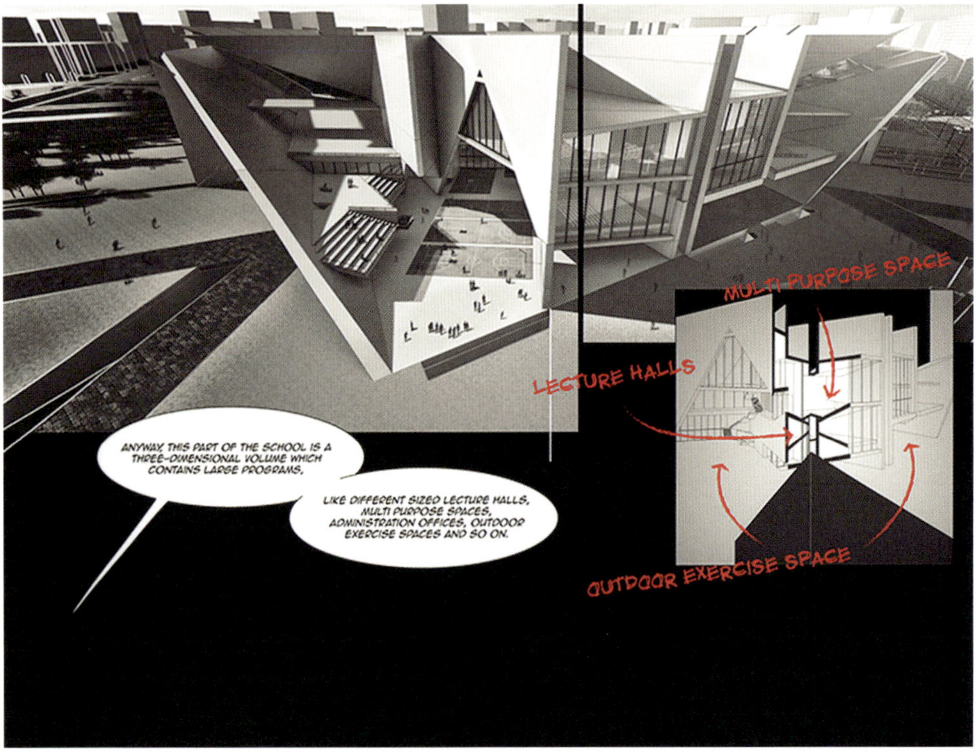
ANYWAY, THIS PART OF THE SCHOOL IS A THREE-DIMENSIONAL VOLUME WHICH CONTAINS LARGE PROGRAMS,
LIKE DIFFERENT SIZED LECTURE HALLS, MULTI PURPOSE SPACES, ADMINISTRATION OFFICES, OUTDOOR EXERCISE SPACES AND SO ON.
MULTI PURPOSE SPACE
LECTURE HALLS
OUTDOOR EXERCISE SPACE

THE GROUND FLOOR IS THE LOBBY, DISCUSSION AND MIXED USE AREAS WITH SMALL SEMINAR ROOMS ON THE SIDE.
THE LIBRARY HAS THREE MAJOR LEVELS... THE BOOK STORAGES ARE ON THE TOP. ON THE SECOND FLOOR IS THE READING ROOM AND STUDY AREA.
NOW WE ARE ON THE SECOND FLOOR OF THE LIBRARY.
BOOK STORAGES
READING ROOM AND STUDY AREA
LOBBY, DISCUSSION AND MIX USED AREAS

Collin Daniel Barrington Gardner (MArch I AP)
Advisors: Antoine Picon and Ingeborg Rocker

This thesis is about authorship. It is a thought experiment in search of an opening. It is an attempt at formalizing something that will forever resist formalization. The aim is to outline a framework for thinking about authorial stances and to trace how these stances produce theoretical and practical dilemmas for contemporary architects.

Michael Peguero (MArch I)
Advisor: Timothy Hyde

Viewing images of spaces, capturing images of spaces on our phones, uploading images of spaces to our Instagram accounts, navigating through the city from our phones—we spend an increasing amount of time spatially engaging and adding to universal data through the medium of the screen. UX.POSTXT explores the potential of this data for collective space making.

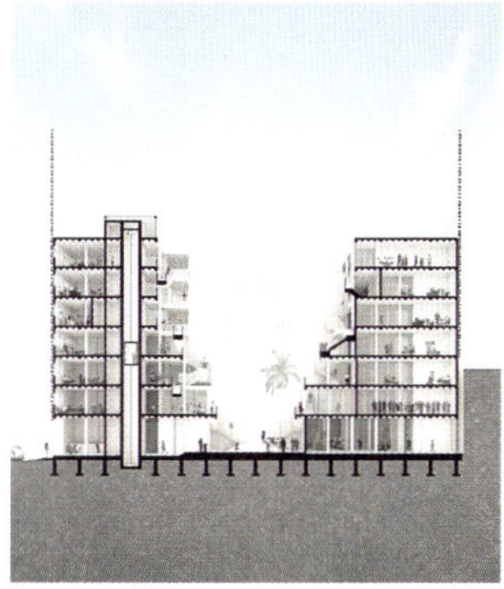

Joanna Rodriguez-Noyola (MArch I)
Advisor: Mack Scogin

All architectural projection is science fiction: informed speculation about an imaginary yet likely future. The Ministry of Illicit Technologies is such a projection: an institution existing in a collectively imaginable near future in Cuba. The narrative that generated the project showcases the layers of simultaneous, non-synchronous, surreal realities of Havana.

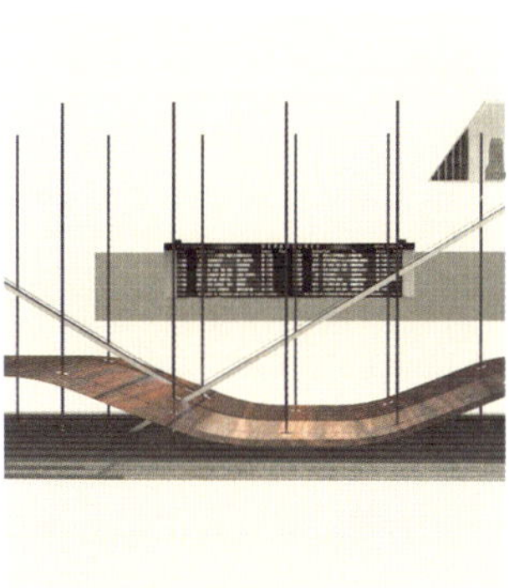

Elle Gerdeman (MArch I)
Advisors: Eric Höweler and Ingeborg Rocker

Within the field of architecture, there is a divide between those who celebrate the influx of consumptive tendencies, who embrace the generic, and those who ignore it. By exploring consumption in its most pure typological form, shopping, I intend to highlight and subvert architecture as both spatially and physically consumed.

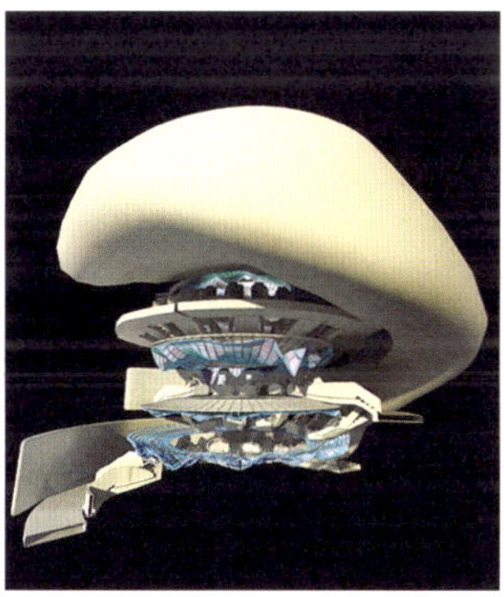

Joanna-Maria Helinurm (MArch II)
Advisor: Sanford Kwinter

Technological innovation is said to be the leading force behind the development of economy and society. While taking care that architecture not take measures as extreme as those that the Behaviorists used, a better understanding of how different brains function can enrich and enhance the uniqueness and individuality of the users, ultimately opening unexpected paths to innovation.

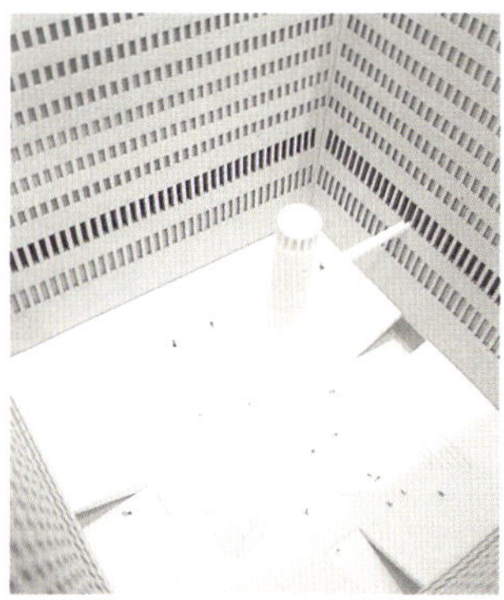

Jennifer Ly (MArch I AP)
Advisor: Florian Idenburg

With data growing at an exponential rate, questions of its physical manifestation in the built environment become unavoidable. This thesis considers the legibility of monumentality as the architectural means to confront the ostensibly immaterial. The Monument for Personal Data in Lower Manhattan is a project that explores the mechanisms of legibility to produce a heightened awareness of the data within.

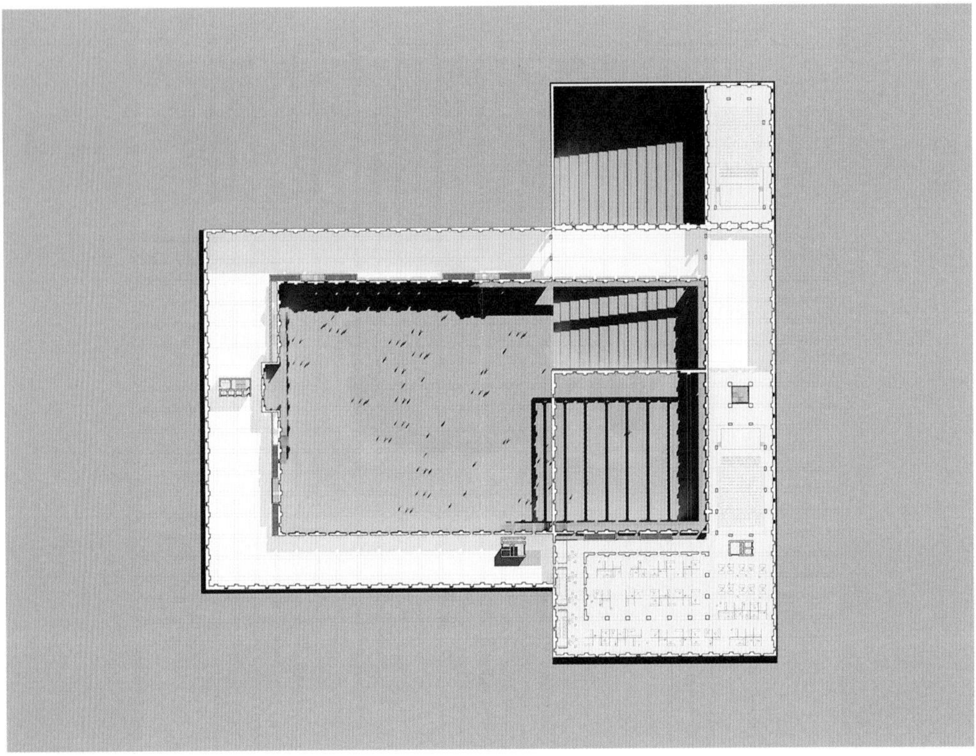

With(out) Memory | Uncanny Reflections
<u>Linda Yifei Zhang</u> (MArch I AP)
James Templeton Kelley Prize
Advisor: Mack Scogin

The uncanny, as a vehicle for architectural design, offers a means of addressing memory and constructing identity that simultaneously conjures and negates history: with (out) memory. It offers a means of addressing the incommensurability between the binary opposition of memory and active forgetting, between the fabrication of history and an equally fictitious severance from the past, between nostalgia and amnesia, between reconstruction and development. Utilizing the concept of the uncanny, the thesis moves beyond this hierarchical distinction by constituting identity through the logic of both/and, which is beyond actual history and beyond the stabilization of false memories. It destabilizes the imagined unity of self by placing exteriority at the center, at the interior; the foreigner comes from within, the other is actually another—another you. The uncanny unsettles and questions origins rather than constructing false new origins. It emerges as a toxic outgrowth of Enlightenment rationality, with the emergence of modern nation-states based on an imaginary logic of identification.

Reconciling the Everglades Edge
Victor Perez-Amado
(MArch I/MAUD)
Clifford Prize
Advisor: Leire Asensio Villoria

This thesis seeks to capitalize on this fragile border and threshold and sees an opportunity to retool dated infrastructures by designing new dynamic, flexible, and adaptive urban interfaces between the Everglades and its urban contexts.

This thesis aims to convert the back-swamps of Southern Florida into a new and resilient frontage for the city, blurring artificial and engineered boundaries between the Everglades and the city, creating an interface capable of knitting the park with its urban contexts and offering a cultural connection to one of the largest parks in the United States. This thesis seeks to create architectural and urban design typologies capable of responding to the surroundings and coupled with soft infrastructures, flooding control, and natural water fluctuation techniques to provide a landscape and cultural experience of the Everglades.

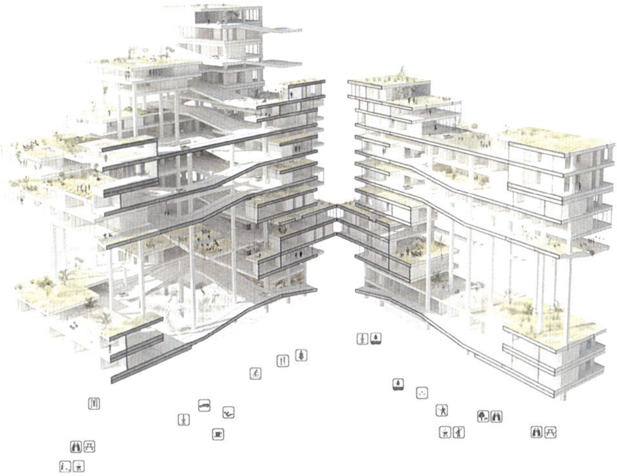

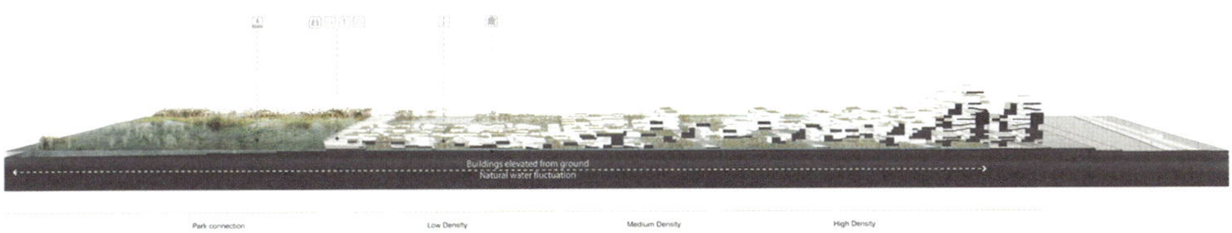
Buildings elevated from ground
Natural water fluctuation
Park connection
Low Density
Medium Density
High Density

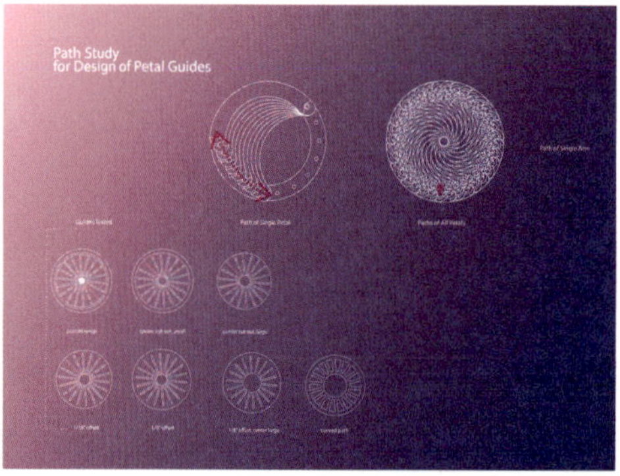

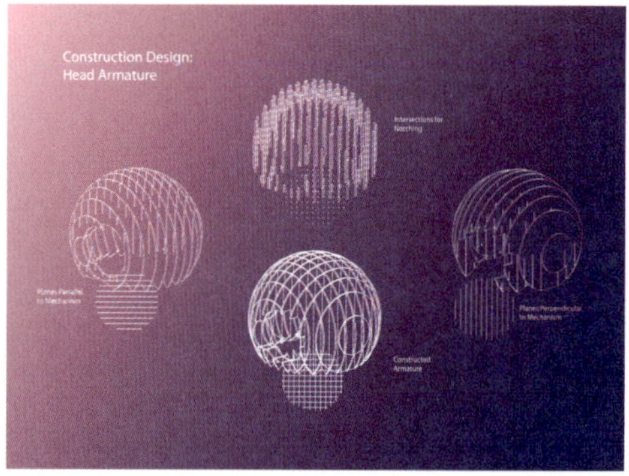

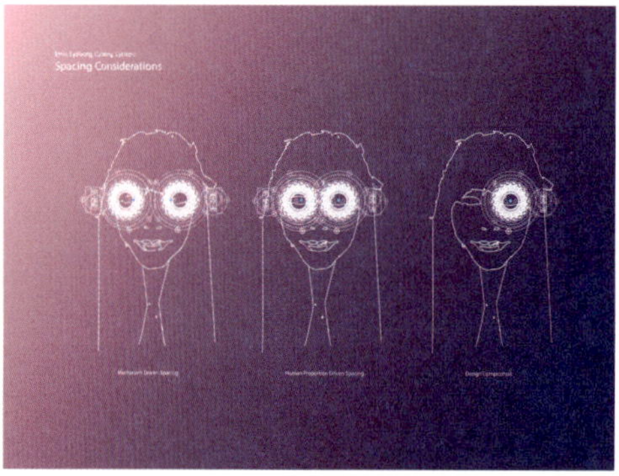

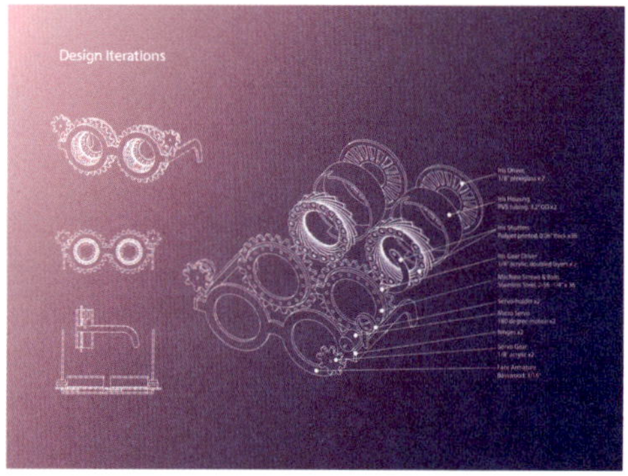

**Cultural Prosthetics:
Didactic Provocations for
Reprogramming Perception**
Anne Liu (MArch I)
**Advisors: Ingeborg Rocker
and Krzysztof Wodiczko**

What is architecture divorced from building? In exploring this provocation, we come to reevaluate the context and agency of the architect practicing in an era of relentless technological advancement. Architecture has historically been an essential manifestation and expression of humanity. Today, a new media of technological determinism has emerged, challenging the current paradigm of architecture. Architecture itself needs to broaden its definitions to recapture its relevance.

Technology has become the ultimate prosthetic. All technology has become assistive technology, and we are living with a myth of digital autonomy. Since the beginning of time, humans have been creating devices and methods to enhance natural abilities, amalgamating technology until it has ultimately become an extension of ourselves. In recent times this augmentation has allowed us to evolve ourselves with ever-increasing speed, to possess engineered abilities that no other species has ever had. This interaction between humanity and technology has fundamentally changed who we are, impacting our abilities, our perception, and the very makeup of our cognitive organization. We are on the cusp of a second wave of body modification,

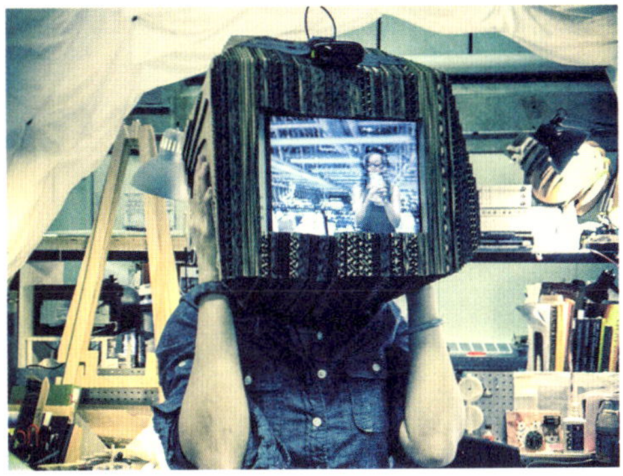

a new wave of industrialization: the next hacking frontier is the body. Thus through prosthetics, on the body itself, has emerged the ultimate site for projections of utopia.

The aim of this thesis is to produce work that expresses current cultural changes and critically reflect our reality, in which technology has become a cultural prosthesis and extension of humanity. To achieve this, I began by examining and reprogramming our conduits of perception. Perception is fundamental to architecture, as it is through our bodies, sensorial organs, and cognition that architectural experiences exist. The artifacts produced by the research of this thesis reconstruct spatial perception from within the human sensory system, becoming a means of forcing us to reconsider the very constructs of our own points of view.

The discourse of philosophers, design theorists, anthropologists, and architects in the last decade has concerned itself with the dissolution of the self, coining terms such as posthumanism, noosphere, and cybernetic organism. This thesis reconfigures technology to address what technology has stripped from our identities as humans, including interdependency, patience, slowness, physical interaction, and engagement in the present moment. Capitalism has manufactured numerous commercial technologies to increase productivity and manage our time. But is there technology that helps us manage our emotions? Can wearable technology extend dignity? Could we develop

technology that protects us from technology itself?

It is my stance that technology co-creates: machines are not taking over, but they can help us become more human. My thesis is not concerned with the metaphor, semiotics, or aesthetics of technology. Instead I employ prosthetics as a tool to apply a social and cultural lens to the effects of technology, using the same medium as the message: technology. Through investigating systems of perception, this thesis aims to reframe and reveal a more nuanced and ineffable understanding of the human experience within our networked cultural and spatial constructs, both as inhabitants and designers.

01 Krzysztof Wodiczko coined the term "Cultural Prosthetics"

02 Thesis Prep Classes: Art, Design and the Public Domain, Krzysztof Wodiczko, Fall 2013 Project Development, Transformable Design Methods Class, Chuck Hoberman, Fall 2013

Chana Haouzi (MArch II)
Advisor: Mack Scogin

Despite modernity's obsession with function and measurable results, any truly meaningful contribution to architecture begins within uselessness, in the space beyond function. The thesis confronts the calculated performance of an active reservoir in downtown Montreal by creating a purely useless moment in the city, yet one capable of representing greater powers and larger meanings.

Michael Burton (MArch I)
Advisors: Cameron Wu and Andrew Witt

This thesis invents a new mode of kinetic design. The flexagon system allows for variation in geometry and arrangement of a series of tetrahedrons that cyclically rotate and tumble, redefining the space. Within this system, variations on the tetrahedrons can start to emulate floors, walls, and ceilings, invoking a transformative architecture.

Rachel Dao (MArch I)
Advisor: Cameron Wu

The urban mosque is situated within an evolving historical and typological narrative, liturgical and site constraints, and a range of visual expressions. Developed within a preexisting structure, the mosque becomes a key to the design of the whole, mediating between the needs of the secular and the requirements of the sacred while addressing Islam's image in New York City.

Joe Liao (MArch I)
Advisor: Panagiotis Michalatos

What are the ethical responsibilities of an architect? The luring glory of publications has heightened architectural concerns for beautiful images; novel fabrication technologies are ever-more liberating and seductive. Resisting such temptations, this is a real architecture project for people who are dear to me, with constraints I must confront and a burden of privilege I cannot ignore.

Sunggi Park (MArch I AP)
Advisor: Eric Höweler

Infrastructure can be understood as a permanent installation addressing a functional necessity. The old paradigm evaluated transport infrastructure primarily on efficiency, speed, and affordability, yet traffic congestion, maintenance deferrals, and a lack of mobility for nondrivers followed as problems. How can we utilize obsolete transport infrastructure while improving traffic flow and lessening congestion?

Katherine Chin (MArch I)
Advisor: Maryann Thompson

The double-loaded corridor ubiquitous in the American multifamily housing market, is often overlooked as merely a developer's tool to increase efficiency and achieve a high financial return on investment. This thesis investigates how the corridor, commonly considered a leftover space, can be shaped into a civic realm in multifamily housing to support the needs of a modern family structure.

Daniel Urban Kiley Lecture:
James Corner
April 15, 2014

"[...] If I, in Field Operations, have been associated in the past with themes of productive, working landscapes, with time-based landscapes, with indeterminacy and process, with unfinished ecological processes of landscape that evolve and grow complexity over time, broader models of landscape urbanism, then this is probably, for the most part, still true. All themes tied to systematic and pragmatic thinking, as well as to poetic experience through occupation and use. The kind of focus I wanted to hit on tonight is the equal importance of form, design, spectacle, and delight, especially in the urban public realm. These are the ingredients that fire up the imagination, inspire the public toward new forms of interaction with the natural world, and are perhaps ultimately the most powerful ecological instruments we have in forging more symbiotic forms of urban settlement, and environmental responsibility. [...] Design is an ingredient in the charging up of ecological and social enrichment. And the urban public realm is perhaps the most critical and urgent for design's import right now."

"[...] As political theorist Benjamin Barber asserts, 'We understand cities as naturally conducive to public space because we understand them to be ur-democratic spaces. Their diversity mandates tolerance; their openness invites immigration from without and mobility from

© Katherine Taylor, 2014.

"Design is an ingredient in the charging up of ecological and social enrichment."

within; their interdependence makes their borders porous and their behavior interactional and transactional; their friction-inducing density ignites imagination and creativity; their anonymity and liberty inspire innovation and entrepreneurship.'

He's arguing for the primacy and the importance of the public realm in the city today, and he goes on to lament the increased loss of the public realm, through surveillance, and through over-regulation of public space. However, with regard to his notion of interdependence, codependence, transactional porosity issues in the city, you could say the same for a healthy ecosystem. Its very systematization is what produces bewildering effects, qualities, and changes over time. Similarly the city, and especially the urban public realm, is a designed ecosystem that demands porosity, mobility, interconnectedness, and a sort of open platform that is both anonymous and spectacular in its effects."

"This is the most urgent task for contemporary landscape architecture, landscape urbanism, and design more broadly, and I urge you all to work hard to make our public realm what it needs to be."

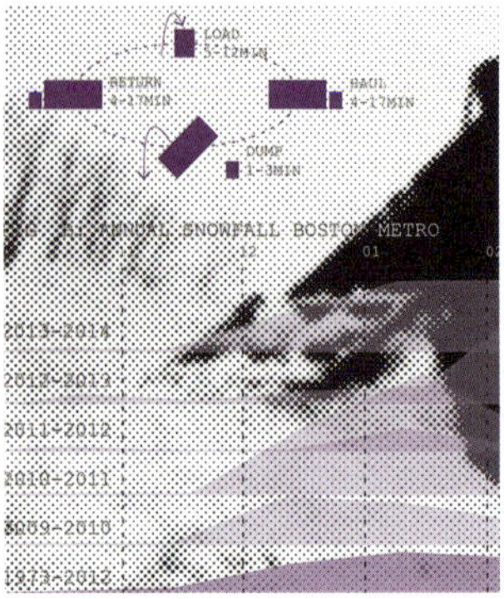

Cali Pfaff (MLA I)
Advisor: Jane Hutton

The procedures and protocols that make up a city's maintenance regime have profound spatial implications. Flora and fauna expand and contract; invisible boundaries, such as city limits, become legible; and aesthetic preferences are codified. These practices are so commonplace that they largely go unseen. This thesis reimagines maintenance as a generative rather than suppressive force for at-risk urban ecologies. Using networked test sites along the rail corridor in Somerville, Massachusetts, an examination of these practices aims to expand habitat for a target population (pollinator species) while testing the bounds of acceptability for wildness in urban landscapes. Counter-ordinance explores three types of maintenance practiced by Somerville's Department of Public Works: snow removal, overgrowth management, and wildlife management. By aligning plant palette with a specific maintenance practice and pollinator population, color becomes a signifier of intentionality, counterbalancing the necessary disorder of habitat. Ultimately, this project looks at how targeted revisions of established practices can have immense impacts on the quality, biodiversity, and craftsmanship of public landscapes, as well as how we perceive them.

Gabriella Rodríguez (MLA I / MLAUD)
Advisor: Silvia Benedito

"The act of crossing space stems from the natural necessity to move to find the food and information required for survival. But once the basic needs have been satisfied, walking takes on a symbolic form that has enabled man to dwell in the world. By modifying the sense of the place crossed, walking becomes man's first aesthetic act, penetrating the territories' chaos, constructing an order on which to develop the architecture of situated objects.."
—Francesco Careri, *Walkscapes* (2002)

Referencing the Puerto Rican territory across multiple scales of engagement by unraveling a territorial narrative, in abstraction, through close interaction with the specific, this thesis proposes a 90-kilometer transecting walkway through the western part of Puerto Rico. Experiencing the island through the walker's perspective reveals the often overlooked and neglected aspects of the territory. The nuances in the transitions and shifts through the Puerto Rican landscape are essential to the structure of the sequences choreographed across the proposed transect, in which multiple types of walking and engagement take form. By engaging the land with a haptic consciousness, a new geography emerges, unfolding through time and in motion. This thesis explores a contemporary notion of landscape as journey.

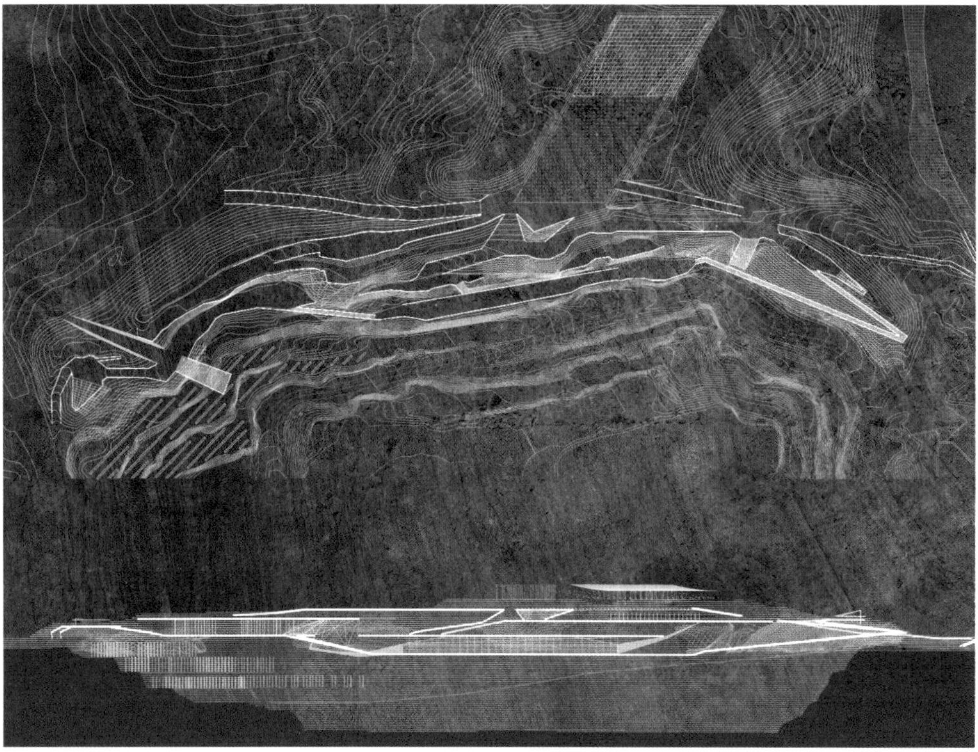

Incomplete Landscapes:
Quarries as Cyclic Terrain
Cara Walsh (MLA I)
Advisor: Anita Berrizbeitia

Incomplete Landscapes explores the potential to reconceive aggregate quarry futures in urban contexts from a conversation of post-use and closure to the possibility of continuous use and hybrid occupation over multiple scales of time.

Active landscapes of aggregate extraction are necessary features in any urban land-use mosaic, as they supply the materials needed to build and rebuild the cities that have grown around them, yet they remain squarely and intentionally out of view of the public.

The project emphasizes both the intent of continuous use and flexibility of these sites (a flexibility inherent in urban ground), reimagined and overlaid with hybrid uses. These uses themselves can expand or contract based on the fluctuations of economy and incident. Yet they also question what it means to design under terms that are not finite or complete, conditions that can be built and rebuilt, assembled and disassembled—pretenses under which landscape architectural projects are not generally conceived.

The project explores the incomplete at several scales. As fragment, the quarry is a landscape that is in constant metabolic flux with the city around it and its own resultant internal topographic register.

As overlay, hybrid program connects public and private space that would otherwise be left as terrain vague. As insertion, light structures are designed to support slopes, to make the unoccupiable occupiable, to promote vegetative growth (while material specificity is calibrated to a gradient of permanence), under the pretense that quarry operations may need to expand in the future.

Finally, as experience, the cumulative effect of topography, industrial ruin, access to the monumental, and ambiguity of typology results in a singular experience within a public space.

Employing the measured scale of quarry operations alongside the tools of the landscape architect—through earth moving, planting, accessibility, and the design of experience—the thesis exploits the borrowed landscape of the quarry to cobble together a new shared landscape of production and experience in the public realm.

01 Geometrical Connection
02 The Archipelago of Floating Villages
03 Linear Rural Development
04 Organized Uses and Linear Development
05 Informal Configuration and Edge Public Uses
06 Informal Configuration
07 Floating Urbanization
08 Public Interfaces

01

02

03

04

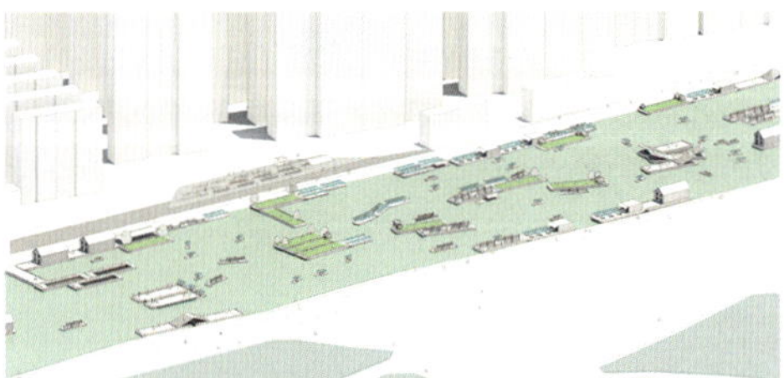

05

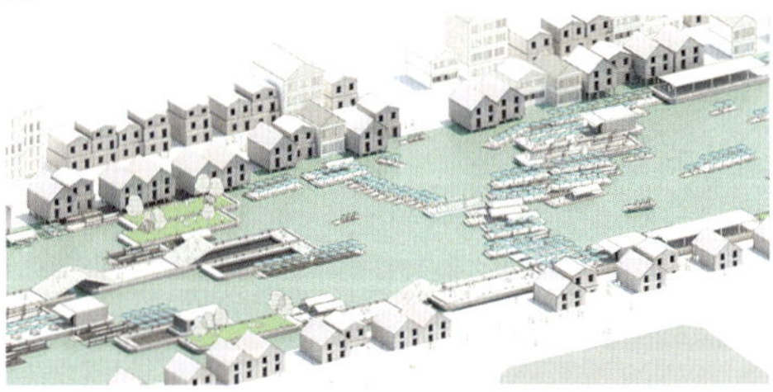

06

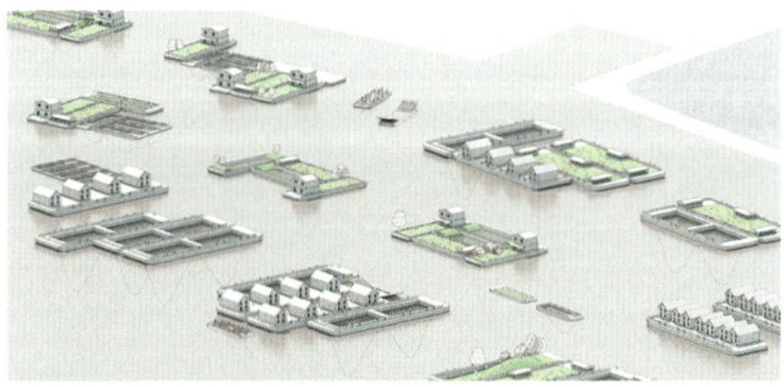

07

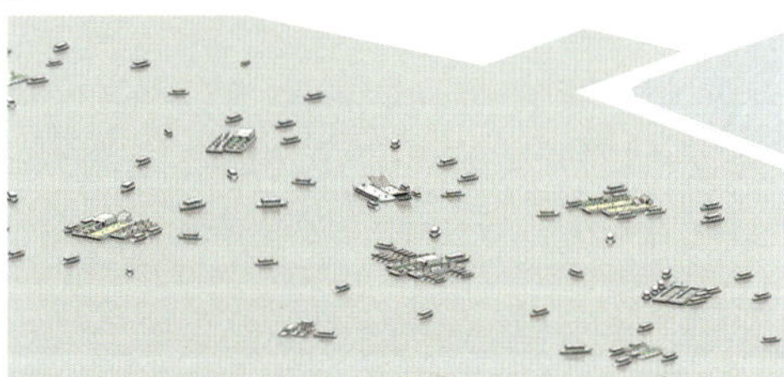

08

Traversal Landscape: Curating a New Public Realm in the Pearl River Delta
Taehyung Park (MLA I AP)
Advisor: David Mah

This thesis addresses four questions. 1. "How can we develop public realms in contemporary growing cities shaped in between extreme industrialization of landscape and urbanization?"

The territory of the Pearl River Delta has been transformed into a landscape machine for globalized seafood production. Meanwhile, relentless urbanization has been deployed over the territory without any evidence of how the relationship between the region's urbanization and its aquacultural landscapes may be organized. This tension between urbanization and industrialization of landscape raises questions as to how landscape architects can design a new form of public realm in this hyperdense mixture.

2. "Can we design a new model of public realm that generates vibrant interfaces across dynamic and fragile urban conditions?"

Traversal Landscape rejects developing general landscape types as a form of public realm. This intermixed urban landscape needs a new model of public space. The thesis imagines landscape as a medium for projecting public realms across the Pearl River Delta's urban environment and aquacultural landscape. The ambition is to leverage the fragmented urban conditions to set a relation between infrastructures and the

mobile cultural practices that shape the Pearl River Delta's lifestyles. It is envisioning an extreme and radical collective form of public culture.

3. "What if we speculate to develop mobile landscapes that catalyze cultural practices and public life, acting like a parasite activating all over the territories as an alternative form of public realm?"

The thesis aims to design traversal platforms that can be deployed across the territories of the Pearl River Delta for opportunistic and flexible public uses—a model that synergizes a temporal mode of vernacular as well as urbanized lifestyles. Typologies of platforms can be deployed in a wide range of different strategies all over the territories. The ranges of spatial configuration begin from highly common and informal forms of public uses—a bottom-up way of configuration and operation to rigid and geometrical top-down forms. The platforms navigate beyond existing commonalities to create public vibrancy that can catalyze the archipelago of the floating cultures.

4. "And, in the end, can it drive a parasitic urbanism that may inform how we shape adaptive and temporal forms of urban spatial realms?"

I explore three scenarios of the sites based on the feasible scale and varied forms of water infrastructure, lifestyle, economies, and level of urbanization. The scenarios envision how floating public realms catalyze not only interface of lifestyles but also drive a new form

of urbanization. It mobilizes the idea of a "typical" public realm as a constellation of individuality that may culminate in a model for a new shared territorial lifestyle.

01

02

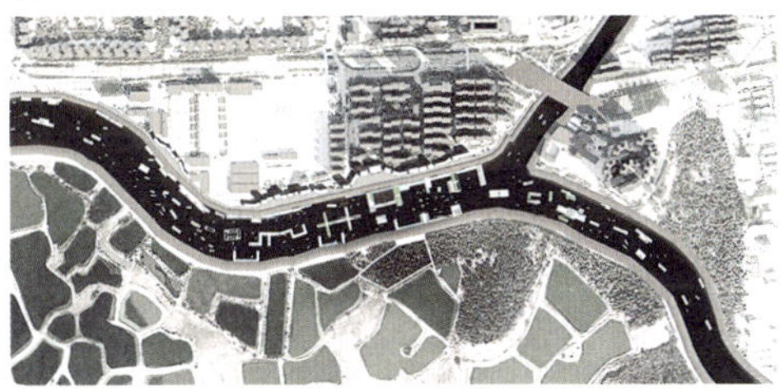

03

01 Floating Urbaniztion in Dongguan, Guangdong
02 Floating Public Space and Rural Development in Nansha Island, Guangzhou
03 Projecting to Urban Waterfront and Linear Development in Shenzhen River, Guangdong

"...it is possible
to design openness
in a city..."

Lecture: Richard Sennett
The Open City
September 09, 2013

"[...] For me, my thinking about urbanism has moved from, if you like, the Jane Jacobs's view to something that wants to take [Lewis] Mumford—not take his side, but to take seriously the notion that urbanism is not just about spontaneity, it's not just about the local, and most of all that design itself can make a city that has a socialist character. That's the long prelude to explain why I got interested in open city issues, and in open systems, which are systems designed to be open, to be complex, and that can scale up. Which is, I think, is the business we're in, which is scaling up."

"[...] But what an open city is dealing with is that it takes noise seriously—all those elements of disruption, chaos emergence, latent consequences, which deform a system. And I don't think that those can be understood simply in terms of freedom of form. I think they have a shape."

"[...] To understand about emergence, and more largely about open systems—they focus on immanence rather than transcendence. They are not about vision, literally and figuratively. They are not about having a vision of what society should be. And just to bring that idea up to date, emergence is about the interaction of practice and form. [...] This is a real issue for us, about design. In a city, emergence occurs when density and adjacency combine. And the chemical reaction depends on putting unlikes close to each other. How they'll interact is open. [...] But the idea is, you don't know what's going to happen. It's immanent, rather than a transcendent ideal of form." Furthermore, in terms of time, they must be co-present rather than serial, these conditions of density and adjacency. This is against the idea of the fill-in, which is the Garden City idea of urban development. And it's a trope for us in urbanism, that gradually, diverse people or functions are brought near to each other. That's a serial form of management, of adjacency and density. Co-present, rather than serial, means that you are willing to take the risk of something being there all at once, that you know you're not regulating the staging of an event. And co-presence assumes that density and adjacency have different functions in particular, intertwined from the start. And this is how we produce an urban habitus."

"[...] My view of what happens when a city really works as an open system is that you scale up. You can sometimes scale down, and keep it open. But more normally, scaling down is a form of closure, and scaling up is a form of openness in this way. I hope this is enough to give you an idea of what I mean by an open city. It's based on systems theory. I think we have a lot to learn from it. It takes us beyond a debate that marked the middle of the twentieth century, about local versus design, and says that it is possible to design openness in a city, just as much as we do in certain forms of technology."

Too Many Plans: A Study of Rapid Urbanization and Its Management in Ulaanbaatar, Mongolia
Raven Anderson (MUP)
Advisor: Michael Hooper

This thesis uses the experience of Ulaanbaatar, Mongolia, as a lens to examine the process of urban planning as it is practiced in a rapidly urbanizing developing-world city. Ulaanbaatar is experiencing a unique set of urban problems, which diverse organizations have converged on the city to try to address. This thesis examines the strategies adopted by these actors as they seek to provide services to Ulaanbaatar's residents and combat the externalities imposed by rapid urban growth. Interviews were conducted with seventeen organizations working on urban development in Ulaanbaatar. The results demonstrate that, despite strong agreement about the problems facing the city, there is a lack of consensus about how best to tackle them. This has led to a proliferation of plans, as each organization obeys its own institutional prerogatives at the expense of widespread coordination. This is in line with longstanding theories regarding bureaucratic politics and culture. The interviews also suggest that local actors' perspectives on urban management are not reflected in many of the resulting plans or policy documents. Local government, for instance, responds to particular Mongolian perspectives on land use and housing, leading to a divergence between plans and implementation. This thesis argues that this divide between international development organizations and local actors is likely to lead to poor service provision and reduce the city's ability to cope with rapid urban change.

01

02

03

04

01 A Ger district Ulaanbaatar
02 Sunrise with air pollution
03 On the outskirts of Ulaanbaatar
04 Ger district industry

Afroditi Stathopoulou (MAUD)
Advisors: Hashim Sarkis and Luis Callejas

Charted territories that have transformed over time tend to present trajectories of persistent traces, which traverse land across ridges, in close relationship to its geography. Focusing on the Athens (Attica) region, the proposal regards these as carriers of change in the long term. The design entails a series of quasi-objects to reconstitute a collective narrative for the city.

Noam Dvir (MAUD)
Advisors: Hashim Sarkis and Judith Grant Long

This thesis is an original study of emerging patterns of vacation urbanism in the Mediterranean. The thesis introduces two core contributions: first, the identification of the Mediterranean Strip, and second, the extraction of three principal typologies of vacation urbanism that inhabit the basin, on both the continental side and the islands.

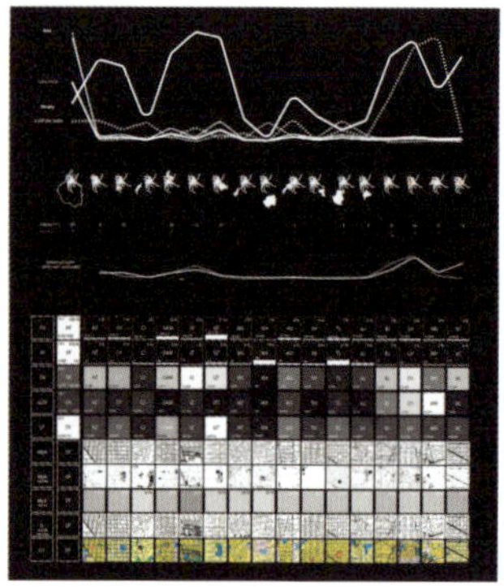

Miguel Lopez Melendez (MAUD)
Advisor: Joan Busquets

Morphologic is an analysis of the relation between population density and urban morphology. Using Mexico City as a case study, it questions how population density is measured today (giving equal value to each land unit). This analysis uses a new way to measure it that gives equal value to each person, suggesting the capacity of our cities in relation to urban form.

Beth Lundell Garver (MAUD)
Advisors: Alex Krieger and Peter Rowe

Sweet Limin[AL]ity explores how lessons from southern porch culture may inform new urban development strategies that extend the "sphere of belonging" from the domicile to the public arena. The thesis introduces several characters that serve to reframe public space in the narrative landscape of the Post-Panamax port city of Mobile, Alabama.

Santiago Orbea (MAUD)
Advisor: Hashim Sarkis

This thesis draws on western Quito's archaeological findings to extract urban design guidelines to organize the territory. The historic elements intersect with a recreational program to configure a new National Archaeological Park, bridging the current system and the ancient configuration to create an economical and sustainable space.

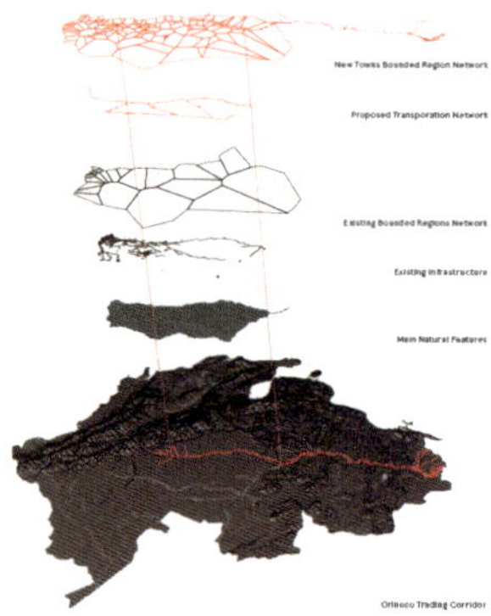

Manuela Guzmán Ramírez (MAUD)
Advisor: Joan Busquets

This framework developed a design tool that can be used for increasing the number and quality of populated areas in the Altillanura. Using a grid that categorizes the territory and a set of rules determined by proximity to and distance between urban and natural features, this thesis proposes a system that enables the emergence of new populated areas that promote productivity and environmental sustainability.

Neo-Volcanic Regional Orders: Eastern Mexico City and Repurposing Infrastructure as an Interface between the Territory and Architecture
Victor Manuel Rico Espínola (MAUD)
Advisors: Diane Davis and Hashim Sarkis

Focusing on Eastern Mexico City, this thesis is a projective reconstruction of a forgotten landscape by reintroducing water to the city's basin and by associating disparate infrastructural fragments into a coherent body, hence constituting a "return to the amphibious city." It is an example of how to protect cities from losing an overall sense of identity in the face of a pronounced horizontal growth across vast territories, while suggesting that infrastructures and thick-porous urban edges are tasked with interfacing between the scale of the territory and that of architecture.

Three historic phenomena help explain Mexico City's monstrous yet fascinating growth. 1) A sixteenth-century insistence on consolidating the capital in the middle of a lake culminates in its drainage. 2) Ambivalence about territorial ordering and connectivity between local and national politics in the aftermath of the 1910 revolution led to an industry-driven polarized growth that exacerbated squatter occupation on land "unsuitable for urbanization." 3) Efforts to impose social and spatial order in the modern era derived from ambiguous property rights and

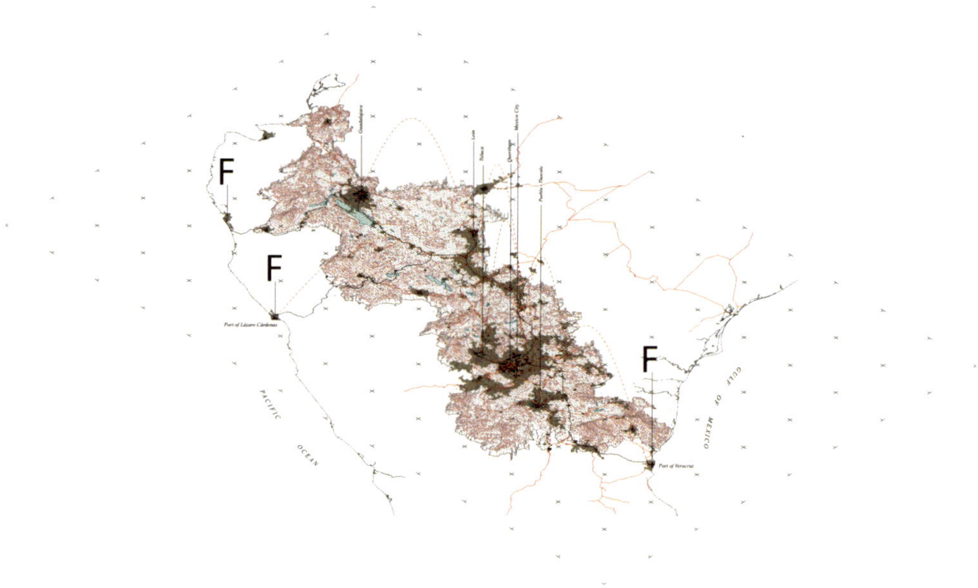

uneven distribution of urban services.

Overlooking ecological, scalar, and local cultural attributes in Mexico City led to a confrontation of the city with its geography, epitomized in the tremendous disparity between its east and west. Current processes of urbanization in Mexico differ from those of "suburbanization." New spatial forms show qualitative changes: spatial fragmentation of productive processes affecting rural areas, large cities dissolving into their hinterlands, the emergence of new centrality patterns, and a network of cities that interact unconstrained by distance. In Mexico, this is best exemplified in the emerging urban patterns along the Neo-Volcanic Axis. Decentralization policies, communication networks, and export-oriented infrastructures have reduced polarization of the dominant cities in the core region, giving way to one continuous city that stretches across 10,000 kilometers.

Under the allegory of Mexico's mythic relationship between its volcanoes and lakes, this thesis suggests that it is counterintuitive to plan for cities as bounded domains. It is imperative that any future plans for Mexico consider a new regional order between spatial forms of agglomeration and dispersion. Integration of ecology, technology, industry, and housing, under the supervision of an urban governance body committed to managing larger regions, will be critical.

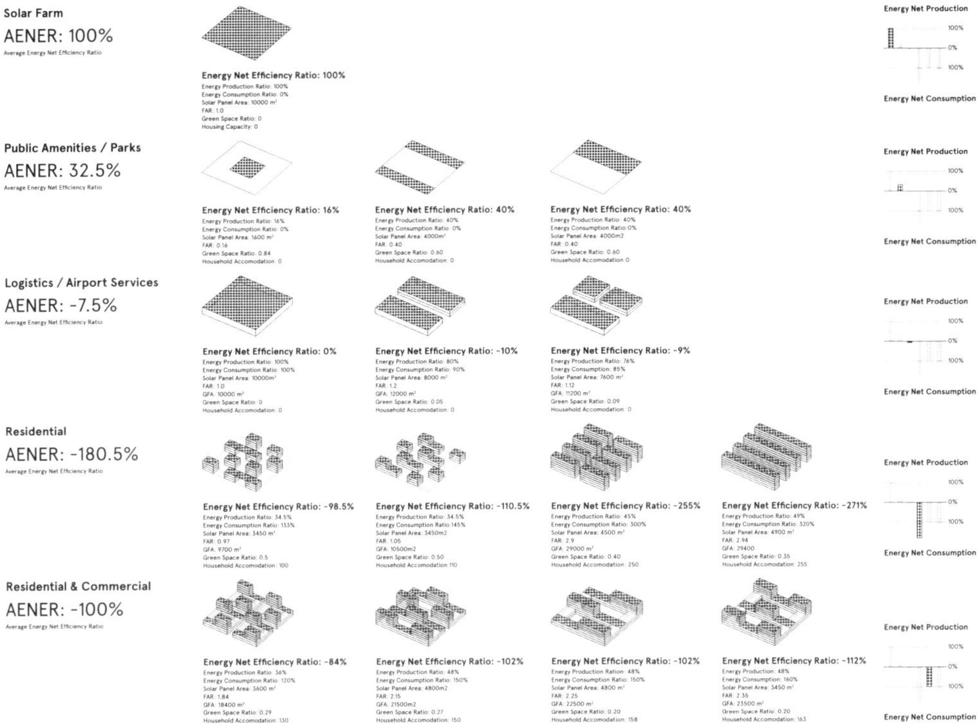

Townization: In Search of a New Paradigm of Urbanization in China
Dingliang Yang (MAUD)
Advisor: Peter Rowe

On March 17, 2013, the new Premier of China, Li Keqiang, announced a new policy on "Chinese Townization." This marked a shift from central government policy since 1978, which focused on the urbanization of cities rather than towns. Realizing this significant policy reorientation from "city making" to "town making," my thesis commits to the issue of "Townization" by researching three salient questions: (1) Why switch the focus of urbanization from "city" to "town" (2) What is "Townization" and why has it been established as a key Chinese urbanization paradigm? And (3) What urban planning and design strategies can effectively implement this "Townization" policy and contribute to reconfiguring Chinese new towns?

Based on my preliminary empirical research and data analyses, I conclude that megacity problems, environmental deterioration, urban-rural disparity, and the continuous demand that urbanization stimulate the economic development of China are the four main reasons behind the central government's policy reorientation. As a strong response to those issues, the thesis provides a new "Town Network" as the complementary network to the existing "City Network." Together these constitute the new "Urban Network" of China. The proposed town network consists of 19,683 existing designated towns. The efficiently planned, designed, and managed town network can help absorb the 300 million people (the fifteen-year target of the new central government) who would otherwise be additions to urban populations, relieve pressure on large cities, provide alternatives for citizens, and stimulate the development of surrounding rural areas and cities.

This is actually the fourth time that the central government has tried to pursue town making. Learning from their previous failures, I strongly argue that China's townization should be based on the existing towns, with the primary task to upgrade existing towns instead of creating new towns in the middle of nowhere. Further, the thesis examines a series of successful town precedents, including the famous river towns, historical towns, and TVE (Township-Village Enterprise) towns, and then generates a set of fundamental planning and design principles for China's town-making proposals.

These principles take into account demographic and population criteria, scale, suitable distance to major cities, and appropriate support industries. The thesis translates its quantitative and qualitative analysis, and its policy and spatial research into concrete urban design projects on two experimental sites.

Through these two specific projects, my thesis tries to

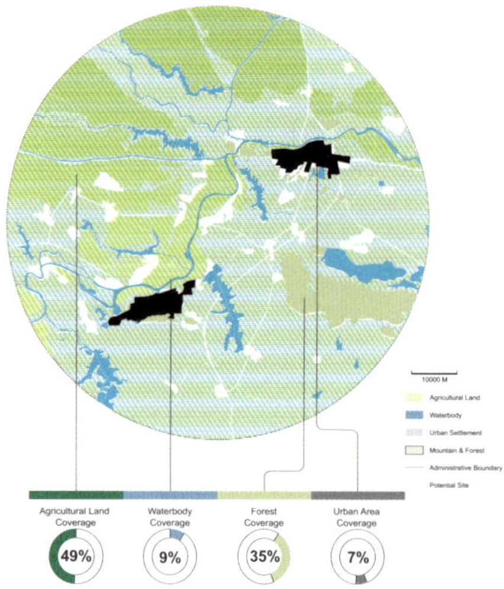

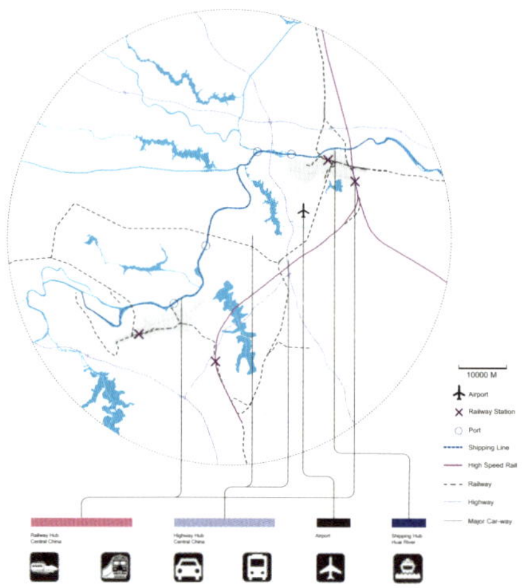

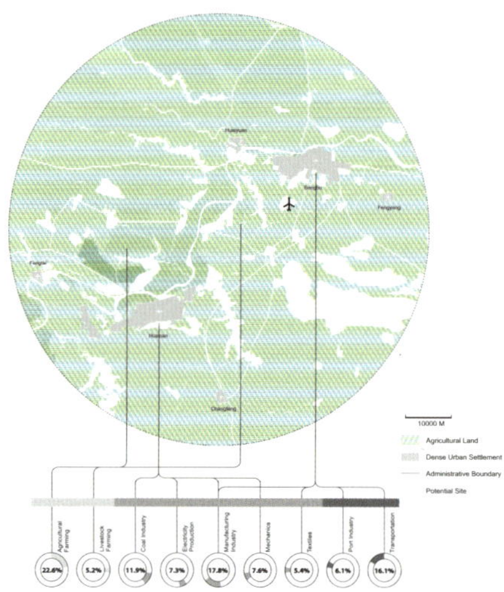

demonstrate, during this emergent "Townization," how urban design strategies can contribute to improving the built environment while reducing environmental pollution and protecting agricultural land and natural resources to enhance the quality of town life.

The first of these studies concerns Xiaoyi New Town in Bengbu, Anhui Province, an exemplary case of rural consolidation where village clusters are being transformed into a new town. The second is Beijiazao New Town in Datong, Shanxi Province, an extreme case in which the town undergoes industrial transformation from traditional coal-dependent villages to a renewable energy-dependent town.

In conclusion, this thesis offers five key suggestions for the urban planning and design strategies for the implementation of "Townization" policy:

(1) Emphasis should be placed on upgrading existing towns and townships in China.

(2) Faster transportation infrastructure should connect the larger urban network.

(3) Standard living should include of technology and amenities.

(4) Both urban and rural populations should have lifestyle options.

(5) Local industry (rather than resource extraction and agricultural production) should provide employment opportunity.

"...I've looked at technology more as a means of expression..."

Nicholas Negroponte

Nicholas Negroponte in Conversation with Mohsen Mostafavi
October 29, 2013

NN: "And so I decided that what I should do is go to architecture school. And again, maybe an illustration of gall, I went to see the headmaster, and told him this. And I said, "You know, I decided I'm going to go study architecture, because I do well in math, and I do well in art." And he looked at me, and he said—I remember it distinctly—he said, "You know, I like gray suits. And I like pinstriped suits. But I hate gray pinstriped suits." It completely went over my head. Totally. And I went to architecture school. Which was wonderful. I would never do it differently. But it took me a while to figure out that the intersection of those two fields wasn't necessarily architecture, it was computers.

[...] But in architecture school, what I learned was not to solve problems but to ask questions. When I look at all of my colleagues in engineering at MIT and other departments, they actually think of themselves as problem-solvers, and they even use the term 'problem-solving' sort of interchangeably with the word 'design,' and I think what I learned was to ask questions."

MM: "You are referring to bringing machines whose uses are not quite clear together with examples from art, which suggests that there is also a poetic project somehow at work. And the emphasis on the role of the human, and the kind of participatory aspect of this. It wasn't quite like that with a lot of people who are using computers; you were arguing against the kind of domination of the machine, and seeing the machine much more in kind of a liberative manner. It's very evocative, in terms of what one assumes you are imagining, these kinds of juxtapositions between art, architecture, machinery."

NN: [...] "For me it begins with thinking, 'How many scientists do I know who can hang out with Andy Warhol? And how many people in computers had Bucky Fuller as a professor?' I can name-drop down that list of people who affected my life that had nothing to do with computers. And so, maybe it was really the pinstriped suit at work."

MM: [...] "You were saying that when you started the Media Lab, you actually didn't imagine it lasting for a very long time, or at least you didn't want it to last for a long time, because you deliberately wanted it as a kind of short-term exercise or project. What was that about?"

NN: [...] "Well, it turns out—and I didn't know it before this evening—we were both influenced by the same person, Gordon Pask. And when people would ask me, at the time, I said that the Media Lab should be like cybernetics. It was a field that only lasted, depending on how you count, fifteen, twenty years. But it just kept producing new fields and subfields, and different things would spin out of it. And some people would argue that computer science came out of it, a lot of developmental psychology, and I thought that was a pretty good model. I would actually tell people that I wanted it to be like cybernetics, that it would come and go, and then have all this generative sort of value."

NN: [...] "I've always thought of technology not as sort of a tool for the institutional side of the equation but more for the sort of learning by playing and learning by doing. I've looked at technology more as a means of expression than communicating or transference."

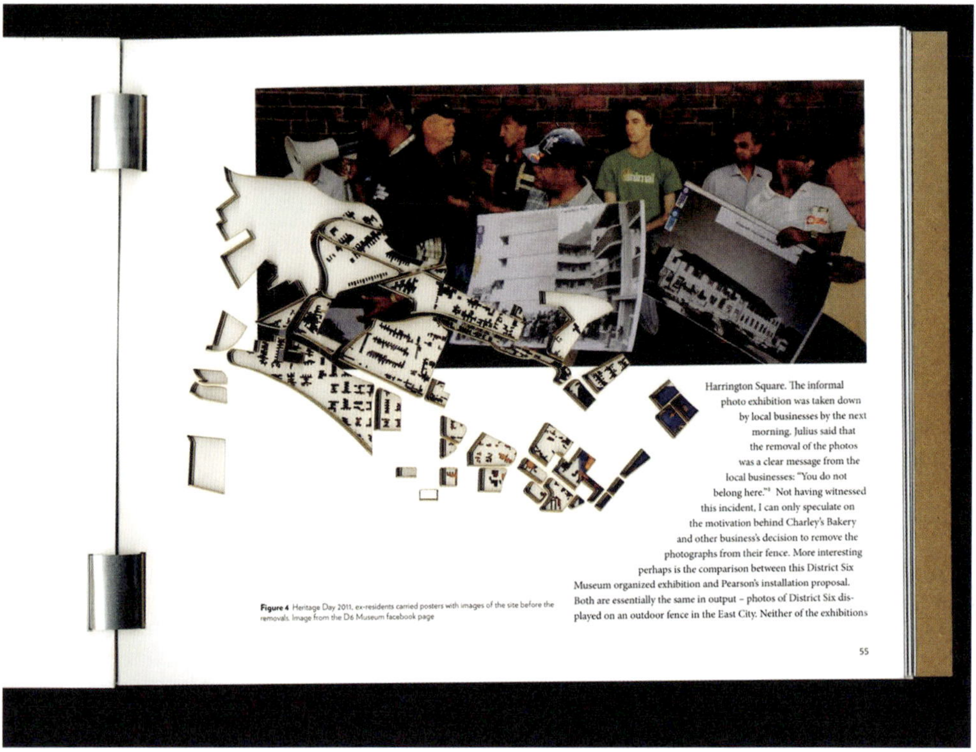

Learning from District Six: Drawing on Cape Town
Ashley Mendelsohn (MDes)
2014 Urban Project Prize Winner
Advisors: Susan Snyder and George Thomas

District Six is an infamous example of the forced removals of the South African apartheid regime. The vibrant, integrated district was declared white and 66,000 people were forcibly removed over the course of two decades. Almost all traces of life were eliminated. Today, decades after the fall of apartheid, the site remains a visible scar on the landscape. Its redevelopment is contingent upon the new generation of Capetonians' ability to critically engage and empathize with the history and heritage of the former District Six community. The identity of District Six will never be understood in a simple, concrete way. The fragmented landscape, however, provides the opportunity to look forward and backward.

After a year of research, the site revealed multiple registers of District Six: the extent to which it is represented and misrepresented, contested and forgotten. The future of District Six depends on changing the perception of the site as a place and as a concept. Making the distinction between learning about and learning from District Six, this thesis is a book that catalogs and unpacks elements from the urban fabric that contribute to future development and understanding of the broader city.

01 Learning from District Six
02 Positioning
03 Recognizing
04 Remembering
05 Storytelling
06 Imagining

01

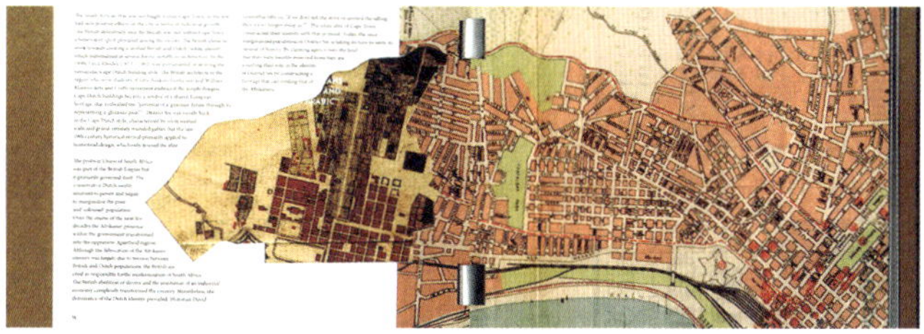

02

03

04

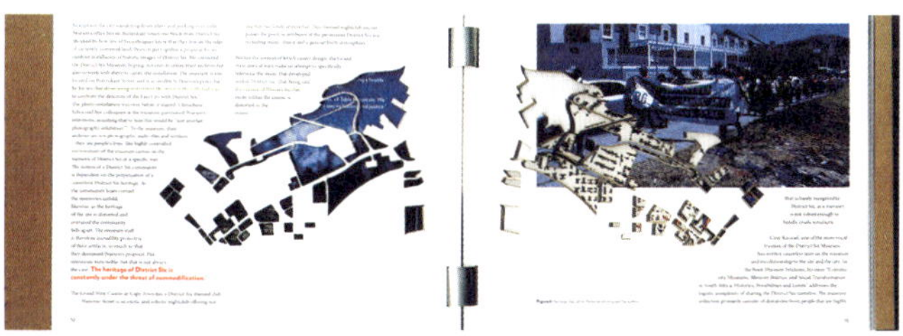

05

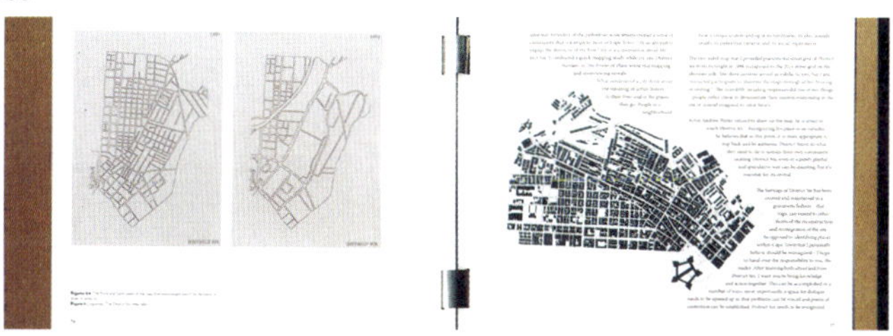

06

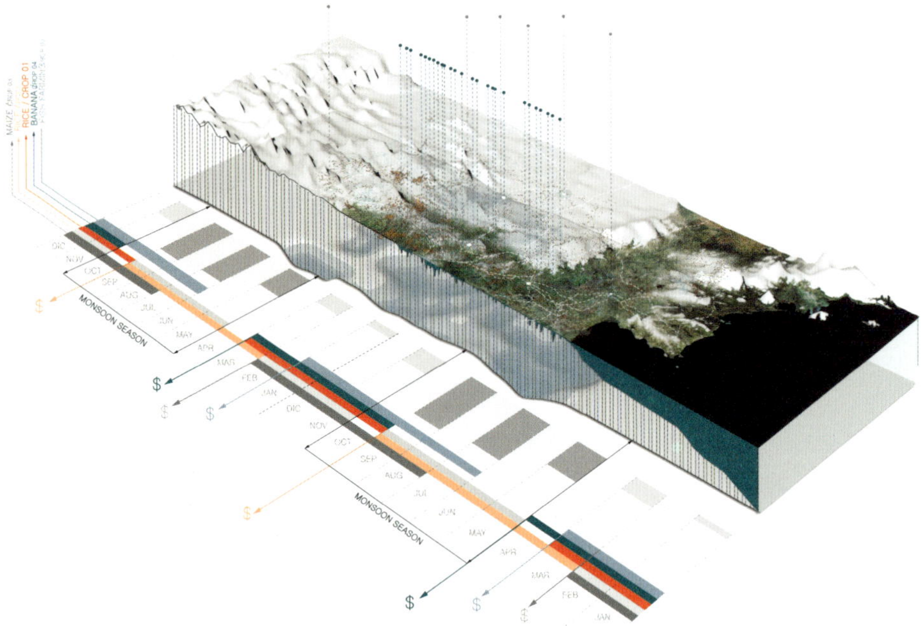

Wet Grounds: Emerging Landscapes of Storage
Adriana Chávez Sánchez (MDes)
2014 Urban Project Prize Winner
Advisor: Pierre Bélanger

According to the United Nations Human Development Report (2007), one of the most significant challenges of contemporary urbanization is water scarcity. However, development dynamics in industrializing parts of the tropics suggest that the most important challenge is that of water storage.

To capitalize on the opportunity for economic revitalization in emerging tropical economies, this thesis investigates and suggests the development of qualified patterns of urbanization that are characteristic of the tropical region and support the growth of hydraulic accumulation methods throughout the region.

Looking toward storage as both an ecological and economic strategy, this project develop ways of managing effluents, liquids, and fluids within the context of urbanization occurring in manufacturing corridors throughout inter-tropical deltaic regions and storm basins.

This thesis reveals the opportunity for new webs of urbanization within a landscape replete with industrial growth and climate complexities, where varied water storage infrastructures will work to support emerging industries and farms.

In a critique of the classic hydraulic hypothesis put forth by Karl Wittfogel in 1956, this thesis proposes a requalification of

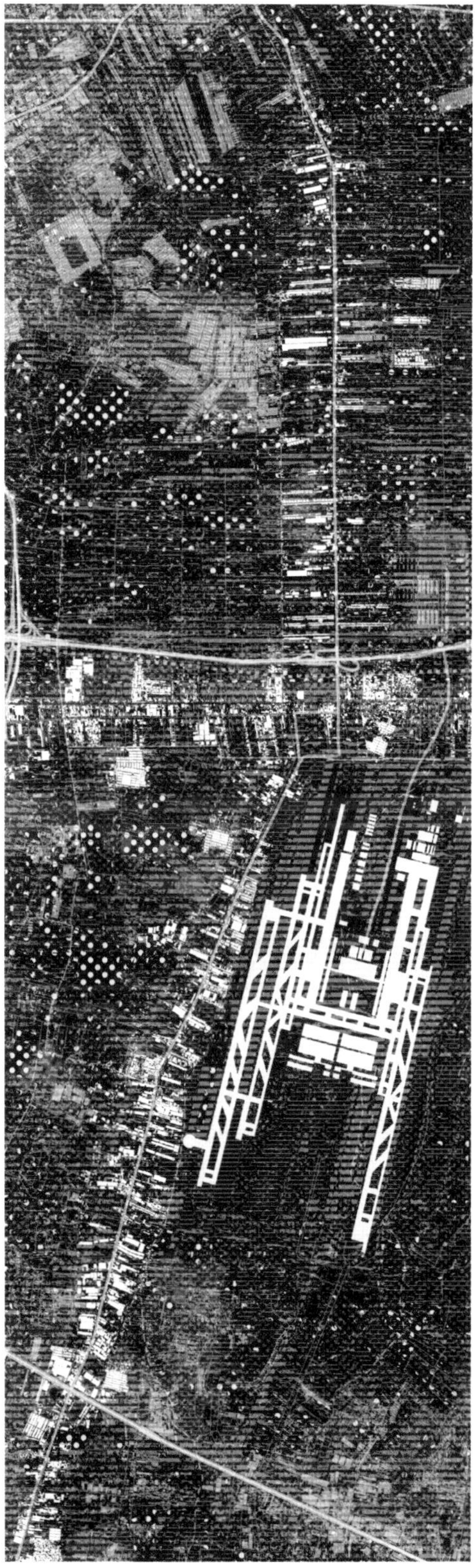

hydraulic determinacy. It does this while recognizing external hydrological processes of rain precipitation, water storage, irrigation, evaporation, and their attendant biotic processes of ecological growth as intrinsic parts of industrial and agricultural production.

By building a contemporary climatic and spatial language for the growth of economic zones in tropical regions, hydrologic accumulation becomes essential to the flexibility of international development of industrial archipelagos in between the cycles of saturation, circulation, and storage.

From Object to Agent: A Software Platform for Designing Behavior, Imbuing Traits, and Facilitating Object Learning in Interactive Environments and Artifacts
Michael Degen (MDes) and Jason Tucker (MDes)
Digital Design Award
Advisors: Panagiotis Michalatos and Allen Sayegh

This thesis focuses on the design and execution of a software platform for designing and manipulating behaviors in physical objects. The software facilitates a new conceptual framework through which designers can conceptualize interactive systems and behavior. The system allows designers to more easily implement nondeterministic behavior, growth, and learning in an object, while also providing the means of deployment through an arduino microprocessor. The current workflow for interactive projects involves an engineer-oriented process of object response creation through traditional coding environments and minimal processing of sensor data and actuation commands. Variable seeks to alleviate this problem through abstracting the data in the system, allowing the user to shift focus to the interaction and the qualities of the actuation via visual cues. Through machine learning, signal processing, and behavior trees, the user is able to create engagement between occupants and their interactive environments.

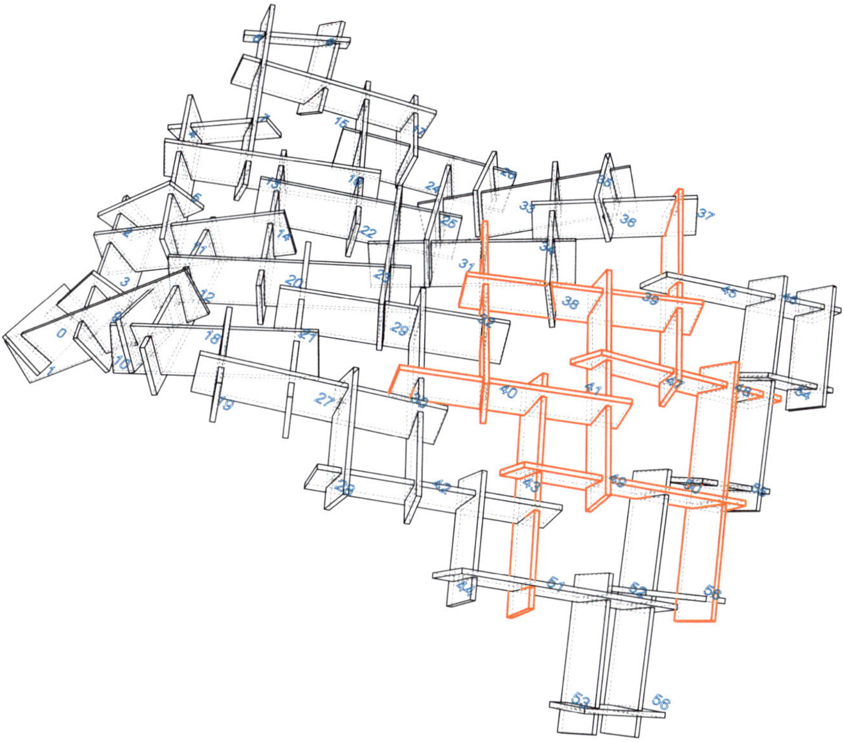

Mass Customization of Reciprocal Frame Structures: Digital Optimization and Robotic Manufacture
Ana Garcia Puyol (MDes)
Peter Rice Prize for Innovation in Architecture and Structural Design
The Daniel L. Schodek Award for Technology
Advisors: Leire Asensio Villoria and Martin Bechthold

This thesis creates digital workflow that uses computational design tools to automate the generation of planar reciprocal frame (RF) structures. This research covers the structural behavior of linear members present in conventional reciprocal frames and develops those designed with planar elements. In the latter, the boards can be mass-customized according to their position and function within the structure. Designed using optimization algorithms, RF structures incorporate notching techniques to accomplish joinery. The three-dimensional nature of the intersections between members is conceived computationally in consideration of the constraints of the fabrication process, where the elements are manufactured by means of a six-axis robot.

A reciprocating system uses relatively short members to build a structure with a span longer than that of its individual parts, where each beam supports and is supported by other beams in the structure. Other expressions used to describe this type of structure are reciprocal frame, mutually

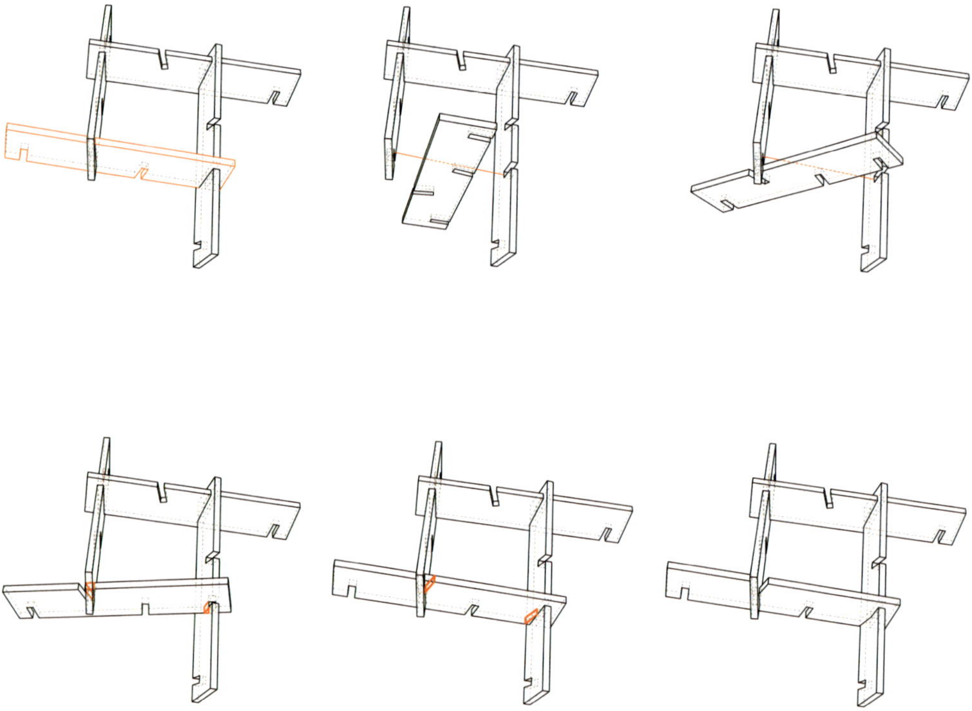

supported beams, nexorades, and mutually supported element systems.

Olivier Baverel and Alberto Pugnale explain the origin and development of reciprocal structures as linear elements in Europe and in the East. In the former, the goal of covering large spans with the available short elements proliferated these wooden structures. In the latter, large structures called "mandala roofs" were created as a result of scaling up the system used in traditional interwoven bamboo baskets [2013].

Adhesive technology in timber products made glue-laminated timber trusses and plywood widely available in the construction industry and replaced the reciprocal frames built of shorter elements with structures of long spanning beams. However, wooden reciprocal frame structures have recently become the focus of extensive research as they present an opportunity to empower eco-friendly design for their properties of recyclability, and ease of disassembly and reassembly of parts elsewhere. Mutually supported systems also appear in nature in weaver birds' nests, providing another reason for exploration of these structures within the increasing biomimetic approach to architectural design.

FOUNDRY

01 Weather
02 Email
03 Spotlight
04 Communication

Ambience Augmentation
Wenting Guo (MDes)
Advisor: Panagiotis Michalatos

Ambience Augmentation is an interaction design project that reconstructs a responsive environment in an indoor space. With ambience as a sensory intervention, the project utilizes a programmable light source, projecting lights onto the ground, while multiple speakers that provide three-dimensional sound to intuitively give users necessary information. In contrast to the current trend in digital technology of compressing information, Ambience Augmentation rethinks the interior ambient condition as a platform that diffuses information and communicates it at the highest level of latency and abstraction. It establishes a new paradigm of interaction with information that is more tangible and less attention demanding, through a dynamic and customizable ambience.

The design of this ambient environment draws on research in the related fields of vision, art, image processing, and information architecture. Five applications are prototyped to demonstrate the use of this platform, all of which take real-time data as inputs and generate lighting and sound effects as outputs to unobtrusively apprise the occupants of relevant information.

01

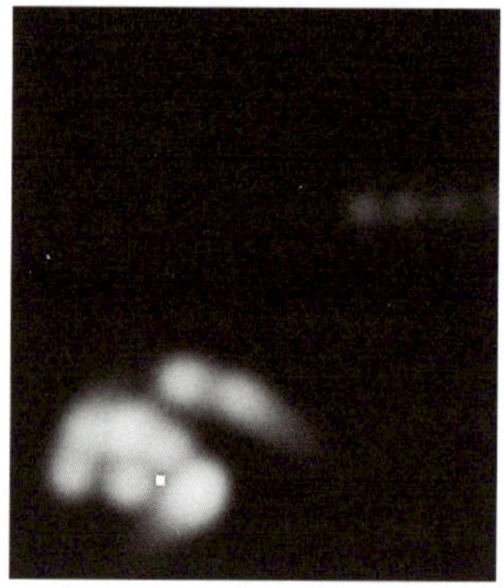

02

03

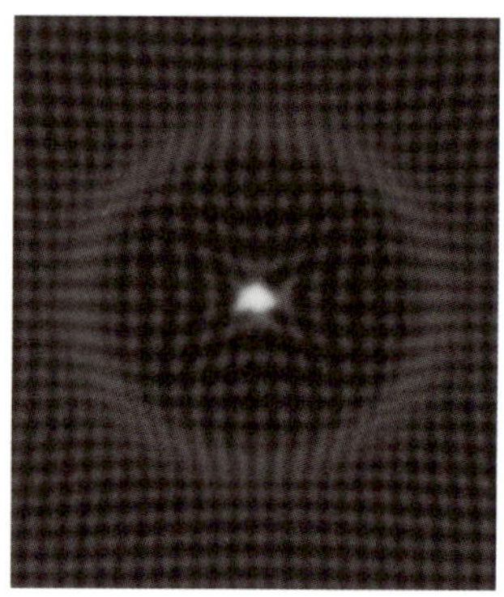

04

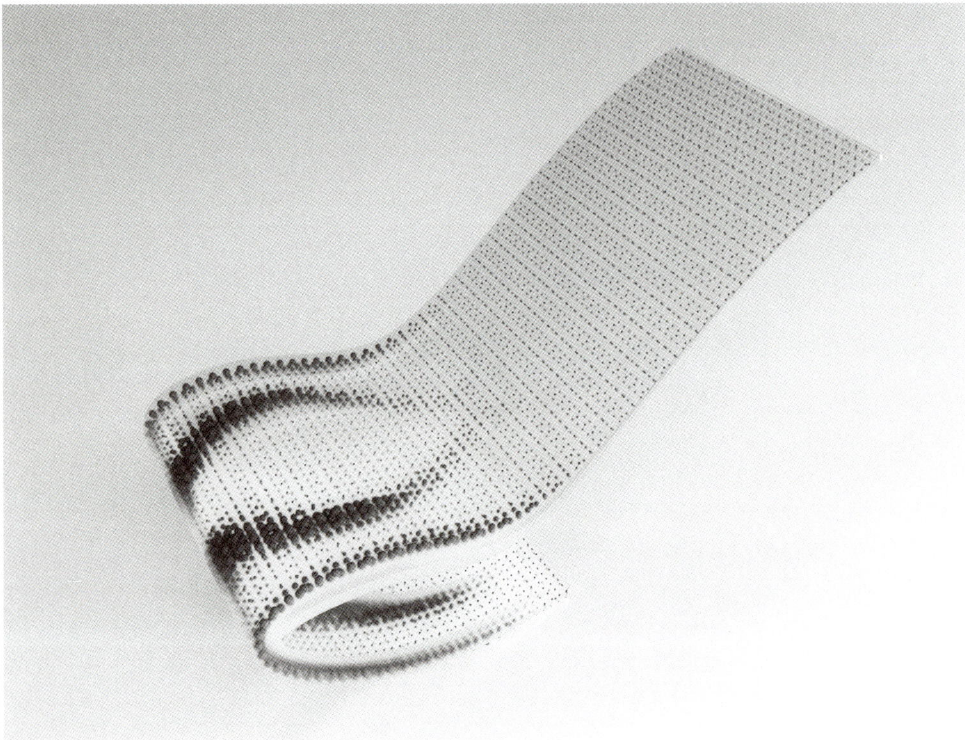

Unveil the Story Inside of It: Structural Optimization and Material Distribution as a Design Solution
Juhun Lee (MDes)
Advisor: Panagiotis Michalatos

Each of the objects we use in our daily life, such as a chair or a wine rack, deals with a structural behavior within itself. Although structural issues on this scale are not problematic in terms of safety or stability, there is interest in exploring the aesthetics of structural behavior in the design process. There has been much research on the application of structures to the design process, and various computational tools have become available to designers to handle this study. However, these analyses and programs remain out of reach for those unfamiliar with the specific expertise.

MiniPede is a computation tool that performs the analysis and optimization of structure and modifies input geometry based on its findings. MiniPede was developed for three types of users according to their degree of computational knowledge.[01] The basic MiniPede operates in Grasshopper for Rhino, one of the most commonly used programs by designers. Minipede uses Millipede[02] libraries to perform the analysis and optimization of structure and Rhinocommon.dll for modifying geometries inside the Rhino3d platform.

MiniPede takes a surface design input and converts it to a mesh for analysis. A user then sets intended thickness, support region, and area of the load, enabling MiniPede to run initial calculations. With these few inputs, the user receives information and verification of the design's structural validity. In addition, MiniPede offers two optimization steps to adjust the structural design via thickness redistribution.

Supplementary functions of MiniPede are available to designers who are not familiar with parametric design. MiniPede has seven components that generate modified surfaces, various patterns, fiber placement, material separation, and density fields closely related to the optimization result. Each component has input parameters controlled through simple number sliders, enabling exploration of even more design alternatives.

The final version of MiniPede operates on the user-friendly interface of application and web-based commands. In this version, the user can set up all critical information by intuitive gestures such as touch, drag, click, and slide. MiniPede calculates other detail inputs internally and provides users with the various design options.

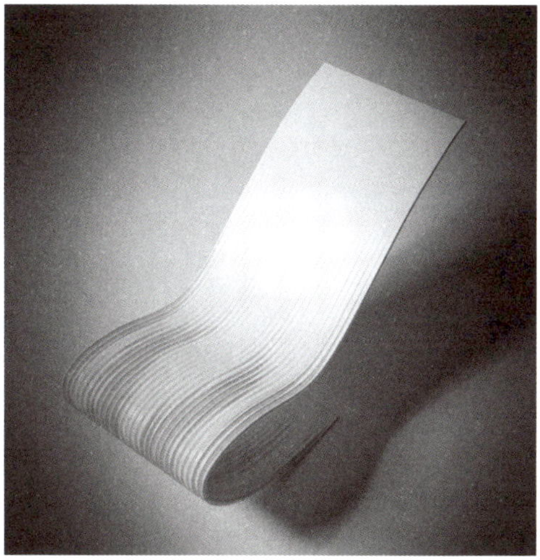

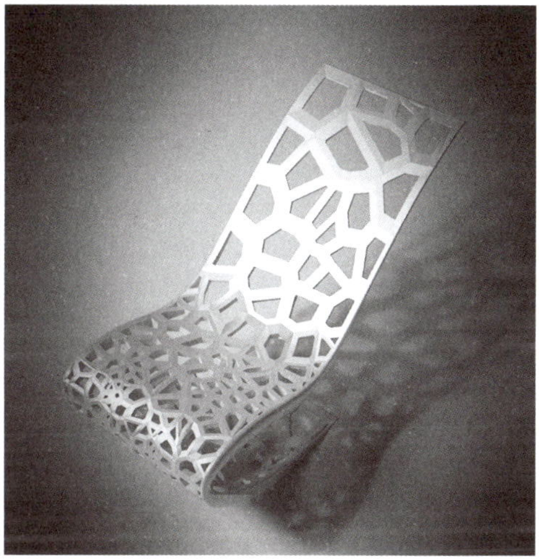

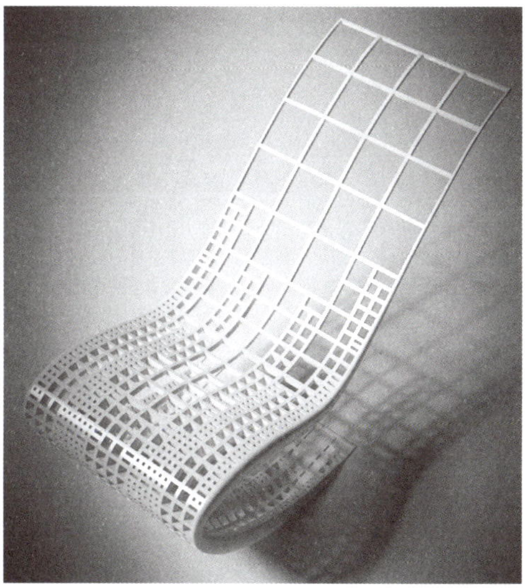

01 First target user: Designer has computational ability. Second target user: Designer has minimal computational ability. Third target user: General public with no experience in CAD but strong intentions toward customized designs.

02 Millipede is a Grasshopper™ component developed by Prof. Panagiotis Michalatos focusing on the analysis and optimization of structures. The component's core is a library of very fast structural analysis algorithms for linear elastic systems.

 Chuck Hoberman with Anne Liu and her prosthetic prototype

01

01 Ahmed Hosny (MDes)
Nicholas Jacobson (MDes)
Charlotte Lipschitz (MArch I)
Nina Sinatra (SEAS)
Emily Kappes (MArch I AP)
02 Zachary Seibold (MDes)
Yingyi Wang (MDes)
Malika Singh (MDes)
LingLi Tseng (MDes)
03 Arta Yazdanseta (DDes)
Saurabh Shrestha (MDes)

02

03

Material Systems

Instructors
Nathan King
Rachel Vroman

Digital fabrication, deeply embedded in today's architectural discourse, has enabled new modes of practice and informed design pedagogy on a global scale. Through workflow optimization and automation, designers are increasingly able to move seamlessly between digital environments and physical realization by leveraging advanced tooling. This rapidly changing field continually offers architects and designers new opportunities. This course pursued positioning and testing technology as a driver in the creative design processes, while providing an outlet for critical evaluation.

Ceramic material systems provided the framework for contextual discussion, research, and experimentation surrounding digital design and fabrication technologies. Newly emerging methods of assembly and digital fabrication have challenged the dominance of the ubiquitous ceramic tile. Ceramics have the potential to produce a great diversity of shapes through a variety of material processes. Craft-based manufacturing and high-volume industrial production of clay-based ceramics are both affected by digital and robotic fabrication techniques. These opportunities were explored in group research projects in collaboration with the Harvard Ceramics Program and with support from the Spanish Ceramic Tile Manufacturers' Association (ASCER).

04

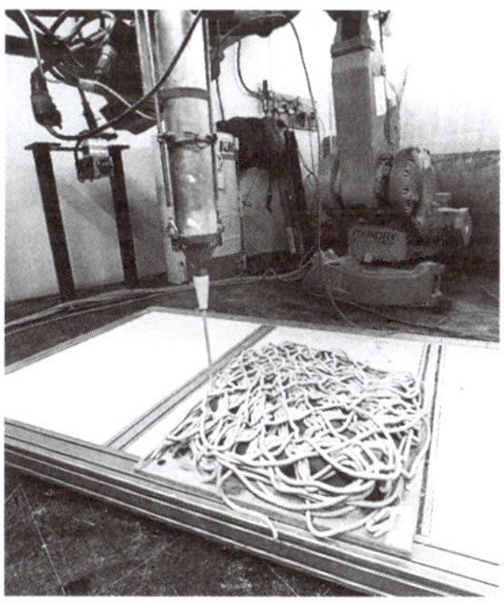
05

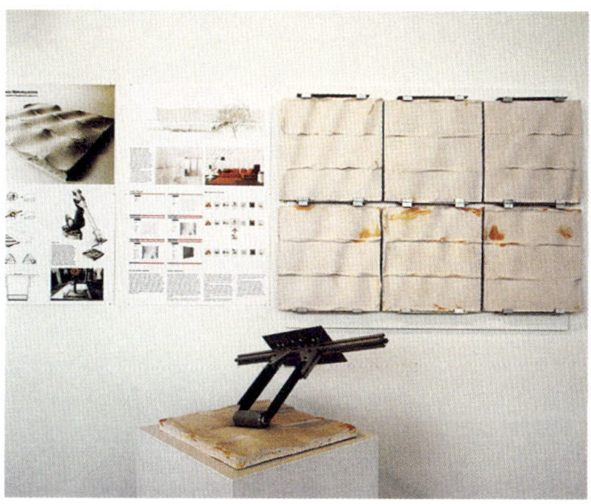
06

04 Material Systems Exhibition
05 Jared Friedman (MDes)
Hea Min Kim (MDes)
Olga Mesa (MDes)
06 Peter Sprowls (MArch I AP)
Bongjai Shin (MArch I)
Rossitza Kotelova (MArch I)
Sekou Cooke (MArch II)

The Practice as Project

Instructors
Florian Idenburg
Matan Mayer

The role of the architect today is constantly shifting. While well-rounded licensed and affiliated architects will continue to be required to provide core professional services, an increasing number of hybrid practitioners will apply an architectural skill set—for example, the ability to synthesize and orchestrate—in areas such as design consultancy, technology, and other cultural spheres. Furthermore, novel practice models are emerging based on a single agenda or the exploration of a specific field of interest. Understanding the extent of this shifting array of opportunities, and how to operate within this dynamic field, is vital for the graduates of tomorrow.

Kevin Murray (MArch I)
Evan Cerilli (MArch I)
"Comparison of New York City Firms"

Kanika Arora (MDes)
Christopher M. Johnson (MArch I AP)
"Redesigning 80 Walnut"

Environment, Economics, and Enterprise

Instructors
Holly Samuelson
Frank Apeseche

How can one optimize the benefits of environmental sustainability while generating a higher return on investment in buildings? Where are the opportunities for real estate initiatives that are highly functional, healthy, aesthetically pleasing, and financially rewarding? The challenge for designers, developers, environmental consultants, and other professionals lies in finding and communicating these synergies. This cross-disciplinary course gave students an approach to problem solving to help them contribute to thoughtful, high-impact decisions about design and construction that are both environmentally and socially influential and economically effective.

In Search of Design through Engineers

Instructors
Hanif Kara
Andreas Georgoulias

This course taught, stimulated, and demonstrated "design-led" opportunities that exist in the zone between architecture and engineering, through the paradigm of design engineering. Positioned within the space of interdisciplinary boundaries, the course invited both GSD and MIT students to encourage and pioneer a joint discourse.

The course covered a broad spectrum of architectural approaches that allowed students to respond to each unique derivative position, from concept to construction. Accessing unpublished original material, students engaged with the early conceptual stages through to the detailed design process and construction. The process brought the students as close as possible to the original premises of the case-study method: the presentation of a "piece of reality" and the expansion of one's experience base. The students were given exposure to the materials of the project team for some of the most challenging buildings of contemporary architecture. Placed in the middle of the process, the students were no longer passive receivers of information but gained firsthand experience of the design issues at play when architects and engineers come together.

01

Nelson Byun (MArch II)
Roland Faust (MArch I AP)
Melissa Han (MIT MEng HPS)
01 Site
02 The Water Loop

02

Computational Material Distributions

Instructor
Panagiotis Michalatos

This course explored the role of computational structural analysis and form-finding methods in design and fabrication problems. Such techniques indicated a structurally consistent way of assembling and distributing materials with implications for geometric, aesthetic, and tectonic expression. The concept of optimization operated as an abstraction of the digital model, but became problematic in the wider design challenge, partially because digital models are imperfect approximations of reality. Also, for real-world problems, the optimal is multiple. The transition from model to material artifact was not straightforward and required design interpretation.

The course explored the role of the designer in the creative interpretation of such quasi-optimal outcomes and speculated on how engagement with such methods can alter the intuitive understanding of structural challenges. This year's theme was compliance gradients and how architects can think about the differentiation of flexibility and rigidity within a structural system. New analysis, design, and fabrication techniques allowed us to consider properties of "rigidity" outside of the traditional binary system of a rigid component and frictionless joint. Rather, rigidity was viewed as a compliant and flexible mechanism, as a gradient of intentional deformations. The compliance of the structure and its response under different loads thus became the object of design.

01

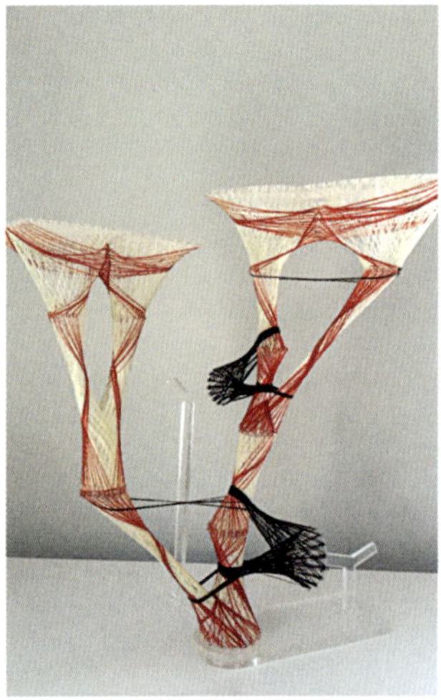

02

01 Saurabh Mhatre (MDes)
Malika Singh (MDes)
Yingyi Wang (MDes)
02 Jeonghyun Kim (MArch II)
03, 04:
Dongah Cho (MArch II)
Hea Min Kim (MDes)

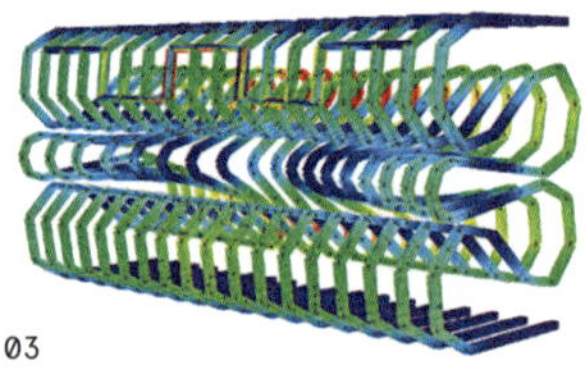

03

04

01

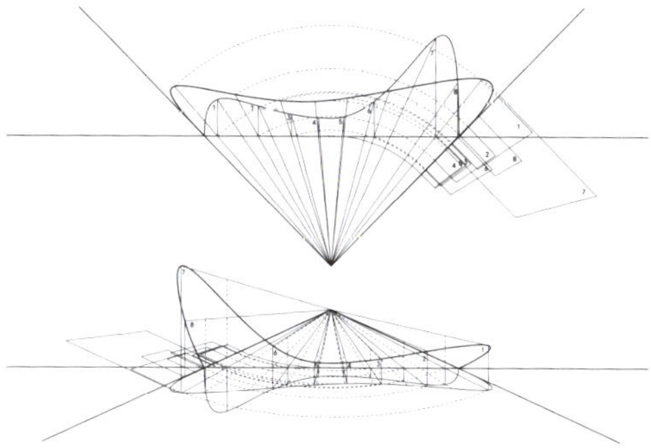

02

01 Nancy Nichols (MArch I) "Developable 'H-Unit' Aggregation"
02 Arthur Terry (MAUD) "Stereotomic Development"
03 Iman Fayyad (MArch I) John Morrison (MArch II) "2-Cone Geodesic Laminate Model"

03

Conic and Developable Surfaces

Instructor
Cameron Wu

In terms of differential geometry, developable surfaces are defined as those with vanishing Gaussian curvature that can be unrolled to a plane without distortion. The advent of complex surfaces in recent architecture has necessitated the use of developables to post-rationalize surfaces of double curvature for increased economy and constructability. Although these surface classes comprise only a small subset of all surfaces, they are capable of producing a remarkable amount of complexity and continuity when deployed in specific and precise permutations.

In this seminar, students engaged in the mathematical description and behavior of tangential developables, generalized cones, and generalized cylinders as the a priori building blocks of a (periodic) architectural language. Also of interest were the mathematically related doubly ruled surfaces of the hyperbolic paraboloid and the hyperboloid of revolution. In-depth analysis of historical precedents of form and construction methods served as the geometric and discursive springboard for a set of design exercises that culminated in a final prototype fabrication. Design propositions exhibiting discrete aggregations of surfaces may challenge or reinforce current fascinations with the smooth and continuous.

(Re)fabricating Tectonic Prototypes

Instructor
Leire Asensio Villoria
Structural Consultant
Hanif Kara
Teaching Assistants
Ana Garcia Puyol
Felix Raspall
Juan Pablo Ugarte

The course was framed by a general ambition to develop explorations in digital design, fabrication, and parametric tools that were informed and enriched by historical precedent while still maintaining a speculative and novel outlook. Primarily focused on the development of conceptual skills and techniques, the course also addressed technical understanding of the application of digital processes and tools in the development of tectonic and construction systems in architecture.

Students completed projects using a number of emerging and established digital techniques and processes to develop new prototypes for construction systems. System precedents were studied and reconsidered during the course to inform and inspire the development of each project. Students were encouraged to rethink existing systems to produce novel expression as well as performance.

A period of analysis and documentation of prevailing systems and their associative geometric and material relationships initiated the development of a rigorous analytical understanding of specific construction and tectonic systems, as well as proficiency in applying this knowledge to construct associative/parametric digital models. These models constituted the tools to generate alternative variations of the analyzed systems. A subsequent phase of prototyping used the GSD fabrication laboratory's tools. Prototype fabrication allowed students to gain knowledge in and explore the new potentials and capabilities of tools in the emerging field of digital fabrication. These digital design and parametric tools allowed for the reconsideration and expansion of the potential applications of exemplary construction and tectonic systems today.

01

02

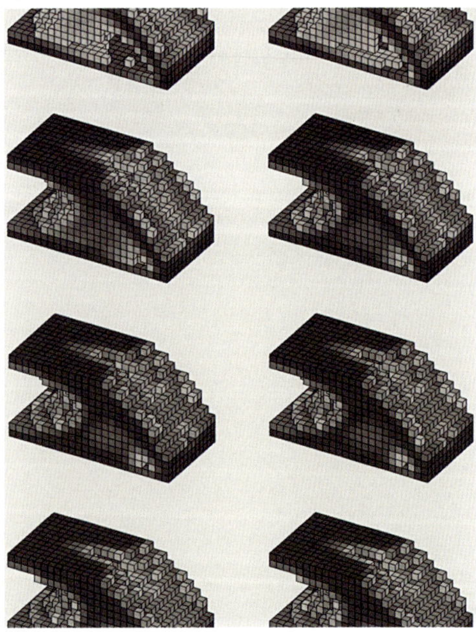

03

01,02:
Luke Booth (MLA II)
Keojin Jin (MDes)
Wilfred Leung (MAUD)
"Huesos Fusión"

03 Ahmed Hosny (MDes)
Nicholas Jacobson (MDes)
Zachary Seibold (MDes)
"Voxelbeam"

04,05:
Rachel Dickey (MDes)
Olga Mesa (MDes)
LingLi Tseng (MDes)
Xin Li (MArch I)

04

05

$\text{endI} := 120 \qquad \text{endJ} := 40$

$\text{in} := 0, 1..\text{endI} \qquad \text{jn} := 0, 1..\text{endJ}$

$$A_{in,jn} := \operatorname{asin}\left(\sin\left(\frac{in}{endI} \cdot 2\pi\right)\right) \cdot \frac{16}{\pi} \qquad B_{in,jn} := \operatorname{asin}\left(\cos\left(\frac{in}{endI} \cdot 2\pi\right)\right) \cdot \frac{16}{\pi} \qquad C_{in,jn} := \operatorname{asin}\left(\cos\left(\frac{jn}{endJ} \cdot \frac{45}{100}\pi\right)\right) \cdot \frac{4}{\pi}$$

$$a := \cos\left(\frac{\pi}{4}\right) \qquad b := \sin\left(\frac{\pi}{4}\right) \qquad c := \frac{\sqrt{2}}{2}$$

$$DEF\_I_{in,jn} := \sin\left(\frac{in}{endI} \cdot 2\pi + \frac{\pi}{4}\right) \cdot 2$$

$$X_{in,jn} := 13 \cdot \frac{jn}{endJ} + \frac{in}{5}$$

$$Y_{in,jn} := \begin{cases} \left|(A_{in,jn} \cdot b) + (B_{in,jn} \cdot a)\right| \cdot c \cdot C_{in,jn} & \text{if} \quad endJ \cdot \frac{1}{2} \le jn \le endJ \\ \left|(A_{in,jn} \cdot b) + (B_{in,jn} \cdot a)\right| \cdot c - 4 - DEF\_I_{in,jn} & \text{otherwise} \end{cases}$$

$$Z_{in,jn} := \begin{cases} \left|(A_{in,jn} \cdot a) + (B_{in,jn} \cdot -b)\right| \cdot c \cdot C_{in,jn} & \text{if} \quad endJ \cdot \frac{1}{2} \le jn \le endJ \\ \left|(A_{in,jn} \cdot a) + (B_{in,jn} \cdot -b)\right| \cdot c - 3 & \text{otherwise} \end{cases}$$

<ins>Jeonghyun Kim</ins> (MArch II)
<ins>Julia Michalski</ins> (MArch II)
"The Little House
on the Prairie"

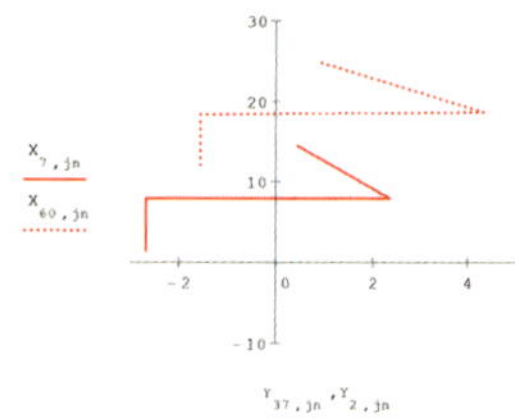

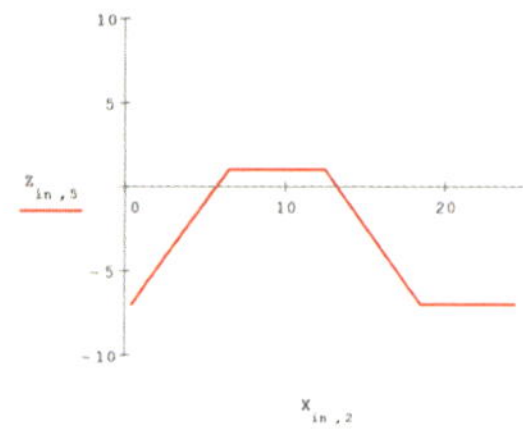

Superficial Spaces

<ins>Instructor</ins>
George L. Legendre
<ins>Teaching Assistant</ins>
Michael Leef

At a time when architectural discourse and practice are (still) brimming with references to new geometries, this course investigated the architectural potential of abstract three-dimensional surfaces. In accord with the practical ambition of the option studios, this seminar helped students devise formal prototypes for architectural consumption while broadening their understanding of the rigors of abstract formal analysis.

With equal emphasis on theoretical reading, graphic analysis and diagramming, elementary mathematics, numerically controlled fabrication techniques, and theoretical writing, the seminar orbited, in increasingly tight loops, the surface as object of knowledge.

01

02

Nano Micro Macro

Instructor
Martin Bechthold
Teaching Fellow
Daekwon Park

This course explored design research methods and techniques through the microcosm of newly emerging biologically inspired material systems and their applications in buildings. Focused on technologies and systems developed by researchers of the Adaptive Materials Technology Platform (led by Professor Joanna Aizenberg) at the Wyss Institute for Biologically Inspired Engineering, the course served as an interdisciplinary platform for students to interact with material scientists and chemists from Wyss. The course introduced ideas-to-innovation processes in a hands-on, project/product-focused manner. Emphasis was on the use of "inspirational objects"—somewhat autonomous artistic artifacts that balance thematic effects with promising real-world opportunities. Alternating between guided discovery and focused development, between bottom-up and top-down thinking, the course helped students establish generalizable frameworks as researchers and innovators with a focus on new and emerging material systems.

Kurt Fischer (MArch II)
Jonathan Grinham (DDes)
Jeff Mansfield (MArch I)
Puja Patel (MDes)
"Fluidform"
01 Ceramic tile prototype
02 Acrylic tile prototype
03 Fluid-magnet relationship

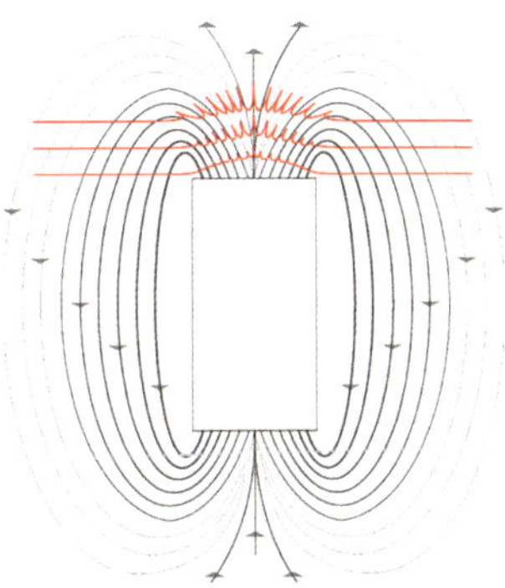

03

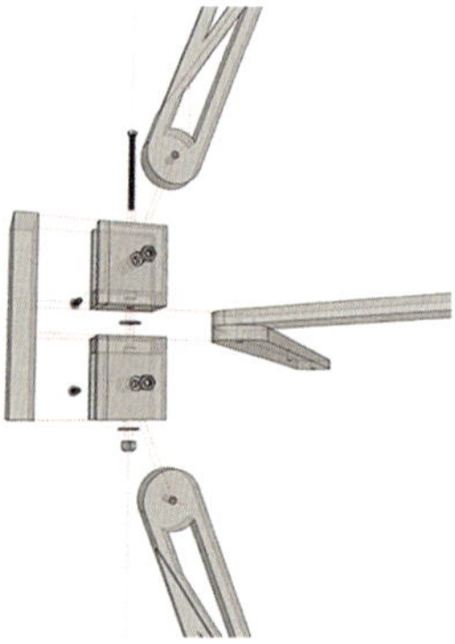

Joon Hyuk Choe (MArch II)
Mitch Crowder (MAUD)
Jina Kim (MArch II)
Sunchung Christine Min (MArch II)
"Watch Your Fingers: How a Bench Can Transform to an Exhibit"

Transformable Design Methods

Instructors
Chuck Hoberman
Nathan King

Portable buildings, retractable coverings, kinetic façades, and spaces that morph: these transformable structures have become part of the lexicon of dynamic architectural possibilities. Still, examples of truly dynamic buildings are few, and architectural design remains focused on objects that are essentially static. How can we understand transformation itself as a design parameter that can be shaped, crafted, and optimized?

This course provided a theoretical overview and practical methods for designing objects that can change size, shape, and surface. Our goal was to introduce new ways of thinking about design by developing structures that demonstrated real-time changes of morphology. We applied a systematic methodology for the creation and development of transformable mechanisms. We started with purely geometric tools and moved to the basics of kinematic analysis and synthesis. Ultimately, a parametric approach joined form and movement through an integrated design process.

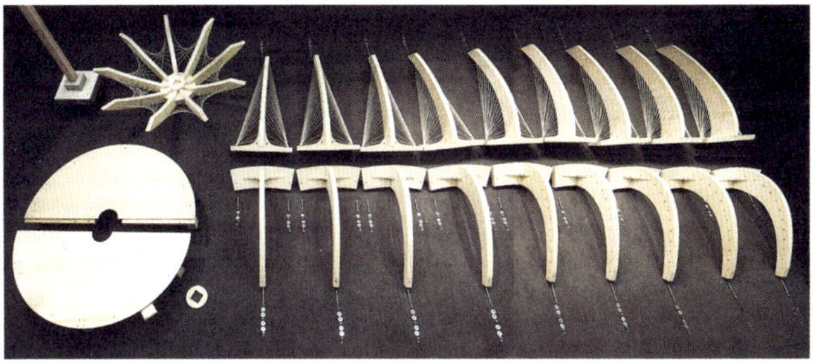

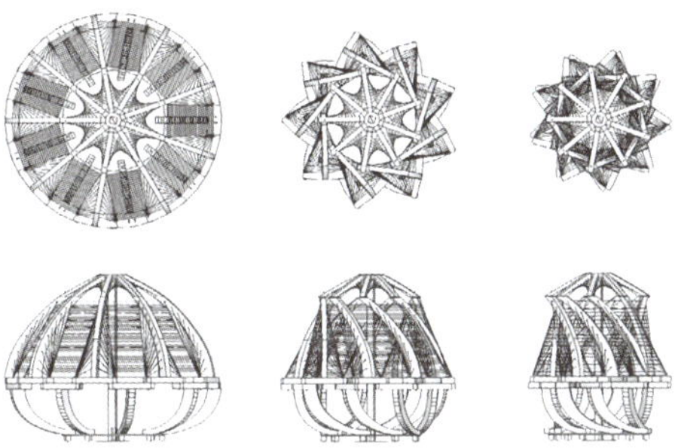

LingLi Tseng (MDes)
Aiko Nakano (MIT SMBT)
Fernando Rodriguez (MIT SDM)
Wendy Engler (Harvard Nieman Foundation Affiliate)
"Bloom: Deployable Sculpture"

Designed Porous Media

Instructor
Salmaan Craig
Teaching Assistant
Saurabh Shrestha

This seminar focused on designing porous surfaces and materials to orchestrate the flow of heat through buildings in novel ways. The primary aim was to inspire interest in the phenomenology of heat and the possibilities of "doing architecture" at the material scale. Ideas and design methods from materials engineering and the thermal sciences (thermodynamics, heat transfer, and fluid dynamics) were introduced, with a focus on design-led learning through practical application and experiment.

Teams were organized and tasked with:

[Cellular elements] Developing and testing a system of hollow-core construction elements whose cellular cavities are optimized to control convection heat transfer in a given climate.

[Breathing wall] Developing and testing a 3D printed porous wall element that recaptures outgoing heat when external air is passed through it.

[Thermo-active surface] Developing and testing a porous heat-exchanger surface for cooling or heating a space, made from a folded composite of metal and polymer, and "activated" by small-diameter water tubing.

[Dew-harvesting canopy] Developing and testing a surface array of funneling pores, optimized to maximize the yield of dew or cold air in a given climate.

01

Nancy Nichols (MArch I)
Madeline Gradillas (MIT SMArchS)
Rachel Moranis (MArch I)
"Radiative Roof"
01 Geometry and construction
02 Experimental study

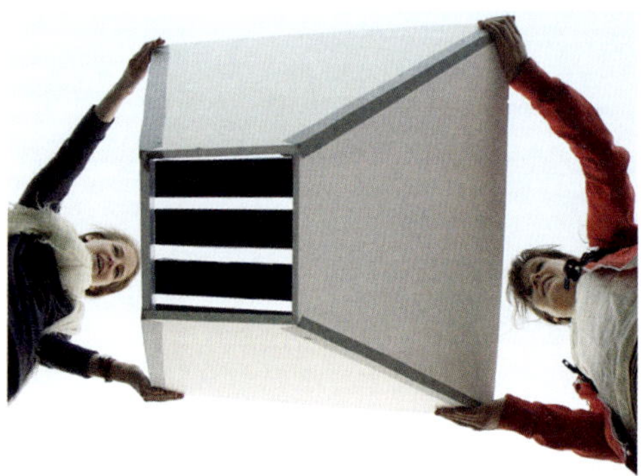

02

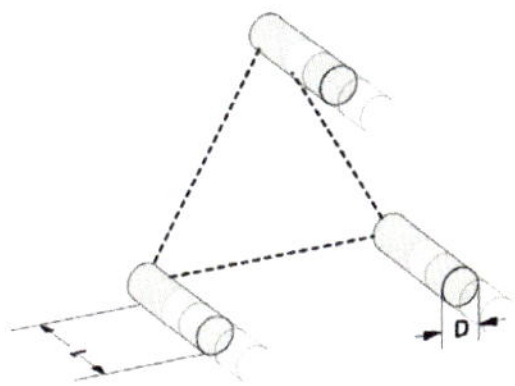

Set L at desired length and solve for D

Pin Design
The form of the pins themselves is optimized to maximize the conductive transfer between the pins and the thermal mass based on a pin efficiency formula.

Nelis & Klein
Heat Transfer
1.6.7 Fin Optimization

$$mL = \left[\frac{4 \times \bar{h}}{k_s \times D}\right]^{\frac{1}{2}} \times L$$

Increasing the length of the pin increases its convective heat transfer to the air, but the increase in length must be accompanied by an increase in diameter that ensures the pin will be able to conduct heat from the thermal mass at one end to the air at the other. Optimal performance of the pin occurs when mL ~ 1.4

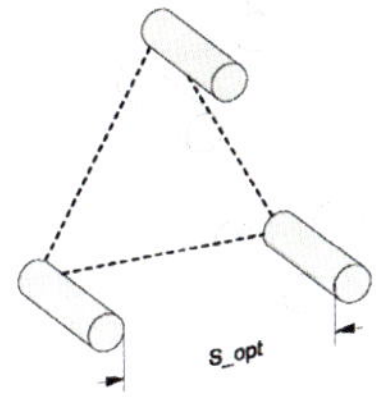

With D set, we can now solve for S_opt

Array Design
The spacing of the array is optimized to maximize convective heat transfer between the air and the pins.

Adrian Bejan
Design with Constructal Theory 3.3
Optimal Spacing of Staggered Pins

$$Ra_H = \frac{9.807\ m/s^2 \times \beta \times \Delta T \times H^3}{\alpha \times v}$$

$$\frac{S_{opt}}{H} \simeq 2.72\left(\frac{H}{D}\right)\mathrm{Ra}_H^{-\frac{1}{4}} + 0.263\frac{D}{H}$$

By plotting the asymptotes which predict heat transfer at small and large spacings it is possible to calculate a theoretical maximum value for q_max which occurs at the intersection between the two. The following formula can be used to calculate the theoretical maximum cooling power of the design:

$$\frac{q_{max} \times D^2}{k(T_{max} - T_0) \times H \times L \times W} \simeq 0.448\left[\left(\frac{H}{D}\right)^{\frac{1}{3}} \times Ra_D^{\frac{1}{4}}\right]^{-1.6}$$

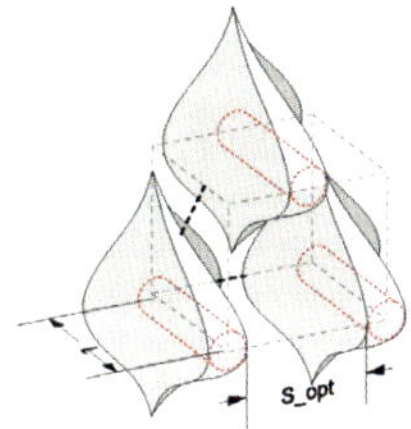

Optimized Morphology
These relationships establish an order of magnitude for the geometric definition of the design. We introduced a geometry which is wider at the base so the pins will not be fragile, and rounded to reduce drag on the flow. Additionally, the pointed ends of the fin-pins provide a more aerodynamic shape that minimizes drag.

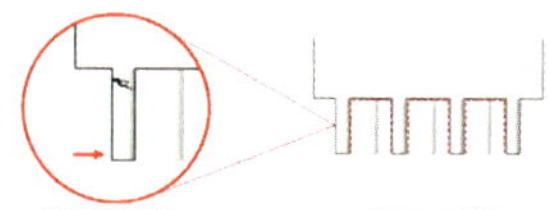

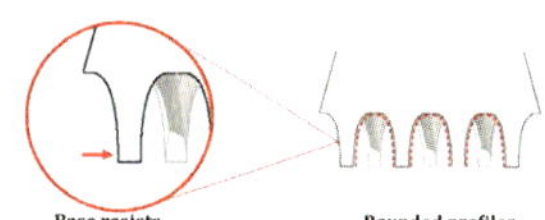

03

Jared Friedman (MDes)
Alex Jacobson (MArch I)
Julia Michalski (MArch II)
"External Walls"
03 Optimal size and stagger
04 Variables in relation to proposed geometry
05 Nesting of hexagonal blocks

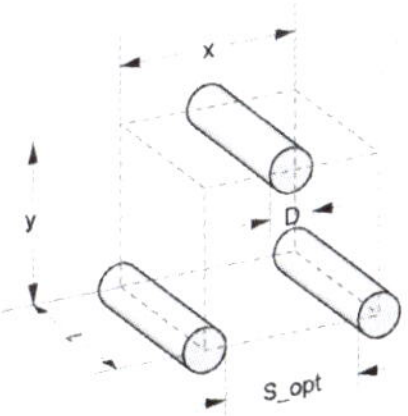

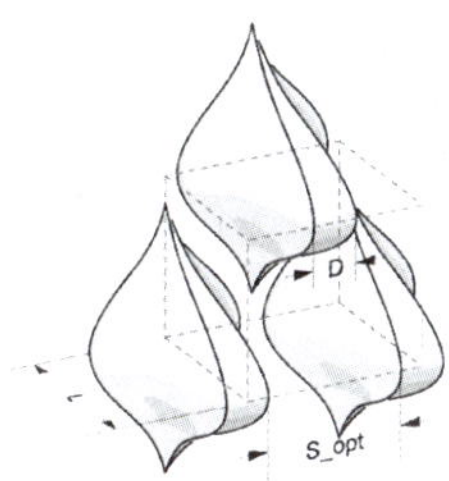

Bejan Model

$$Ra_H = \frac{9.807\ m/s^2 \times \beta \times \Delta T \times H^3}{\alpha \times v}$$

$$\frac{S_{opt}}{H} \simeq 2.72\left(\frac{H}{D}\right)\mathrm{Ra}_H^{-\frac{1}{4}} + 0.263\frac{D}{H}$$

Ra_H = Rayleigh Number according to height
β = Coefficient of volumetric thermal expansion
ΔT = Difference in ambient and pin surface temperature
α = Thermal diffusivity
v = Kinematic viscosity of air
H = Height of overall wall

Nellis and Klein Pin Lengths Model

$$mL = \left[\frac{4 \times h}{k_s \times D}\right]^{\frac{1}{2}} \times L$$

mL = Pin performance parameter (set to 1.4)
h = Average heat transfer coefficient on pins
k_s = Thermal conductivity of solid
L = Length of pin
D = Diameter of pin

04

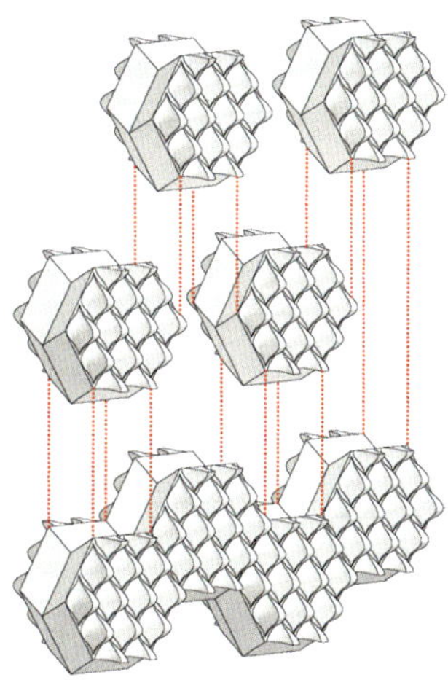

05

Hitchhiker's Guide to Hyperreality

Instructor
Neil Leach
Teaching Assistant
David Pearson

Contemporary postmodern culture is dominated, according to French cultural theorist Jean Baudrillard, by simulation and hyperreality. The image has become the new reality—or hyperreality—a virtual world floating above the real world in its own hermetic envelope. It is a culture that has lost touch with its referents in the real world, and one where, paradoxically, the term "real" has been hijacked by multinational conglomerates. It's the "real thing," a Coca-Cola world of industrially manufactured "natural" ingredients. In a world where the imaginary becomes the "real," there is no longer a place for the real. In the "perfect crime" of the twentieth century, reality itself has been stolen. Nowhere has the cover-up been more obvious than in Disneyland, the archetypal dream center of this culture of consumption, and Los Angeles—the city that produced Disneyland—the epicenter of this culture of hyperreality.

This course in contemporary cultural theory interrogated the theme of hyperreality not only through a close reading of various theoretical texts but also through films about LA and visits to iconic sites around the city. The course treated Los Angeles as a laboratory of the immediate present, an experimental breeding ground for possible realities. Los Angeles itself became the classroom and studio for this course.

David J. Pearson (MArch II)
"Thermo LA"

2013 - 2014 is California's driest period since it was granted statehood in 1850.
In 1999 Los Angeles moved its downtown weather station 6 km closer to the beach, thus instilling a millenial discontinuity in the historical weather record.
Sensors attached to a bike recorded the following: CO, Ozone, Methane, LPG & Temperature
CO
Ozone
Methane
LPG
Temperature
A general rule for "standard atmosphere" temperature drop with height is 6.5 degrees Celsius (3.57 degrees Fahrenheit) per 1000 meters (1000 feet).
0

Quantitative Aesthetics: Attention

Instructors
Panagiotis Michalatos
with Cristina Caprioli
Teaching Assistant
Wenting Guo

This course examined computational approaches to digital media that analyzed and reinterpreted our environment as a signal, creating interactive interventions that distorted the limits of the sensible. "Aesthetics" had less to do with judgments of beauty and more with its original meaning on the discourse "of the senses." Our experience of cultural, social, and physical environments is increasingly influenced by digital media that form cascades of filters and surfaces of interaction. Understanding the totality of what can be seen, said, or heard within these environments (what Jacques Rancière might call "the distribution of the sensible") leads into the realm of signal analysis: a conceptual framework for making sense of and intervening in an environment that exists in a superposition of states that can be analyzed and recombined in different ways.

Stockholm-based choreographer Cristina Caprioli helped us to frame the scope for this year. Currently organizing a new type of traveling conference on dance and politics that tests modes of speech delivery and retention, she has contributed to rethinking the communication and media organization of the conference space. In particular, contemporary discourse on dance helped us address the problem of maintaining attention. We tested the idea that achieving a heightened state of attentiveness and engagement by speakers and audiences alike involved placing them in unfamiliar situations characterized by discomfort. At the least, a strategic impediment to perception required more effort, physical labor, and investment from speakers and listeners. As Pier Paolo Pasolini would say, he expected from the viewers of his films as much attention and effort as he had put into making them.

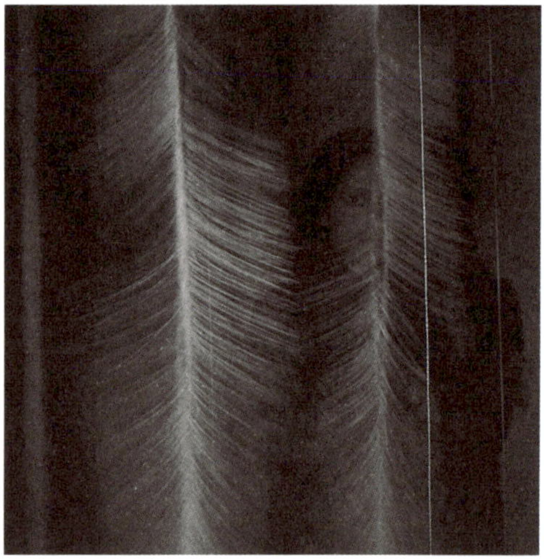

Chungseok Baek (MLA I AP)
Olga Mesa (MDes)
LingLi Tseng (MDes)
Yingyi Wang (MDes)
"Feather"
01 Tonal scale detection
02 Gesture detection

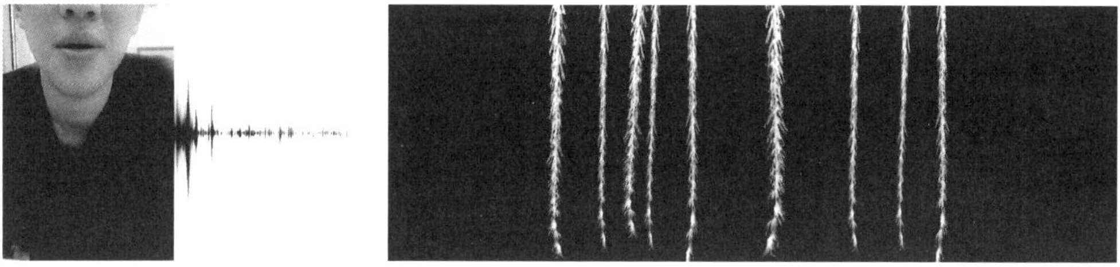

01

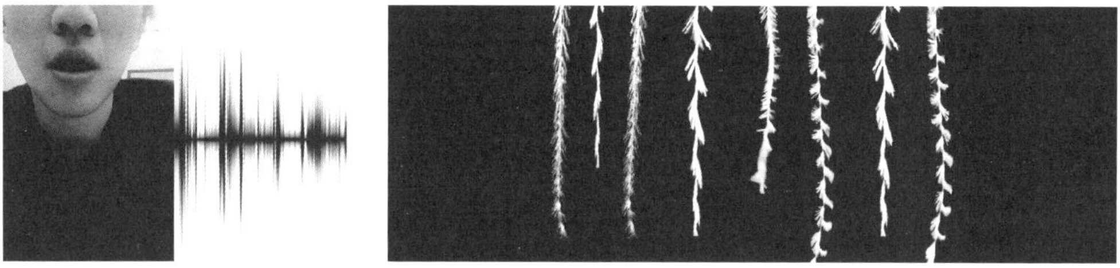

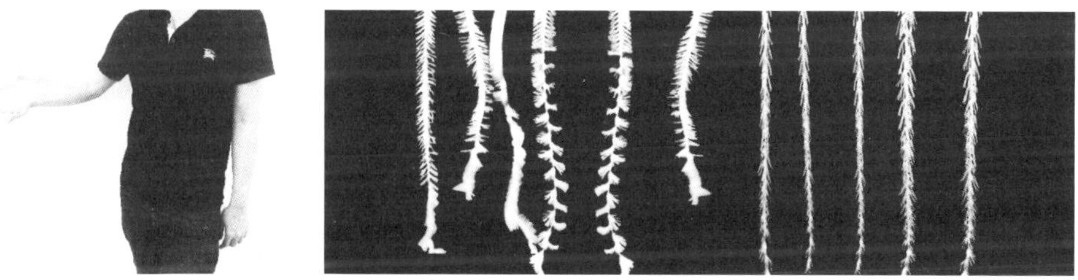

02

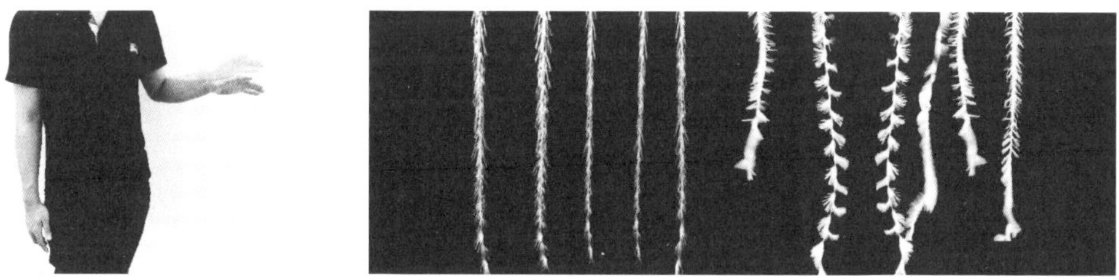

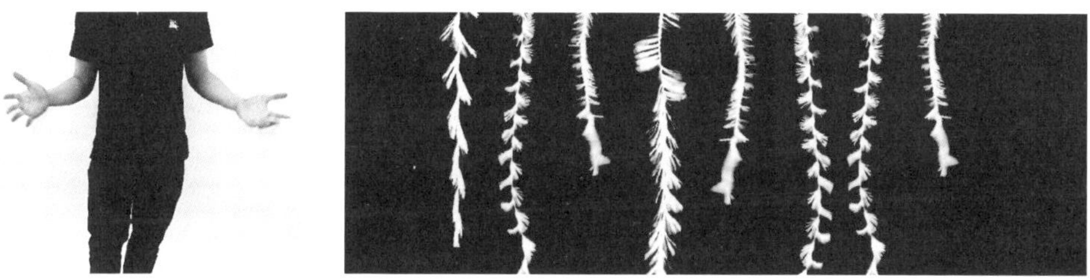

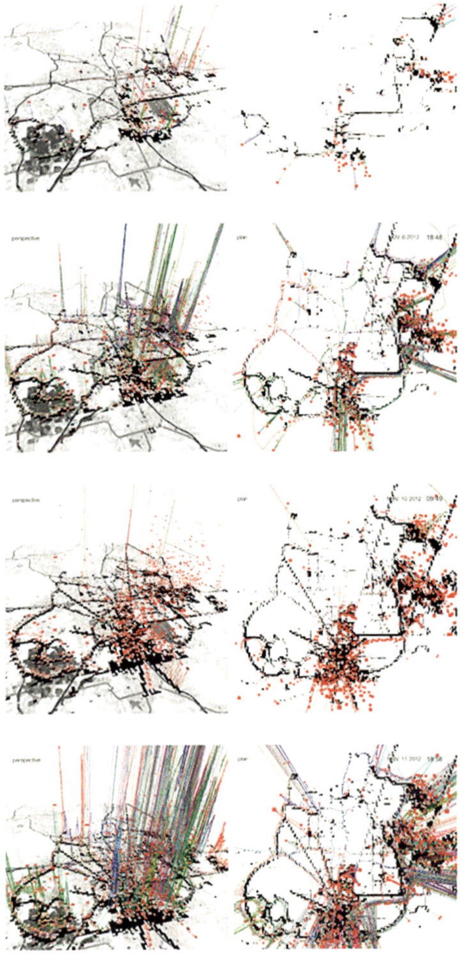

Krystelle Denis (MArch I AP)
"(in)visible trails"

Mixed-Reality City

Instructors
Yanni Alexander Loukissas
with Matthew Battles

The contemporary city is constituted by multiple overlapping, intermixing realities articulated across built form and imagined space, individual experience and collective memory, embodied sensation and digital mediation. Often these multiple realities are invisible or illegible, with certain narratives dominating particular environments. However, realities always leave traces, to be excavated and reconstructed. The Mixed-Reality City was an exploratory research seminar and workshop in which students pursued studies of urbanism-in-the-making through means and methods emerging in the digital arts and humanities, including: data narrative, digital ethnography, adversarial design, and critical technical practice. The course focused in equal parts on unpacking discourses and developing interpretative digital artifacts.

This year, the course examined the mixed reality of natural and artificial environments, principally in the Northeastern United States. Projects focused on historical and contemporary controversies over troubled natural or wild places and phenomena by exploring their associations and effects within cities. The class pursued questions about the co-construction of the "natural" and the "artificial" as well as feral presences in cities: places and phenomena once domesticated, now returned to nature. Moreover, we examined the relationship between natures and networks. What happens to technology in the wild? Can technology itself become feral?

Real-Time Cities: An Introduction to Urban Cybernetics

Instructor
Nashid Nabian
Teaching Fellow
Stefano Andreani

Urbanity merges with digital information in real-time cities. The built environment is dynamically sensed and synchronously actuated to perform more efficiently and intelligently; we can repurpose systems developed for other reasons to collect information about urban operations. Additionally, each urbanite can be considered a human sensor, an agent for reporting individual experiences. The crowd then becomes a distributed network of sensors that allows us to understand the dynamic patterns of the real-time city and the experiences of its citizens.

The course provided the theoretical grounding and technical skills required to design, develop, and implement prototypical urban cybernetic mechanisms that sense or actuate the city, with the promise of creating a "smart city" that is a desirable, safe, and sustainable place to live and work.

HEARTFELT

It'll sense your heart rate...

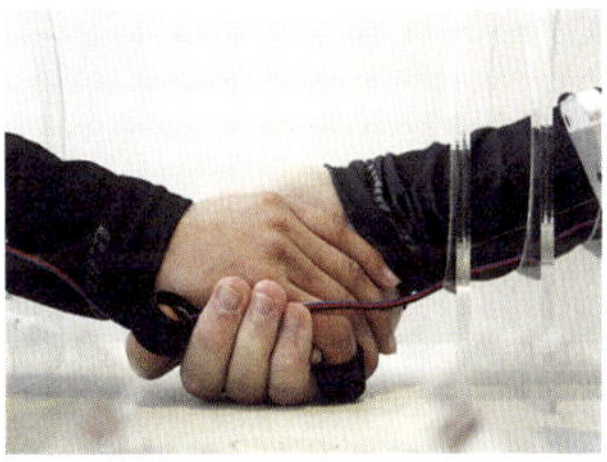

...and show it to your partner.

Make dating a science.

01

02

01 Tiffany Chen (MArch II)
Jason Lipshin (MIT CMSW)
"Heartfelt"
02 Maria Soledad Cano (MDes)
"Like Me"

The Community Façade

Student
Joungwon Lee (MDes)
Advisor
Krzysztof Wodiczko

The major problem of U.S. public housing projects, besides the reality of concentrated poverty, is the negative image of the projects. Public housing projects are seen as places to fear and stigmatize residents through implied association with criminal activity; those who live there are made to feel isolated from the rest of society. The building typology of housing projects intensifies this stigma by becoming the symbolic figure of the televisual landscape of housing projects while providing a physical environment that fosters a public neighborhood, as opposed to a community. This project aims to redress the stigma of housing projects by performing a physical intervention on this building typology. Specifically, the project attempts to reshape the image of public housing without negating the existing building typology, unlike the recent trend of redevelopment projects.

Recent public-private interventions to deal with the negative image of housing projects have included demolition, replacement, and redevelopment. Denying the current situation, however, is not a solution; instead, denial could intensify the crisis by treating the stigmatized buildings and communities as deserving of destruction. Upon acknowledging the building form as it stands, this intervention adds elements currently lacking in the public housing building typology. By installing a temporary window box, this project encourages residents to go to their window and connects their interior activities to a public space. The planter box would also provide fresh vegetables to the residents.

In this project, the exterior of the building is not transformed by superficial wrapping materials but by the activities of the residents. Each household maintains its own planter box so that the façade reveals residents' collective efforts to maintain the building. A planter box accompanies the frame of each window, forming a "decorative" window-box unit. Although it is a redundant decoration, it is different from other attempts at "window dressing" or "spring beautification" in that the window box is an apparatus that mirrors the resident's identity. Specific strategies to carry out this goal include using the planter-box unit as a "canvas" to externalize the interior spaces or individual characters of the residents. By doing so, this project tries to recognize the individuality of residents and defy the negative label collectively attached to them. Also, residents will have stronger attachments to the objects and the place where they are installed. The building exterior with its various planter-box units displays the residents' emotional connection to their living space. In sum, this test installation is a statement about reshaping the image of public housing through acknowledging the value of the individuals who live in it.

A test installation was made to the building exterior of the Franklin Field public housing project in Dorchester, with permission from the Boston Housing Authority. The installation was designed and developed with the help of four households who volunteered to participate in the project. The process of realizing a physical intervention to the public housing building required various tactics: to gain the residents' attention, to overcome community apathy, and to actualize the idea and solve the practical obstacles in construction. Sophisticated architectural details was devised to install the window unit without using glue or nails that might damage the building. The hanging structure inserted between window jambs, the only available structure on the wall, is integrated into the window system, allowing for the operation of windows and mosquito netting.

The test installation was approved on March 19, 2014, and completed on May 5, 2014. Once the design was placed in public, it became an object to which the owner actively tried to impart a new meaning. It became a part of participants' identity to the extent that they wanted to include them in their interior spaces when they were detached from the exterior wall. Likewise, people who noticed each installation saw the residents living within.

Panchito!

J M P Garden

01

01 Kelly Murphy (MLA II)
Karol Malik (MLA I)
02,03:
Malika Singh (MDes)
Saurabh Mhatre (MDes)

Landscape Material Design Practice and Digital Media

Instructor
David Mah
Teaching Fellow
Felix Raspall

The course fostered conceptual as well as technical approaches to the integration of digital design and fabrication techniques with design and construction processes. This project introduced a wide range of techniques that informed and enriched the process from design conception to various design application scenarios and finally, to prototype fabrication of construction and material systems in contemporary landscapes. The course expanded on digital design skills in three-dimensional modeling, scripting, and parametric tools, as well as digital fabrication. Precedents were studied to inspire the projects to address novel expression as well as performance criteria.

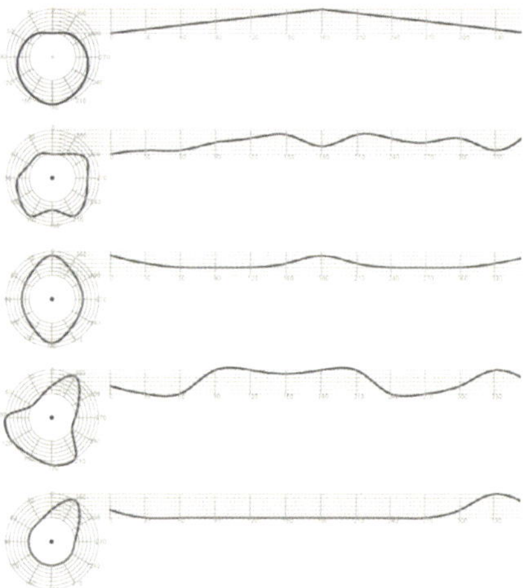

02

03

04

05

04 Kelly Murphy (MLA II)
Karol Malik (MLA I)
05,06:
Hea Min Kim (MDes)
Heng Zhang (MLA I)
Zhenhuan Xu (MArch II)

06

01

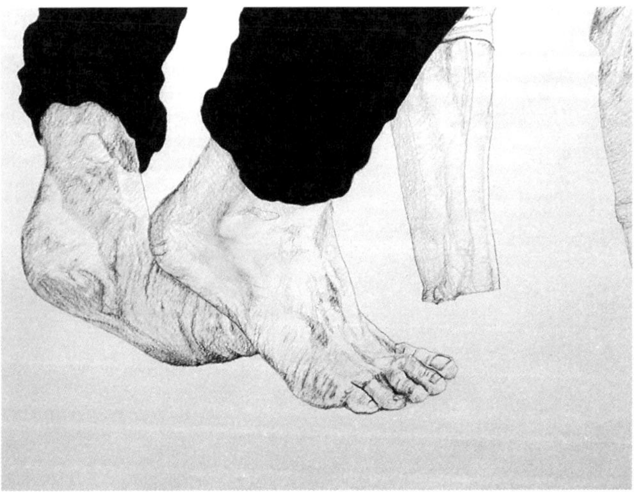

02

04

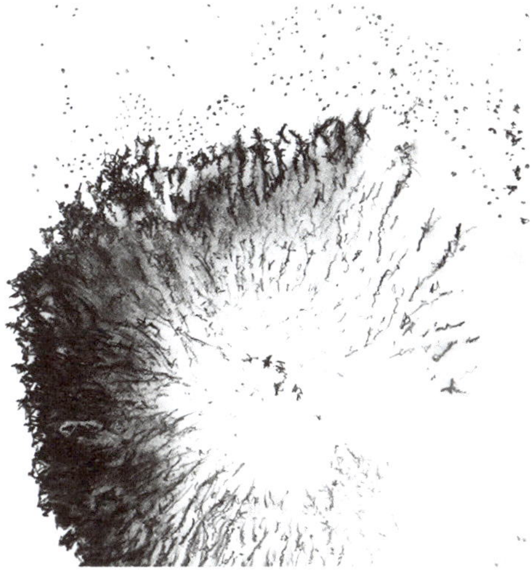

03

01 Emily Margulies (MArch I)
02 Jinhyun Jun (MLA II)
03 Justin Jackson (MLA I AP)
04 Hao Chen (MAUD)

Drawing for Designers

Instructor
Ewa Harabasz
Teaching Assistant
Lara Mehling

This course focused on drawing as a tool to advance students' visual skills in artistic representation and creative imagination. Main objectives included mastering technical and artistic skills in hand drawing, refining sensitivity to all details of what one sees, and developing greater capacity to articulate ideas in a visually convincing and evocative form. Projects included drawing in both outdoor and indoor situations and drawing of live models.

In the process of drawing, students focus on the world of lines, textures, shapes, light, shade, and values. We used various tools, materials, and artistic techniques such as pencils, vine charcoal, conté pastels, markers, ink, and other media. Ultimately, these media were combined with the use of camera, press imagery, and computer renderings.

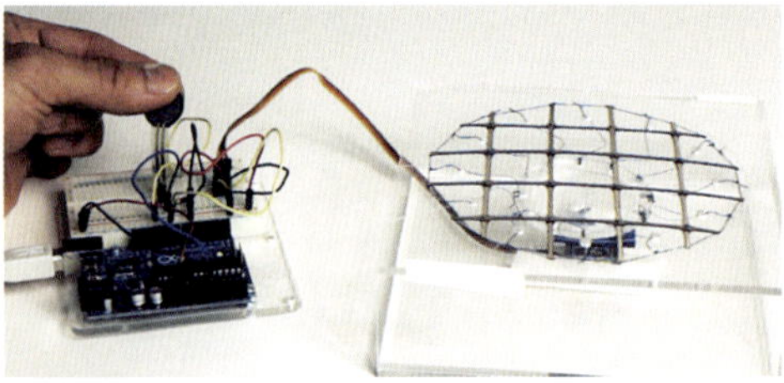

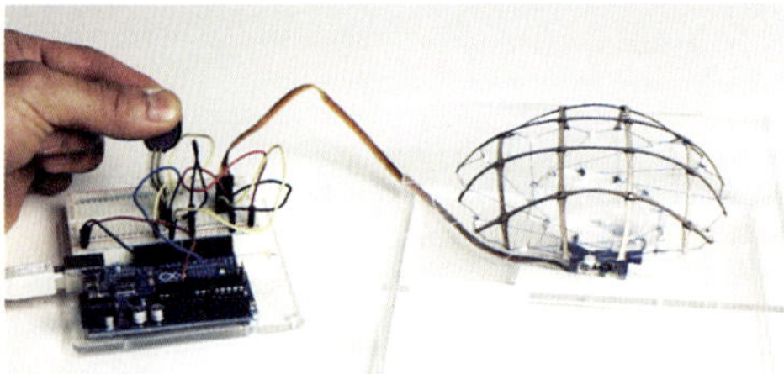

01

01 Brian Chu (MArch II)
Conor Coghlan (MArch II)
02 Patrick Burke (MArch I AP), "Animation Still," Continually Forming Agent-Based Polygon Mesh
03 Ren Tian (MArch I)
04 Zheng Cui (MArch II)
05 Bennett Gale (MArch I) "Off-Axis Circular Breaking," Rotational Movement of Figure along Cylindrical Axis

Digital Media for Design

Instructor
David Mah
Teaching Fellow
Joëlle Bitton
Teaching Assistants
Zi Gu
Zhewen Dai

The interrogation and acquisition of emerging and established digital design approaches was the focus of this course. Students gained knowledge of digital design media as well as the wide range of design approaches that constitute the larger field of digital/computational work in landscape, architecture, and urban design. Exercises and techniques were explored that illustrate varied methods, from associative to generative design.

Along with an investigating digital modeling, an emphasis was placed on exploiting the capacity for design software and diagramming techniques to model and integrate both complex material and time-based difference and transformation in landscape, architectural, and urban patterns, behaviors, performance, and formation processes.

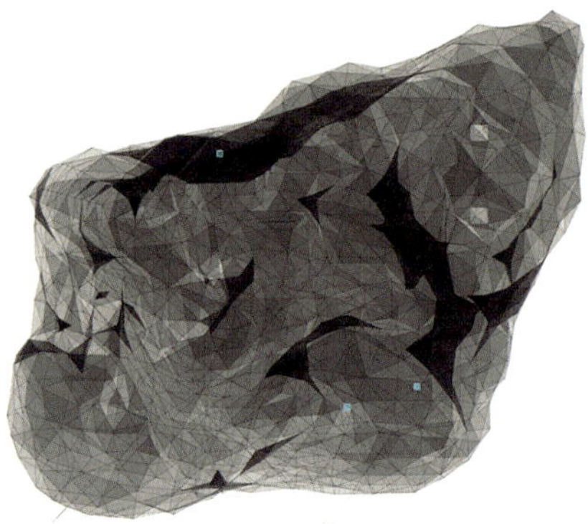

02

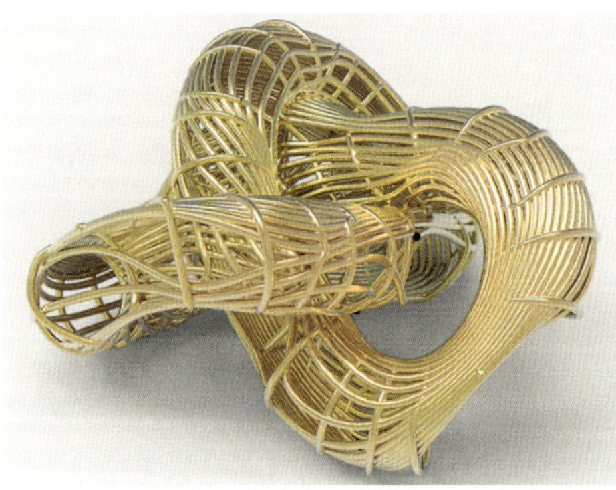

03

04

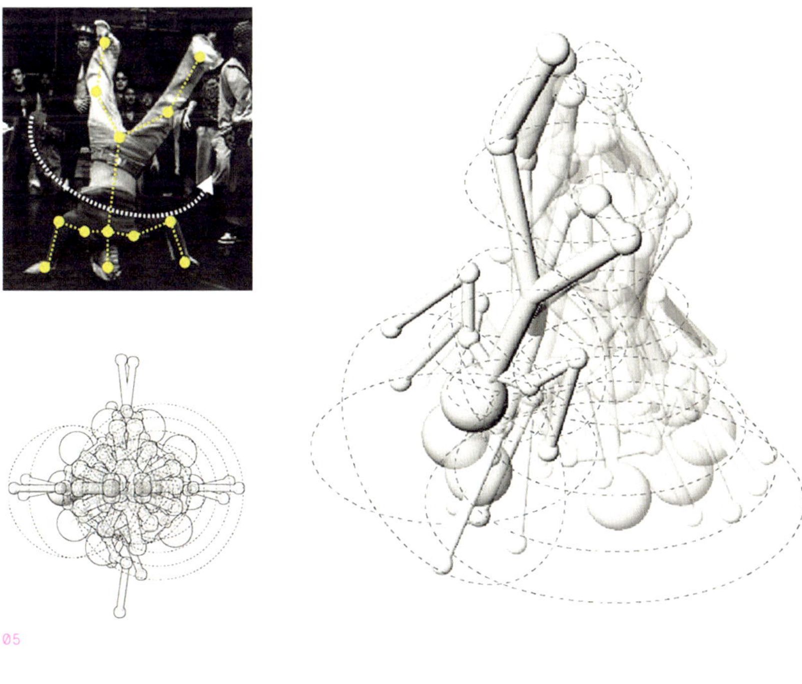

05

01

02

03

04

05

03

07

08

01 Patricia Semmler (MArch I)
02 Jennifer Corlett (MLA I)
03 Patrick Sunbury (MLA I AP)
04 Hyeyun Jung (MArch I)
05 Manuel Colon Amador (MLA I AP)
06 Miree Song (MLA I)
07 Alicia Gomez Jimenez (MLA I AP)
08 Haiyun Wang (MLA I AP)
09 Hao Chen (MAUD)
10 John Frey (MLAUD/MLA I)

09

10

Landscape as Painting

Instructor
Ewa Harabasz
Teaching Assistant
John Kirsimagi

The course advanced students' visual skills in artistic representation and creative imagination through painting. Assigned and generated by students, projects focused on emotional perception, bodily experience, and metaphoric interpretation of landscape. The course emphasized visual sensitivity and the capacity to articulate and convey perceptions through painting in a visually convincing and evocative form. Projects addressed both natural and built environments, with assignments focused on the world of colors, textures, composition, mood, light, shape, and values. Various media were used, including acrylic and oil paints, watercolor, and gouache. As a whole, playful experimentation emphasized and encouraged innovative combinations of various painting materials, methods, and techniques.

Cities by Design II

<u>Instructors</u>
Rahul Mehrotra, Christine Smith, Peter G. Rowe, Jose Castillo, Ricky Burdett, Eve Blau, Jana Cephas, Erkin Özay
<u>Teaching Fellows</u>
Ozlem Altinkaya Genel
Olga Touloumi
<u>Teaching Assistant</u>
Michael Leef

Cities by Design studied urban form and provided a synthetic overview of the factors affecting the design of contemporary cities. In this second course in a year-long series, students examined twelve cities as case studies to explore a range of urban design parameters in various geographical contexts. The course investigated cities' processes of evolution that shaped the urban formation as a whole, along with the particularities of urban fragments and projects. The two main pedagogical goals that guided the course were: (1) to engage students in a comparative study of cities that will broaden their definition of the "urban," and (2) to build a historical framework within which they will identify the urban characteristics and design strategies that render particular cities distinct.

01

Resource Extraction Urbanism II: Recasting the South American Hinterland

John Frey (MLAUD/MLA I)
"Shale: Urbanization in the South American Hinterland"
01 Global markets of natural gas and consumption
02 South American natural gas networks

Instructor
Felipe Correa

As development pressures continue to transform the hinterlands at an unprecedented rate, it has become crucial for the design disciplines to actively engage and conceptualize alternative futures for decentralized geographies and unbound territories. This faculty research seminar utilized the Initiative for the Integration of Regional Infrastructure in South America (IIRSA) to gauge the potential role that transnational mobility infrastructure can play as the backbone for a more integral mode of urbanization within South America's hinterland.

This seminar served as a platform to investigate the physical inscriptions of the most salient resource extraction industries, and affiliated infrastructures, which have reconfigured the South American hinterlands throughout the twentieth century, and the diverse models of urbanism that these industries have generated. This overview became a point of reference for understanding the physical effects of the IIRSA initiative throughout the South American hinterland, to conceptualize urbanization models that can synthesize the relationships across resource extraction, infrastructure, landscape, and urbanism.

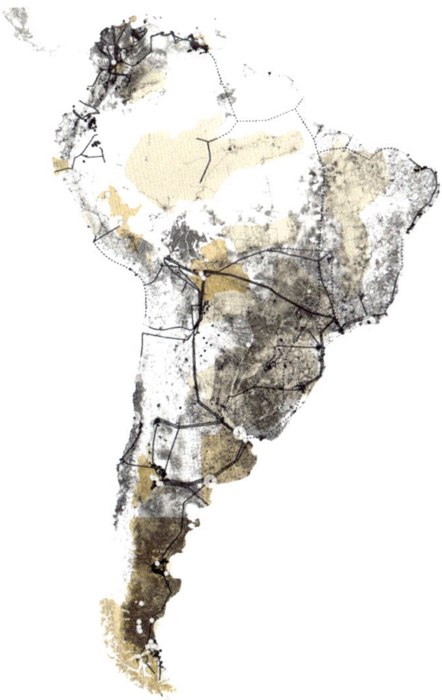

02

Healthy Places

Instructor
Ann Forsyth

It seems obvious that there is a link between environments and health, but how important is it? What are the key health issues that should concern those in planning and related fields? Does incorporating health issues into planning and design processes always add value?

This course focused on how to make places healthier in an evidence-based, inclusive, and efficient manner. We examined the extent to which environments determine health outcomes and how this relationship between people and places evolved over time. The class studied several key topics where location and built environment contributed to health outcomes, from air quality to the geography of vulnerable populations, to address questions of design and healthy places.

Photo Credit Health Impact Assessment (HIA)

Modern Housing and Urban Districts

Instructors
Peter Rowe
Har Ye Kan

This seminar addressed "modern housing" from 1990 to the present. Housing projects were discussed in the context of contributing to the making of "urban districts" or of being shaped by the districts in which they are placed. Case studies examined pairings of underlying urban conditions with architectural projects that also took into consideration historical circumstances and housing development lineages. Concluding discussions observed various dimensions across projects and urban conditions to identify strengths and weaknesses, but also to set contemporary housing apart from modern housing in prior eras.

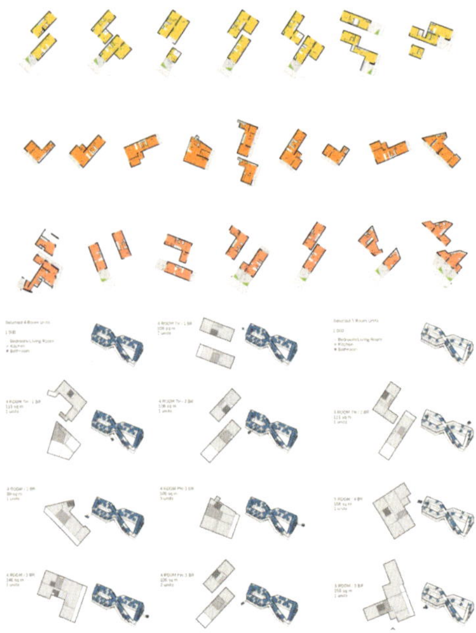

Jaime Daroca (MArch II)
Jerome Byron Hord (MAUD)
"Big Buildings/Submultiples"

Global Leadership in Real Estate and Design

Instructors
Bing Wang
Eugene A. Kohn

This research course investigated synthesizing real estate and design education to provide a forward-looking analysis of and exposure to the complexity and interconnection in current real estate design, development, and investment processes. The course integrated domestic and international urban development projects and interactive process to rethink, anticipate, and reinvent practice paradigms in both real estate and design fields that respond to exigent and projected transformative environmental, market, economic, and cultural changes.

Chen Ling (MAUD), Emmanuel Torres (MAUD), Hang Zhang (MAUD) "Downtown Boston Waterfront Development Towers"

Ryan Bouma (MDes), Zhenhuan Xu (MArch II), Elisa Saccenti (University of Bergamo), Roberta Allevi (University of Bergamo). "GROWin BERGAMO" with Jock Herron

Smart[er] Cities

Instructor
Nashid Nabian
Research Associate/Teaching Fellow
Stefano Andreani

With the objective of developing alternative models of urbanization framed in the context of technologically enhanced cities, this course addressed the emerging areas of Smart[er] Knowledge and Smart[er] Health. Students explored new opportunities offered by innovative technologies for the redefinition of knowledge creation and the distribution of ecosystems of innovation for the enhancement of health solutions and practices. The course investigated how new networks, enhanced immersive and interactive spaces, and novel computational technologies contributed to tackling questions of learning and health care through design of smart architectures, infrastructures, and ultimately artifacts, as well as technologically retrofitting our built environments. The course was conducted in academic collaboration with the University of Bergamo.

 Working with the robots in the fabrication laboratory

ABB
FOUNDRY
PLUS

INFORMAL MATERIAL FORMATIONS: RESPONSIVE DESIGN-TO-FABRICATION METHODS FOR IRREGULAR AND IMPRECISE MATERIAL PROCESSES

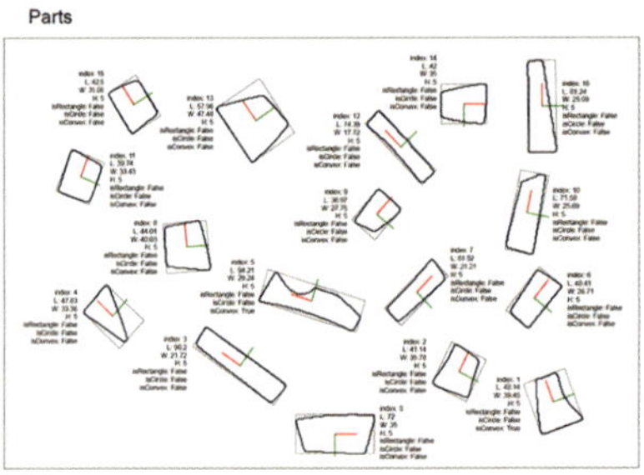

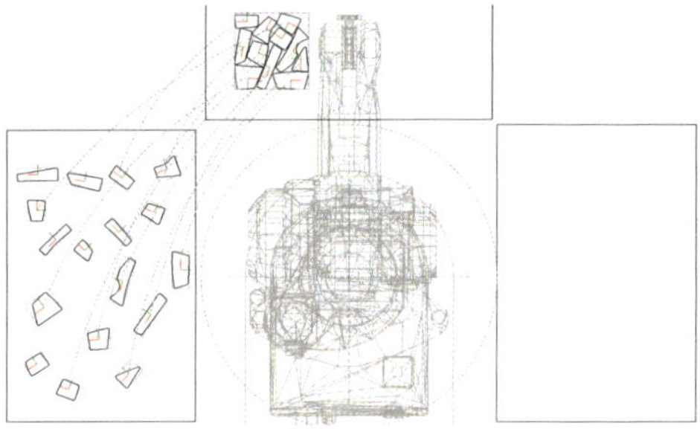

Design and construction practices in the informal city and in the work of designers who produce with found objects are often praised by architects for their resourcefulness. Their creative process, "informal production," creates useful and often expressive designs out of what is immediately available, despite (and by virtue of) the large irregularities of the materials at hand and the imprecisions of construction. While the discipline of architecture encourages complete and fixed designs before construction and requires standard and predictable construction methods, "informal production" leaves designs open-ended until the very moment of fabrication, when material uncertainties are finally resolved.

This thesis investigates the creative process in "informal production" from a theoretical perspective and proposes methods to implement its "responsiveness"—its capacity to adjust the design during construction—into the professional model. The research is organized into three parts. The first part studies "informal production" practices from a theoretical perspective. The core is the comparative analysis of a selection of case studies of informal practices vis-à-vis the well-established professional model. Based on this empirical evidence, the research constructs a vocabulary and a conceptual framework, discussing the concepts of material uncertainty, material feedback, responsiveness, control, process design, and nonstandard construction methods.
The second part proposes design and fabrication strategies, technologies, and workflows to incorporate the "responsiveness" of informal practices into the discipline of architecture. To this aim, the thesis develops a design and fabrication workflow and the enabling technologies to coordinate material scanning, design computation, and online fabrication in real time. Three sets of design and fabrication experiments test the efficacy of the proposed system in designs that take advantage of variable material inflows such as discarded streams. The accessibility and customizability of the proposed system is tested by untrained students in a workshop.

The third part of the thesis discusses the implications of an informal method for the discipline of architecture and debates the specific challenges and limitations of the developed technologies. It studies future applications in architecture and construction, in particular and design with reclaimed materials and in human-machine collaborations in construction.

The thesis concludes by organizing future lines of research. This research contributes to advancing the understanding of "informal production" and demonstrates a possibility of reproducing their "responsiveness" within the disciplinary model. Several design and fabrication experiments prove the initial feasibility of this approach for design reusing discarded materials.

Advisors: Martin Bechthold,
Panagiotis Michalatos, Sergio Forster
Felix Raspall (DDes)

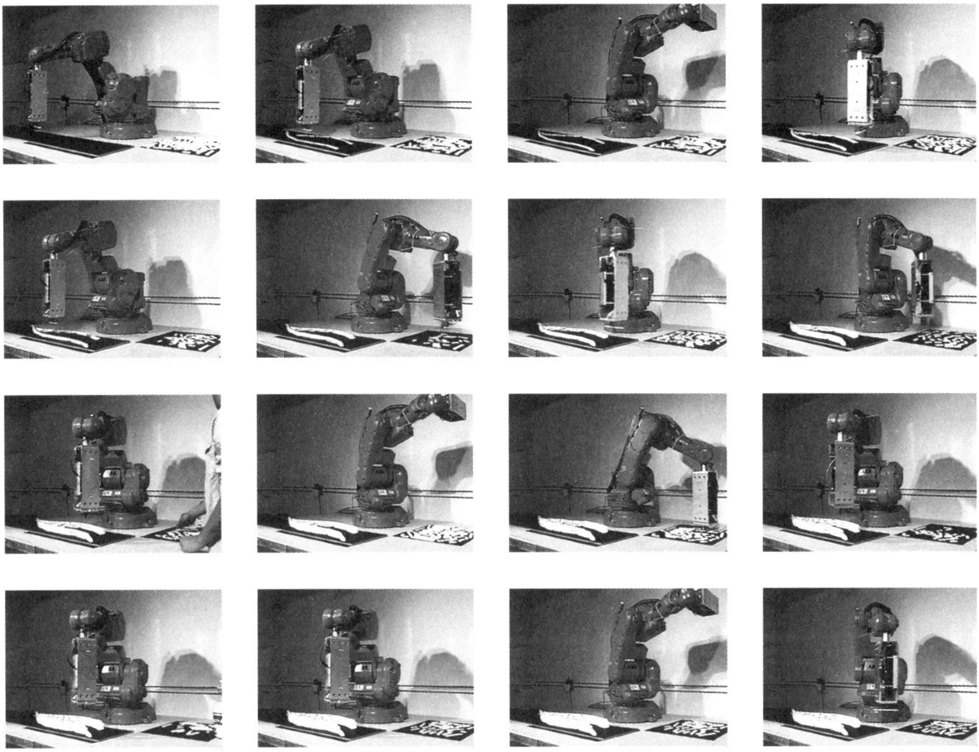

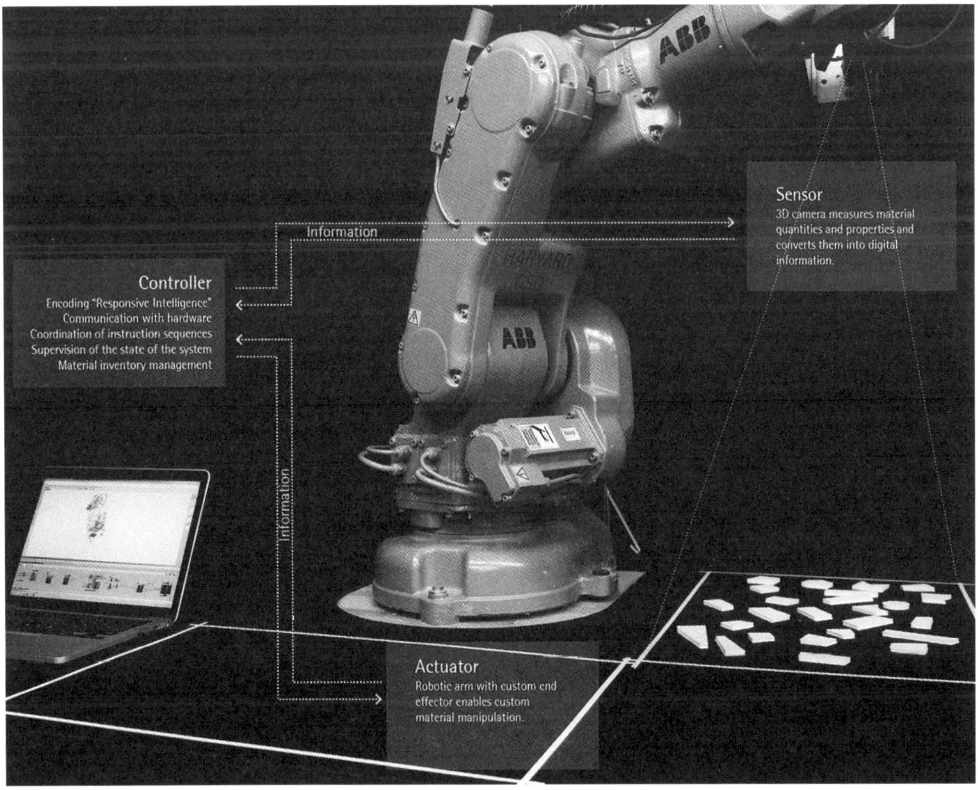
Sensor
3D camera measures material quantities and properties and converts them into digital information.
Information
Controller
Encoding "Responsive Intelligence"
Communication with hardware
Coordination of instruction sequences
Supervision of the state of the system
Material inventory management
Information
Actuator
Robotic arm with custom end effector enables custom material manipulation.
ABB

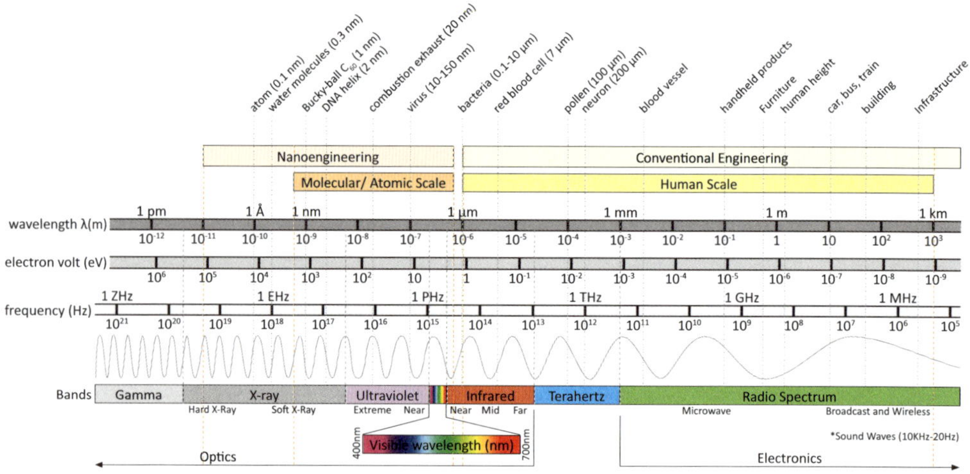

PERCEPTUAL MATERIAL INTERFACE: DESIGN OF PHYSICAL BOUNDARY LAYERS IN THE AGE OF BIOLOGICALLY INSPIRED MATERIAL TECHNOLOGY

This research is intended to formulate a comprehensive conceptual framework for designing material systems across multiple design scales based on the physiological and psychological perception of humans. One of the key goals is to investigate the strategies for overcoming the scale discrepancies between the design disciplines (industrial, fashion, and architectural design) and the enabling technologies (material science, nanotechnology, and biotechnology). The distinction is substantial since the enabling technologies operate substantially below the micrometer scale, and the design applications operate above it. In the context of this study, physical boundaries include the material interface of artifacts and environment within the immediate area that is perceivable to humans. At any given moment, we are interacting with a number of physical layers simultaneously and dynamically, and it is those systematic interactions that create microenvironments or zones that we can experience. Therefore the interactions between us and a collection of physical boundary layers, as well as the interactions between the layers themselves, are critical to the research.

The study is further focused on a group of closely related factors in the design of physical boundaries that mediate between electromagnetic stimuli and visual-thermal sensation. The key environmental factors are light and heat in the context of thermal radiation, which is a subdomain of the electromagnetic spectrum and includes a portion of ultraviolet radiation and all visible and infrared radiation. The experiential factor of interest is visual-thermal comfort based on human sensation and perception relating to vision and thermoception. Finally, material systems that operate between 100 nm and 100 µm will be the main focus of this study.

Above: Preliminary conceptual framework diagram
Various scale relationships between electromagnetic spectrum, operation, and application.
Advisors: Martin Bechthold, Joanna Aizenberg, Salmaan Craig
Daekwon Park (DDes)

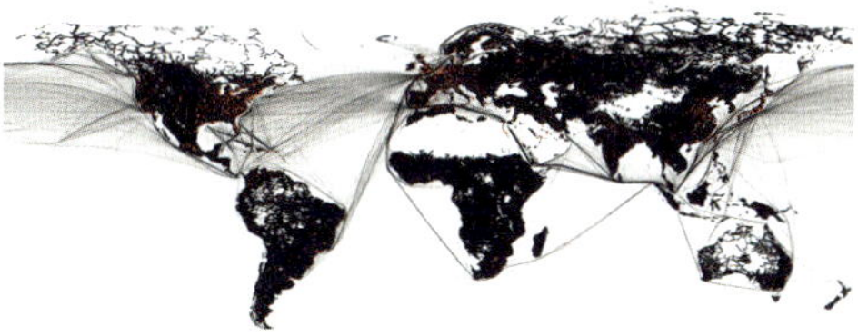

FROM HINTERLAND TO HINTERWORLD: TERRITORIAL ORGANIZATION BEYOND AGGLOMERATION

Urbanization can be characterized by a continuous process of socio-material exchange between agglomerations and complex webs of (dis)continuous supply and service hinterlands. Historically confined at the regional scale, this relationship has become extremely hard to define under globalization. While the systems of "global cities" coevolve with an equally unprecedented reorganization of systems of global hinterlands, the latter remain largely dissolved in the operations of logistical networks. Multidisciplinary approaches have tried to address the socioeconomic and, recently, ecological dimensions of these global hinterlands. Yet the processes of their construction and restructuring remain largely "external" to the study of urbanization, which has continued to focus on territorial organization of agglomerations. Through a hybrid methodology of historical research and critical cartographic experimentation, this research explores how the geographical, social, and technical processes of the construction of the hinterworld can be integrated into the study of urbanization.

Above: The total "used" area of the planet and the global system of agglomerations. Nikos Katsikis, Urban Theory Lab.
Advisors: Hashim Sarkis, Neil Brenner
Nikos Katsikis (DDes)

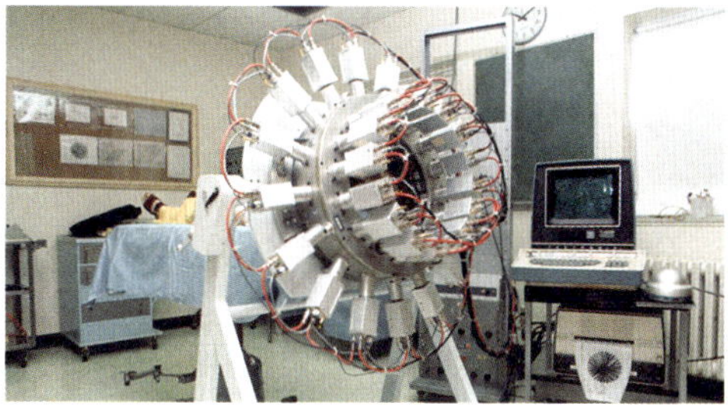

TOWARD A NEW HOSPITAL: ARCHITECTURE, MEDICINE, AND COMPUTATION, 1960–1975

This dissertation provides an account of how computing left behind its origins in academic and military research to become part of the hospital equipment setting. I examine the efforts of reformers, including administrators, planners, architects, and computer consultants, to provide appropriate accommodation for modern biomedicine. I explore three stories to untangle the admixture of architecture, medicine, and computation as they intertwined through a mutual engagement with automation, operations research, cybernetics, and biomedical research in the postwar hospital. In London, architects Llewelyn Davies Weeks used computer algorithms to help design Northwick Park Hospital. In Boston, pioneering research consultants Bolt Beranek & Newman collaborated with the Massachusetts General Hospital on an experimental total information system known as the Hospital Computer Project. Lastly, in Canada, the Montreal Neurological Institute adopted computing to transform its expertise in clinical brain imaging research.

Above: A prototype positron emission scanner, the Positome, installed at the Montreal Neurological Institute, ca. 1975. Courtesy Christopher Thompson. Advisors: Allan Brandt, Peter Galison, Michael Hays, Antoine Picon
David Theodore (PhD)

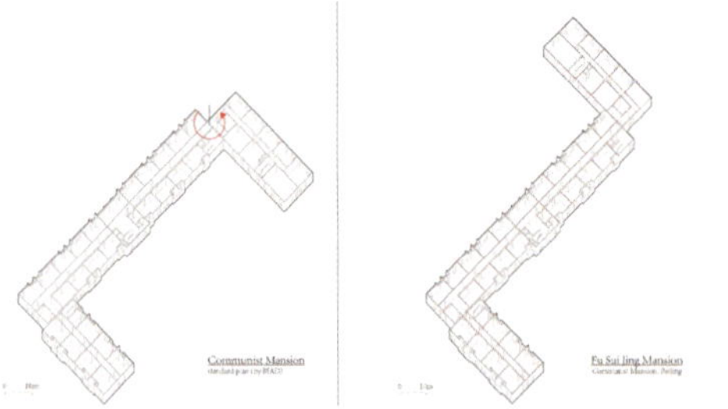

ARCHITECTURE FOR THE MULTITUDE: THE LOGIC AND DIALECTICS OF URBAN FORMS IN BEIJING IN THE 1950s

To define a position on the city as architects is to make a claim for architecture's relevance for the city. This dissertation rethinks the contemporary Chinese city via the dialectics between built architectural forms and the urban spaces of Beijing in the 1950s. From state-driven planning economy (1950s) to state-driven market economy (2000s), the logic of the Chinese city remains unchanged: the city is "the spatialization of the collective." I theorize China's urban forms through the dialectics of the "state-collective-individual" relationship. Instead of focusing on the city as a whole, I concentrate on three exemplary urban forms in Beijing. Adopted under modernist ideals and remaining pivotal in the contemporary city, they are the Mansion (Communist Mansion), the Square (Tiananmen Square), and the Factory (Beijing No. 2 Textile Factory). These examples are not normative but "singular formal events that serve to define the possibility of a milieu of forms." These urban forms are instrumental in their function in the city, what they confront, and what the effects are, not abstractions of rules or principles. Thus the possibility exists to appropriate these archetypes as critiques against the conventional notion of urban design as a master plan.

Advisors: Peter Rowe, Eve Blau, Joan Busquets
Ling Fan (DDes)

ARCHITECTURE, EXPERTISE, AND THE GERMAN CONSTRUCTION OF THE OTTOMAN RAILWAY NETWORK, 1868–1919

The dissertation examines the production of knowledge and architecture through the German-sponsored construction of the Ottoman railway network to critically reconsider the epistemological tenets of expertise in broader political, economic, and cultural structures distinct from the normative creative processes that dominate the historiography of empires. The dissertation capitalizes on the ambiguous colonial nature of the German role in the architecture, engineering, and urbanism of the late Ottoman Empire and situates it as a variegated model of European cultural expansionism through a process identified here as ambiguous transmutation. Wider findings emerge from this study. First, a burgeoning interdependency of modernity and secular rationalism with geopolitical strategy is manifest. Second, a new paradigm of the power/knowledge genre privileges the transnational "expert" in the production of design knowledge in an early globalizing world order. Third, the railways' construction reveals new insight into the geo-pragmatic origins of multiculturalist logic. Lastly, the German construction materialized a site for paradigmatic mutations in architectural form. The dissertation serves as instructive: explaining the dynamics of ambiguity as a way of negotiating innovation in knowledge amid the excitement and duress of modernity.

Above: Guillaume Gustave Berggren, View of the Anatolian Railway, tunnel at Bekdemir (Pékdemir), c. 1893. Niedersachsisches Landesarchiv, Ernst Mackensen Nachlass, 240 N Nr. VIII 6.
Advisors: Eve Blau, Gülru Necipoğlu, Antoine Picon Peter Christensen (PhD)

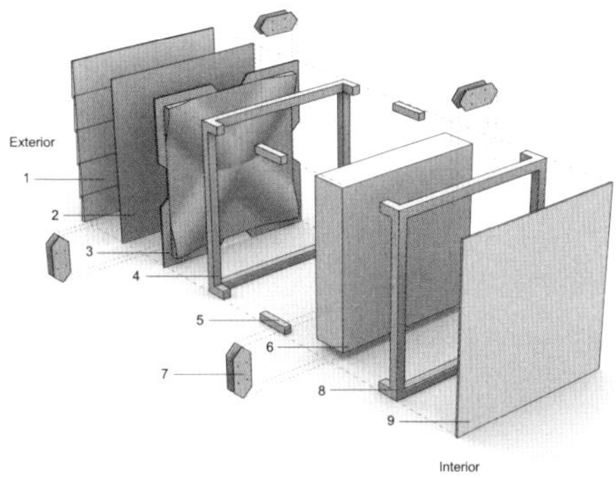

DESIGN METRICS FOR DISASSEMBLY AND MATERIAL RECOVERY

The dissertation presents the Material Recovery Potential Index (MRPI), a composite indicator for analyzing and designing highly recoverable building assemblies. The index provides a multi-criteria evaluation platform with which designers can compare a wide range of assembly and material types on a single material recovery potential scale. Consisting of a product-oriented and an assembly-oriented assessment modules, the MRPI employs both established and new metrics for measuring material-level recyclability, toxicity, biodegradability, rapid renewability, and other environmental impacts, as well as assembly-level separation damage, disassembly time and tool type, connection type, access, and integration level. In addition to explaining the theoretical and scientific underpinnings of the presented metrics, the dissertation demonstrates their application in a comparative study of building envelope assemblies. Lastly, the exploratory use of the index in an envelope assembly design process is discussed.

Above: Highly recyclable residential envelope assembly.
Advisor: Martin Bechthold
Matan Mayer (DDes)

ARCHITECTURES OF GLOBAL COMMUNICATION, 1941–1970

This dissertation examines architectural constructions of globality within the framework of mid-twentieth-century efforts to institutionally organize the world and engineer media democracies. I interrogate the aural modernities that architects constructed in collaboration with engineers, officials, and acousticians, along with the architectural strategies that informed them: the theater, the concert hall, the cinema. These interiors reconfigured the international community as a networked audience and the institutions of world organization as the main stages of international diplomacy. The dissertation foregrounds architects' role in negotiating the electroacoustic spaces of communication in the post–World War II period. Loudspeakers, multichannel consoles, and microphones point to dialogues between networks and environments, engineering, and midcentury aesthetic theories. Through the design and construction of assembly halls, courtrooms, and World Expo pavilions, architects participated in the mythopoetics, the myth-making, of "global village" narratives in the postwar period.

Above: United Nations Assembly at Flushing Meadows, 1947. UN Photo.
Advisor: Antoine Picon
Olga Touloumi (PhD)

© Maggie Janik, 2013. Review meeting for Exuma research project, October 04 2013.

EDUCATION

A Rapidly Expanding Field

The rapid development of research ranks among the most striking recent evolutions of the Graduate School of Design. In less than five years, the research income of the school has increased from approximately half a million dollars to more than $8 million. In response to this changing context, various structures have been added to established programs and centers such as the Aga Khan Program for Islamic Architecture and the Harvard Joint Center for Housing Studies. In addition to the new Harvard Center for Green Buildings and Cities, eight Design Labs are currently investigating issues ranging from architectural design and technologies to urban and landscape questions. Some of the current explorations of the Labs are featured in the following pages. They epitomize the challenges of research in a design school.

The first of these challenges regards the complexity of the objects and processes investigated. Buildings and construction techniques, cities and urbanization processes, landscape and ecological milieus are intrinsically multidimensional and require truly interdisciplinary approaches. The composition of the Labs reflects this growing need for interdisciplinarity.

A second challenge is linked to the largely felt urgency to find solutions to some of the most pressing problems facing our natural and built environment. The need to identify more sustainable modes of development permeates many research agendas. It raises questions regarding the necessary but always complicated relation between academic research and practice.

In a diverse environment such as the GSD, these challenges also represent opportunities to bridge the gap between the various dimensions of design education, in particular between lectures and seminars, on the one hand, and studios and workshops on the other. The active participation of students in the Labs—through productions ranging from texts to diagrams, and from maps to projects—bears testimony to the new possibilities for transcending traditional boundaries. In the years to come, research will appear more and more as an essential common ground between the diverse components of design education.

Its thematic range will also greatly expand. Joining well-established fields of inquiry such as construction and building technologies; the future of cities; and energy, environment, and climate change, domains like new spaces for work, leisure, and education; the problems raised by housing in relation to domesticity and interiority; and the need to rethink design at the threshold of art, engineering, and sensory media will require in-depth exploration. This expanded research landscape will also give full place to the histories and theories of the built environment beyond the current perimeter. Architecture, landscape architecture, urban planning, and urban design are disciplines in need of this continued historical and theoretical perspective.

Antoine Picon
Director of Research
G. Ware Travelstead Professor of the History of Architecture and Technology

Above: Olga Mesa (MDes), LingLi Tseng (MDes), and Yingyi Wang (MDes), "Star Labyrinth"

Members: Allen Sayegh, Edith Ackermann, Stefano Andreani, Jock Herron, Nashid Nabian, Panagiotis Michalatos

REAL
Responsive Environments and Artifacts Lab

The Responsive Environments and Artifacts Lab (REAL) at the Harvard Graduate School of Design pursues the design of digital, virtual, and physical worlds as an indivisible whole. It recognizes the pervasive nature of digital information and interaction at scales ranging from our bodies to the larger urban contexts that we occupy and the infrastructures that support them.

REAL takes an interdisciplinary look at the design of the physical environment from the lens of technologically augmented experiences.

Putting the human being at the center, from the micro (bodily sensors, smart product design) to the macro (information infrastructures, communication frameworks), researchers at REAL examine the emerging ways in which technology fuses with the ways we live, work, and play.

What kind of interfaces embrace our social, cultural, and natural landscapes? How does mediated matter permeate our environments, our surroundings, and our personal space? Which experiences are truly physical, and which are truly digital today? How can we design for an audience that is rapidly adopting new technologies, and what approaches can we take to embody responsiveness in our design decisions?

REAL develops a design-led approach and understanding of new media methods, technologies, and techniques that affect different aspects of our everyday lives and built environments.

Harvard Center for Green Buildings and Cities

The Harvard Center for Green Buildings and Cities aims to transform the building industry through a commitment to a design-centric strategy that directly links research outcomes to the development of new processes, systems, and products.

Through partnerships with cities, governments, and industry thought leaders, the Center will both disseminate findings and continue to explore the role that building efficiency plays in the larger urban context of sustainability.

By strongly emphasizing innovation and multidisciplinary collaboration, the Center will work to promote holistic change within the built environment—namely, the creation and continued improvement of sustainable, high-performance buildings and cities.

The Center's agenda involves four categories of research: Design and Operation, High-Performance Materials and Construction, Technology Adaption and Diffusion, and Sustainable Planning.

Students and experts from the Graduate School of Design will collaborate with researchers from various Harvard institutions including the School of Engineering and Applied Sciences, the School of Public Health, the Business School, the Kennedy School, the Law School, and the Faculty of Arts and Sciences.

Above: Alexander Jacobson (MArch I)

Members: Ali Malkawi, Richard Freeman, Iñaki Abalos, Martin Bechthold, Stephen Ervin, Eric Höweler, Jerold Kayden, Panagiotis Michalatos, Kiel Moe, Toshiko Mori, Richard Peiser, Antoine Picon, Spiro Pollalis, Chris Reed, Holly Samuelson, Allen Sayegh, Andrew Wang, Beth Pollack, Matan Mayer, Bin Yan, Salmaan Craig, Yujiao Chen, Gosia Sklodowska, Blanca Dasi Espuig, Jonathan Grinham, Alexander Jacobson, Karol Malik, Alejandra Romo, Bing Wang, Ching-Wen Xiao, Arta Yazdanseta, Michael Yuan, Liuwei Zhao, Jenna Bjorkman, Stefan Riley

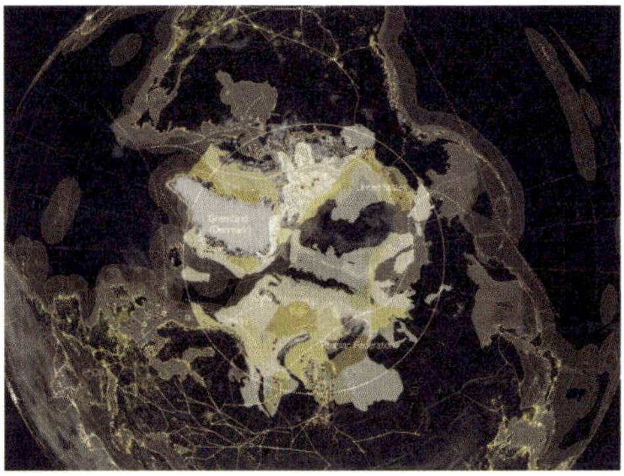

Urban Theory Lab

From top: Christopher Bennett (MDes), Grga Basic (MDes), and Vineet Diwadkar (MLA I AP/MUP)

Members: Neil Brenner, Robert Gerard Pietrusko, Daniel Ibañez, Nikos Katsikis, Ali Fard, Kian Goh, Marianne Potvin, Adam Tanaka, Dalal Musaed Alsayer, Shirin Barol, Grga Basic, Chris Bennett, Matthew Brown, Vineet Diwadkar, Leif Estrada, Ana Maria Quiros

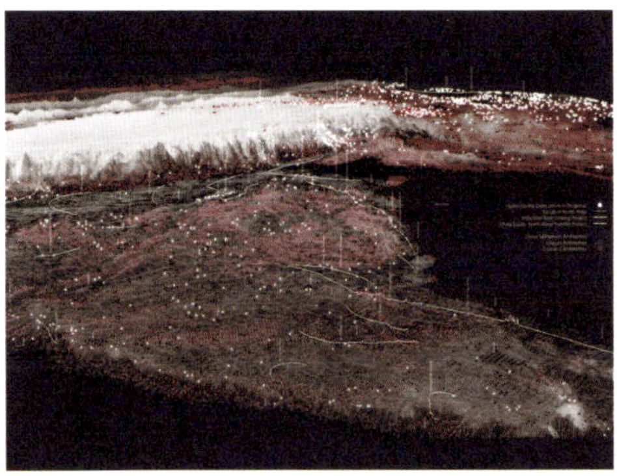

In the early 1970s, Henri Lefebvre put forward the radical hypothesis of the complete urbanization of society. This required, in his view, a profound shift from the analysis of urban form to the investigation of urbanization processes. The Urban Theory Lab-GSD builds on Lefebvre's approach to investigate emergent sociospatial formations under early twenty-first-century capitalism.

Our research proposes that inherited frameworks of urban knowledge must be reinvented to illuminate emergent forms of twenty-first-century urbanization. In contrast to the urban/suburban/rural distinction that has long underpinned the major traditions of urban research and cartographic practice, we argue that the urban today represents a worldwide condition in which all political-economic and socio-environmental relations are enmeshed, regardless of terrestrial location or morphological configuration. This emergent condition of planetary urbanization means, paradoxically, that even spaces that lie well beyond the traditional centers of agglomeration—from worldwide shipping lanes, transportation networks, and communications infrastructures to resource extraction sites, alpine and coastal tourist enclaves, offshore financial centers, agro-industrial catchment zones, and erstwhile "natural" spaces—are integral to a worldwide operational landscape for (capitalist) urbanization processes.

Through a conceptual distinction between concentrated urbanization (agglomeration) and extended urbanization (operational landscapes) developed in collaboration with Prof. Christian Schmid of the ETH-Zurich, we aim to investigate the historical geographies of the capitalist urban-industrial fabric in ways that supersede inherited metageographical binarisms while opening up new sociological, cartographic, and political perspectives on the contemporary global-urban condition. Our work combines conceptual and representational experimentation, theory-driven research, and research-based pedagogy, as well as various forms of outreach and events programming within the Harvard-GSD community and at scholarly conferences and workshops around the world.

Social Agency Lab

The Social Agency Lab is a research group at the Graduate School of Design that examines the ways in which individuals, institutions, and organizations shape social outcomes in cities. The lab leads a number of funded research efforts related to this theme. For example, lab members Raven Anderson and Aldarsaikhan Tuvshinbat, together with lab director Michael Hooper, are conducting research on the politics of urban planning in Mongolia. Based on extensive interviews with planners and residents of Ulaanbaatar, the coldest capital city on Earth and the planet's most polluted city, the team is attempting to understand the tensions between Mongolian and international efforts to constrain rapid urban growth. In Haiti, the lab has been involved in a long-term study of the politics of post-disaster reconstruction. Drawing on extensive interviews with organizations involved in the reconstruction of Port-au-Prince, the team is investigating three linked question: how are reconstruction priorities determined, what are the spatial assumptions that drive reconstruction efforts, and how do organizations grapple with the complex issue of rubble removal? In addition to these two projects, the lab is also conducting research in Ghana, Canada, and Sweden. The lab also brings together graduate students and researchers working on related topics and hosts a weekly seminar where members of the group can discuss their research and emergent findings.

Members: Michael Hooper, Brian Goldberg, Andrew Perlstein, Julia Cadaval Martins, Pamela Sitko, Andy Gerhart, Martha Pym, Maria Ignacia Arrasate, Raven Anderson, Batjin Boldbat, Aldarsaikhan Tuvshinbat

Above and below: "Policy Levers and Urban Growth: Rapid Urbanization and Its Management in Ulaanbaatar, Mongolia"

Principal Investigator: Michael Hooper
Lead researcher: Raven Anderson
Researcher: Aldarsaikhan Tuvshinbat

Funders: William F. Milton Fund, Joint Center for Housing Studies of Harvard University, American Planning Association

Above and below: "Priority Setting Amid the Rubble: Organizational Approaches to Post-Disaster Reconstruction in Haiti"

Principal Investigator: Michael Hooper

Funders: Harvard Academy for International and Area Studies

Above and below: "The Dynamics of Grassroots Mobilization: Social Movements, Eviction, and Involuntary Resettlement"

Principal Investigator: Michael Hooper
Collaborators: Jenny Cadstedt, Swedish Red Cross University

Funders: Social Sciences and Humanities Research Council (Canada), American Planning Association (International Division)

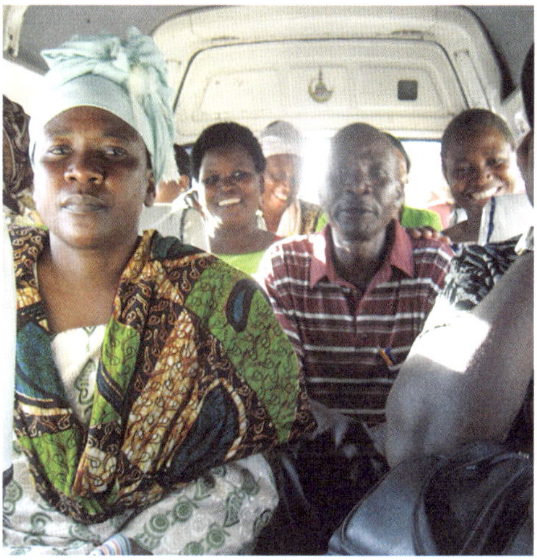

Harvard Joint Center for Housing Studies

Left: John Skurchak, "The Rental Squeeze, 2013"

Members: Ann Forsyth, Ali Malkawi, Rahul Mehrotra, Peter Rowe, Barbara Alexander, William Apgar, Michael Berman, Rachel Bratt, Michael Carliner, Karl Case, Kent Colton, Daniel Fulton, George Masnick, Shekar Narasimhan, Mark Richardson, Matthew Furman, Jackelyn Hwang, Robert Wellburn, Chris Herbert, Pamela Baldwin, Kermit Baker, Kerry Donahue, Angela Flynn, Elizabeth La Jeunesse, Mary Lancaster, Irene Lew, Karen Manning, Ellen Marya, Daniel McCue, Jennifer Molinsky, Rocio Sanchez-Moyano, Abbe Will

The Harvard Joint Center for Housing Studies (JCHS), formed in 1959 as the Joint Center for Urban Studies of MIT and Harvard, took up the challenge of addressing intellectual and policy issues confronting a nation and a world experiencing widespread demographic, economic, and social changes, with dramatic and far-reaching effects on cities in particular.

Today, JCHS is a collaborative unit affiliated with the Harvard Graduate School of Design and the Harvard Kennedy School. Through its research, education, and public outreach programs, the Center advances understanding of housing issues and informs policy making at all levels of government, business, and the civic sectors. Through graduate and executive courses, as well as fellowships and internship opportunities, the Joint Center trains and inspires the next generation of housing leaders to effectively address the needs of cities and communities in the United States and in the global economy.

The Center researches housing supply and demand, conditions in rental and owner-occupied markets, trends in housing affordability, developments in the mortgage finance system, efforts to support community development, and patterns of urban development. Many of these themes are represented in the Center's signature annual report, *The State of the Nation's Housing.*

Above: Matthew Conway (MArch I), Robert Daurio (MArch II), Carlos Cerezo Davila (MDes), Mariano Gomez (MArch II), Natsuma Imai (MArch I), Takuya Iwamura (MLA I), Ana Garcia Puyol (MDes), Thomas Sherman (MDes); "Horizon House," Kiel Moe, Mark Mulligan

Energy, Environments & Design Lab

Members: Kiel Moe, Jane Hutton, Sekou Cooke, Carlos Davila Cerezo, Kurt Fischer, Sofia Koutsenko, Nicholas Rivard, Tom Sherman, Mike Smith, Anne Weber, Arta Yazdanseta
Anne Weber, Arta Yazdanseta

The Energy, Environments & Design Lab investigates novel agendas for materials and energy at a range of design scales. From overlooked thermal parameters at the molecular level to global-scale emergy analysis, the design disciplines urgently need alternate intellectual frameworks, research methodologies, and practices for energy in the twenty-first century. Materials, buildings, landscapes, cities, and urbanization are all overtly connected energy hierarchies that must be lucidly understood as the basis of any design agenda for energy today.

To be certain, buildings, landscapes, and cities are fundamentally not sustainable entities. Instead, they are inextricably bound to large-scale material and energy systems. The aim of this design lab is to expand and deepen our understanding of energy in relation to buildings, environments, and design. To best understand the relationship of design to energy and environments, the lab focuses on projects that range in type from historical, geographic, and ecological to the design, analysis, and fabrication of full-scale prototypes and designs. Overdetermined by neither building science nor ecosystem theory, this lab presumes that both are essential to designing agendas for energy that fit the obligations and opportunities inherent in this century.

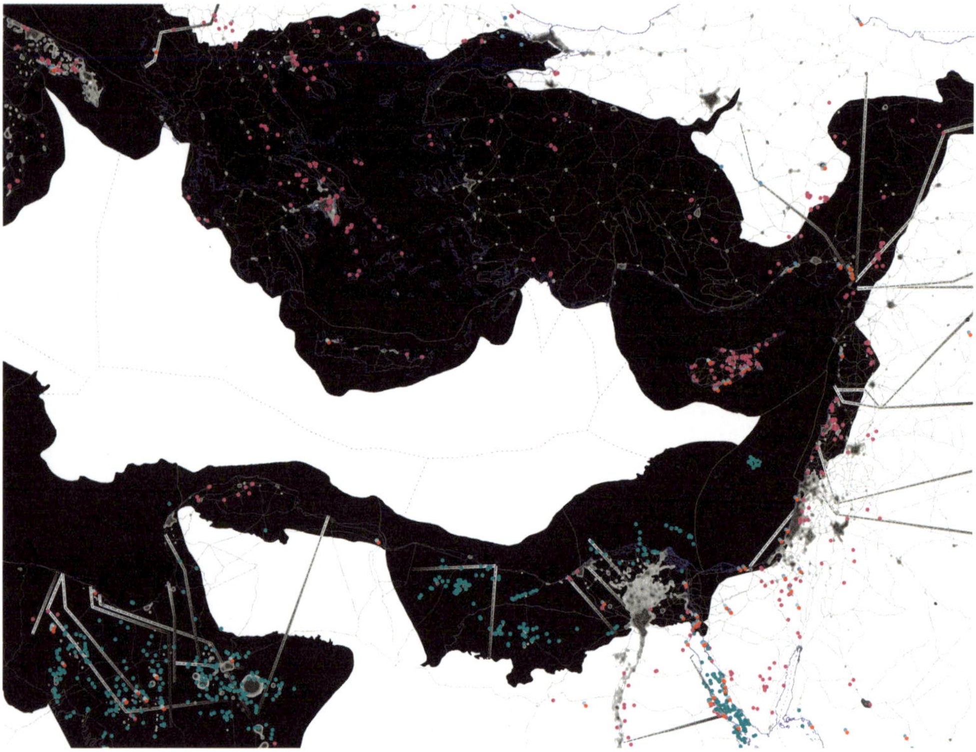

Above: Shirin Barol (MDes), Micheal Leef (MArch II), Gavin Robb (MArch I), "Port Peninsulas of Eastern Mediterranean"

Members: Hashim Sarkis, Nikos Katsikis, Roi Salgueiro Barrio, Daniel Daou, Ali Fard, Daniel Ibañez, Taraneh Meshkani, Pablo Pérez Ramos

New Geographies Lab

During 2013, the New Geographies Lab research seminar explored new potentials for architecture at a larger territorial scale, focusing on extracting new tropes out of the territories surrounding historical cities in the eastern Mediterranean. A parallel aim was to reconsider the very categories of city, metropolis, and territory and to propose new organization schemes.

The emphasis was on developing hybrid tropes combining artifacts such as roads, viaducts, walls, or canals with geographic elements such as coastlines, valleys, and hills. Out of the NG sequence, this was the first time that we ventured collectively and methodically to identify larger-scale architectural elements that could help organize the form of the territory. The lab is committed to the idea that territorial form could be recovered as a means for urban organization. This form is at once given and superimposed. We looked for it as historical recurrence over geographic territory, as a figure made of formations that could not have been connected because they were not seen together before, or because they correspond to new forms of life that are emerging but not yet articulated.

(Re)Planned Obsolescence: Rethinking the Architecture of Waste

Left and below: "A clear plate means a clear conscience," by James Fitton; printed for HM Stationary Office by Wm Brown and Co., Ltd., London, c.1939-45; "We Want Your Kitchen Waste," by John Gilroy, c. 1939-45. Ministry of Food (UK).

Members: Hanif Kara, Andreas Georgoulias, Leire Asensio Villoria

Currently architecture and design play a minor role in the design and construction of industrial building types. Except for a small number of exemplary projects, architecture and design have largely been excluded from the development of these pervasive structures and the integration of these buildings within the larger constructed and natural environments. As major parts of industrial production are outsourced to developing countries and to the East, Waste-to-Energy (WTE) infrastructure will continue to be needed locally in cities. As densities increase and consumption patterns change, innovation will make WTE an acceptable and affordable source of renewable energy to diversify a portfolio of other sources (solar, wind, and biomass) for the future.

Using WTE facilities as a vehicle, this research lab proposes to reengage interdisciplinary design and architecture with industrial buildings and facilities. The WTE research lab conducts design research on novel and effective ways to rethink the relationship of architecture and waste—a (re) planned obsolescence.

Pathways to Urban Sustainable Housing in Mexico: PUSH Mexico

Successful national urban policies and plans often require state and local actions. This project explores how Mexican housing and urban policies and plans that influence the cost, location, and feasibility of affordable housing development are implemented by various levels of government across Mexico. Based on that assessment, it proposes ideas for policy improvements to increase housing production and the quality of urban life.

The research lab answers several interrelated questions. What are some strategies for better coordinating various levels of government to produce and renovate social housing in urban Mexico? What kinds of regulatory and technical tools, or urban planning and design interventions, can be used to improve practice and successfully implement the new national housing policy? What levels of government would have to embrace them and how can they be mobilized? What are the challenges in coordinating the new national housing and urban policies with state and local government actions critical to the success of the national policies?

Above and below: "San Luis Potosi": "Rehilete Celaya, Guanajuato." Photo credit: Jose Castillo

Members: Diane Davis, Ann Forsyth, Jose Castillo, Eric Belsky, Erica Blonde, Sarah Bolivar, Charlie Brennan, Kate Casey, Tim Czerwienski, Lydia Gaby, Jennifer Lee, Marcela Orozco, Margaret Scott, Jessica Sevilla, Sofia Viguri

HAPI: Health and Places Initiative

There are many links between health and the built environment, from air quality to food access. The Health and Places Initiative (HAPI) helps create and synthesize the evidence base linking landscape, urban design, planning, and health. In its current phase, the project is developing templates for alternative models of urban development, stressing their impact on health and aging. Bringing together experts from the Harvard Graduate School of Design and the Harvard School of Public Health, the project creates a forum for understanding the multiple issues that face cities in light of rapid urbanization and an aging population worldwide.

The first component of the project focuses on education, including courses taken by students in both the design and public health schools; Harvard Extension School courses opened to a limited number of professionals; and a series of seminars and events. Second, the research dimension includes investigations at the building, neighborhood, and city scale, including innovative analyses of datasets from Chinese studies to better understand the connections between health and places; the development of new tools for both evaluating and making places and processes healthier; and the translation of research on the connections between environments and health into guidelines and prototypes for practice. Overall, the project will create a forum for further work on the connections between built environments and public health.

Above: Photo credit: Ann Forsyth

Members: Gary Adamkiewicz, Ann Forsyth, Andreas Georgoulias, Peter Rowe, John Spengler, Julia Kane Africa, Leire Asensio Villoria, Rachel Banay, Jack Dennerlein, Chenghe Guan, Robert Herrick, Joseph M. Hunt, Peter James, Har Ye Kan, Linyan Li, Yingying Lü, David Mah, Yannis Orfanos, Ramon Sanchez, Ping Shao, Laura Smead, Linda Powers Tomasso, Chuan Hao Chen, Heidi Youngha Cho, Sang Cho, Lydia Gaby, Merissa Grenon, Joyce Lee, Wei Li, Weishun Xu, Dingliang Yang

Zofnass Program for Sustainable Infrastructure

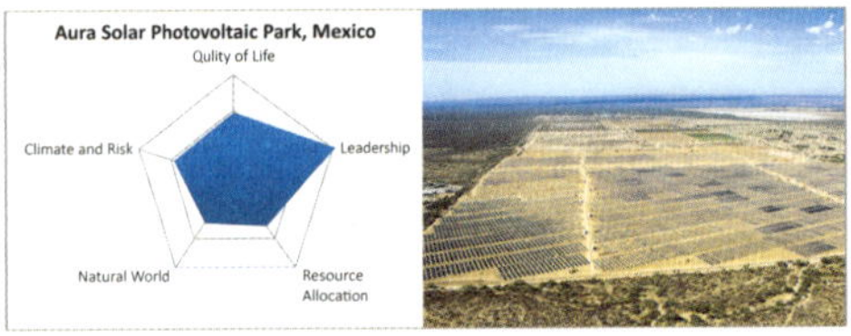

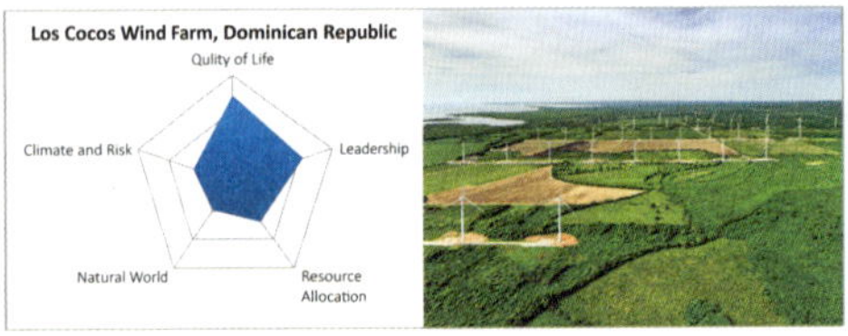

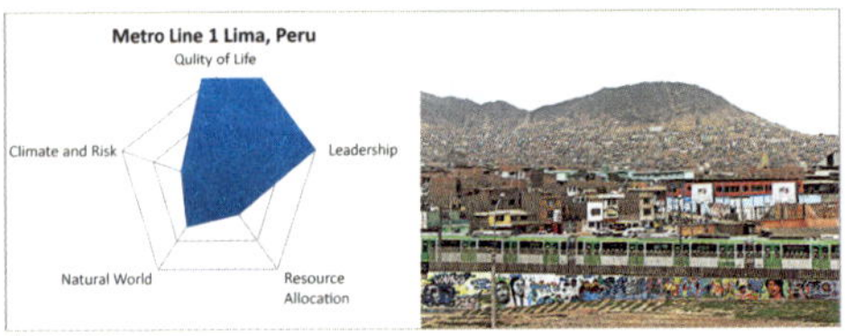

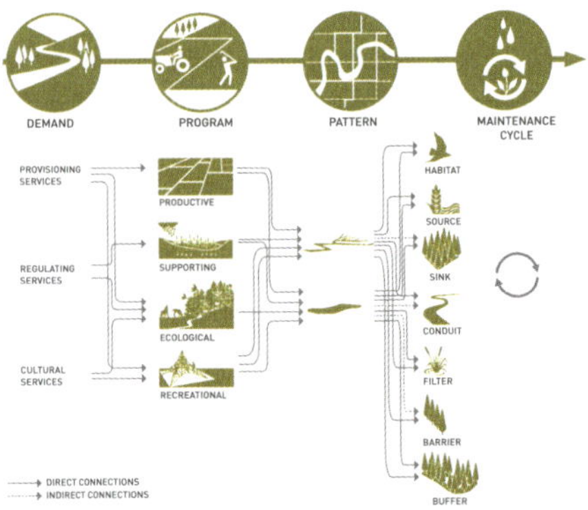

The mission of the Zofnass Program for Sustainable Infrastructure is to develop and promote methods, processes, and tools that quantify sustainability for infrastructure. Its goal is to facilitate the adoption of sustainable solutions for infrastructure projects and systems, and expand the body of knowledge about sustainable infrastructure.

The program is housed at the Harvard Graduate School of Design and extends its activities throughout the University, including the School of Public Health, the Kennedy School of Government, the Business School, and the Center for the Environment. It is supported by the private sector through an Industry Advisory Board and by foundation grants.

The key contribution of the program is the Envision Rating System, guidelines that aid in optimizing the sustainability of an infrastructure project during the planning and preliminary design phases, as well as a means to quantify the relative performance of the project through sixty factors that cover environmental, social, and governance dimensions and impacts. Envision was developed in collaboration with the Institute for Sustainable Infrastructure, which represents the major professional societies of the architecture, engineering, and construction industry. Envision is widely deployed in the United States, with several applications throughout the world.

The program is comprised of research initiatives that include the application of Envision at the Infrastructure 360 Awards program in Latin America (in collaboration with the Inter-American Development Bank), the online Zofnass Economic Process tool, research and development of planning guidelines for infrastructure, and research on the Zofnass planning tool for sustainable cities.

From top left: Andreas Georgoulias, Cristina Contreras, Hatzav Yoffe, Judith Rodriguez; project photos courtesy of project owners: Spiro Pollalis, Richa Shukla, Yannis Orfanos

Members: Spiro Pollalis, Andreas Georgoulias, Cristina Contreras, Anthony Kane, Yannis Orfanos, Judith Rodriguez, Richa Shukla, Hatzav Yoffe

From top left: "Mexico City"; "Stockholm"; "Seoul"; photo credit: Onesimo Flores Dewey

Transforming Urban Transport

Members: Diane Davis, Onesimo Flores Dewey, Justin Stern, Fallon Samuels, Brian Chang, Anneli Tostar, Amy Rader Olsson, David Ginsberg, Theodore Conrad, Antya Waegemann

Networked transport systems that produce low-carbon mobility patterns and integrated land uses are key to producing environmentally sustainable cities. The challenge is how to achieve these aims. It is one thing to know the positive impacts of sustainable transport systems and the technologies that produce them, and quite another to understand the political negotiations and governance strategies that make such outcomes possible.

This ongoing research initiative, Transforming Urban Transport—The Role of Political Leadership, examines the spatial, political, and economic enablers and constraints on building sustainable urbanism. Focused on transportation innovations and the actions of citizens, state authorities, and private sector actors, our expanding research team explores the conditions, conflicts, and coalitions that have made Stockholm, Mexico City, and Seoul global leaders in transforming urban transport and advancing sustainability.

Introducing congestion charges in a charged political context of opposition from automobile users, implementing bus rapid transit against the wishes of small private transport providers, and removing highways and building extensive subway networks for the purposes of making a high-tech city of the future—these three cases examine the interactions among transport modalities, land-use changes, political conflicts, and urban development strategies. Concurrent research on Paris, London, Stuttgart, Portland, Los Angeles, São Paulo, and Philadelphia inform the project's larger aims.

Members: Martin Bechthold,
Leire Asensio Villoria, Felix Raspall

Contributors: Stefano Andreani, Amanda Lee,
Jose Luis Garcia del Castillo Lopez, Kevin Hinz,
Andreas Trummer (TU Graz)

The Material Processes and Systems Lab

The Material Processes and Systems Lab (MaPS, formerly called Design Robotics Group) pursues applied research at the intersection of building technology, science, and design. The lab is a collaborative of faculty, researchers, and graduate students at the Harvard University Graduate School of Design, with strong ties to the School of Engineering and Applied Science and the Wyss Institute for Biologically Inspired Engineering at Harvard. The work of the lab looks at material-centered design questions from the nano to the macro scale, researching material and resource flows, digital and robotic fabrication, structural systems, adaptability, and related computational questions. The emphasis is on innovation for advancing knowledge about the design of better built environments. Funded research is the core of MaPS, complemented by courses and graduate student thesis projects.

The group currently focuses on three topics:

- Adaptive Living Environments (ALIvE)
- Architectural Ceramics
- Design Robotics

In 2014 the ceramics research focused on developing novel approaches to the structural use of ceramics. An early mockup was installed as the centerpiece of the international ceramics show in Valencia, Spain. Sponsored by the Valencia Trade Fair Association and ASCER Tile of Spain, the suspended tile system represents the first iteration of a structural ceramic and concrete shell system being developed in collaboration with the Institute for Structural Design at TU Graz, Austria. The structure's large stoneware elements enclose channels that form a perpendicular network of fiber concrete ribs.

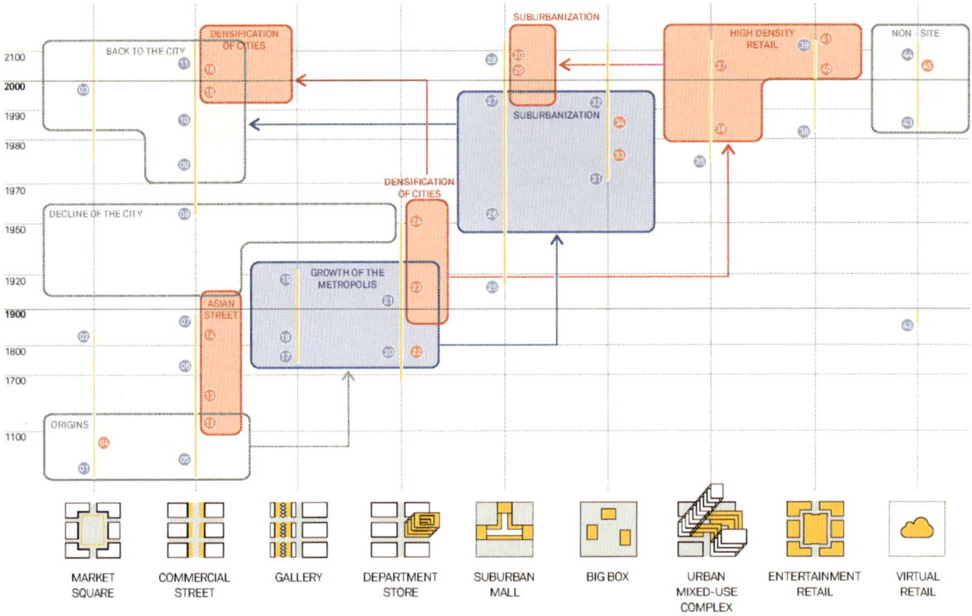

Real Estate and the Built Environment

Above: Bing Wang, Hugh Clark, Yonatan Cohen, Yong Kim, "Interaction between Urban Form and Retail Typologies in the West and in Asia"

Right: Bing Wang, Yong Kim, HyperBina Design Group, "Office Development as a Synthetic Urban Organism"

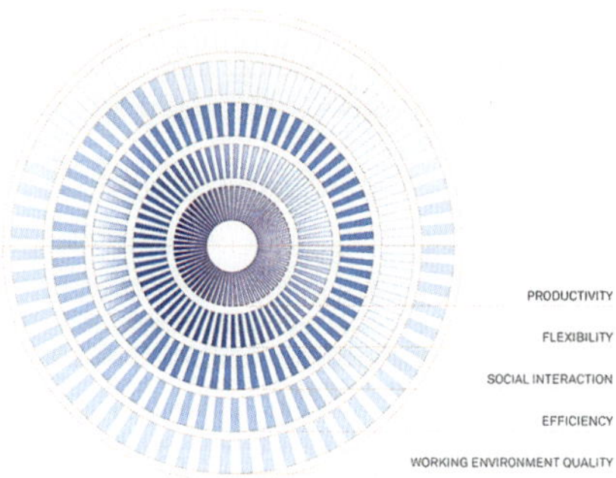

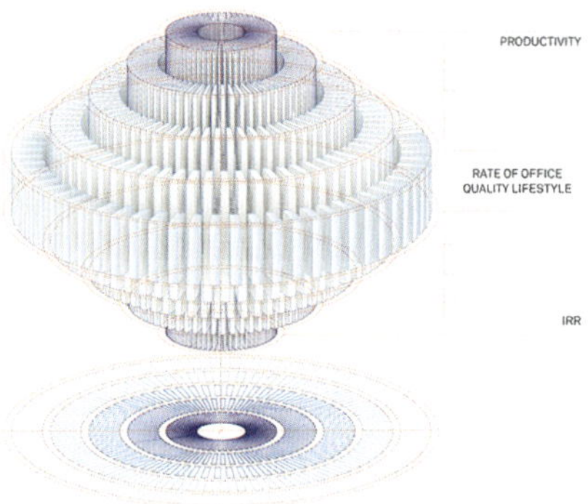

Prestige retail typology research and a related publication (*Prestige Retail Design and Development*, to be published by the International Council of Shopping Centers in 2014) focus on the dynamic evolution of spatial morphologies and trends within physical and digital retail typologies. The research critically documents both historical and contemporary trajectories of retail forms and strategies in the West and East, and projects their future impacts on urban form, retail trends, and lifestyles in the context of globalization.

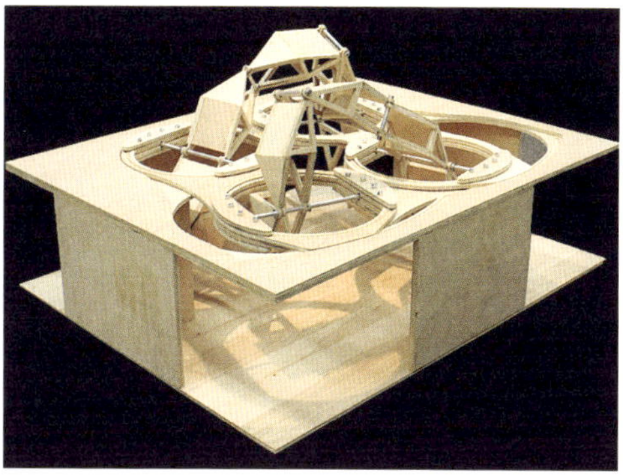

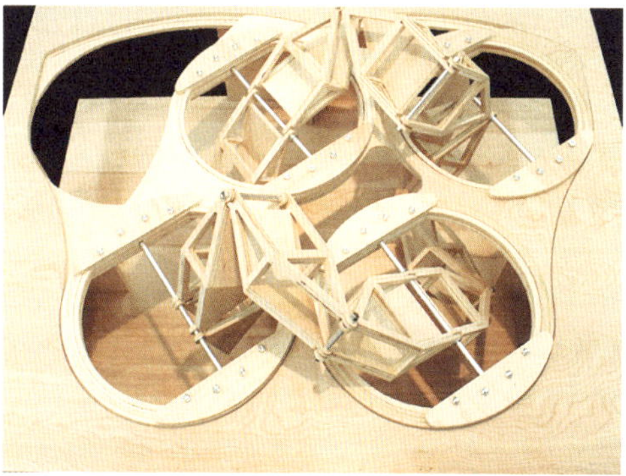

Geometry Lab

Left: Michael Burton (MArch I), "Architectural Kinematics": Andrew Witt, Cameron Wu, Chuck Hoberman; Nick Gu (MArch I), Qi Su (MDes), Nathan Shobe (MArch I), "Automated Hammer Forming: Zebra Panel Fabrication (2013)"

Members: Preston Scott Cohen, Andrew Witt, Cameron Wu, George Legendre, Panagiotis Michalatos, Mariana Ibañez, Chuck Hoberman, Michael Burton, Iman Fayyad, William Gavin Robb

The Geometry Lab is a new research unit that engages core questions of architectural geometry and computational design. Focused on the use of advanced geometry in the discipline of architecture, the research scope of the lab includes issues of digital fabrication, constructability, structural geometry, performance and infrastructural optimization, formal research, and the historical role of geometry in design. The objective of the lab is to produce and disseminate new knowledge, to generate broad scalable solutions to big problems, and to explore the cultural and human implications of geometry in design.

© Justin Knight, 2013. Packing crates for the GSD exhibitions team

ARD
SCHOOL
ESIGN

01

02

04

05

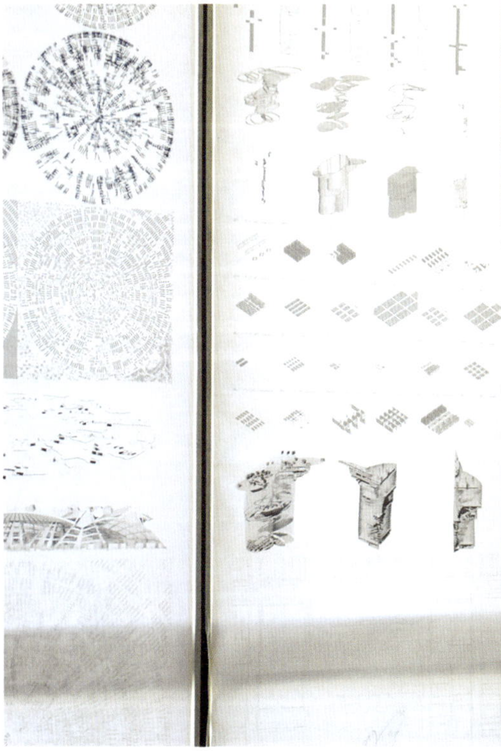

03

06

07

01 ChinaGSD 2014
02 STU1212 MLA Core IV
03 STU1318 Borrominations
04 SCI6423 (Re)Fabricating Tectonic Prototypes
05 STU1306 Material Performance
08 VIS2446 Drawing for Designers and VIS 2448 Landscape as Painting

Exhibits at 40 Kirkland:

06 Craig Reschke (MLA I AP) and Ann Lui (MIT), "Wall Strike"
07 Adam Tanaka (PhD, Urban Planning) and Carly Gertler (MArch I AP/MLA I AP), "spiraLondon & Beyond the West and the Western"
09 GSD Student Publications at Open House, "Paper Party"
10 Michael Lee (MDes), "Space Is Power"

08

09

10

01

02

03

04

05

06

07

01,07:
STU1507 Design and Politics: Managing Risks and Vulnerabilities
02,10:
STU1211 MLA Core III
03 STU1606 Los Angeles Studio: The Possibilities of the Wrong Scale
04 STU1305 Parametric Semiology
05 STU1601 Macau Cross-Border Cities
06 STU1212 MLA Core IV
08 STU1202 MArch Core IV
09 Anne Liu, Thesis review, with Krzysztof Wodiczko

08

09

10

01

03

welcome
Welcome!
Pick a Need
Pick a Place
Continuum of Care

04

02

© Katherine Taylor, 2013.

05

06

07

08

09

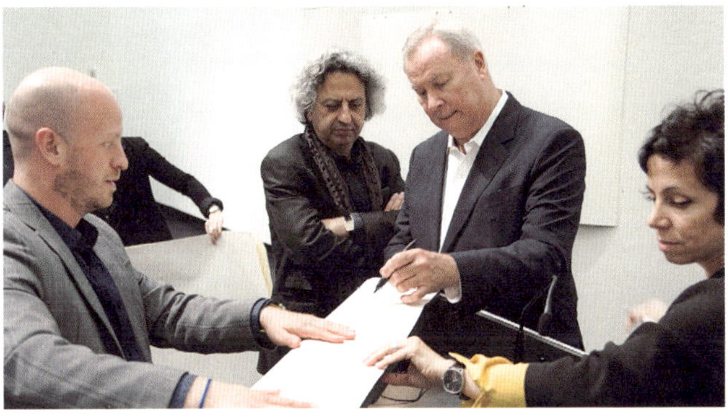

10

01 Javier Martin (MDes) testing model stresses
02 VIS2446 Drawing in action
03 Zofnass SIAB Workshop, May 19-20, 2014
04 Caroline James (MArch I), "Cambridge: Open City" Kiosk for VIS2481
05 Celebrations and cheers
06 MLA students testing drones and GIS mapping
07 Fabrication Lab
08 GSD Women in Design visit Novartis construction site with Toshiko Mori
09 International Women's Day
10 Robert Wilson visits GSD

↑ **KANYE WEST DROPS BY THE GSD**
Kanye West met with the GSD African American Student Union on invitation to discuss the "the trajectory of design discourse and practice." West also achieved the seemingly impossible: clearing out Gund Hall on a Sunday night with free tickets to his concert that evening.

01

02

03

04

01 GSD African American Student Union and Kanye West
02 Beer + Dogs, Open House
03 Thanksgiving Dinner, Piper Auditorium
04 Halloween 2013
05-09: Commencement Day (Images © Justin Knight)

05

08

06

07

09

01

02

03

05

04

01 Jamaica Bay, New York
STU1212 MLA Core IV
02,06:
Amsterdam
STU1302 Unfinished Work III
03,04:
Los Angeles, CA
STU1606 The Possibilities of the Wrong Scale
05 Switzerland
STU1311 Après Ski: Eco Village Les Diablerets
07 Argentina
STU1314 In the Land of Ñanduti
08 ChinaGSD JTerm Travel
09 Beijing, China
STU1409 Negative Planning in Nanshahe

06

07

08

09

→ CELEBRATING TRANSFORMATIVE URBAN DESIGN: THE VERONICA RUDGE GREEN PRIZE
Pritzker laureate Eduardo Souto de Moura accepts the Veronica Rudge Green Prize in Urban Design at a ceremony held at the GSD in September.

↑ DAN BORELLI (MDes 12) RECEIVES ARTPLACE GRANT

↑ ↗ RADCLIFFE UNVEILS PUBLIC ART INSTALLATION BY GSD STUDENTS
The Radcliffe Institute for Advanced Study unveiled a public-art installation designed by GSD students Keojin Jin and Juhun Lee (both MDes), "Saturate the Moment"

→ THE THINKING HAND EXHIBIT
Japanese woodworking tools were displayed at CGIS Harvard in an exhibition co-curated by Mark Mulligan and History of Art and Architecture Professor Yukio Lippit.The collection was a gift from the Takenaka Carpentry Tools Museum in Kobe and will be part of the GSD Loeb Library's permanent collection.

→ HE SAID, SHE SAID: WOMEN IN DESIGN TAKE ON PRITZKER
WiD's 2013 petition garnered over 18,000 signatures, spurring a conversation about equality in the design community. In October, the discussion continued when Denise Scott Brown visited the GSD and shared her insights at an open forum.

↓ LAUNCH OF REDESIGNED *HARVARD DESIGN MAGAZINE* "DO YOU READ ME?" AT THE VENICE BIENNALE

© Katherine Taylor. 2013.

↑ JOHN E. IRVING FAMILY DONATION KICK-STARTS HARVARD GSD CAMPAIGN

← AGA KHAN PROGRAM CELEBRATES 10TH ANNIVERSARY
In March, the GSD celebrated with "The Space Between Development and Conservation" symposium. The symposium gathered leading experts from MIT's Aga Khan Program, the Faculty of Arts and Sciences, and the Aga Khan Trust for Culture to discuss a comprehensive approach to conserving the region's historic cities and natural landscapes as living, vibrant spaces.

© Yusuke Suzuki. 2014.

→ GSD TEAM CELEBRATES THE OPENING OF RETREAT IN NATURE HORIZON HOUSE
From left: Jury member Tomonari Yashiro (Deputy Director and Professor at the Institute of Industrial Science, the University of Tokyo), Thomas Sherman (MDes), advisor Mark Mulligan (Professor at the Harvard University Graduate School of Design), jury member Kengo Kuma (Professor at the Graduate School of Architecture, the University of Tokyo), Ana Garcia Puyol (MDes), Carlos Cerezo Davila (MDes), jury member Darko Radović (Professor of Architecture and Urban Design, Keio University)

← "HERE TODAY, GONE TOMORROW": GSD TEAM WINS TOHOKU RECOVERY COMPETITION
From left: Trevor Johnson (MUP), Kristen Hunter (DDes), Elise Baudon (MUP), Maria Arrasate (MDes), Karina Gilbert (MAUD), Natalia Gaerlan (MUP) (not pictured). The team, led by Hunter and advised by Jerold Kayden (Professor of Urban Planning and Design), traveled to Japan in February to receive the $10,000 award.

↓ GSD TEAM WINS 16TH ARQUINE INTERNATIONAL COMPETITION
The team led by Daniel Daou (DDes) won 1st place with their entry "Umbral de las Américas". Collaborators: Adriana Chavez (MArch II/ MDes), Oscar Malaspina (MAUD), Nicolas Rivard (MAUD), Einat Rosenkrantz (MAUD), Elizabeth Añaños, and Gabriel Morales (AA)

↑ INFRASTRUCTURE 360 AWARDS
An interdisciplinary team of 12 Harvard GSD students worked with Andreas Georgoulias (Lecturer in Architecture and Research Director of Zofnass Program for Sustainable Infrastructure) to deliver the Inter-American Development Bank (IDB) Private Sector Infrastructure Sustainability Awards, or Infrastructure 360. The IDB research team included Maria Ignacia (MDes), Juan Cristaldo (MAUD), Arianna Galan (MArch I), Jennifer Lee (MAUD), Emanuel Torres (MAUD), Isabella Royo (MLA), Marianne Barrera (MAUD), Manuela Guzman (MAUD), Judith Rodriguez (MLA), and Julie Mercier (MDes). Research associates Hatzav Yoffee (MLA) and Cristina Contreras worked with the students to use the Envision rating system developed at Zofnass to conduct detailed project assessments and develop case studies.

↓ SURDNA FOUNDATION AWARDS ZOFNASS PROGRAM $300,000 FOR 2 YEARS OF RESEARCH ON SUSTAINABLE ENVIRONMENTS

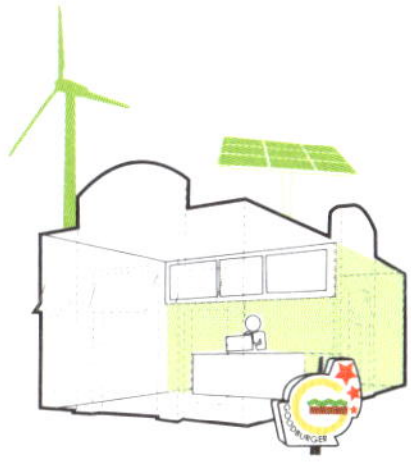

↑ HARVARD TEAM WINS DEPARTMENT OF ENERGY'S BETTER BUILDINGS CASE
Led by Jordan Smith (GSAS), the Harvard team comprised of David Henning (MUP), Brian Vargo (MDes), Arta Yazdanseta (MDes), Lauren Hartle, Benjamin Franta, and Eliza Morris (all of SEAS) won the "most innovative" for their proposal "Crown Joules." The proposal focused on improving policy, strategy, and design of energy efficiency in quick service restaurants. Advisor: Holly Samuelson

↑ MDES TEAMS WIN NET-ZERO ENERGY DESIGN COMPETITION
Kanika Arora (MDes), Abhinay Sharma (MDes), Baha Sadreddin (MDes) and Rohit Goyal (GSAS) won for residential new construction. Advisor: Holly Samuelson

Johannes Staudt (MDes), Saurabh Shrestha (MDes), and Tom Sherman (MDes) won for commercial renovation. Advisor: Kiel Moe

↓ GSD ESTABLISHES THE HARVARD CENTER FOR GREEN BUILDINGS AND CITIES

↑ WHEELWRIGHT PRIZE 2014
The $100,000 travel grant was awarded to Jose Ahedo, Barcelona-based architect and GSD alum (MArch II). Finalists' work from top left: Masaaki Iwamoto; Ana Dana Beros; Jose Ahedo; Alison Crawshaw; Jimenez Lai; Kaz Yoneda; Sean Lally

↗ INGE SAFFRON (LF) TAPPED FOR PULITZER PRIZE FOR HER WORK AS ARCHITECTURE CRITIC

↗ SARA ZEWDE (MLA I) NAMED NATIONAL OLMSTED SCHOLAR

→ SEEKING OBSOLESCENCE: JAMES LENG (MArch I AP) WINS SOM PRIZE
Also among the 8 finalists were Arielle Assouline-Lichten (MArch I) and Edward Becker (MArch I)

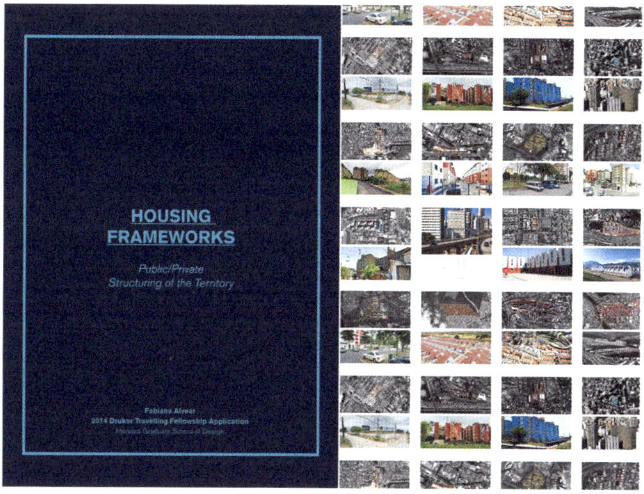

← FABIANA ALVEAR (MAUD) AWARDED DRUKER TRAVELING FELLOWSHIP

↓ GSD ALUMNA RECOGNIZED FOR DESIGN WORK
Andrea Cochran Landscape Architecture, based in San Francisco, was founded by Andrea Cochran (FASLA, MLA 79). Cochran received the 2014 Cooper-Hewitt National Design Award and the 2014 ASLA Design Medal.

← DEANS' DESIGN CHALLENGE URBAN LIFE 2030
Of the 18 finalists, the GSD was represented by: 1st runner up Wendy Fok (DDes) for "Resilient Modular Systems", pictured with Eileen Sun (GSAS); Dimitris Papanikolaou (DDes) for "Cloudcommuting" (2nd runner up); and Matan Mayer (DDes) for "MateriaLEASE"

↑ FACULTY AND ALUMNI RECEIVE GRAHAM FOUNDATION GRANTS
Iñaki Abalos, with Renata Sentkiewicz; Gareth Doherty; Daniel D'Oca, with Tobias Armborst and Georgeen Theodore; Zaneta Hong, with Michael Leighton Beaman (MArch); Forbes Lipschitz (MLA) (Image: Zaneta Hong/Michael Leighton Beaman)

↑ FACULTY DESIGN AWARD FOR MArch II AWARDED TO JOSÉ MAYORAL MORATILLA

↓ TRANSFORMATIVE MOBILITIES: PORTO & MEDELLÍN
August 26, 2013 - October 13, 2013
Curated by Rahul Mehrotra

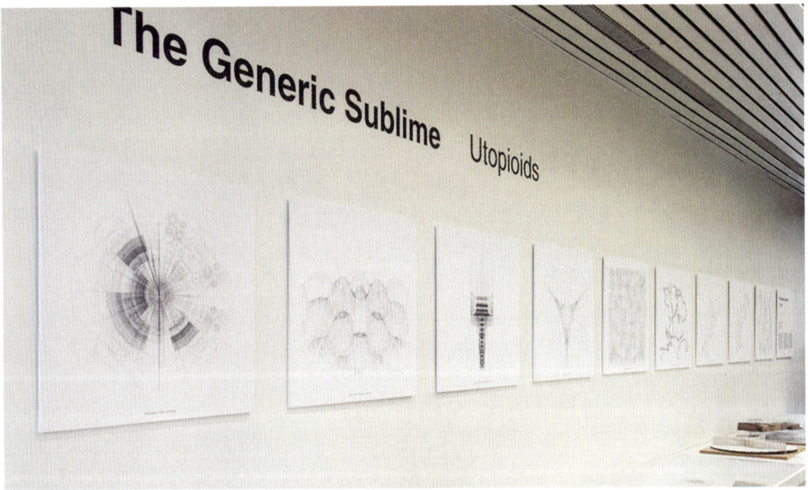

↓ THE GENERIC SUBLIME: UTOPIOIDS
September 02, 2013 - October 04, 2013
Curated by Ciro Najle

↓ COMPOSITES: RENEWED OPTIMISM IN THE AGE OF DIGITAL FABRICATION
September 02, 2013 - October 04, 2013
Curated by John Nastasi and Rachel Vroman

↑ SOM PRIZE AND TRAVEL FELLOWSHIP AWARD IN ARCHITECTURE, DESIGN, AND URBAN DESIGN: JAMES LENG (MArch I)

September 16, 2013 - October 04, 2013

↑ AIRPORT LANDSCAPE: URBAN ECOLOGIES IN THE AERIAL AGE

October 30, 2013 - December 19, 2013

Curated by Charles Waldheim and Sonja Duempelmann

↑ AIRPORT LANDSCAPE: FROM AIRFIELDS TO GREENFIELDS

October 30, 2013 - March 25, 2014

Curated by Sonja Duempelmann

↓ ANOTHER NATURE: JUNYA ISHIGAMI

January 20, 2014 - March 09, 2014
Curated by Junya Ishigami

↓ MATERIAL PERFORMANCES: FIBROUS TECTONICS

January 27, 2014 - March 23, 2014
Curated by Achim Menges

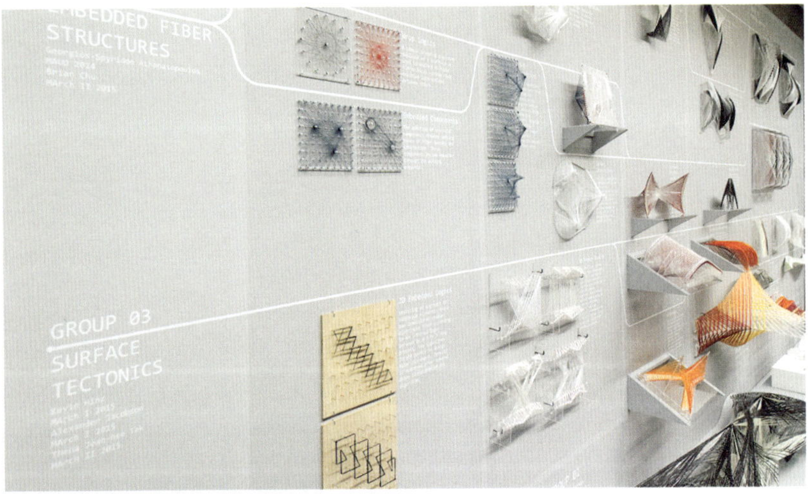

↓ SILVIA GMÜR RETO GMUR ARCHITEKTEN

February 17, 2014 - March 23, 2014
Curated by Silvia Gmür

↑ HORIZON HOUSE

April 02, 2014 - May 16, 2014

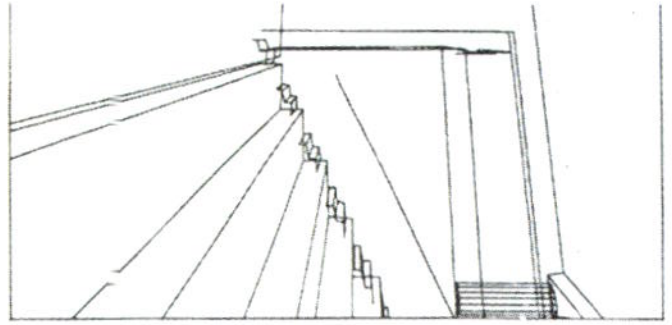

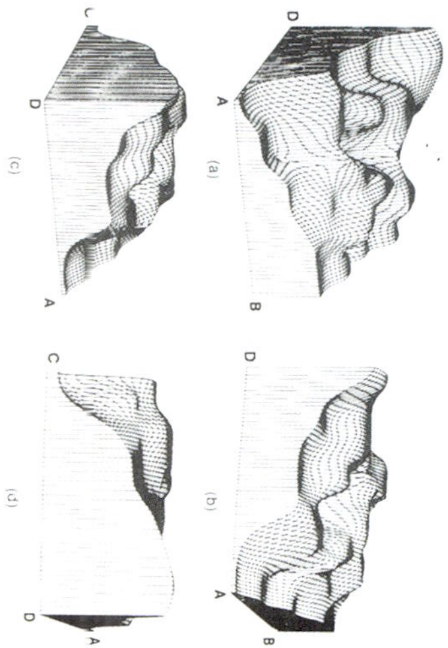

↑ WHEN THE GSD DESIGNED SOFTWARE: EXPERIMENTS IN COMPUTER VISION, 1965-1991

April 03, 2014 - May 16, 2014
Curated by Matthew Allen (MArch)
Assisted by Sophia Panova

↑ ANIMATING THE ARCHIVE

April 02, 2014 - May 16, 2014
Curated by Matthew Allan (MArch)
Assisted by Sophia Panova

→ LECTURE BY TAKAHARU TEZUKA
October 10, 2013

"When you do science, you try to focus onto one truth, right? But there is not one truth, you know? Architecture exists in the balance of many factors."

©Yusuke Suzuki, 2013.

→ LECTURE BY KATHERINE BOO
FEBRUARY 20, 2014

©Yusuke Suzuki, 2014.

→ LECTURE BY JUNYA ISHIGAMI
"My Work"
February 02, 2014

©Yusuke Suzuki, 2014.

©Katherine Taylor

↑ LECTURE BY DAVID ADJAYE
March 28, 2014

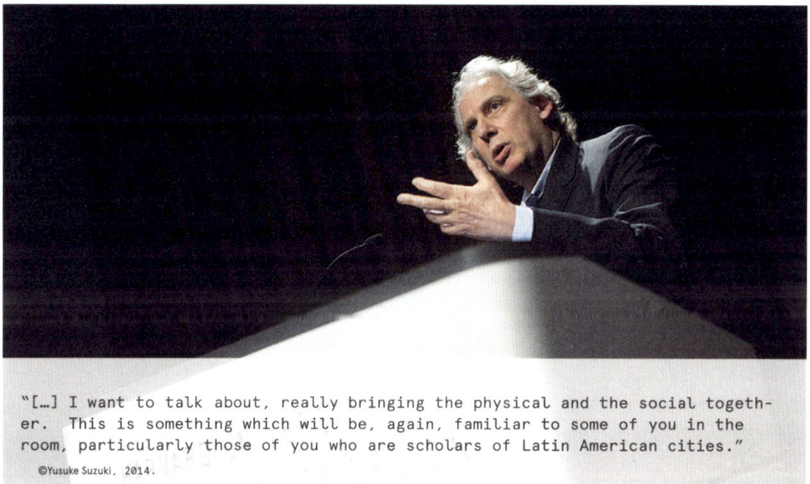

"[…] I want to talk about, really bringing the physical and the social together. This is something which will be, again, familiar to some of you in the room, particularly those of you who are scholars of Latin American cities."

©Yusuke Suzuki, 2014.

↑ LECTURE BY RICKY BURDETT
February 22, 2014

©Anita Kan, 2014.

↑ LECTURE BY TADASHI YANAI
"Design + Management = Innovation"
April 22, 2014

© Jozef Sulik, 2014. *Harvard Design Magazine* launch party at the 2014 Venice Biennale

Projective Ecologies
Edited by Chris Reed and Nina-Marie Lister
Copublished with Actar, 2014
Designed by Ramon Prat
ISBN 978-1-940291-12-3

The past two decades have witnessed a resurgence of ecological ideas and thinking in discussions of urbanism, culture, and design. The field of ecology has moved from classical determinism and a reductionist Newtonian concern with stability and order in favor of more contemporary understandings of dynamic systemic change and the related phenomena of adaptability and resilience.

In the Life of Cities
Edited by Mohsen Mostafavi
Copublished with Lars Müller Publishers, 2012
Designed by Integral Lars Müller
ISBN 978-3-03778-302-3

What is it that gives places their individual qualities and defines the life of a city? Architects and urbanists are accustomed to describing and creating the organizational structures, the layouts and physical attributes of our cities. But what are the relations between the design of a city—its form—and the life engendered by that form? Portfolios of contemporary photography assert the layered realities of urban life today. With text contributions by Arjun Appadurai, Eve Blau, Svetlana Boym, Felipe Correa, Rahul Mehrotra, Antoine Picon, Gyan Prakash, Nasser Rabbat, Rafi Segal, Jorge Silvetti, and AbdouMaliq Simone, among others.

Instigations: Engaging Architecture, Landscape, and the City
Edited by Mohsen Mostafavi and Peter Christensen
Copublished with Lars Müller Publishers, 2012
Designed by Integral Lars Müller
ISBN 978-3-03778-307-8

This volume celebrating the first seventy-five years of the GSD presents episodes in a rich history along with selected looks at current and future lines of teaching and research; these views reflect the constant oscillation between the pragmatic realities and the imagined yet never realized ideal that lies at the heart of design.

Kenzō Tange: Architecture for the World
Edited by Seng Kuan and Yukio Lippit
Copublished with Lars Müller Publishers, 2012
Designed by Integral Lars Müller
ISBN 978-3-03778-310-8

Kenzō Tange (1913–2005) is a peerless figure among 20th-century Japanese architects. This unique assemblage of new scholarship reframes Tange according to the contingencies of Japanese modernism as well as contemporary discourses of cultural identity, technology, urbanization, and the synthesis of the arts. With contributions by Yatsuka Hajime, Fujioka Hiroyasu, Seng Kuan, Kawaguchi Mamoru, Yasufumi Nakamori, Ken Tadashi Oshima, Toyokawa Saikaku, and Sarah Teasley.

Harvard Design Magazine No.37: Urbanism's Core?
Guest edited by Eve Blau and Rahul Mehrotra
Designed by Allon Kaye
ISBN 978-0-9916117-0-6

"Urbanism's Core" makes an argument for bringing theory into closer dialogue with practice, design into collaboration with planning.
The issue highlights strategies, processes, and practices of intervention that are being proposed in response to emerging environments, and explores new directions for research and theoretical formation emerging from the condition of the urban. It explores frameworks for understanding processes of urbanization across a broad geography; that engage issues of scale, publics, governance, poverty, social inequality, violence, extreme differentiation, abandonment, risk and resilience, informality, temporality, hybridity, media,and network cultures. Other contributions propose strategies for intervening at multiple scales; they show the diversity of critical approaches and practices emerging in response to contemporary states of urbanization.

Harvard Design Magazine
No.38: Do You Read Me?
Edited by Jennifer Sigler
and Leah Whitman-Salkin
Designed by Jiminie Ha,
with Projects, Inc.
ISBN 978-0-9916117-1-3

"Do You Read Me?" invites "reading" across disciplinary boundaries, and stakes out an expanded arena for architecture and design dialogue. This issue is about reading and misreading, and the role of design in streamlining or garbling the exchange between sender and receiver, writer and reader, maker and user. Whether written or rendered, engineered or enacted, both message and messenger are designed, and it is the relation between craft and comprehension that is explored here. With contribution by Homi K. Bhabha, Sanford Kwinter, Eileen Myles, Jeffrey T. Schnapp, Denise Scott Brown, Kazys Varnelis, and Ines Weizman, among others.

New Geographies, No.5:
The Mediterranean
Edited by Antonio Petrov
Distributed by Harvard
University Press, 2013
Designed by Tomas Celizna
and Daniel Harding
ISBN 978-1-934510-33-9

New Geographies 5 aims to recast "the Mediterranean" as a contemporary phenomenon and spatialize its formation as a larger geographic entity in the 21st century.

New Geographies, No.6:
Grounding Metabolism
Edited by Daniel Ibañez and
Nikos Katsikis
Distributed by Harvard
University Press, 2014
Designed by Rob Daurio and
Chelsea Spencer
ISBN 978-1-934510-3-7

Design disciplines have always recognized the potential of urban metabolism to shape spatial strategies. Today's generalized urbanization is characterized by an unprecedented complexity and planetary upscaling of metabolic relations. *New Geographies* 6 aims to trace alternative, synthetic routes to design through a more elaborate understanding of the relation between metabolic models and concepts and material specificities of spatial structures across scales.

Ecological Urbanism
(Chinese Edition)
Edited by Mohsen Mostafavi
with Gareth Doherty
Ifeng Space Media, 2014
ISBN 978-7-55370-143-1

While climate change, sustainable architecture, and green technologies have become increasingly topical, issues surrounding the sustainability of the city are much less developed. The premise of this book is that an ecological approach is urgently needed as an imaginative and practical method of addressing existing as well as new cities. The book brings together practitioners, theorists, economists, engineers, artists, policymakers, scientists, and public health specialists.

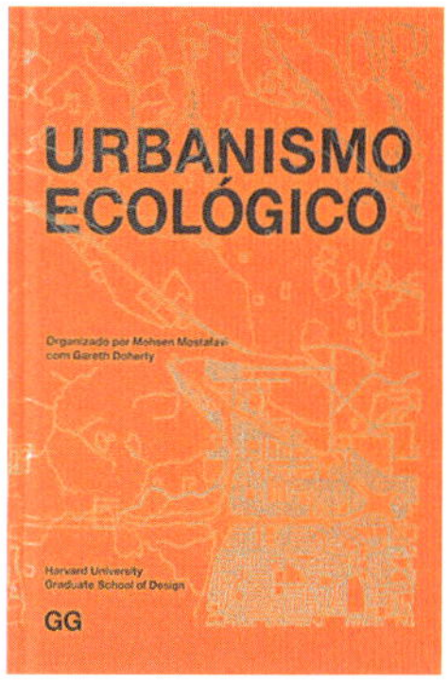

Urbanismo Ecológico
(Portuguese Edition)
Edited by Mohsen Mostafavi
with Gareth Doherty
Copublished with Editorial
Gustavo Gili, 2014
ISBN 978-8-56598-550-5

Urbanismo Ecológico
(Spanish Edition)
Edited by Mohsen Mostafavi
with Gareth Doherty
Copublished with Editorial
Gustavo Gili, 2014
ISBN 978-8-42522-742-4

HARVARD UNIVERSITY GRADUATE SCHOOL OF DESIGN

Drew Gilpin Faust President of Harvard University
Mohsen Mostafavi Dean of the Graduate School of Design
Patricia Roberts Executive Dean
K. Michael Hays Associate Dean for Academic Affairs
Beth Kramer Associate Dean for Development and Alumni Relations
Benjamin Prosky Assistant Dean for Communications

Iñaki Abalos Chair of the Department of Architecture
Rahul Mehrotra Chair of the Department of Urban Planning and Design
Charles Waldheim Chair of the Department of Landscape Architecture
Martin Bechthold Co-Director of the Doctor of Design Program
Pierre Bélanger Co-Director of the Master in Design Studies Program
Anita Berrizbeitia Director of the Master in Landscape Architecture Program
Felipe Correa Director of the Master of Architecture in Urban Design and the Master of Landscape Architecture in Urban Design Programs
Ann Forsyth Director of the Master in Urban Planning Program
Kiel Moe Co-Director of the Master in Design Studies
Mark Mulligan Director of the Master in Architecture Programs
Erika Naginski Co-Director of the PhD Program in Architecture, Landscape Architecture and Urban Planning
Antoine Picon Co-Director of the PhD Program in Architecture, Landscape Architecture and Urban Planning and Doctor of Design Program

FACULTY OF DESIGN

Iñaki Abalos Professor in Residence and Chair of the Department of Architecture
Martin Bechthold Professor of Architectural Technology
Pierre Bélanger Associate Professor of Landscape Architecture
Silvia Benedito Assistant Professor of Landscape Architecture
Anita Berrizbeitia Professor of Landscape Architecture
Eve Blau Adjunct Professor of the History of Urban Form
Neil Brenner Professor of Urban Theory
Joan Busquets Martin Bucksbaum Professor in Practice of Urban Planning and Design
Preston Scott Cohen Gerald M. McCue Professor in Architecture
Felipe Correa Associate Professor of Urban Design
Diane Davis Professor of Urbanism and Development
Peter Del Tredici Associate Professor in Practice of Landscape Architecture
Jill Desimini Assistant Professor of Landscape Architecture
Sonja Duempelmann Associate Professor of Landscape Architecture
Edward Eigen Associate Professor of Architecture and Landscape Architecture
Danielle Etzler Assistant Professor of Architecture
Susan Fainstein Senior Research Fellow
Ann Forsyth Professor of Urban Planning
José Goméz-Ibáñez Derek Bok Professor of Urban Planning and Public Policy
K. Michael Hays Eliot Noyes Professor of Architectural Theory
Gary Hilderbrand Professor in Practice of Landscape Architecture
Michael Hooper Assistant Professor of Urban Planning
Eric Höweler Assistant Professor of Architecture
Jane Hutton Assistant Professor of Landscape Architecture
Timothy Hyde Associate Professor of Architecture
Mariana Ibañez Associate Professor of Architecture
Florian Idenburg Associate Professor in Practice of Architecture
Hanif Kara Professor in Practice of Architectural Technology
Jerold Kayden Frank Backus Williams Professor of Urban Planning and Design
Niall Kirkwood Professor of Landscape Architecture
Rem Koolhaas Professor in Practice of Architecture and Urban Design
Alex Krieger Professor in Practice of Urban Design
Sanford Kwinter Professor of Architectural Theory and Criticism
Grace La Professor of Architecture
Mark Laird Senior Lecturer in Landscape Architecture
Christopher Lee Associate Professor in Practice of Urban Design
George Liaropoulos Legendre Associate Professor in Practice of Architecture
Judith Grant Long Associate Professor of Urban Planning
Ali Malkawi Professor of Architectural Technology and Founding Director of the Harvard Center for Green Buildings and Cities
Rahul Mehrotra Professor of Urban Design and Planning and Chair of the Department of Urban Planning and Design
Panagiotis Michalatos Assistant Professor of Architectural Technology
Kiel Moe Assistant Professor of Architectural Technology
Rafael Moneo Josep Lluis Sert Professor in Architecture
Toshiko Mori Robert P. Hubbard Professor in Practice of Architecture
Mohsen Mostafavi Dean and Alexander and Victoria Wiley Professor of Design
Farshid Moussavi Professor in Practice of Architecture
Mark Mulligan Associate Professor in Practice of Architecture
Erika Naginski Professor of Architectural History
Paul Nakazawa Associate Professor in Practice of Architecture
Richard Peiser Michael D. Spear Professor of Real Estate Development
Antoine Picon G. Ware Travelstead Professor of the History of Architecture and Technology
Spiro Pollalis Professor of Design Technology and Management
Chris Reed Associate Professor in Practice of Landscape Architecture
Ingeborg Rocker Associate Professor of Architecture
Joyce Klein Rosenthal Assistant Professor of Urban Planning
Peter Rowe Raymond Garbe Professor of Architecture and Urban Design and Harvard University Distinguished Service Professor
Holly Samuelson Assistant Professor of Architecture
A. Hashim Sarkis Aga Khan Professor of Landscape Architecture and Urbanism in Muslim Societies
Allen Sayegh Associate Professor in Practice of Architectural Technology

Matthias Schuler Professor in Practice of Environmental Technology
Martha Schwartz Professor in Practice of Landscape Architecture
Mack Scogin Kajima Professor in Practice of Architecture
Jorge Silvetti Nelson Robinson Jr. Professor of Architecture
Christine Smith Robert C. and Marian K. Weinberg Professor of Architectural History
Laura Solano Associate Professor in Practice of Landscape Architecture
John Stilgoe Robert and Lois Orchard Professor in the History of Landscape Development
Maryann Thompson Professor in Practice of Architecture
Matthew Urbanski Associate Professor in Practice of Landscape Architecture
Michael Van Valkenburgh Charles Eliot Professor in Practice of Landscape Architecture
Charles Waldheim John E. Irving Professor of Landscape Architecture and Chair of the Department of Landscape Architecture
Bing Wang Associate Professor in Practice of Real Estate and the Built Environment
Elizabeth Whittaker Assistant Professor in Practice of Architecture
Jay Wickersham Associate Professor in Practice of Architecture
Krzysztof Wodiczko Professor in Residence of Art, Design and the Public Domain
Cameron Wu Assistant Professor of Architecture

VISITING FACULTY

Frank Apeseche Lecturer in Architecture & Urban Planning and Design
Steven Apfelbaum Lecturer in Landscape Architecture
Gerdo Aquino Design Critic in Landscape Architecture
Leire Asensio Villoria Lecturer in Architecture and Landscape Architecture
Bridget Baines Design Critic in Landscape Architecture
Vincent Bandy Design Critic in Architecture
Katy Barkan Design Critic in Architecture
Frank Barkow Lecturer in Architecture
Rodney Barnett Visiting Professor in Landscape Architecture
Stephen Bates John T. Dunlop Visiting Professor of Housing and Urbanization
Peter Beard Design Critic in Landscape Architecture
Eric Belsky Lecturer in Urban Planning and Managing Director of the Joint Center for Housing
Solano Benitez Design Critic in Architecture
Imola Berczi Instructor in Architecture
Andre Bideau Lecturer in Architecture
Adrian Blackwell Visiting Associate Professor in Landscape Architecture and Urban Design
Sibel Bozdogan Lecturer of Architectural History
Jeffry Burchard Design Critic in Architecture
Ricky Burdett Visiting Professor in Urban Planning and Design
Luis Rodrigo Callejas Mujica Lecturer in Landscape Architecture
José Castillo John T. Dunlop Design Critic of Housing and Urbanization
Chiara Cavallieri Design Critic in Landscape Architecture
Jana Cephas Instructor in Urban Planning and Design
Christine Cheng Design Critic in Architecture
Leena Cho Lecturer in Landscape Architecture
Philippe Coignet Design Critic in Landscape Architecture
Betsy Colburn Lecturer in Landscape Architecture
Jürg Conzett Lecturer in Architecture
Salmaan Craig Lecturer in Architecture and Research Associate
Lawrence Curtis Lecturer in Urban Planning and Design
Renée Daoust Design Critic in Landscape Architecture
Eric de Broche des Combes Lecturer in Landscape Architecture
Pierre de Meuron Arthur Rotch Design Critic in Architecture
Timothy Dekker Lecturer in Landscape Architecture
Michel Desvigne Peter Louis Hornbeck Design Critic in Landscape Architecture
John Dixon Hunt Visiting Professor in Landscape Architecture
Daniel D'Oca Design Critic in Urban Planning and Design
Gareth Doherty Lecturer in Landscape Architecture and Urban Planning and Design
Kelly Doran Lecturer in Landscape Architecture
Rosetta Elkin Lecturer in Landscape Architecture
Erle Ellis Visiting Associate Professor in Landscape Architecture
Stephen Ervin Lecturer in Landscape Architecture and Urban Planning and Design
Teman Evans Lecturer in Architecture
Teran Evans Lecturer in Architecture
Onesimo Flores Dewey Lecturer in Urban Planning and Design
David Gamble Lecturer in Urban Planning and Design
Carlos Garciavelez Alfaro Lecturer in Urban Planning and Design
Ana Gelabert-Sanchez Design Critic in Urban Planning and Design
John Gendall Instructor in Urban Planning and Design
Andreas Georgoulias Lecturer in Architecture
Shauna Gillies-Smith Design Critic in Landscape Architecture
Inessa Hansch Design Critic in Landscape Architecture
Andrea Hansen Lecturer in Landscape Architecture
Ewa Harabasz Lecturer in Architecture and Landscape Architecture
Ron Henderson Visiting Professor in Landscape Architecture
Jacques Herzog Arthur Rotch Design Critic in Architecture
Alison Hirsch Visiting Assistant Professor in Architecture
Chuck Hoberman Lecturer in Architecture
Zaneta Hong 2013-2014 Daniel Urban Kiley Fellow and Lecturer in Landscape Architecture
Eelco Hooftman Design Critic in Landscape Architecture
Christopher Hoxie Lecturer in Architecture
Ying-Yu Hung Design Critic in Landscape Architecture
Junya Ishigami Kenzo Tange Design Critic in Architecture
Sharon Johnston Design Critic in Architecture
Brian Kenet Lecturer in Landscape Architecture
Kathryn Kennen Lecturer in Landscape Architecture
Matthew Kiefer Lecturer in Urban Planning and Design
Jonathan King Instructor in Architecture
Eugene Kohn Lecturer in Urban Planning and Design

Max Kuo Design Critic in Architecture
Neil Leach Lecturer in Architecture
Mark Lee Design Critic in Architecture
Mia Lehrer Design Critic in Landscape Architecture
Réal Lestage Design Critic in Landscape Architecture
Enriqueta Llabres Valls Design Critic in Landscape Architecture
Sergio Lopez-Piñeiro Visiting Assistant Professor in Landscape Architecture
Yanni Loukissas Lecturer in Architecture
Kathryn Madden Design Critic in Urban Planning and Design
David Mah Lecturer in Landscape Architecture
Michael Maltzan John C. Portman Design Critic in Architecture
Edward Marchant Lecturer in Urban Planning and Design
Sebastien Marot Lecturer in Architecture
Fadi Masoud Lecturer in Landscape Architecture
Christopher Matthews Lecturer in Landscape Architecture
Matan Mayer Instructor in Architecture
Giancarlo Mazzanti Design Critic in Urban Planning and Design
Patrick McCafferty Lecturer in Architecture
Alistair McIntosh Lecturer in Landscape Architecture
Karen M'Closkey Visiting Assistant Professor in Landscape Architecture
Achim Menges Visiting Professor in Architecture
Carles Muro Design Critic in Architecture
Nashid Nabian Lecturer in Urban Planning and Design
Ciro Najle Design Critic in Architecture
John Nastasi Lecturer in Architecture
Sheila O'Donnell Design Critic in Architecture
Chad Oppenheim Lecturer in Landscape Architecture
Henk Ovink Design Critic in Urban Planning and Design
Erkin Özay Instructor in Urban Planning and Design
Megan Panzano Design Critic in Architecture
Katharine Parsons Lecturer in Landscape Architecture
Robert Pietrusko Lecturer in Landscape Architecture and Urban Planning and Design
Damon Rich Design Critic in Urban Planning and Design
Eduardo Rico Carranza Design Critic in Landscape Architecture
Jennifer Riley Lecturer in Architecture
Thomas Ryan Lecturer in Landscape Architecture
David Sanderson Visiting Professor in Urban Planning
Deidre Schmidt John T. Dunlop Lecturer of Housing and Urbanization
Patrik Schumacher John C. Portman Visiting Professor in Architecture
Richard Sennett Visiting Professor in Urban Planning and Design
Renata Sentkiewicz Design Critic in Architecture
Jonathan Sergison John T. Dunlop Visiting Professor of Housing and Urbanization
Gullivar Shepard Design Critic in Landscape Architecture
Shohei Shigematsu Design Critic in Architecture
Robert Silman Lecturer in Architecture
Mitchell Silver John T. Dunlop Lecturer of Housing and Urbanization
Graciela Silvestri Robert F. Kennedy Visiting Professor of Latin American Studies
Michael Smith Instructor in Architecture
Susan Snyder Lecturer in Architecture
Kathy Spiegelman Design Critic in Urban Planning and Design
James Stockard Lecturer in Housing Studies
Belinda Tato Design Critic in Urban Planning and Design
George Thomas Lecturer in Architecture
Raymond Torto Lecturer in Urban Planning and Design
Stephan Truby Instructor in Architecture
John Tuomey Design Critic in Architecture
Jose Luis Vallejo Design Critic in Urban Planning and Design
Ben Van Berkel Design Critic in Architecture
Keith VanDerSys Design Critic in Landscape Architecture
Christian Veddeler Instructor in Architecture
Luis Felipe Vera Benitez Instructor in Urban Planning and Design
Spela Videcnik Design Critic in Architecture
Paola Vigano Visiting Professor in Landscape Architecture and Urban Planning and Design
Alexander von Hoffman John T. Dunlop Lecturer of Housing and Urbanization
Emily Waugh Lecturer in Landscape Architecture
Ann Whiteside Lecturer in Architecture and Librarian
Simon Whittle Teaching Associate in Urban Planning and Design
Matthew Wilson Visiting Assistant Professor in Landscape Architecture and Urban Planning and Design
Andrew Witt Lecturer in Architecture
Kongjian Yu Visiting Professor in Landscape Architecture

LOEB FELLOWS

Baye Adofo-Wilson Planner, Developer, Lawyer, Co-founder Lincoln Park Coast Cultural District, Newark
Angelyn Chandler Architect, NYC Parks Capital Program Manager, Freshkills Park, New York
Arana Hankin Community Economic Development Specialist, President Queens West Development Corp., NY State Manager Manhattanville Project
Alexandra Lange Architecture and Design Critic and Author, New York
Helen Lochhead Architect and Urban Designer, Director Strategic Developments, Sydney Harbor Foreshore Authority
Matt Nohn International Development and Poverty Reduction Consultant, Berlin
Florencia Rodriguez Architect, Critic, Editor and Publisher Piedra Papel & Tjera, Buenos Aires
Eli Spevak Residential Communities Developer, Owner Orange Splot, Portland
Alexie Torres-Fleming Community Organizer, Co-founder Bronx River Alliance, Southern Bronx Watershed Alliance, New York

STAFF

Ashley Alberts Building Services
Joe Amato Building Services
Kathleen M. Anderson Executive Education
Nader Ardalan Architecture
Alla I. Armstrong Academic Finance
Samantha Arsenault Development
John Joseph Aslanian Student Services

FACULTY AND STAFF

Lauren Baccus Human Resources
Kermit Francis Baker Joint Center for Housing Studies
Pamela H. Baldwin Joint Center for Housing Studies
Kate Bauer Dean's Office
Lauren L. Beath Finance Office
Eric S. Belsky Joint Center for Housing Studies
Todd Belton Computer Resources
Jenna Bjorkman Harvard Center for Green Buildings and Cities
Shantel Blakely Communications
Susan Boland-Kourdov Computer Resources
Sarah Bordy Development
Dan Borelli Exhibitions
Laura Briggs Development
Stacy J. Buckley Faculty Planning
Kevin Cahill Building Services
Bonnie Campbell Development
Tom Brent Childs Building Services
Joanne M. Choi Library
Anna Cimini Computer Resources
Carra Lyn Clisby Development
Sean Kelliher Conlon Registrar
Anne Creamer Career Services
Andrea Croteau Architecture
Jennifer De Merode Research Administration
Kevin Derrick Development
Sarah Willoughby Dickinson Collections
Kerry E. Donahue Joint Center for Housing Studies
Barbara Cecile Elfman Advanced Studies Program
Stephen McTee Ervin Computer Resources
Angela Kelly Flynn Joint Center for Housing Studies
Rena Fonseca Executive Education
Porscha Fontellio Human Resources
David B. Ford Development
Nicole Crawford Freeman Development
Jennifer S. Gala Executive Education
Heather Avery Gallagher Executive Education
Erica L. George Landscape Architecture & Urban Planning and Design
Keith Alan Gnoza Financial Assistance
Mark Goble Finance Office
Meryl Golden Academic and Student Services
Julia Goldmacher Finance Office
Sara Gothard Landscape Architecture & Urban Planning and Design
Hal Andrew Gould Computer Resources
Lindsey D. Grant Development
Norton Greenfeld Development
Arin Gregorian Academic Finance
Deborah L. Grohe Building Services
Kimberly Joy Gulko Architecture
Gail Joy Gustafson Admissions
Mark Hagen Computer Resources
Barry J. Harper Building Services
Cynthia Henshall Real Estate Academic Initiative
Christopher Edward Herbert Joint Center for Housing Studies
Thomas Bickford Keen Hewitt III Academic Finance
Maggie Janik User Services
Nancy J. Jennings Executive Education
Pilar E. Raynor Jordan Academic Finance
Johanna Rose Kasubowski Abe Visual Services
Karen J. Kittredge Finance Office
Jeff L. Klug Career Discovery
Sarah H. Knight Development
Ardys J. Kozbial Library
Beth Kramer Development
Elizabeth A La Jeunesse Joint Center for Housing Studies
Mary C. Lancaster Joint Center for Housing Studies
Ashley Marie Lang Academic Services
Kevin Lau Library
Burton LeGeyt Computer Resources
Sharon Marie Lembo Real Estate Academic Initiative
Irene Lew Joint Center for Housing Studies
Theresa A. Lund Dean's Office
Judy Mai Computer Resources
Karen Manning Joint Center for Housing Studies
Stephanie Marvel Development
Ellen Tracy Marya Joint Center for Housing Studies
Anne Mathew Research Administration
Daniel T. McCue Joint Center for Housing Studies
Beth Alison Millstein Development
Jennifer Hrabchak Molinsky Joint Center for Housing Studies
Margaret Moore De Chicojay Executive Education
Maria Moran Advanced Studies Program
Janina Mueller Library
Michelle Muliro Human Resources
Maria Ann Murphy Student Services
Gerilyn Sue Nederhoff Admissions
Caroline Paquette Newton Landscape Architecture & Urban Planning and Design
Christine G. O'Brien Communications
Trevor D. O'Brien Building Services
Terri Park Development
Jacqueline Rose Piracini Academic Services
Lisa E. Plosker Human Resources
Beth Pollack Harvard Center for Green Buildings and Cities
Benjamin Prosky Communications
Julia Alexandra Reiskind Visual Services
Carlos Reyes Student Services
Stefan Riley Harvard Center for Green Buildings and Cities
Patricia Roberts Executive Dean
Holly Rozanski Landscape Architecture & Urban Planning and Design
Rocio Sanchez-Moyano Joint Center for Housing Studies
Meg Sandberg Communications
Madelin R. Santana Executive Education
Ronee Saroff Communications
Jennifer L. Sigler Communications
Gosia Skodowska Harvard Center for Green Buildings and Cities
Matthew Smith User Services
Laura Story Snowdon Student Services
Melinda Starmer Faculty Planning
Jennifer M. Swartout Architecture
Aimee L. Taberner Academic Services
Ellen Tang Financial Assistance
Kelly Anne Teixeira Wisnaskas Student Services
Emily Caroline Thompson Development
Rachel Tolano Dean's Office
Richard Tursky Computer Resources
Jennifer Vallone Finance Office
Edna Van Saun Research Administration
Melissa Vaughn Communications
Rachel Stefania Vroman Computer Resources
Antya E. Waegemann Research Administration
Liz Ann Walat Finance Office
John Kenneth Watts Finance Office
Juliet Ciel Wendel Student Services
Ann Whiteside Library
Leah Whitman-Salkin Communications
Sara J. Wilkinson Human Resources
Abbe H. Will Joint Center for Housing Studies
Janet L. Wysocki Executive Education
Sarah U. Young Loeb Fellowship
Ines Maria Zalduendo Library
David W. Zimmerman-Stuart Exhibitions

AS HEARD AT THE GSD

"FORM IS VERY IMPORTANT. IT IS CRUCIAL IF YOU'RE TRYING TO BUILD ENVIRONMENTS THAT MOVE PEOPLE. THERE'S A HIGH DEGREE OF IMAGINATION, VISUAL ACUITY AND A HIGH SENSITIVITY TO TACTILITY, TO MATERIALS, TO DETAIL."

April 15, 2014
Daniel Urban Kiley Lecture: James Corner

"How many scientists do I know who can hang out with Andy Warhol? And how many people in computers had Bucky Fuller as a professor? That list of people affected my life."

October 29, 2013
Nicholas Negroponte in Conversation with Mohsen Mostafavi

"I really do believe that the world can be saved through design."

November 17, 2013
Kanye West

"We want to create great architecture, and we want to not go bankrupt. Okay, that's enough of a target."

April 3, 2014
Sheela Maini
The Project as Practice Lecture

"To focus teaching on the act or art of inhabitation is appropriate, because it holds the essential in architecture. It forms the basis of urbanity and a background atmosphere of living, of possible happiness and comfort."

March 25, 2014 - Jonathan Sergison and Stephen Bates - On Continuity

HARVARD GSD SPRING 2014

Evening Program

1/28 Lecture
Iwan Baan
Photographer, Amsterdam

1/29–1/30 Film Program
Highlights from the Architecture and Design Film Festival
Organized in collaboration with Kyle Bergman, AIA, founder, ADFF
gsd.harvard.edu/events/adff

2/4 Kenzo Tange Lecture
Junya Ishigami
Junya.ishigami+associates, Tokyo
2014 Kenzo Tange Design Critic

2/6 Conversation
William Anderson
FAICP, MCRP '83
Principal/Vice President, AECOM, San Diego
Mitchell Silver
Planning Director, City of Raleigh

2/7 DDes Conference
Projective Views on Urban Metabolism
gsd.harvard.edu/events/urban-metabolism

2/11 Sylvester Baxter Lecture
Bruce Kuwabara
KPMB Architects, Toronto
Christopher Glaisek
Vice President for Planning and Design, WATERFRONToronto

2/13 Alumni Insights Lecture
Teddy Cruz
MDes '97, Estudio Teddy Cruz, La Jolla

2/18 Lecture
Manuel Castells
University Professor and Wallis Annenberg Chair in Communication Technology and Society, University of Southern California, Los Angeles

2/20
Senior Loeb Scholar Lecture
Katherine Boo
Writer, London

2/21
Panel Discussion: Thesis at the GSD
Wes Jones
MArch '84
Jones Partners Architects
Eric Bunge
MArch II '96, nARCHITECTS
Gia Wolff
MArch '08
Architect, New York
Moderated by Edward Eigen, Associate Professor of Architecture and Landscape Architecture, GSD

2/25 Lecture
Ricky Burdett
Professor of Urban Studies, London School of Economics

2/27 Lecture
Teresita Fernández
Sculptor, New York

3/3 Lecture
Silvia Gmür
Silvia Gmür Reto Gmür Architekten, Basel

3/7 Aga Khan Program Symposium
The Space Between Development and Conservation: In Celebration of 10 Years of the Aga Khan Program at the GSD and ArchNet
gsd.harvard.edu/events/agakhansymposium

3/11 Lecture
Christopher Benfey
Andrew W. Mellon Professor of English, Mount Holyoke College, Amherst
Part of the series Then and Now: Walter Gropius and the Lineage of the Bauhaus, sponsored by the Breger Fund in honor of Walter Gropius

3/13 Lecture
Erika Naginski
Professor of Architectural History, GSD

3/25 Lecture
Jonathan Sergison Stephen Bates
Sergison Bates, London

3/28 Lecture
David Adjaye
Adjaye Associates, London

3/31–4/1 Symposium
Waste Convened by
Frank O. Gehry
Gehry Partners, Los Angeles and
Mohsen Mostafavi
Dean, and Alexander and Victoria Wiley Professor of Design, GSD
gsd.harvard.edu/events/waste

4/4 Open House Lecture
Michael Murphy
MArch '11, MASS Design Group, Boston
Alan Ricks
MArch '10, MASS Design Group, Boston

4/2 Lecture
Vijay Iyer
Composer, Pianist, Producer
Franklin D. and Florence Rosenblatt Professor of the Arts, Department of Music, Harvard University

4/8 Lecture
Grace La
MArch '95, LA DALLMAN, Professor of Architecture, GSD
James Dallman
MArch '92, LA DALLMAN

4/10 Lecture
India Pierce Lee
LF '10, Program Director for Neighborhoods, Housing & Community Development
The Cleveland Foundation, Cleveland

4/11 Cambridge Talks VIII
Framing Architecture: Environment, Institutions, Practice
gsd.harvard.edu/events/cambridgetalks

4/15 Daniel Urban Kiley Lecture
James Corner
James Corner Field Operations, New York

4/22 Lecture
Tadashi Yanai
CEO, UNIQLO, Tokyo

4/24 Lecture
Renée Daoust
Daoust Lestage Inc., Montreal

Noontime Program

2/10 Alumni Insights Noontime Talk
Manifest 2 In Progress: The Architecture of Religion
with
Justin Fowler
MArch '10
Anthony Acciavatti
MArch II '09
gsd.harvard.edu/events/manifest

2/27 GSD Talks
On the Legacy of Manfredo Tafuri
Michael Hays, Eliot Noyes Professor of Architectural Theory
Erika Naginski, Professor of Architectural History
and Pier Vittorio Aureli, DOGMA; Yale University; Architectural Association, London

3/11 GSD Talks
Rosetta Elkin
Kiley Fellow in Landscape
In Conversation with Charles Waldheim, John E. Irving Professor of Landscape Architecture, GSD

3/27 Innovate / Award-Winning Projects by Two GSD Student Teams
Horizon House: A 21st-Century Sustainable House in Rural Japan
moderated by Mark Mulligan, MArch '90
Adjunct Associate Professor of Architecture
Near-Zero: Simulation-Aided Design of a Low-Energy House
moderated by Holly Samuelson, DDes '13
Assistant Professor of Architecture

4/1 Innovate
Ali Malkawi
Professor of Architectural Technology, GSD

4/9 GSD Talks
Jane Thompson
Jane Thompson Design Group, Boston
in conversation with
Alexandra Lange
MDes '14 Architecture Critic, New York
Part of the series Then and Now: Walter Gropius and the Lineage of the Bauhaus, sponsored by the Breger Fund in honor of Walter Gropius

4/14 GSD Talks
Projective Ecologies; Chris Reed
Associate Professor of Practice in Landscape Architecture, GSD
in Conversation with Charles Waldheim, John E. Irving Professor of Landscape Architecture, GSD

Exhibitions

1/20–3/9 Main Gallery
Another Nature
Curated by Junya Ishigami, 2014 Kenzo Tange Design Critic

1/20–3/23 Experiments Wall
Fall 2013 Studio: Material Performance —Fibrous Tectonics
Curated by Achim Menges, Visiting Professor in Architecture, GSD

3/24–5/16 Main Gallery
Platform 6
Curated by Rosetta Elkin, Lecturer in Landscape Architecture, GSD

2/27–3/23 Library
A Hospital is a House for Man
Curated by Silvia Gmür Reto Gmür Architekten

3/31–5/16 Experiments Wall
Horizon House: A 21st Century Retreat in Nature
Curated by Mark Mulligan, MArch '90, Adjunct Associate Professor of Architecture, GSD
Kiel Moe, MDes '03, Assistant Professor of Architectural Technology and Student competition team

4/2–5/16 Library
Animating the Archive
Curated by Matthew Allen, MArch '10, Assistant Professor, University of Toronto

Harvard University
Graduate School of Design

For up-to-date information:
www.gsd.harvard.edu/events
www.gsd.harvard.edu/exhibitions

Anyone requiring accessibility accommodations should contact the events office two weeks in advance at 617 496 2414 or events@gsd.harvard.edu

Designed by Masayoshi Kodaira, FLAME Inc. 2014